100 Years on the Road

100 Years on the Road

The Traveling Salesman in American Culture

Timothy B. Spears

Yale University Press   New Haven and London

For Nancy

Published with assistance from the foundation established in memory of Philip Hamilton McMillan of the Class of 1894, Yale College.

Designed by Sonia L. Scanlon

Set in Baskerville type by The Composing Room of Michigan, Inc., Grand Rapids, Michigan.

Printed in the United States of America by Thomson-Shore, Inc., Dexter, Michigan.

Library of Congress Cataloging-in-Publication Data

Spears, Timothy B., 1957–

    100 years on the road : the traveling salesman in American culture / Timothy B. Spears.

      p.   cm.

    Includes bibliographical references (p.   ) and index.

    ISBN 0-300-05908-6 (alk. paper)

    1. Traveling sales personnel—United States— History.   2. Travelng sales personnel in literature.

   3. American literature—History and criticism.

  I. Title. II. Title: One hundred years on the road.

  HF5441.S64   1994

  381'.1—dc20   94-6070

             CIP

A catalogue record for this book is available from the British Library.

10 9 8 7 6 5 4 3 2 1

Contents

Preface

From advertising to public relations to politics, sales personnel and selling strategies pervade American life. Fuller Brush men, Avon ladies, retail merchants, door-to-door canvassers, telemarketers, even presidents constitute a partial list of people who have something to sell. On television and radio, in magazines and newspapers, the figure of the salesman—or saleswoman—is always before us—assuming a familiar form of address, persuading us to answer our heart's desire, and buy. Indeed, salesmanship may seem so much a part of American society that to study its cultural significance is akin to disrupting the natural order, a futile attempt to understand the way we are. In this study I reject the notion that we cannot escape the bonds of discourse to understand the marketplace that apparently creates us. By offering a historical perspective on the dynamics of salesmanship, I suggest that the contemporary cliché "Everyone is a salesman" is the product of time and culture. As a study of traveling salesmen and their role in American culture during the years 1870–1925, this book does not offer an all-inclusive view of personal selling practices. I would be disingenuous, however, if I did not admit to believing that the conflicted nature of the relation between American society and salesmanship is both reflected and rooted in the development and reception of commercial traveling.

At various times I have been tempted to think of the traveling salesman's story as uniquely American, the last great ode supporting the now academically suspect effort to illuminate "American exceptionalism." The appearance of commercial travelers in eighteenth-century England, the "commis voyageur" in France, and a host of literary types ranging from Dickens's one-eyed Bagman in *The Pickwick Papers* to Balzac's "illustrious Gaudissart" in *La Comédie humaine* to Kafka's Gregor Samsa in "The Metamorphosis" chastens this temptation.[1] Until more is known about how commercial traveling developed in—and across—these and other cultures, readers are advised to weigh any implied claims to cultural exceptionalism found in the pages that follow.

A preliminary qualification concerning the identity of "my" salesmen deserves mention here. For most Americans the traveling salesman inhabits a variety of fictional contexts: Broadway plays, short stories and novels, dirty jokes, Norman Rockwell paintings, and Hollywood films. From glimpses snatched in childhoods spent in small towns and rural areas, older Americans may remember the traveling man as a flesh-and-blood creature who periodically appeared in local retail stores. The business community and, of course, people who sell things may have an even more specific conception. Yet not even the contemporary commercial traveler, nor, for that matter, the historian knee-deep in nineteenth-century sources, can be wholly free from the welter of images generated by modern popular culture. As the offspring of cultural production, a larger-than-life traveling man always threatens to subsume all real salesmen. In the terms made familiar by the French critic Roland Barthes, the traveling salesman has become a "mythical" figure, a "type" whose cultural identity outstretches the historical world that made him.[2] Although one object of this book is to explain the evolution of this type, I can hardly begin to address the ways in which his contemporary image or images have affected my perspective, except perhaps to acknowledge the influence and, letting the sources be my guide, strive to clarify the relationship between real and represented salesmen.

Adjusting this perspective likewise involves problems of scale: how to see the traveling salesman within and against a changing cultural landscape. Broadly construed, the history of commercial traveling proves inextricable from the larger, more familiar story of the emergence of a national market economy and a consumer culture in the late nineteenth and early twentieth centuries. Add to these developments the looming prospects of rapid urbanization, shifting demographics, widespread changes in the built environment —in short, the defining characteristics of a modernizing nation on its way to becoming a mass culture—and the traveling man's role, let alone his importance, can disappear from sight.

Traveling men, Arthur Miller has observed, "lived like artists, like actors whose product is first of all themselves, forever imagining triumphs in a world that either ignores them or denies them altogether."[3] Locating the salesman's significance at the volatile intersection of cultural, economic, and personal power, Miller suggests a commercial version of the self that historians of consumer culture have only begun to address. In *Counter Cultures: Saleswomen, Managers, and Customers in American Department Stores, 1890–1940,* Susan Porter Benson traces the emergence of the retail sales culture, focusing on the twentieth century; and in *Worlds Apart: The Market and the Theater in Anglo-American Thought, 1550–1750,* Jean-Christophe Agnew examines the elusive grounds of signification shared by market relations and dramatic performance, leading up to the development of the American context. But beyond these studies, a few essays, and several scattered discussions, the cultural history of the face-to-face economy remains uncharted, especially between 1870 and 1900. Although histories of American business—ranging from Lewis E. Atherton's and Thomas D. Clark's classic studies of country merchants and general stores in the 1930s and 1940s to Alfred D. Chandler, Jr.'s, definitive study of business management—have long stressed the commercial traveler's significance in the development of the nineteenth-century market, no scholar has explained how or why, in Chandler's words, traveling men "became familiar figures in rural America and the nation's folklore."[4] Among the still-emerging histories of consumer culture, traveling men have died a kind of scholarly death; they have almost been ignored. And where they do appear, even as key players in the marketplace—for instance, in Susan Strasser's recent examination of the mass market and Olivier Zunz's social history of the corporation—they play supporting roles in studies that explicate broader commercial developments.[5]

The lack of a comprehensive study that takes into account not only the traveling salesman's economic importance but also his place in the broader culture is remarkable, especially in light of the attention that modern American writers have given him. Ironically, the traveling salesman's death in fiction, drama, and film has led to his continued vitality as a cultural icon. There is Willy Loman—a man "way out there in the blue, riding on a smile and a shoeshine"—whose dreaming, both misguided and self-deceiving, "comes with the territory."[6] And there are others: the protagonist of Eudora Welty's first published story, "Death of a Traveling Man" (1936), who dies in a farmhouse; Hickey, the life of the party, who kills himself in Eugene O'Neill's 1946 play, *The Iceman Cometh;* George Brush, the book salesman in Thornton Wilder's novel of 1935, *Heaven's My Destination,* who nears death after losing his religious faith but, after regaining it, continues his saintly life. Either in contrast to the impersonal nature of twentieth-century commercial life or in protest against it—or both—these and other representations of the traveling salesman provide a human-scaled view of economic culture that scholars have tended to ignore in favor of a larger historical picture.

The terms of this exclusion surface in Daniel Boorstin's 1973 book, *The Americans: The Democratic Experience,* one of the first studies to take a comprehensive look at consumer culture. In a concluding summary of how "consumption communities" underwent a signal transformation during the late nineteenth and early twentieth centuries, Boorstin characterized the rise of the mail-order business as "the triumph" of a large, rapidly expanding commercial community over a much smaller one. "It was," he argued, "a victory of the market over the marketplace. And it spelled the defeat of the salesman by advertising. In a word, it was a defeat of the seen, the nearby, the familiar by the everywhere community."[7]

Although scholars have revised Boorstin's notion of commercial democracy, by a strange twist of Whiggish history they continue to confirm Boorstin's vision of a triumphant mass market, the effect of which has been to occlude an earlier, equally vital chapter in the history of consumer culture. *100 Years on the Road* is an attempt to redress this omission. By examining the traveling salesman's role in American culture between the 1830s and the 1930s, I argue that the triumph of the everywhere community cannot be understood without knowing the history of face-to-face commercial relations. The great irony of the story I tell—a historian's version of "the death of the salesman"—is that commercial travelers paved the way for a modern mass market only to see their own relative economic importance decline. Yet as the following pages demonstrate, the salesman always had to contend with his diminished value in the eyes of society. Indeed, it is this sense of struggle, illuminated in texts by and about salesmen, that accounts for the traveling salesman's special status in American cultural history.

Hints of this struggle and its importance for the development of a modern commercial self sometimes surface in advertising histories. Nowhere has the romance of the mass culture exerted more fascination or produced more creative scholarship than in the study of modern advertising, for it is through advertising that the modern marketplace appears most persuasive, and most capable of guiding the culture and shaping the self. As Roland Marchand, Jackson Lears, and others have shown, the peculiarly personal, often fantastic appeals to psychological needs that characterized early twentieth-century advertising helped "make way for modernity" by naturalizing the expanding marketplace and thus easing the historical transition from a producer-oriented economy to a bureaucratic consumer culture. Outlining the argument for hegemony that has come to dominate studies of consumer culture, Lears observes that although this transformation "was never complete" and although public discourse remained a "contested terrain," the rhetoric and symbols of advertising ultimately "play[ed] a major role in sanctioning values appropriate to a new corporate system." Even though historians have suggested that such rhetoric evolved from vernacular modes of persuasion and that much of the contest focused on the transformation of face-to-face selling strategies to a new medium—hence, the common early-twentieth-century definition of advertising as "salesmanship in print"—they have generally left those origins unexamined. Put another way: if modern advertising, as Michael Schudson shrewdly describes it, has fostered the "decontextualization" of personal selling strategies, the original context remains a mystery.[8]

In a 1986 review of Roland Marchand's book *Advertising the American Dream: Making Way For Modernity, 1920–1940,* Lears noted this gap in the scholarship, observing that there are "many links between the commercial theatricality of the patent medicine era and the later, more systematic manufacture of appearances."[9] And in his own work he has traced the origins of the theatricality to the magical appeal of the antebellum peddler, a trickster figure whose commercial improvisations look back to the wily Greek god Hermes and forward to the more rationalized, though equally slippery, surfaces of modern advertisements. In effect revising Constance Rourke's concept of the "mask" as a mediating, changeable form—passed down like "a portable heirloom" from one pioneer itinerant to another, as Rourke describes its diffusion in her seminal 1931 book, *American Humor: A Study of National Character*—Lears, and to a certain extent Jean-Christophe Agnew, have been less concerned with the quest for an indigenous, integrated national culture than with the ways market forces impinge on the construction of that culture. In the absence of any "autobiographical record of market experience," the focus shifts from a consideration of actual market behavior to an analysis of how that behavior is represented in texts.[10] Like the confidence man dramatized in Herman Melville's 1857 novel, *The Confidence Man: His Masquerade,* the peddler serves as a represented figure and hence a lightning rod for ante-bellum anxieties—and fantasies—about involvement in the marketplace. The significant issue is not whether the depicted commercial practices were real but how economic behavior was perceived, meaning was apportioned, and the boundaries of consumer culture were established in the great crucible of class dynamics.

The challenges posed by emerging studies of marketplace culture extend beyond the methodological shift that commentators have tied to the way historians and literary critics position and treat texts. At issue is the familiar Marxist question of how economic forces guide consciousness, shape culture, and generate the kind of worries about what is real that ultimately inform even the most arcane academic debates over representation.[11] At stake in this book, however, are at least two concrete questions related to these more ab-stract problems. First, I ask who or what historical forces were most responsi-ble for developing the modes of persuasion that we now associate with mod-ern advertising. To focus this question, I have begged the implications of the early twentieth-century adman's dictum: If advertising is salesmanship in print, what then is salesmanship? How did it evolve? What role did the travel-ing salesman play in its development? Second, in approaching the broader and in many ways more difficult question of historical context, I ask how much freedom traveling salesmen had to develop their sales methods and the customs of their profession. Related to this is the question of social control, or cultural hegemony. What conflicts accompanied the growth of commercial traveling? Were the modes of representation that traveling salesmen claimed for their own truly theirs, or were they the diffusion—or perhaps the projection—of presentations common in the culture at large?

Without claiming too decisively to have found the missing link, I argue for the traveling salesman's place in the evolution of commercial theatricality and seek to restore some sense of human scale in the history of consumer culture. As the descendant of Constance Rourke's Yankee peddler, the traveling sales-man inherited his improvisational ways and, more important, expanded and refined them within the new economic context of the late nineteenth and early twentieth centuries. Neither peddler nor door-to-door canvasser, the commercial traveler—or drummer, as he was often called—almost always sold to the trade and was the aggressive, logical consequence of the expanding national market system, a figure who from an economic standpoint remained inseparable from the growth of the railroad and other developments that strengthened the "visible hand" of business. No other occupational group concerned with selling drew so heavily—or represented so dramatically—the nascent power of modern business enterprise. Yet, as I emphasize throughout the book, the traveling salesman's relation to these forces did not wholly determine the development of his sales techniques nor make him the pawn of institutional forces. In fact, it often provided him with a modicum of freedom, although not without some cost.

Writ large, the history of commercial traveling thus lies in the structural

innovations that marked the emergence of the corporation as the most powerful institution in the United States and in the rationalization of commercial
practices that transformed all kinds of business organizations between 1840
and 1920. The following chapters take shape in light of such changes, tracing
the opening of American society in the 1830s and 1840s, when the traveling
salesman's most immediate predecessor, the city drummer, steered visiting
country merchants toward the showrooms of wholesalers; the rise of a national market system after the Civil War, when drummers took to the road in
great numbers; and the subsequent incorporation of American manufacturing interests just before and after the turn of the twentieth century, when
forward or vertical integration led to the formation of corporate sales forces
and, in some industries, the elimination of the wholesaler's drummer.

Yet readers hoping to find in this account a detailed examination of sales
organizations, company records, and developing markets are urged to revise
their expectations. In providing what William R. Taylor calls a history of
perception, I take an ethnographic view of the marketplace, highlighting the
traveling salesman's historically shifting role in "commercial culture"—a term
that designates my concern with the development of sales techniques within
the business community itself rather than the broader, less easily identified
"consumer culture."[12] Autobiographies, trade journals, advice manuals, letters, and diaries establish this view of market practices and also a framework
for understanding the meanings that Americans attached to them. On the
other hand, periodical literature, legal writing, photographs and illustrations,
and a wide variety of fiction provide an imperfect but far-reaching gauge of
what the traveling salesman represented to late nineteenth- and early
twentieth-century Americans and of how the nature of this representation
changed.

Although no one kind of text holds an absolute premium on objective
truth, I maintain the line between actual market practices and represented
behavior, and not only because of the availability of a wide range of autobiographical writing on commercial traveling. The distinction provides a crucial point of contrast between developing sales techniques on the one hand
and reactions to those emerging practices on the other, as well as a stable
context for examining those moments of historical transition when the dialectic breaks down and the two opposing spheres appear to overlap. Asserting
this difference also emphasizes the importance of volition and autonomy for
market behavior, illuminating the possibilities—and the limitations—of the
improvisational powers that Miller ascribed to the traveling salesman. Rather
than collapse Miller's portrait into a textual vision of commercial artistry and,
in effect, leave salesmanship in print, I root it in a social-historical setting, the
face-to-face economy of the late nineteenth and early twentieth centuries.
More than a decade ago, in his path-breaking discussion of personality, Warren I. Susman described a similar self—malleable, improvisational, and
fluid—whose emergence as a concept around 1900 he linked to the rise of
mass urban culture. In this book I argue that the lineaments of this modern

self appeared as early as the 1870s and 1880s and developed along the peripheries of American culture, far from urban centers, sustained always by a burgeoning commercial culture, further accentuated by the conflicts that took place within and around that culture, and nurtured through the institutional supports of the rapidly expanding, nearly all-male profession of commercial traveling.[13] The apotheosis of this self, embodied in the hundreds of salesmanship manuals published between 1900 and 1925 and later epitomized in Dale Carnegie's 1936 best-seller *How to Win Friends and Influence People,* was a traveling man who knew that his personality was his "capital" and that for each new sale he would have to "get on the customer's side of the fence" and "sell himself" anew.

Between 1870 and 1920, following the career trajectory described by Burton Bledstein and other historians of the middle class, traveling men shaped the culture of their profession—sharing, rationalizing, and codifying existing sales practices. By 1950, if not before, according to C. Wright Mills's *White Collar,* these practices were at the heart of American middle-class culture, a territory that Mills corrosively dubbed The Personality Market.[14] In figurative terms, then, the traveling salesman's place may be said to have moved steadily away from the margins of culture and toward its center when the relationship between drummer and merchant shifted away from the antebellum urban marketplace, and the salesman became a familiar sight on Main Streets across the nation. Yet even during the 1830s and 1840s, although city drummers sparked the same kind of fears (of "Protean" forms of self-representation) that Karen Halttunen has associated with the confidence man, this movement was well under way as salesman and merchant forged the relationship around which the customs of commercial traveling developed. Departing from historians who have persuasively demonstrated the gradually leveling impact of the commercial economy but, to my mind, overstated its placelessness, I emphasize the regional, physical, and visual dimensions of the commercial traveler's evolving place in the culture.[15]

Throughout the nineteenth and twentieth centuries, salesmen typically and tellingly called their field of work "the road," literally a market*place,* and it was on this commercial landscape that salesmanship evolved. As anthropologists, sociologists, and historians continue to demonstrate, physical gestures and everyday routines can acquire both instrumental and cultural significance, simultaneously developing within and shaping their immediate environment.[16] For salesmen the customs of traveling and selling were similarly related. I argue not only that the commercial traveler's sales practices logically followed from his movements from place to place but also that traveling men played a significant role in helping create the visual and physical spectacle that began to characterize consumer culture—and American culture in general—during the late nineteenth century.[17]

In this sense, the boundless, abstract market that some historians associate with twentieth-century consumer culture emerged, paradoxically, by virtue of the salesman's ability to negotiate the cultural and regional differences that his very presence ultimately effaced. As the business historians Glenn Porter and Harold Livesay have argued, in some industries nineteenth-century distribution methods persisted into the twentieth among "diffuse," remote markets—that is, among isolated, small towns. Porter and Livesay's analysis helps explain why the traveling salesman's place in American culture remains rooted in the landscape of the small town. There the salesman stood out, whereas in "concentrated" markets—cities—he slipped from sight.[18] It also suggests why the transformation of the marketplace into a market—what Boorstin called the everywhere community—did not take place in the late nineteenth century or in some places well into the twentieth. Nor would it have taken place at all without the commercial traveler's understanding of what distinguished one small town from another or one customer from another, a concrete knowledge on which the central directive of modern salesmanship—"Be everything to everyone"—was based.

This understanding was what animated the traveling salesman's dramatic presence on and around Main Street and framed his role in nineteenth-century local-color literature and twentieth-century remembrances of rural childhoods. It was also what carried the traveling man away from the putative margins of culture and toward the center and infused his relationships with the paradoxical combination of "closeness and remoteness" that the German sociologist Georg Simmel associated with the movements of a "stranger."[19] To be sure, vernacular forms of persuasion persisted, however residually, in even the most "scientific" sales techniques, as evidenced by twentieth-century salesmanship manuals that include instructions on how to read character according to phrenological principles. But what finally distinguished the commercial traveler's presentation of samples from the street-corner "fakir's" sleights-of-hand were his substantially different audience—the trade—and his position within a profession that was determined to assimilate and standardize vernacular sales practices and modes of self-representation. Seen in this context, the salesman's proximity both to established commercial centers and to those marginal itinerants whose very presence threatened his claims to professional legitimacy simultaneously made him a middleman in the commercial landscape of the late nineteenth and early twentieth centuries and the key link between traditional folk figures, like the peddler, and twentieth-century advertisers.

I have also tried to show how an emergent commercial culture clashed with and eventually reshaped dominant cultural values. As historians continue to demonstrate, one response to rapid social transformation among nineteenth-century middle and upper classes was to erect barriers between the marketplace and culture, creating a distance between vulgar commercial activities—frequently associated with the working class and immigrants—and established social practices and institutions. In some places, like those isolated pockets of rural Georgia that, according Steven Hahn, gave root to Southern populism, resistance to the market was even more pronounced, if wholly different in character.[20] Salesmen experienced this resistance at first hand, from the purely existential hardships of life on the road to the pervasive licensing laws that impeded mobility throughout much of the late nineteenth century. The deprecating images of the traveling salesman that circulated within nineteenth- and twentieth-century popular culture—in fiction, humor writing, and even advertising trade-cards—show a similar, if subtler, form of opposition. In treating these texts I take up the figure of the salesman as a represented site of conflict: first as an agent of an emergent, intrusive market during the nineteenth century and then, in the twentieth century, as the agent of an already entrenched consumer culture. By this rough division I mean to highlight two kinds of cultural criticism that developed around the market economy—one associated with "island communities" anxious about change and defensive of local traditions, the other provoked by a profound disillusionment with the ascendant mass culture.

At the same time, many such documents evince a mix of humor, envy, and even sympathy for traveling men that qualifies these critical categories and clarifies their development. Attributes that condemned the traveling salesman in the eyes of late nineteenth-century middle-class readers—for instance, his apparent disregard for domestic ideology—coexist with features that were cause for admiration, for example, his ability to travel and his seemingly glamorous freedom. This sense of complicity suggests that what, in anthropological terms, made the traveling salesman "good to think" within late nineteenth- and early twentieth-century culture was not an immutable set of features associated with the marketplace but rather a cluster of attributes pointing to larger social conflicts, such as emigration from small towns and rural areas, evolving concepts of home and work, and emerging gender constructions.

But what made salesmen good to think also made them hard to understand. Henry James aptly expressed the difficulty that observers had in assessing the significance of the ubiquitous commercial traveler. Like other aspects of the American scene that puzzled and shocked him upon his return to the United States in 1904 after an absence of twenty-one years, the salesman "loomed." The drummer's "completely unchallenged possession" of dining cars and hotels, his "primal rawness of speech" and "air of commercial truculence," threatened "to block out of view almost every other object." The crowds of traveling men insisted on a "category" of their own and, for James, became "types" or "specimens" of the intrusive commercial culture in America. He wondered about the terms of a world that could create these "extraordinarily base and vulgar" men. Whom did they call on? How did they establish confidence? "What women did they live with, what women, living with them, could yet leave them as they were?" James could not imagine answers to these questions. Still, he did not despise the commercial travelers but instead pitied these "victims and martyrs, creatures touchingly, tragically doomed" by the demands of American business culture. After all, James reflected, they had not chosen "to be almost the only figures in the social landscape—hadn't wanted the fierce light to beat all on themselves."[21]

James's ambivalent possession of this type speaks directly to the salesman's paradoxical status in late nineteenth- and early twentieth-century literature. Both repelled and fascinated, writers placed traveling men at a remove while they simultaneously struggled to understand (and conceded) his cultural significance. For the writers whose work I consider in some detail this ambivalence suggests a complicated emotional relationship to the literary marketplace. On the one hand, their fiction documents the leveling effect of an expansive market economy; on the other hand, their portraits of traveling men place a remarkably personal face on the medium of exchange, qualifying Michael T. Gilmore's conclusion (in his study of romantic literature) that "market society thrives on indirection and impersonality."[22]

One explanation for these younger writers' softer attitude toward market forces has to do with historical timing. Born after the Civil War, many of them lacked personal knowledge of the producer-oriented culture whose dramatic contrast drove Thoreau's and Melville's criticism of market capitalism. More to the point, however, at least for such writers as Theodore Dreiser and Sherwood Anderson, their small-town upbringing provided an intimate view of market relations that informed both their fictional subjects and their sense of professional writing. As the figure for at least two exchange processes—one explicitly commercial, the other implicitly cultural—the traveling man occupied the center of this view. His presence in fictional landscapes represented the continued power of the human element in the marketplace—bodied forth, however, to exemplify the writer's own cultural exchange, often a migration from a small town to a city and a literary vocation.

As a figurative middleman in literature, the salesman thus provided writers a point of "direct confrontation with the elusive process of social change," to borrow a phrase from Amy Kaplan's study of literary realism. Yet this encounter was not limited to realists, nor did it confront all realists. As the Bibliography makes clear, I have searched for the salesman's presence with the zeal of a collector and ignored the generic distinctions that inform recent studies of the relation between the marketplace and literary representation.[23] One goal of the search was frankly quantitative: I wanted to establish the salesman's circulation in popular cultural texts. Another, more important goal was to establish a context that, in breaking down distinctions among kinds of texts and between high and low forms of representation, would allow me to recover, if only in part, the rich and variegated efforts to depict and review the traveling man's place on the cultural landscape. Over time, the nature of these representations changed, imperfectly reflecting the salesman's evolving role in the marketplace. But as much as I depend on this dialectic exchange to show a concrete, materialist base for the texts considered here, I likewise show how it might have worked the other way—for instance, how during the late nineteenth century traveling men responded to their unsavory reputation and struggled to fashion a more acceptable professional image based on sentimental, domestic values. Whereas Jackson Lears has stressed the importance that such values had for cultural elites attempting to exercise social control over the marketplace, I offer a somewhat different view, arguing that the response of the profession to resistance was not simply to capitulate to dominant values but also to assimilate and even transform them. In making the road their home, commercial travelers thus hewed to public sentiment—and hence stabilized their apparent subversiveness—but they did so in terms that reinforced their improvisational powers and structured the commercial practices of modern consumer culture from the bottom up.

Among certain scholarly discourses, even to look for conflict in a capitalist market or to suggest a separation of commerce from some more general field of culture is already to misunderstand the relation. For how—as Walter Benn Michaels states the problem in *The Gold Standard and the Logic of Naturalism*—can expressions of opposition to consumer culture signify any viable alternative when the very terms of resistance are by definition inscribed in a market system? Similarly, how can scholars critical of the emergence of this culture—whose accounts are consumed objects themselves—presume to transcend the rhetorical and perceptual boundaries of their own society? Michaels's extended meditations on these questions—the short answer is that they cannot—like other New Historicist readings of economic culture, offer a salutary view of the sense of complicity that unites oppositional rhetoric to historical dynamics.[24] But his refusal to grant conflict any authenticity depends on a straw-man argument that sees resistance as a force that is real only when it resides outside capitalism. What Michaels is less willing to entertain are the more prosaic conflicts that develop within the capitalist marketplace in a social-historical context whose emergence precedes and shapes the literary text. The naturalist discourse whose logic Michaels so powerfully demonstrates is indeed a historicized construct, but it is built on a history of conflict, which he elides.

In much of what follows, I emphasize these conflicts, not to argue that modern consumer culture as we know it could have been different but rather to show that the naturalized marketplace now taken for granted evolved from human endeavor that poststructural examinations of texts as history tend to ignore. Because I am intent on presenting a historical narrative of the traveling salesman's place in American culture, I synthesize and range broadly, a method that inevitably gives short shrift to extended readings of discrete texts (an exception is my discussion of *Sister Carrie*). My reluctance to focus principally on literary texts (which is another possible way of organizing this study) and subordinate all other (historical, ephemeral) material to them also stems from my belief that the texts of professional writers and the texts of professional salesmen—for all their similarity in an increasingly commercialized society—represent different kinds of work, each deserving interpretive room of its own. The contrast boils down to the difference between the productive labor of literary representation, an ideal that late nineteenth-century writers continued to associate with authorship, and the distributive work of sales representation, an enterprise that in part led to the salesman's objectification in literature.

I have sought to recover the history of commercial travelers—as subjects. The traveling men whose autobiographies, diaries, and letters dominate my citations were real enough, if their imagined counterparts—the Willy Lomans of literary history—were not. And where I let these men speak for themselves, I intend to tell something of their struggles and show what it was like to be a traveling salesman during the late nineteenth and early twentieth centuries. Of more than antiquarian interest or nostalgic import, my recovery of this history follows the examples set by hundreds of contemporaneous authors and artists who sought to understand the salesman's place in American culture. At issue in their efforts and more consciously in mine is the changing face of market capitalism—a form of commercial representation that emerged from the antebellum cities, developed in regional markets during the late nineteenth century, and was gradually "incorporated" after 1900. Alan Trachtenberg's important discussion of incorporation serves to frame this last development but is less useful for understanding why the traveling man's face-to-face selling strategies thrived on a decentralized commercial landscape.[25] In fact, at least for between 1875 and 1895 or so—what might be called the glory days of commercial traveling—salesmen contended with, but remained surprisingly free of, controlling directives.

Sometimes such freedom proved somewhat illusory, but given fairly wide parameters to "make towns" and sell goods, traveling men had room enough to create their own culture. The endurance of this apparently unencumbered, all-male culture, whether as a residual force or just plain nostalgia, is at the heart of contemporary notions of traveling salesmen. Yet it may also mask a historical irony that this study is at pains to reveal. Although commercial travelers may be said to have triumphed by sustaining the growth of their profession, after 1900—as the sales strategies that they had developed and refined were absorbed into the national consumer culture and as their own status was diminished by the rise of advertising and other modern commercial practices—the traveling man appeared to be just one salesman among many.

Acknowledgments

My interest in traveling salesmen began in the basement stacks of Baker Library at Harvard Business School, where I discovered *Only a Drummer,* a turn-of-the-century account of life on the road written by "one of the profession," Wilbur Castelow. Like a piece of Americana found at a flea market and brought home to sit among familiar objects, Castelow's tongue-in-cheek celebration of the special vision that traveling salesmen share changed the way I looked at books that I thought I knew. It served as the starting point for a dissertation completed in the History of American Civilization Program at Harvard, which in turn became the basis for this book.

One thing I have learned from badgering relatives, friends, and acquaintances about the possibilities of this project is that scholarship, like salesmanship, builds on the work and knowledge of many people. I am indebted to the individuals and institutions that helped bring this book to market. Financial support from the Summer Travel Fund of the History of American Civilization Program and the National Museum of American History of the Smithsonian Institution sustained my research. A grant from the Mrs. Giles Whiting Foundation allowed me to finish writing the thesis. The Middlebury College Faculty Professional Development Fund helped me turn a manuscript into this book.

I thank the librarians and curators at the various research institutions that I visited and corresponded with, especially the staffs at the American Antiquarian Society, the Chicago Historical Society, the Strong Museum of American Life, and the Archives Center at the National Museum of American History. I am grateful to Daniel Aaron and Alfred D. Chandler, Jr., who provided crucial guidance in the early stages of my research; to Susan Strasser, who shared her own research on salesmen; to Malcolm Levison, who discussed his work as a commercial traveler; and to Jackson Lears, who read portions of the thesis and made valuable suggestions. I also thank Andrew Delbanco, Bob Kenzer, Janice Knight, and Marguerite Shaffer, who provided constructive commentary on selected chapters. Fellow travelers David Leviatin, Rafia Zafar, and, in particular, Steve Szaraz—whose ear I continue to bend—read and listened and made graduate study a collective pleasure. In Alan Heimert and John R. Stilgoe I was lucky enough to have advisers whose own searching engagement with primary materials encouraged me to take advantage of the boundless resources at Harvard. Their examples as scholars and teachers are still before me.

During the four years that it has taken to bring the dissertation to book form, I have incurred new debts and extended old ones. My editor at Yale University Press, Judy Metro, has borne with me as I have worked to revise and expand the manuscript. Working in the natural splendor of Vermont has brought me wonderfully supportive colleagues in the Department of American Literature and Civilization at Middlebury College. John McWilliams has provided wise general counsel, Ken Myers gave a valuable critique of my chapter on antebellum New York, and Nancy Schnog not only read several chapters in draft but helped me to think through the importance of domestic ideology for traveling salesmen. Outside Middlebury, correspondence and stray conversations with Pamela Laird, Charles McGovern, Roland Marchand, and others have sustained my interest in consumer cultural history. And I appreciate the time Willard F. Gordon and Carl W. Albrecht took to talk with me about the painter Archibald M. Willard.

Like so many of the salesmen whose words appear in this study, I am acutely aware how much I have relied on my family in completing this work. For their generous hospitality, support, and interest I would like to acknowledge William H. Rehnquist and the late Natalie Rehnquist. I would also like to thank my own parents, Carolyn and Robert Spears, whose unqualified support of my education has made all the difference. Finally, however inadequately, I thank Nancy Rehnquist Spears. From listening to graduate papers in the bathtub to holding children as I punched keys, she never stinted in her support. With love, I dedicate this book to her.

Introduction: A Rare Bird of Passage

After the Civil War, as the railroad system expanded and business interests reached out to new markets, the traveling salesman staked his claim on the American imagination. Hauling his gripsacks and sample trunks through railroad depots, hotel lobbies, and general stores, linking retail merchants to wholesalers and manufacturers, he played a vital role in the creation of a national market economy. A highly visible figure on the increasingly busy thoroughfares joining urban centers to small towns, he appeared to observers of all sorts as both the agent of cultural change and its representative—a touchstone for the contradictory impulses and meanings that Americans attached to the forces of modernization. Yet by 1900 the commercial traveler, or drummer, as he was often called, seemed part of an irretrievable past. "Lest this order of individual should permanently pass," eulogized Theodore Dreiser in *Sister Carrie,* "let me put down some of the most striking characteristics of his most successful manner and method."[1]

The economic factors allied against the salesman were several. Mail-order houses like Sears and Montgomery Ward, selling directly to consumers, bypassed the dreaded middleman and eliminated traveling salesmen from their marketing processes. National retail-store chains, buying directly from suppliers, challenged local retailers and threatened the salesmen who serviced them. And in some industries, manufacturers who had once depended on wholesalers—and scattered legions of traveling men—to market their products began, as early as the 1880s, to create their own sales forces.

For the most progressive businessmen, the terms of the drummer's passing were clearer still: the salesman now traveled in the shadow of the printed page. Advertising promised to revolutionize the marketplace and supplant older, face-to-face selling methods with more efficient, powerful modes of persuasion. In a 1904 *Atlantic* article, "The Psychology of Advertising," the industry consultant Walter Dill Scott presented the crux of the argument. During the nineteenth century the "separation of buyer, seller, and commodity made the commercial traveler with his sample case a necessity." But now that "the market-place has given way to the office," the advertisement "has superseded the market-place, and is, in many cases, displacing the commercial traveler." Traveling men would still be part of the distribution process—taking orders from customers and sales managers—but as influential factors in the creation of consumer desire, their glory days were over. The mysteries of persuasion now belonged to advertising, in those New York or Chicago offices where the "good features" of the marketplace—chiefly the salesman's personal appeal—were preserved and transformed.[2] As Roland Marchand has shown in *Advertising the American Dream: Making Way for Modernity, 1920–*

Cover, *A Drummer's Diary* (1906), by "Milton." (By permission of Houghton Library, Harvard University.)

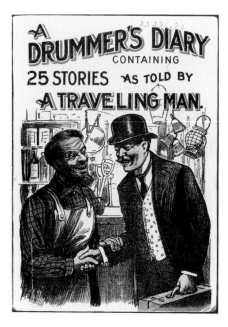

1940, ad agencies might welcome salesmen as copywriters, they might even require writers to serve time on the road, but they had little reason to acknowledge the genealogy of selling practices that stood behind their own work; as purveyors of modernity, backed by an arsenal of visual and psychological strategies, their goal was to efface all signs of the middleman and adapt the subjective nature of human relationships to the new medium of mass communication.[3] Modern advertising would henceforth be "salesmanship in print."[4]

Commercial travelers announced their own death with hardly a trace of irony. Beginning in the 1890s and continuing through the 1920s, trade journals like the *Sample Case* and the *Commercial Travelers Magazine,* as well as hundreds of salesmanship manuals, carried the arguments of traveling men that an "inflexible law of evolution" had banished the "old-time drummer" from the marketplace and spawned "scientific" sales techniques.[5]

On the one hand, the widespread evocation—and dismissal—of the drummer by twentieth-century salesmen suggests that progress did not bypass the traveling salesman, that "business enterprise"—Thorstein Veblen's term for calculating, corporate values—permeated all aspects of the marketplace, and that modernity galvanized face-to-face selling methods as much as it sped the rise of advertising techniques.[6] On the other hand, the tension between old and new methods reflected well-founded concerns over the changing nature of the economy, and a concerted effort by the profession as a whole to construct a genealogy of commercial practices recognizing the salesman's place in the development of modern American business. According to this genealogy, salesmanship, not advertising, and the salesman's psychological powers, not the advertiser's, anchored the new era in business. For progressive sales

2

avatars, the death of the drummer was good news: it signaled the regeneration of face-to-face selling methods and the birth of the modern salesman.

Contrary to Walter Dill Scott's claims, the traveling salesman did not disappear—in fact, the number of commercial travelers working in the United States rose dramatically during the first quarter of the century. Nor did his appeal as a cultural type wane; that appeal would hardly have pleased twentieth-century business reformers, however. By mid-century there was no need to explain the traveling salesman's function, his past, or his cultural significance, no point in distinguishing the drummer from the modern scientific salesman. The traveling salesman, the drummer, and the traveling man collapsed into a composite figure—a paradoxical icon bearing the imprint of the past and the gloss of modern mass culture. On Norman Rockwell magazine covers, where he occasionally appeared during the 1930s and 1940s, he became a quintessential American character, alternatively evoking gentle nostalgia and stoic loneliness. Moviegoers beheld the salesman's improvisations turned to heroics, comedy, and villainy. The 1920s alone yielded at least ten films featuring traveling salesmen in lead roles. Mostly silent and now out of print or unavailable for viewing, films like *Confidence* (a "rural comedy") and *Sunset Legion* (a "western melodrama") depended on the salesman's mobility for plots of mistaken identity and outlawry.[7] Resembling in effect the nineteenth-century dime novels in which the drummer's role was tailored to conventional story lines, such films—and later *The Music Man*—carried the image of the traveling salesman to an ever-widening audience and helped break down the finer distinctions that separated one kind of traveling salesman from another.

Despite the efforts of salesmen to recast the reputation of their profession, many productions cast the traveling salesman as an ambivalent, even scurrilous character. Eugene O'Neill's Hickey, featured in the 1946 play *The Iceman Cometh,* and Arthur Miller's Willy Loman. who premiered in 1949, remain perhaps the best-known representatives of this sullied figure, but they were not the first—or last. In Ring Lardner's "Haircut" (1926), T. S. Stribling's novel *Birthright* (1922) and his 1933 Pulitzer Prize winner, *The Store,* and Robert Tallant's *Southern Territory* (1951) readers discovered profligate jokers and untrustworthy salesmen.[8] Even where writers acknowledged the influence of modern salesmanship, as both Thomas Wolfe and Sinclair Lewis did in their fiction, the traveling men they depicted, however fleetingly, are often coarse, insincere, or savagely opportunistic.[9] By 1919, as H. L. Mencken noted in *The American Language,* "drummer" was one of many "commonplace Americanisms" that the public took for granted. In his own use of the word, Mencken was more pointed about its connotations: in "The National Letters" he twice condemned American popular literature, once because "it is addressed primarily to shoe-drummers and shop-girls" and again because "it is written by authors who are, to all intellectual intents and purposes, shoe-drummers and shop-girls." As a generic term evoking cheap commercialism or as an actual figure rehearsing tawdry dramas, *drummer*—the word and the

FLIRTING WITH CHAMBERMAID

THE INDEPENDENT SALESLADY

THE INDEPENDENT **SALESMAN.** TAKES ORDERS FROM NO ONE.

Instead of working to earn your pay,
You're boozing or sleeping half the day,
You're out playing poker every night
And flirting with chambermaids is your delight.
You try on the railroad to beat your way
And a lot of fake jewelry you display,
As a salesman you are only a bluff;
Go get a move on, and sell some stuff.

MADE IN U. S. A.

Despite the emergence of more efficient sales practices and notwithstanding efforts by the business community to reform the public's view of the traveling salesman, images like this greeting card from the 1920s dominated American imaginations. (Courtesy of Strong Museum, Rochester, N.Y.)

type—was part of a vocabulary that Mencken ironically shared with the low-brow publications that he condemned. At bottom, Mencken's highbrow condescension drew from the same stock of allusions that shaped "A Drummer's Prayer," which appeared in a 1921 issue of the humor magazine *Captain Billy's Whiz Bang:* the supplicant asks the "Good Lord" to "curb our tendency to flirt with the married women; the single ones don't count, and they expect it."[10]

Whether or not a majority of traveling salesmen actually did drink to excess, chase women, and generally flout middle-class notions of respectability is unclear; the production of any stereotype—concerning race, creed, ethnicity, gender, or even occupation—owes as much, if not more, to cultural perceptions and the social conditions that surround those perceptions as it does to objective social facts. It is clear, however, that the basis for the salesman's image in twentieth-century America shifted away from social reality and toward the increasingly visible institutions of modern popular culture. According to Booth Tarkington, writing in *Penrod,* his 1914 novel about boyhood indiscretions, the reproduction of this image was part of a heterodox process that yielded real salesmen but had nothing to do with reality. One of Penrod's offenses, for example, involves spending church money on a film about "a company of loose travelling men." After this movie "made a lasting impression on him" and after he caused a disruption in school, Penrod attributes his behavior to lack of sleep—a lack, he tells his teacher, precipitated by a family crisis: his Uncle John's drinking spree. "It all commenced," explains Penrod, "from the first day he let those travelling men coax him into the saloon."[11]

Like many of Tarkington's readers and like many Americans born at the turn of the century, Penrod learned of the drummer second- and even third-hand; then he passed his lesson on, as though it derived from his family's social history. Tarkington captured the uniquely modern terms of the traveling man's presence in twentieth-century America. Thirty, even twenty years earlier, lessons like Penrod's took place on the Main Streets of small towns or along the corridors of the nationwide rail system—places where people knew the commercial traveler by sight. But by the 1920s, if not sooner, such lessons had less to do with direct observation than with the vast panorama of sources and artifacts—literature, language, jokes, oral history, and film—in which the traveling man appeared, reappeared, and circulated. This, indeed, is how contemporary Americans have come to know the traveling salesman—as a mythic figure cut loose from the bonds of history.

The years between 1900 and 1925 constitute an important prelude to this disappearance from history, a moment when the traveling salesman's past and future opened up for public scrutiny. The immediate occasion for a historical evaluation was economic: the transformation of the old-time drummer into the modern salesman. But the transition resonated beyond specialized business needs to encompass some of the principal social developments of the early twentieth-century United States: the continued expansion and maturity of consumer culture, the rise of corporate and bureaucratic institutions and ways of thinking, the ongoing modernization of the transportation system and the built environment, the demographic shift from rural to urban centers, the cultural and literary embrace of various modernisms, and more. The salesman preoccupied writers and critics by appearing to mediate these transformations and occupying a rather nebulous territory that separated an older America from a newer one. In best-selling books like George Horace Lorimer's *Letters from a Self-Made Merchant to His Son* and Edna Ferber's series of business novels, including *Emma McChesney and Co.* and *Personality Plus*, in fiction by such writers as Sherwood Anderson and Willa Cather, and throughout periodical literature of the era, the commercial traveler played the paradoxical role of cultural middleman; he figured not only as a representative of modern business success but also as a remnant from the past.

In even the most ebullient portrait of the up-to-date salesman, *Letters from a Self-Made Merchant to His Son*, there were signs of the past and indications of the tensions that accompanied the progress of business. First published in serial form by the *Saturday Evening Post* in 1902 and loosely based on the author's own experiences working for P. D. Armour, Lorimer's *Letters* highlighted the business education of a meat-packing executive's son and the importance of modern business methods.[12] The Harvard-educated son is prone to wasteful habits when he begins working, but rises through the ranks of his father's company in large part by spending time on the road and unlearning the romance associated with being a traveling salesman. "A real salesman is one-part talk and nine-parts judgment," the self-made Graham tells his son. "Real buyers ain't interested in much besides your goods and your prices," and "mighty few men work up to the position of buyer through giving up their office hours to listening to anecdotes. I never saw one that liked a drummer's jokes more than an eighth of a cent a pound on a tierce of lard."[13]

It is clear from such advice that success in the modern era depends on relinquishing the colorful methods of yesteryear and adopting a more direct, efficient way of doing business; so Pierrepont succeeds and is eventually promoted to a managerial position. Yet it is equally clear that the past persists in residual form, as in old Graham's storytelling and his shrewd, cracker-barrel wit—a vernacular that is at odds with the kind of modern business rhetoric that he recommends to his son. Indeed, as Lorimer's recent biographer has argued, Lorimer's object as a writer and as the editor of the *Post* was to create and promote a modern America made by commonplace business success. Although stories about captains of industry appeared in the *Post*, Frank Norris's *Pit*, for example, the immense success of the magazine and the popularity of the *Letters*, whose publishing success rivaled that of *Uncle Tom's Cabin*, stemmed from the depiction of commonplace business habits and businessmen, especially salesmen—subjects, in other words, that appealed to the magazine's middle-class audience.[14]

The tremendous growth of white-collar corporate jobs around the turn of the century created the subject and the audience for the trade in business romances, but the emphasis was less on innovation than on the transition from old to new. Thus Lorimer promoted the values of modern business enterprise in nineteenth-century terms, trying to encourage efficiency without sacrificing common sense, character, or hard work—traits that he associated with his own generation. Edna Ferber likewise dramatized the tension between old and new commercial methods in generational terms. Jock McChesney, the young adman portrayed in her novels, is up-to-date, modern, and, at times, overconfident. But as if to answer celebrants of modern advertising, Ferber qualifies his success, or at least complements it, by insisting on his mother's ability to command the marketplace where advertising cannot. Emma McChesney is a traveling saleswoman. And her success in a story of modern business enterprise, not only in promoting and nurturing her son's career but also in affirming the continuing power of face-to-face sales methods—though they might appear obsolete—reflects the ambivalent nature of the traveling salesman's persistence in twentieth-century America.

By 1900 there seemed to be two salesmen fighting for the commercial traveler's identity—one the representative of a older, "residual" face-to-face marketplace, the other the agent of an "emergent" corporate economy, both of which, according to Raymond Williams's formulation of the terms, posed potential threats to established cultural values.[15] For business reformers the choice was obvious. Flashy clothing, dirty jokes, and treating for drinks— the most frequently criticized aspects of the old-time drummer's ways— threatened the rationalizing thrust of modern business enterprise. Yet no matter how fiercely proselytizers called for the transformation of commercial practices, even they had difficulty separating old from new. Not only did the new appear organically linked to the old in ways that resembled the generational relationship described by Lorimer and Ferber, but the one distinguished and defined the other. Without the old, there could be no new, so to promote the modern salesman, progressive businessmen almost always returned to the drummer. But old and new were not merely value-free formal distinctions. Modern salesmanship's emphasis on cooperation and rationalization conflicted with broadly held notions of individualism, autonomy, and freedom. This emphasis was complicated by the fact that even the most standardized selling strategies required some independence and initiative. In dramatizing the importance of teamwork and systematic effort, however, early twentieth-century sales experts rarely acknowledged this irony. To do so would highlight the contradictions built into this most unself-conscious, most personal of professions. According to the bulk of literature published between 1900 and 1925, the modern salesman was expected to adapt his personality to a variety of customers, follow prescribed steps in making a sale, and dispel any sign of conflict during that sale—all without drawing attention to himself.

Despite the claims to modernity that ran throughout the literature, the salesman remained only human, which is to say that no matter how scientific his rhetoric or approach appeared, he represented the continuity of face-to-face relationships in a world increasingly given to effacing them. Janus-faced, the twentieth-century traveling man was neither drummer nor scientific salesman, but frequently and sometimes tragically he was both. The poignance of Arthur Miller's *Death of a Salesman* and the savagery of Eugene O'Neill's *Iceman Cometh* derived from this paradox: in selling product and self, the salesman proved humanly fallible, yet he constantly tried to create himself anew and become something more. The contradiction dates to Greek tragedy; in the twentieth-century United States its power rested on the wide range of tensions generated throughout the culture by the expansion of modern business enterprise. For many writers and critics the traveling salesman's ambivalent links to the past and the future, and to residual and emergent commercial methods, represented the mixed blessings of modernization.

Although the traveling salesman provided the occasion for dramatization and criticism of economic and cultural change during the late nineteenth century, it was only in the first years of the twentieth century that he became a creature of historical consciousness. In portraits that emerged around 1900, observers figured the salesman as a somewhat overdetermined middleman in a transaction that exchanged youth for adulthood, stasis for mobility, and small-town or rural existence for urban life. These autobiographical, elegiac studies of the past often located modernity where we would least expect it: in an intimate landscape set apart in time and space from the anonymous mass market—in what Scott and other business writers called a marketplace. "Where will you find such a market-place in modern days?" asked Bruce Barton in his popular 1925 paean to advertising, *The Man Nobody Knows*. "A corner of Fifth Avenue? A block on Broadway?" Whereas Barton argued that advertisements were now "the cross-roads where the sellers and buyers meet," he found the origins of commercial power in the "small and leisurely" cities of the biblical past, in a world that fostered face-to-face selling strategies. And whereas he viewed Jesus as a vigorous precursor to modern advertisers, he claimed that Jesus "brilliantly exemplified" the "principles of modern salesmanship"—indicating that Barton's search for the origins of twentieth-century business had less to do with ancient history than with his own small-town background and a vivid memory of traveling salesmen pursuing the trade along Main Street.[16]

Reconstructing the salesman's place in the nineteenth-century market-place was most immediately a reaction to the abstract nature of twentieth-century commercial practices. In the long run, however, it was the perceptual problem of a self-consciously modern culture struggling with the loss of a decentralized, human-scaled landscape. The traveling salesman had not disappeared. "He is everywhere—this modern nomadic missionary of commerce —everywhere, yet elusive," wrote Forrest Crissey in a 1909 article for *Everybody's Magazine*. But despite "his unfailing presence as part of the public landscape, few of those who touch elbows with him know the manner of man he is, or read the riddle of his existence."[17] How could they? By the early twentieth century, the structures of commercial traveling and of American life itself showed the impact of modernization, enough so that the traveling salesman dropped from sight. Most modern salesmen made smaller territories than their nineteenth-century counterparts, and they worked them more quickly. They used the telephone to conduct business, and, as early as 1905, began to drive automobiles, an innovation that, although it often made travel more efficient, inevitably removed them from scenes they had typically haunted during the nineteenth century: railroad cars, depots, Main Streets, and hotel lobbies.[18] According to the "crack" salesman whom Crissey interviewed, the life of the modern traveling man "is a series of quick commercial contacts, a panorama of hustle, a touch-and-go proposition in which he must impress his personality upon the trade with almost the quickness of an 'instantaneous exposure of a kodak.'" No wonder Crissey promised to explain the mystery of this barely visible existence with a "moving picture of a few days in the life of a commercial traveler." No wonder, by contrast, he compared the surviving "impressions" of the drummer to "old daguerreotypes" bearing little resemblance to modern life. Leisurely, sociable, and "picturesque," the "old time" drummer's existence evoked an era when business opportunities were not nearly so "numerous" or so "widespread," or, Crissey scarcely had to emphasize, so rapidly pursued.[19]

Like many other turn-of-the-century observers, Crissey was struck by the traveling salesman's altered nature, his air of modernity. But rather than account for it in terms of inherent characteristics or business training, transformations isolated within the salesman himself, Crissey emphasized the relationship between the traveling man and his audience. Assuming that people continued to find the traveling salesman an object of fascination but acutely aware that the conditions of perception had changed, Crissey suggested a new visual aesthetic—a way of seeing the salesman's place in the "great system," the "big machine" of modern business that resembled efforts by writers and intellectuals to represent twentieth-century technology.[20]

However forward-looking this speed-sensitive aesthetic seemed, it remained rooted in a nostalgic awareness of the more leisurely, somehow more natural ways of seeing that made the drummer a dramatic figure in the nineteenth-century small town. Similar to the German critic Walter Benjamin, who was fascinated with modern culture—a fascination that was likewise mediated by a poignant recollection of how life used to be—Crissey linked the evolution in business practices to changes in cultural perception. In such essays as "The Work of Art in the Age of Mechanical Reproduction" and "The Storyteller," Benjamin used the emergence of new aesthetic forms as an occasion for considering the relation between artistic object and beholder. This relation, and not simply the object itself, informs Benjamin's understanding of the modern aesthetic experience. Perception is always dialectical, both because the process of seeing is dynamic and because the conditions of seeing are always being shaped by historical forces—hence the waning aura of the art object in a culture of mass reproduction, and the loss of community and intimacy in the breakdown of the oral storytelling tradition. These developments, for Benjamin, remained inseparable from the changing economy. As Frederic Jameson has observed, Benjamin's writings are distinguished by a "painful straining toward a psychic wholeness or unity of experience which the historical situation threatens to shatter at every turn."[21] The autobiographical self's longing for a state that the critical self knows has disappeared or is slipping away is itself a product of cultural transformation and, indeed, one of the distinguishing marks of modernity.

A similar temporal breach—a moment when modern business methods seemed to crystallize and to overshadow the traditions of an older, face-to-face economy—framed turn-of-the-century representations of the traveling salesman. The modern salesman, as Crissey's description suggests, epitomized a new culture—upbeat, urban, and peculiarly abstract—as well as a new way of seeing, for both the salesman and his observers. The death of the drummer, on the other hand, augured the disappearance of a pre-incorporated commercial landscape, a Main Street culture that, at least in retrospect, seemed to place salesman, customer, and onlooker on common perceptual ground. Ac-

New greets old, and metropolitan meets rural, in these turn-of-the-century depictions of the traveling salesman's arrival in a small town.

From Charles N. Crewdson's *Tales of the Road* (1905). (Collection of the author.)

counting for this death as the logical outcome of evolving business practices or the natural consequence of pervasive modernization does not, however, begin to get at the autobiographical character of its representation. The drummer's death served as the occasion for a review of the metaphoric power of the marketplace, which, when conceived in personal, historical terms, highlighted the traveling salesman's talismanic pull on small-town imaginations.

Consider, for instance, Sherwood Anderson's reflections on the traveling salesman, written in 1904, ten years before the publication of his first short story. "About the best thing that can be said about the old dyed-in-the-wool, six-months-twice-a-year traveling man," observed Anderson, "is that he is passing." After several years of writing and selling copy—and often traveling—for a Chicago advertising agency, Anderson knew how to press the advantages of progressive business methods on a midwestern audience. Writing for *Agricultural Advertising*, the trade journal of his agency, which was aimed at advertisers and merchants alike, he told readers that "modern methods, rapid transit, mails, electricity and advertising" would soon make

"The Champion and the Drummer," *Crescent and Grip* (August 1907). (Courtesy of Library of Congress.)

the old-style traveling man obsolete. Looking forward to a commercial landscape shaped by systematic efficiency, a time without drummers, Anderson echoed the bluff optimism of modern sales experts when he concluded that the "winds of time will sweep the old boys into the past, and there will be no new ones in their places, and that's fine."[22]

Underlying this faith in modern business enterprise, however, lay an acute, almost painful sense of changed circumstances. Although Anderson confidently greeted the advent of modern methods, that progressive view remained confined to the last paragraph. In most of the article he focused retrospectively on the drummer and the dim outlines of his "lonely, story telling existence." The memories, by contrast, emphasized the clean, hard efficiency of modern advertising copy. But Anderson's own interests seemed to lie elsewhere and, evoking the memory of "those outriders in the march of commerce," he urged his readers to recall their childhood dreams.

> Were you ever a boy in a corn field on a hot June day, and just as you had come to the end of the row and were taking a long pull at the lukewarm water in the jug by the fence corner, did the afternoon train westward bound at forty miles an hour, pass around the corner of the hill and go roaring and screaming off into the strange land that lay over and beyond Brownville? Or did this happen in the evening when you had washed the stains of the day's work from you and had gone down to the depot to see the train go through? And did

something give a savage tug at your heart so that it hurt, as with big hungry eyes you saw all of these people going so blandly and with such careless mien into that wonderful and enchanted land that lay east of Jasperville?[23]

In posing such questions, Anderson hoped to unite his readers around a shared view of the past. First by presenting certain features of small-town life as commonly known landmarks—the tedious farmwork, the busy depot, the scheduled train—then by describing the desire to escape and transcend those landmarks as a romantic exploration of enchanted worlds, he assumed the reader's participation in the emotional and cultural conflicts that accompanied the great internal migrations of the late nineteenth century. Anderson's appeal to you the reader likewise assumes the continued power of this apparently shared past and transforms the youthful longing to explore worlds beyond the cornfield to its contemporaneous equivalent: nostalgia. Like a dream, Anderson's reminiscence derives much of its power from an integration of concrete details and inward longings that lie outside or beyond the temporal and physical scene. What gives the boyhood fantasies their poignance and enables Anderson to re-create a community of hungry modern readers—whose desires were once circumscribed, in figurative terms at least, by a cornfield fence—is the retrospective knowledge of what leaving that world entails. In this sense, the travelers' careless mien and the screaming of the train simultaneously represent a life yet to come and a world left behind. Between these two stages, auguring the transition from present to future and, in retrospect, bridging the present to the past, was the drummer. "I know a fellow that has crept away by himself on many such nights and there, lying on his back amid the grass and looking at the stars, he had such a hungryness to get on that train that he thought he would die of it. Oh! to step briskly along as did that little round man with grip in his hand!"[24] Underlying the drummer's death were the memory of identifying with his apparent freedom of movement and a longing for the shared feeling that such identification conferred.

Similarly, in a 1929 *American Magazine* article entitled "My Memories of the Old-Fashioned Drummer," the humorist Don Marquis represented the traveling man's powers of attraction from a perspective that only a provincial transplant could fully appreciate. "To those of us who lived in the little inland towns in the Gay Nineties, the Drummer was not primarily interesting in his capacity as salesman." Rather, he commanded attention because he was "a brilliant bird of passage," "a connecting link with the great outside world," "a sentimentalist," a "purveyor of stories," and a "political prophet." Unlike the twentieth-century salesman, who "is a standardized product of modern efficiency" and as "self-contained as a tin of tuna fish," the drummer lived and breathed the issues and personalities of his day. Playing as many roles as his improvisational skills allowed, he brought vaudeville to Main Street. In short, Marquis concluded, it "takes the automobile, the radio, and the salesman to fill the place that once he filled so expansively." In his place on Main Street the drummer appeared in retrospect to have been a precursor of, if not a substitute for, the forces of modernization. Catching him at the peak of his improvisational powers on the cusp of the modern age, Marquis revealed why the drummer "bumped the zenith of his era" and how, just a few years later, he became the very image of his "old-fashioned" decade.[25]

But Marquis also remembered another image from the Gay Nineties. "My memory still retains a picture of myself, as a barefooted, freckle-faced boy of twelve, standing on a plank sidewalk in a prairie town . . . and looking up at one of these magnificent beings."[26] No wonder the drummer appeared larger than life. From the ground, looking up, the young Marquis inevitably magnified the drummer's colorful image and, with childlike awe, accentuated the features that already set him apart from the prairie scenery.

By looking up, a generation of inland Americans came to know something of the historical process that was transforming their world of "loosely connected islands" into a close-knit, modern society.[27] Yet only by looking back—in light of intervening transformations—were they able to recover this childhood vision and re-view the drummer's role in instigating cultural change. Surrounded by the wonders of urban mass culture, they looked to their small-town pasts for some sign of modernity and constructed their own roles as witnesses to history. Marquis, for one, acknowledged his small-town perspective and identified its historical frame. "I speak of the Gay Nineties as they appeared to Massilon, Ohio; Griffin, Georgia; Plumville, Pennsylvania; Walnut, Illinois; Clay Center, Nebraska; and not as they impressed London and Paris and New York City." He also acknowledged the vagaries of memory and conceded that after "looking back on [the drummer] through the haze of thirty years" he "seems somehow less romantic to me now than he did then." Marquis questioned whether this picturesque figure was, "actually or potentially, a devil of a fellow with the girls" and admitted that his description rested on "a composite recollection of some forty or fifty drummers whom I knew." But accuracy hardly mattered. "Whether it is true, or whether it was only an agreeable and exciting fiction, I don't know." The reputation was simply "part of the story" that followed the drummer wherever he went.[28] At bottom, "My Memories of the Old-Fashioned Drummer" spoke directly to the drummer's status as a represented figure and, without seeking to substantiate the drummer's actual behavior, highlighted the cultural dynamics that undergirded his collective, mythic identity in the small town. If during the 1890s the drummer's reputation preceded his arrival in Marquis's inland town—outstripping and perhaps even informing his dramatic presence—in memory it thickened and became old-fashioned, the product of a complicated convergence of sentiments that might simply be called nostalgia.

Of course, nostalgia now smacks of sentimentalism. Its late twentieth-century definition—according to the *American Heritage Dictionary*, "a bittersweet yearning for past circumstances, things, or people"—registers the disdain that modern society often has for retrograde historical thinking. This contemporary meaning, however, elides the original usage of the word. Literally, *nostalgia* means "homesickness," and its Greek roots—*nostos* meaning "return home" and *algai* meaning "painful condition"—point to the social and psychological traumas that once accompanied migration. During the seventeenth, eighteenth, and early nineteenth centuries, for example, Europeans understood nostalgia to be an organic disease that afflicted mercenaries, urban migrants, and other people transplanted beyond familiar environs. By the twentieth century the term no longer referred to a physical condition but rather to a painful, subjective state, whose cure, despite its psychological causes, involved returning to a specific remembered place. In the United States this emphasis endured as late as 1934, when, according to *Webster's New International Dictionary, nostalgia* still meant "homesickness"—a reminder of just how recently the nostalgic object had a place in space as well as time.[29]

Reclaiming the older connotations of *nostalgia* broadens and sharpens the context for understanding turn-of-the-century attitudes toward the traveling salesman. Although the notions of residual and emergent cultures highlight the uneasy tension between the drummer and the modern salesman and point beyond the figures themselves to competing business practices, they do not make sufficiently clear the extent to which contemporaneous representations of the traveling man grew out of a consciousness that was simultaneously historical and geographical. In other words, fascination with the drummer as a residual commercial figure had as much to do with the uneven modernization of the American landscape as it did with temporal distinctions between the old-fashioned and the modern. Marquis acknowledged this conflation of time and space when he claimed "that in many localities"—that is, in places seemingly untouched by urban influences and modern conveniences, like chain stores, electric lights, and paved roads—"the Drummer lingered well into the Twentieth Century."[30]

Marquis's suggestion that the same traveling man could be a drummer in one place and a modern salesman in another belies the assertion, made by Walter Dill Scott and others, that by 1900 the human-scaled, face-to-face marketplace had disappeared. The persistence of the marketplace, however, was hardly an objective fact or a condition that could be measured by strictly economic factors. Rather, *marketplace,* like *modern* and *old-fashioned,* may be best understood as a relative term, dependent not only on regional diversity or varying economic conditions but also on shifting cultural perceptions. The dramatic, uneven pace of change accentuated these perceptions, which gave way to a nostalgic ethos in which historical and geographical differences could be fluid and interchangeable. For the people of a nation still becoming a mass society, especially urban migrants from small towns and rural areas for whom the dislocations and anomie of metropolitan culture seemed a palpable reality, nostalgia constituted a kind of homelessness and gave rise to longings for past landscapes that barely distinguished between time and place.[31] In early twentieth-century America *back home* referred to spatial and temporal distance. Back home was rarely in Boston, New York, or Chicago, but rather, as the popular song pointed out, "in Indiana." Or it was in Willa Cather's Nebraska, Hamlin Garland's Wisconsin, or any number of rural and small-town landscapes that native-born Americans abandoned for urban life but returned to in memory.

Understood in this context, the traveling salesman was the focal point for a structure of feeling that encompassed far more than anxiety over a changing economy. Between the drummer and the modern salesman was an ever-varying metaphorical distance that separated small towns from urban centers, old-fashioned ways from modernity, picturesque views from abstraction, and, in short, life-as-it-was from life-as-it-is-now. But the variation in this distance, the apparent struggle between drummer and modern salesman for the same space—even though the two were supposed to be so different—says as much about the evolving nature of the marketplace as it does about the culture that sought to represent the evolution. American business ways changed dramatically between 1885 and 1920. And the erosion of a personal marketplace and the emergence of more abstract market practices—of which modern advertising was only a part—made the traveling salesman himself nostalgically conscious of how things used to be.

Certainly, no one felt the impact of the modern era more acutely than the veteran commercial traveler. Better than their younger colleagues, the old-timers, whose working lives spanned thirty, forty, even fifty years, understood the double-edged thrust of modernization. Certainly they knew, as trade journals frequently reminded them, that the professionalization of commercial traveling meant breaking old habits and established ways. They knew, for instance, that if the middle-aged salesman "foolishly relies on past individual experiences and does not make an effort to assimilate the ideas of the progressive elements, he is sure to be pushed aside."[32] If only because they learned the ground rules of modern salesmanship, veteran travelers knew the costs, as well as the benefits, of modernization.

But accepting and even promoting the evolution of salesmanship hardly obscured the past. In fact, the advent of modern business enterprise prompted a valuation of the old-timer's place in commercial history. In 1916 the *American Magazine* honored "the Oldest Traveling Salesman" in America, an "eighty-nine-year[-old] veteran" named James Fenlon who "continues to 'look after his trade' with all of the success that has characterized his work in his younger days." Ironically, the trade press, which continually rammed home the lessons of modern business enterprise, likewise highlighted the debt of the profession to the "old grey heads" who "brought it about." So the *Commercial Travelers Magazine* began its 1915 biographical series on "the veterans of the road" by praising "the real present pioneers of our business progress" who "first packed their grips as young men so many years ago." Looking down "the vista of many years to see our grey head as he once was, then as he now is," and "watching beside the highway of life" to "behold a generation pass" conveniently reaffirmed the natural development of modern salesmanship. But not even didacticism could conceal the implicit longing to revisit the past. That lingered in subsequent sketches by and of veteran salesmen, in obituaries, and in the ongoing exploits of the Oracles of Christmas Cove, described in the eponymous column in the *Commercial Travelers Magazine*. Featured in the column were the ancient residents of a declining small town and their occasional visits with the "old timers on the road," with whom they fondly remembered bygone days.[33] But most of all, the desire to capture the past persisted in the autobiographical writings of veteran salesmen.

"Thirty years on the road, where's the travelers I knew, / In that summer of eighteen and seventy-two?" wonders the author of "1872 to 1903," in an issue of the *Sample Case*. "Thirty years on the road, what changes have come, / Since the time I first got into the game." With old friends dead, retired, or "still striving to keep up the pace," the veteran salesman marvels that once "we stopped at the tavern, and rode on the stage" and "thought we were living in a mighty fast age." Just as marvelous, however, are the speed with which these changes took place and the eerie sensation that they happened so recently. For "when I look back, it does not seem far / From the old stage coach to the electric car."[34] Compressed into a single working lifetime, the swift pace of change made the past seem very close indeed.

The poem catches the wistful, autobiographical perspective that dominates so many of the accounts written by veteran salesmen in the decades following 1900. In contrast to the many textbooks on modern salesmanship or the spirited, sometimes tongue-in-cheek views of road life published in the late nineteenth century, these works consciously address the passage of time. They are memoirs, reflections on a lifetime of work that circumscribe the growth of a modern profession in highly personal terms. Of course, storytelling was what drummers did—what modern sales theory forbade—so by narrating their life histories, veteran travelers not only exemplified their connection to an older world but denied the complete hegemony of modern business enterprise.[35] Sometimes ambivalent and often nostalgic, such works as *Tales of a Traveler: Reminiscences and Reflections from Twenty-Eight Years on the Road; A Ranger of Commerce; or, Fifty-Two Years on the Road;* and *Beyond the Swivel Chair: Sixty Years of Selling in the Field* dramatize the attempt to find enduring subjective value in an occupation increasingly devoted to scientific standards and efficient organization.[36]

By remembering, old-timers maintained a grip on the improvisational, aggressive spirit that had distinguished their early days on the road, and memorialized their role in the development of commercial traveling. Instead of making towns, veteran salesmen now struggled to make history of an especially personal sort.

Sometimes the struggle provoked bitterness, when pioneer salesmen demanded recognition that younger men seemed unwilling to give. "Horse and buggy days were an actuality to me in the days that are now held in derision by those who know nothing of them," Frank Smith proudly—and defensively—declared in his 1940 memoir, *Beyond the Swivel Chair*. "It Can't All Be Card

Indexed," he quipped after noting that the modern salesman's "route, his sales talk, and his time making them, are all taken care of by the home office." Yet even Smith, who scorned the lack of initiative in modern sales, like most older salesmen who commented on the advent of new business techniques, welcomed the efficiency and cooperation that now distinguished sales organizations. From experiencing the transformations—which, according to one old-timer's rather bitter reminiscences, confined "real life on the road" to an underappreciated past—veteran commercial travelers well knew the consequences of modernity.[37]

Few memoirists proposed, as one salesmen did, to glimpse their "'Footprints' along 'the shifting sands of time'" so that, combining "retrospect" with "introspect," they might morally judge their past conduct, but practically all writers testified to the tremendous differences generated by history.[38] Many addressed specific commercial and industrial advances. A shoe salesman marveled over modern manufacturing techniques, a flower salesman remarked on the improvements in greenhouses, and a hardware salesman noted the impact of corporate mergers on marketing structures.[39] Alone, such facts denoted important, yet hardly poignant, historical changes. Together, embedded in narratives highlighting personal as well as professional landmarks, they told emotional, sometimes melodramatic stories of success and failure.

These narratives are not bildungsromans. At least they do not focus primarily on the education and rise of callow youths. Nor do they evoke the ebullient, self-creative energy that pervades so many American autobiographies. Rather, they offer a moderate, even chastened view of individual success, emphasizing in first-person singular the necessity of the golden rule in business and the importance of "pulling together" with managers, customers, and other salesmen.[40] Avoiding the cynical self-satisfaction of accounts like Edward Palmer's *Forty Years of Hustling*—a story of door-to-door confidence tricks and street-corner faking dedicated to "the many victims of graft" by an "old codger that has really hit the high spots"—they underscore the shared values of a developing profession.[41] A veteran traveling man like Victor Jacobs, who went bankrupt after establishing his own cloak-manufacturing firm, still remained "gratified" by the continued "respect or good will" of his "old friends and neighbors." Even Harry Nisbet, the shoe salesman whose Bunyanesque view of life in *Footprints* sprang, in part, from his debilitating health and poverty, dreamed happily of "old time customers" and the "fraternity of traveling salesmen" that "never allowed" business rivalry to "be other than a friendly one."[42] In middle and old age, veteran salesmen cherished the steadier, less glamorous benefits of their profession.

Stretching beyond these good feelings, impelling and containing them, was the road. No other image so aptly designates the open-ended freedom that distinguished commercial traveling from practically all other professions. No other image contributed so much to the traveling man's allusive power. Indeed, the road gave the salesman a paradoxical mix of identities—made him a pilgrim, a quixotic knight, a Wandering Jew, a liminal trickster, and more. But

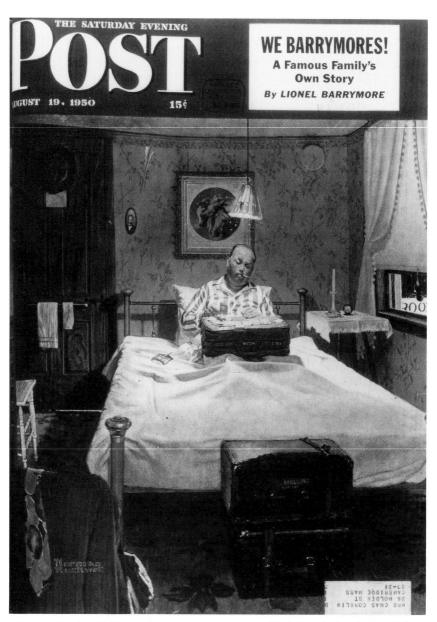

Norman Rockwell's illustration captures the sense of isolation and stoical geniality associated with the traveling salesman's role in twentieth-century American culture. Cover, *Saturday Evening Post*, August 19, 1950. (Printed by permission of the Norman Rockwell Family Trust. Copyright 1950 by the Norman Rockwell Family Trust.)

as commercial travelers inevitably discovered, life on the road demanded as much as it offered. Beyond romance and adventure, making towns frequently bound the salesman to an itinerary, guided his improvisations, and designated his role in a striving, if not embattled, profession. For those who knew it well, the road proved a source of both pleasure and hardship.

Time softened this ambivalence. Nostalgically, veteran salesmen remembered the road as a landscape peopled with valued friends and happy experiences. Territories that they had viewed with increasing familiarity as they mapped its features and met their customers became, in retrospect, adopted homes. Even without returning to the original site, as Howard Peak did when he viewed his old Texas territory from an airplane, veteran salesmen often recollected the landmarks of well-traveled territories with practiced conviction. "I am sure it would be an utter impossibility for any person to recall all the changes that have occurred in the retail shoe business during the last thirty-two years," wrote Harry Nisbet in 1911, "even among those with whom he has personally been acquainted." Yet, "I will endeavor to mention a few of them, starting in at Albany and Troy, then following along the line of the New York Central Railroad in regular order, most of the principal cities and towns terminating at Buffalo."[43] Whatever changes Nisbet missed, he made up for by leading his readers on a detailed tour of the stores and customers that distinguished the Mohawk Valley during the late nineteenth century.

Nisbet's urge to "step over to Lansingburgh" and revisit an "old genial friend and customer" typifies the nostalgia that shaped most salesmen's memoirs. After thirty or forty years on the road, they looked back to recover the physical and emotional features of a waning, even defunct business culture. "Daily I recall the faces and figures of well-remembered friends of the road," wrote Joel Page in his 1916 *Recollections.* Like most old-timers, he devoted pages, even lists, to the memory of fellow salesmen—"the companions of another and earlier generation." Acutely conscious of the age divisions in the modern commercial landscape, veterans recalled a more colorful, less standardized era, a time when sales sense and personal idiosyncrasy appeared to coexist. Simon Skidelsky, for instance, described "one man—let us call him John Smith—who divided his time between his business affairs and bucket shops," and fondly eulogized "others of the type, long gone though not forgotten by their numerous friends," who likewise sold flowers, seeds, and greenhouse equipment during the 1880s and 1890s.[44]

Like exiles from small-town America, old-timers yearned for the old standards and, through memory, attempted to shore up the foundations of their professional and personal identities. Through nostalgia they endeavored to mend a cultural dialogue that, as they well knew, was often fractured beyond repair.[45] "It seems to me in those earlier days we got in closer touch with our customers than we do today," reflected J. P. Bartelle. "The facilities for getting over the territory were not what they are now. As a rule we made but two or three towns daily and therefore had more time for intimate acquaintanceship."[46] Bartelle's memoir, *Forty Years on the Road; or, the Reminiscences of a*

Lumber Salesman (1925), proved an effort to restore this intimacy, to recapture the shared moments that modern business practices, and, indeed, modernity itself, prohibited. Clearly, the drummer's place in the landscape had changed; but, in contrast to Sherwood Anderson or Don Marquis, old-timers described this transformation from the inside looking out. Their view also resonated with broader social change, but the focus remained slightly different. Observers like Anderson and Marquis knew the salesman's story-telling life as a landmark of their small-town childhoods. Traveling men themselves knew it as an indigenous cultural practice, a way of speaking and improvising that sold goods and reinforced fraternal feeling. In addressing audiences, autobiographers assumed this story-telling voice out of occupational custom. No wonder portions of *Footprints on the Road* appeared first in trade journals like the *Boot and Shoe Recorder* and the *Shoe Retailer*.[47] Specifically written for a turn-of-the-century audience whose experiences and memories resembled the authors', such reminiscences exemplified a way of knowing and telling that only drummers could call their own.

Yet as Anderson and Marquis indicated in their own reminiscences, it was precisely this way of knowing that drew writers to the traveling salesman and made his creative powers a touchstone for their own. When Anderson wrote of his childhood admiration for the drummer, he was plainly reconstructing his own desire for freedom and power. And when he recalled the drummer's lonely story-telling existence, he made the connection even more explicit, suggesting that the salesman's perspective as a rover, his vernacular language, and his ability to gather an audience were the attributes of a literary imagination—and, for a would-be writer, worth emulating. Like the oral tradition that Benjamin recalled in "The Storyteller," the drummer's storytelling was peculiarly tuned to local idiom, if only because it was rooted in a marketplace scaled to human gestures and human voices.

This longing for an authentic literary voice grew in the climate of nostalgia that veteran traveling men and their observers shared during the first decades of the twentieth century. In their most sentimental form, nostalgic representations of the traveling salesman became part of a conventional vocabulary that reached toward an unmediated relation with the past and referred elliptically to an unabstracted world of face-to-face relationships. In their least sentimental emanations, in fiction by Anderson, Willa Cather, and, to lesser an extent, Sinclair Lewis, such representations featured the traveling salesman as part of a mediated past, a small-town culture that the narrator encourages the reader to see through the frame of the present. So in Cather's *My Ántonia*, the traveling men shown at the Boys' Home hotel in Black Hawk, Nebraska—and depicted as participants in a warm, domestic scene—appear as commonplace figures momentarily raised to heroic proportions through the poeticizing effects of historical vision. The scene persists in memory, eventually to be resurrected through the act of writing. And as Cather reveals in the novel's frame, the need to repossess in writing a "precious" and "incommunicable past" stems from the troubled present, from the narrator's unhappy life. As the narrator of *My Ántonia,* Jim Burden is aptly named; he emphasizes the anxieties of modern, urban living.[48]

Jim Burden's nostalgia—and Cather's own retrospective vision—might be seen as perfect therapy for the ills of modernity. Nostalgia palliates the contradictions of modern commercial culture and is, at bottom, an emotion of accommodation. The traveling salesman—in his conception both as picturesque, old-fashioned drummer and modern salesman—helped ease the way to modernity, if only because his evolving role epitomized the cultural development of the nation.

Something of this nostalgia would continue to inform fictional portraits of the traveling salesman. In the 1930s Eudora Welty and Thornton Wilder took advantage of the salesman's perspective—Welty in her first published short story, "Death of a Traveling Salesman," and Wilder in *Heaven's My Destination*—to foreground the fragility of human life and the presence of God in a secular world, respectively, features of human life that modern business enterprise all but denied. Yet while these sympathetic, often comic portrayals represent the traveling salesman's world in universal terms, their reversal of the salesman's tawdry image suggests that nostalgia is not always just a reflex of accommodation. Indeed, as Arthur Miller and Eugene O'Neill would later make clear in a line of criticism that includes Sinclair Lewis and even Sherwood Anderson, the drummer's own legacy, the power of face-to-face interactions, could ironically serve as the basis for condemning the effects of modern business enterprise. Though apparently banished to memory, the drummer might also return from the dead and point the way toward more subversive uses of nostalgia.

1 The Perils of Pearl Street

Some traveling men stopped long enough to have their pictures taken behind J. H. Hill's Store in Russell County, Kansas, around 1900. Their pictures are reproduced at the beginning of each chapter courtesy of the Kansas State Historical Society.

The etymology of the word *drummer* is cloudy. In early modern England and Europe both peddlers and military recruiters literally beat a rhythm to drum up trade in the villages they visited. In colonial America peddlers may have continued the custom, but they were never called drummers.[1] In 1830 drumming was still unknown—at least in print—although as a commercial practice, it had begun to emerge in places like New York City, where clerks engaged by wholesale jobbers drummed up custom among retail merchants in town to buy goods. Metaphorically drumming their sales spiels into potential customers' minds, the antebellum city drummer personalized economic power. Laying the groundwork for the commercial travelers who succeeded him, he domesticated an emerging market system by making retail merchants feel at home within the process of buying. During the 1830s and 1840s drumming developed as a marginal, controversial practice, but by 1850 its customs were well established, and its practitioners were a new species of economic man.

If in the context of twentieth-century consumer culture the traveling salesman seems more the product of modern memory than an actual flesh-and-blood creature, during the nineteenth century there was no questioning the drummer's physical presence. When the centrifugal forces of the market propelled drummers beyond urban commercial centers into small towns and villages, salesmen represented the pervasive powers of the market within a vital face-to-face culture. Even when the familiar forms of persuasion involved in commercial domestication distanced the traveling man from genteel conduct and prompted suspicion, the grounds for his transgression rested on a standard scaled to human gestures and endeavors. Understanding how the salesman's paradoxical representative status evolved requires examining the drummer's role in the antebellum mercantile city.

Accustomed perhaps to the familiar figure of the "bagman" in Great Britain, English visitors to the young Republic could not help noticing his absence from American life. "In the United States there are no commercial travelers," Isaac Holmes remarked in 1823; "consequently, shop or store keepers are obliged to repair to the large towns, to procure the different articles they may want."[2] The commercial migrations that brought country merchants to American mercantile centers throughout the first half of the nineteenth century placed the process of exchange in the city, and even though this pattern of trade was later reversed when wholesalers sent salesmen on the road, drumming remained a word and a practice with distinctly urban connotations.

English wholesalers and manufacturers, on the other hand, began using commercial travelers in the eighteenth century. Washington Irving, for instance, characterized the English traveling men whom he featured in *Bracebridge Hall* (1822) as "commercial knights errant, who are incessantly scouring the kingdom in gigs, on horsebacks, or by coach." Impressed by their gentility (they would rather trade than fight) and their social customs (they gathered in

The British commercial traveler, or bagman. (Warshaw Collection of Business Americana, Archives Center, National Museum of American History, Smithsonian Institution, Washington, D.C.)

the "travellers'-room" at inns to drink and tell stories) Irving made the "bagmen" picturesque, even nostalgic figures in the English landscape.[3]

However romantic Irving's attachment to old England was, his sense that these commercial knights were part of a long-standing commercial tradition was well-founded. By 1800, as Neil McKendrick has observed, the birth of English consumer culture was beyond doubt, and the system for growing this market, remarkably strong. Newspaper and magazine advertising, itinerant salesmen representing a variety of industries—Manchester men and Scotch drapers, for instance—an efficient network of canals and roads, and London's role as the the geographical and fashion center of the nation, combined to make a highly integrated, distinctly modern commercial culture, creating the historical conditions that allowed Irving to see the English bagman in nostalgic terms. Such Englishmen as Josiah Wedgewood, the eighteenth-century entrepreneur who manufactured and marketed a wide range of pottery products—first nationally and then internationally—prospered through advertising campaigns and selling strategies that were innovative but by no means idiosyncratic. The eighteenth-century marketplace "still included the humble packman, carrying his goods on his own back," notes McKendrick, but "it also now encompassed world-famous companies using travelling salesmen equipped with illustrated bilingual catalogues, ambassadorial channels exploited for purely commercial purposes, elegant showrooms, foreign warehouses, royal patronage," in short, a "whole battery of commercial techniques designed to make effective a carefully worked out marketing policy."[4]

In early nineteenth-century America such a battery of marketing techniques was impracticable. Throughout the eighteenth century "all purpose" merchants located in port cities along the eastern seaboard controlled the economic life of the colonies, exporting produce, importing a wide assortment of goods, extending credit, and financing nascent manufacturers. As leaders of "face-to-face" societies, communities in which "people of different social conditions frequently interacted within an environment small enough so that they could recognize each other as individuals," merchants often presided over small fiefdoms, deriving their authority from the intersection of business, church, and family.[5] All along the eastern seaboard, aspects of the all-purpose merchant's world lasted into the nineteenth century. Even in the 1820s merchant princes in New York continued to function as village fathers of sorts—minding the business of the community according to precedent and tradition—while apprenticed clerks, typically family members or the sons of other merchants, rose through the ranks to take their place.[6]

Geography alone was enough to keep American merchants from achieving a unified national market. At the time of Washington Irving's English tour, the American economy was vast and diffuse, comprised of regional markets ranging from the household economies of the plantation South to the agricultural frontier of the upper Midwest to the mill towns of New England. And although tremendous internal improvements—canal, road, and railroad building—came in the years between 1820 and 1860, linking villages to cities, accelerating the development of domestic manufacturing, and propelling the transition from mercantile to industrial capitalism, still, in Robert Wiebe's words, "very little in the American economy built upward toward a national pyramid of functions. Almost everything spread outward." Thus the nation's "extensive and distributive" needs stood in the way of consolidated marketing networks like those that distinguished Josiah Wedgewood's success in England.[7]

Yet consolidation could and sometimes did develop where savvy enterprisers created and managed regional markets. Peddlers, for instance, established commercial networks in much of the colonial and antebellum rural North that rivaled the traditional relationship between consumers and local storekeepers. More than humble packmen, they supplemented the flow of urban products to the hinterland and, after the Revolution, circulated goods produced locally by village artisans. As both Jackson Lears and David Jaffee have argued, their canny ability to fashion new identities according to changing circumstances accustomed rural Americans to consumer culture and laid the groundwork for modern—and more centralized—marketing techniques.[8]

The peddler's impact on subsequent marketing structures was inevitably circumscribed by his peripheral relation to stronger mercantile institutions. By the 1860s the peddler was obsolete, retired by the steady growth in economic power of urban wholesalers and manufacturers whose commercial travelers now supplied retailers with mass-produced goods. So the traveling salesman succeeded the peddler in folklore, assuming his aura of mystery, suspicion, and excitement. But in economic terms the genealogical link between the peddler and the traveling salesman was more apparent than real.[9] The commercial traveler's direct ancestor was not the peddler but the urban wholesaler's drummer, and it was the drummer's role (as well as his name) that he inherited when he went on the road.

In this sense, the history of American commercial traveling begins with the emergence of the urban wholesale jobber during the first decades of the nineteenth century. Thus named because he purchased goods in large jobs, or lots, and then sold them in smaller units to retail shopkeepers—and even to manufacturers and other jobbers—the wholesale jobber signaled a crucial shift away from the relatively compact, hierarchical world of the all-purpose merchant toward a more expansive, socially fluid commercial culture. By 1815 the nation was on the brink of what Charles Sellers has called a market revolution.[10]

Increased agricultural production, industrial growth, demographic movement, and rapid urbanization all contributed to the change. The immediate occasion for the wholesale jobber's rise to commercial prominence, however, was the resumption of trade after the War of 1812 and the tremendous influx of cheap imported products into eastern seaports. Nowhere was the commercial impact of the end of the war more dramatically felt than in New York, where the Erie Canal, a deep harbor, packets, and British imports combined in the 1820s to make Pearl Street in lower Manhattan the dry-goods capital of the United States. Chiefly through their sale of foreign textiles—at irresistible prices—Pearl Street jobbers made New York the primary market for U.S. storekeepers. Even after a frenetic period of bargain auctions tailed off in the late 1820s, southern and western merchants continued their visits to New York—and to Pearl Street. Coastal packet lines and canals had made New York accessible enough that merchants visited to buy not just imported goods but domestically manufactured dry goods as well.[11] Hence, although wholesale jobbers in St. Louis, Cincinnati, New Orleans, and Pittsburgh also developed regional markets during the 1830s and 1840s that made their cities stopping places for retail merchants, they were generally unable to match the prices and selection available in New York. In 1832, according to one estimate, the city supplied the storekeepers nationwide with over one hundred million dollars' worth of merchandise, and by 1840, New York wholesalers practically monopolized the western market.[12]

Compared to the face-to-face society of the all-purpose merchant, this expanding economy was "impersonalized," as Alfred D. Chandler, Jr., has pointed out. The ebb and flow of cotton, agricultural produce, and imported and domestic goods, as well as the jobber's extended network of buyers and suppliers, described a market in which invisible hands rather than the personal influence of well-born men determined one's economic fate.[13] Yet to assume the disappearance of the personal from nineteenth- or even twentieth-century mercantile relations would be a mistake. In New York and elsewhere wholesale jobbers carved out a position in the market that lasted well into the twentieth century, in part because they proved willing and able to accommodate their customers. Beginning in the 1820s, the jobber became the retail merchant's principal supplier, offering services that larger import and commission houses could not. By purchasing goods at bargain prices, often at auction, and specializing in certain products—for instance, hardware, textiles, and other dry goods—the jobber was well equipped to meet the individual product needs of country merchants, as well as satisfy their requests for smaller orders. During the 1830s and 1840s inland merchants often traveled great distances under rough conditions to buy goods from wholesale jobbers located in eastern mercantile cities. Indeed, as Lewis Atherton has shown, it was not at all unusual for storekeepers from as far away as Illinois, Kentucky, or the Missouri frontier to make semiannual trips to the eastern seaboard, particularly New York, to purchase hats, dry goods, groceries, drugs, and spices—all from different jobbers.[14]

Jobbers also extended credit to inland merchants, who typically had up to six months to pay the loans. But they often made exceptions, knowing that their ability to collect payments depended on whether the storekeeper's own customers could pay. Hard cash was scarce, and credit, as antebellum businessmen often observed, was the Republic's lifeblood. Hence, the arrangements that jobbers and storekeepers made to maintain the flow of credit—for instance, extending the terms of a debt—went forward in a climate of forgiveness in an economic culture that aspired to systematic efficiency but survived by what Robert Wiebe has termed "an endless series of personal accommodations." Even during the Panic of 1837 and the ensuing depression, when financial structures appeared particularly hard hit and the need for eliminating credit risk seemed of paramount importance, merchants and buyers continued to negotiate credit in an informal matter. And, at least among inland traders, business remained good.[15]

The dunning clerks who began to call on inland storekeepers in the early 1820s are a good example of how the wholesale jobber's apparently impersonalized world was personalized. Like the traveling salesman, the dun was an itinerant middleman, typically traveling twice a year and usually only to collect bills or provide extensions on overdue accounts.[16] Some jobbers' clerks may have alternatively dunned and drummed, sometimes traveling to collect bills, other times staying in the city to solicit custom.[17] Rarely did the collector (as the dun was sometimes called) sell goods. As a Missouri store owner recalled, he "knew but little about the character of the stock at home"— although in the 1830s a few jobbers (and some manufacturers) sent men on the road to both drum up sales and collect bills. As the first commercial travelers in the nation, they were exceptions, part of an "experiment" in marketing that did not take hold until after the Civil War.[18]

Dunning clerks gave urban jobbers their first human face in the hinterland, bringing together the local and the extensive in a paradoxical union that would increasingly distinguish American commercial relations. This ironic integration of interpersonal dynamics into a market system also characterized the credit agencies, which emerged as an institutional alternative to lenders determining credit worthiness on a case-by-case basis. During the 1830s New York credit agencies, especially Lewis Tappan's Mercantile Agency and later R. G. Dun and Company, began supplying systematic credit information about potential customers to their subscribers.[19] Credit rating, based as it was on Franklinian assessments of "character," was hardly an objective science.[20] Agency representatives solicited information at the local level about potential borrowers and provided a credit rating, which, apart from being the product of their own face-to-face interactions, summarized community opinion—for good or for ill—of an individual's business reputation.[21]

Given the strength of belief in republican virtues throughout early nineteenth-century America, it is not surprising that both credit agencies and duns provoked criticism of their threat to individual sovereignty. There were doubtless many merchants who believed, as did a writer for the *Merchant's Magazine and Review* in 1839, that extending credit to unknown customers made trading "a species of gambling."[22] Yet some of these same merchants— and many country traders—would also have agreed, at least in principle, with George G. Foster's conclusion in *New York Naked* that the credit agency was the mercantile community's "organized system of espionage," which "secretly obtain[s] precise information of the property, the associations, the business, the family, and the personal habits of every man engaged in trade." Foster's criticism, coming as it did in 1855, addressed a more "developed" market economy than had existed twenty years earlier. Still, his uncovering of a mercantile conspiracy was representative of an unease that was already in the air in the 1820s. The fear was not only of Wall Street speculation, immoral gambling, and the reckless scramble for wealth but also of the Republic's becoming a commercial "system" capable of surveying and even shaping the character of individual businessmen.[23]

Consider, for example, the view of commercial culture dramatized in "The Philadelphia Dun," a sketch that appeared in the *New York Constellation* in 1830. A dun rides into a small Tennessee town oblivious to his surroundings: a "moving automaton" with "glazed eye and compressed lip." The local innkeeper sizes him up immediately; he can "read" the dun's history "in his motions" and his "immense cravat" and waist "compressed with corsets," which identify him "as a genuine species of that singular genus, the dandy," an eastern, urban creature. The dun incurs the innkeeper's contempt—and his pity. Passing through the crowd assembled in the street for court week, it is clear the dun is not of "the people." And yet here are "the judge . . . the candidates for office . . . the farmer clad in his neatest homespun . . . the hunter with his rifle," all "exhibiting that excitement of feeling which crowds always produce, with a good humor which is only found in countries where all are free and equal." Ignorant of basic democratic traditions, the dun fails to give the "customary" salutation when he rides through the street. He passes by a semicircle of men trading and bargaining without understanding "the serious business" at hand; his "gaze was fixed on vacancy." Offended by the clerk's arrogance, the landlord asks him to leave his inn but does not blame the young dun—"just out of his apprenticeship"—for his rudeness or his disruption of small-town life. Rather, as he tells the author of the sketch, the dun is a generic type, part of "one general denomination" sent out from various cities to collect debts; "some of them are fine young men, but too many are like yonder chap."[24]

Urban and rural, extravagance and simplicity, dependence and independence, effeminacy and manliness, are juxtaposed here to dramatize the dunning clerk's loss of republican virtue. No longer one of the people, the dun is the creature of a corrupt marketplace. No longer responsible for his actions, he carries out another's duties under the influence of a venal urban commercial culture. Figured as a dandy—a creature prey to fashion—and, more importantly, an automaton, linked to larger economic mechanisms, the dun appears in some sense to be the extension of absent mercantile interests. And this is what provokes disdain: the dun has lost the ability to command or possess his own self; his agency is not his own. At the same time, the rhetoric of republicanism used to describe this loss of individuality is insufficient for representing the dun's commercial self. The innkeeper laments the dun's fall from virtuous selfhood but can find no lost self to which the dun might be restored. His self already constituted by the unnatural forces, the dun has evolved into a species of economic man that the critic can understand only in mechanistic terms. Yet these terms further complicate the question of commercial selfhood, for as an automaton, the dun is simultaneously a freestanding, self-motivating entity and a machine-driven cog whose power and reason for being derive from other sources. The logic of the transformation in face-to-face commercial relationships—and the challenge to critics—was that he could be both.

The clerks whom wholesale jobbers hired to drum up custom in mercantile cities presented a more concrete instance of this commercially constructed self, threatening individual sovereignty, as moralists worried might happen, but reinforcing commercial growth, as even critics within the New York mercantile community admitted.[25] From roughly 1830 to 1860 city drummers combed boardinghouses, hotels, saloons, and theaters for out-of-town merchants, whom they then endeavored to lead back to their employers' showrooms.[26] "Drumming, in a mercantile sense," the *Constellation* stated in 1832—in the first American use of the word—"consists in fastening upon every man, whether stranger or otherwise, who labors under a suspicion of having come to the city to purchase goods for the country market; and the object thereof is . . . to obtain as great a share as possible of the wholesale business."[27] Although the term *salesmanship* did not enter usage until the late nineteenth century, the self-conscious, familiar forms of address that words like *fastening* sought to describe represented the emergence of modern selling techniques. As a form of commercial persuasion, drumming codified face-to-face interactions to suit the structures of the urban marketplace and anticipated a conception of the self as personality—as role player and image manager—generally associated with the rise of mass culture in the twentieth century.[28]

Glimmerings of this commercial self in the 1830s and 1840s suggest a different evolutionary process, rooted as much in the institutions of merchant capitalism and the antebellum urban scene as in the structures of modern corporate culture. Adapting face-to-face relationships to the extensive and distributive needs of the market, drummers developed what the critic and humorist Asa Greene identified as the central characteristic of the occupation: the art of "becoming all things to all men, in order to gain some." To attain the confidence of visiting merchants—in Greene's terms, to catch a customer and earn a sum—the drummer exercised protean faculties. In urban settings that rewarded adaptability before all qualities, he learned to improvise.[29] When market conditions changed, he shifted his approach; to accommodate a customer's particular needs and preferences, he altered his demeanor. Thus drumming reinforced the evolution of a theatrical or liminal self and threatened the conceptions of character—steady work habits and moral uprightness—so vital to republican ideology and the spirit of Protestantism.

Drumming was clearly a new kind of commercial work that both typified the wholesale jobber's role in the expansive economy and deviated from time-honored mercantile duties. In the 1830s and 1840s merchants and clerks within the countinghouse continued to perform the same daily chores that their colonial predecessors had—accounting, bookkeeping, and the like—while drummers found their work outside.[30] Especially in New York, this movement outside the countinghouse reflected transformations in the mercantile social order. During the first decades of the century mercantile clerks had boarded with their employers; now a new generation of clerks—composed of as many rural migrants as city natives—resided in boardinghouses and hotels. Abandoning the traditional apprenticeship system for what Allan Horlick has called a "new style of mercantile career" characterized by "more overt aggressiveness and self-promotion," the rising generation of clerks came to symbolize all that was different—and wrong—about the expansive economy.[31] Social commentators worried that unsupervised clerks from the country would degenerate under the influence of those "more initiated youths" with whom they lived in "defective" boardinghouses.[32] And merchants, searching for ways to instill character and maintain social control, founded such institutions as the Mercantile Library Association and the YMCA and urged their clerks to join.[33]

Drummers provoked particular worry because they also worked outside the countinghouse and had to resort "to all feasible means to obtain custom for their employers"—a fact lamented by critics who saw in these duties the seeds of moral backsliding. Jobbers paid drummers liberally, but after hotel board (eight to ten dollars a week at the principal hotels), theater tickets, oyster suppers, and entertainment costs—all spent in pursuit of visiting merchants—they were left with little financial independence. A writer for the *New York Transcript* concluded in 1836 that drummers "must spend their money liberally in the service of those who pay them" or "lose their employment." Under these circumstances, drummers had to fight to maintain their "honor."[34] The subordination of morality to profit making, the subsumption of (morally questionable) leisure activities by work, and the absence of financial autonomy left drummers in a state of venal dependency and spiritual impoverishment.

Drumming's connection to a mercantile order that was itself undergoing transformation accentuated its ambivalent status. While drummers appeared to be marginal figures exempt from the institutional measures that merchants used to accommodate social change, they also epitomized the unabashed self-presentation necessary for getting ahead in the new business world. Because drumming was an emergent market practice that threatened to put the cultural and financial order of the countinghouse on new ground, it met resistance, even within the mercantile community itself.[35] Its eventual adoption by more and more merchants, however, underscores the crucial role of the wholesale jobber in fostering commercial growth and innovation.[36]

Drumming may in fact have been viewed within the mercantile community as meritorious work because it went unsupervised, entailed responsibility, and hence prepared clerks for managerial positions and ownership.[37] But if as nonmanual, incipient white-collar work, drumming contributed to the middle-class ethos that historians see developing in the antebellum period, it also dramatized the looseness and confusion that attended occupational categories at their emergence.[38] As Stuart Blumin points out, the distinction between nonmanual and manual trades, which seemed so clear-cut at the end of the nineteenth century, was a concept that evolved out of commercial and industrial transformations in the early nineteenth-century city. The physical, often visible nature of the changes—for instance, putting commercial and manual occupations in separate work spaces—altered the urban landscape, inevitably making it harder to decipher.[39] The same could be said of the workers who populated this new landscape: although the variety of emerging jobs, especially in the nonmanual occupations, eventually led to distinctions between blue- and white-collar work, the signs of respectability were not always easy to identify.

More than any other commercial occupation to emerge in the antebellum mercantile city, drumming exemplified the ongoing separation of work environments while at the same time eluding identification altogether. Not only did the urban landscape provide the context for the drummer's frequent removal from any specific workplace, but its own fluid dynamics provided the context for the improvisational work that drumming accomplished. Both the product of and a guide to the blurred relations between manual and non-manual labor, rural and urban cultures, and substantive and illusive realities that constituted the mercantile city, the antebellum drummer augured the movement toward a ubiquitous modern market.

From 1820 to 1850 or so, being in the market meant visiting Pearl Street. A "long winding way" in lower Manhattan "choked with bald, high-headed stores," thronged by sharp auctioneers, close Yankee merchants, quill-scratching clerks, and—during the buying seasons—country merchants, Pearl Street epitomized the apparently makeshift commercial order of the nation.[40] Until the late 1840s, when the tall, narrow buildings became warehouses and New York jobbers changed neighborhoods, Pearl Street and its environs thrived on far-flung connections.[41] Rows of sloops and schooners docked at Coenties and Peck slips linked the wholesale district to manufacturers and inland markets. Bales of calico stacked ceiling high or kegs of nails edging out showroom doors declared a jobber's specialty and advertised his economic function in visual terms. By 1834 half a dozen hotels fronted Pearl, Water, and Fulton Streets, flourishing where, in the 1820s, most country traders had stayed in boardinghouses above dry-goods stores.[42] The custom of drumming began in these boardinghouses when, as one merchant recalled, it became "a great object with the jobbers to have one of their salesmen board at a large house for country merchants, so that they could induce them to come to their stores to trade."[43]

If only as a guide to the disorderly landscape of winding, twisting Pearl Street, a drummer could prove useful. By the late 1840s there were over two hundred dry-goods jobbers and virtually the same number of wholesale grocers doing business in New York, many of them located on Pearl Street.[44] Yet the capacity of the street to confuse had less to do with such numbers or with any particular physical element than with the sense of change that enlivened its most visible features.[45] Even more than its parent city, Pearl Street was a place of transitions, part of a constantly shifting marketplace whose immediate tangibility was paradoxically founded on the expanding commercial system.

In his 1845 novel *Big Abel and the Little Manhattan* Cornelius Mathews sought to explain the paradox. Mathews portrayed Pearl Street as a commercial spectacle whose meaning seemed just out of reach, at least to outsiders. Men are shown "hurrying up and down: some reading signs to help them on their journey; others dashing in and out as though they had the whole street at their fingers' ends." Auctioneers and country traders crowd the sidewalks, packed "close and hot" in the Indian summer heat. Portly middle-aged merchants emerge from their stores, among them the silent partner in a firm. Hard by in the slips, Mathews finds sloops, schooners, and brigs, and, pausing, wonders at the meaning of "the tall, smooth, shaven poles, they called 'em masts." The many warehouses, docks, and ships "seem[ed] to say all the time,

The Pearl Street House in New York City, 1831–34. (I. N. Phelps Stokes Collection, Miriam and Ira D. Wallach Division of Art, Prints, and Photographs of the New York Public Library, Astor, Lenox and Tilden Foundations.)

'Here am I, South Street: and here I mean to be for many a day to come.'"[46] Still, for all this physical evidence and despite attempts to decipher the commercial signs and customs, Pearl Street seems mysterious and opaque to Mathews; he cannot successfully unravel what he calls the Working Jacket of the city. Merchants, docks, and ships together constitute an inevitable, natural-seeming order, but by themselves they resist Mathews's analysis. Determined to write an urban epic that evoked a landscape as heroic and sublime as the forests of James Fenimore Cooper's Leatherstocking novels, Mathews only succeeded in further mystifying the relation between the constituent parts of the city and its powerful, commercial order.[47]

As Mathews and others sensed but could not fully explain, the mysterious power of Pearl Street resided in a contradiction: the orchestrated display of seemingly unrelated commercial forces. Ranging from the vessels linking the street with its various markets to the hurly-burly of human activity, Pearl Street demonstrated the capacity of the market economy to express commercial relations in concrete terms. At least by American standards, Pearl Street presented a wholly unprecedented spectacle—a commercial scene whose capacity to enthrall resembled the seductive power evoked later in the century by the urban department store.

Even those who satirized Pearl Street's spectacle of disorder tacitly and sometimes humorously accepted its underlying logic. Works like Asa Greene's *Perils of Pearl Street* (1836) and Anne Stephens's *High Life in New York* (1844) revel in the gap between appearance and reality that Pearl Street jobbers called their business. Wholesalers blocked their store entrances and sidewalks with huge piles of boxes to make people believe "what they boasted themselves, that they sold more dry goods than any house in the city."[48] Or, visitors discovered "heaps of tea boxes and sugar barrels, piled up inside the store." Upon reaching the counting room of his uncle's Pearl Street store, the Yankee hero of *High Life in New York* finds it "carpeted and fixed out like some of our best rooms in Connecticut" but revises his opinion after discovering empty liquor bottles and chewed-off tobacco ends behind the desks and under the tables.[49] Although these descriptions smack of moral indignation, they also contain a sense of play missing from more earnest indictments of New York's "sham" culture. Accepting the insubstantiality of Pearl Street as an indigenous part of the market culture, these more humorous accounts take for granted the viewer's—and the reader's—capacity to interpret the commercial landscape and avoid its perils.

In this respect, representations of the jobber's revolutionary task—uniting the local and the distant, the extensive and the distributive, the abstract and the concrete, the personal and the impersonal—paralleled the wholesaler's own efforts to find the appropriate personal terms for doing business. Observer and participant alike struggled to find a human scale for the large-scale structural transformations in the economy. Notwithstanding the common vocabulary for portraying and constituting commercial practice or even the shared ambivalence for economic growth, a simple but important difference separated the critic from the participant: one contributed far more to the expansion of the market system than the other. And if specific features of the wholesaler's task caused critics unease, there was ample reason. The sporadic, intensive human activity and the movement of finished goods through mercantile establishments designed for the express purpose of selling goods exemplified New York's shift away from the city's lingering village atmosphere and advertised the new market indifference to artisanal culture. The juxtaposition of material disorder and mercantile order on Pearl Street added to the confusion. The bales of calico and kegs of nails clashed with the ship-like order that frequently prevailed within the countinghouses as merchants issued forth from quarterdeck offices to greet important customers and junior clerks attended to routine tasks.[50] As contradictory as these two sights seemed, they were vitally linked and together represented the characteristic pairing of economic system and material drama in the antebellum market.

As the quintessential middleman, the drummer was himself defined by the fluidity of the market. Though closely allied to the effort of the antebellum mercantile community to expand and rationalize the national market, the drummer was as much a spectacle as New York or Pearl Street itself. At the very least, he dressed as a dandy—extravagantly. In Briggs's *Adventures of Harry Franco,* a drummer wears a "lilac calico shirt, with a little ruffle bristling in the bosom, and a cameo breast-pin almost as large as a saucer," and for an evening at the theater the drummer in Richard Kimball's *Was He Successful?* published almost thirty years later, also dresses at the "ridiculous extreme of fashion," covering himself with "rings, pins, and gold chains." Besides their love of extravagant dress, both these figures have an appetite for the immoral pleasures of New York. In *Lectures to Young Men* (1844), a melodramatic though purportedly nonfictional work, Henry Ward Beecher pointed out that the two tastes were logically linked: it was the drummer's "business" to be both "well appointed" in dress and well advised in urban sin so he could escort customers first to theaters and restaurants, then "a little further on" to the city's "high life" of pleasures and "varied phases of lust," and finally to the wholesaler's showrooms.[51] In similarly anxious tones, the Reverend James W. Alexander also condemned the drummer's "smirking, and bowing, and treating" and "playing the spaniel" as mere "grovelling."[52] For both critics, drumming functioned not only as a commercial system and a vehicle for social mobility but also as a dangerous, immoral activity for drummer and customer alike.

In other major cities where drumming took hold—Philadelphia, Boston, Baltimore, Montreal—critics were likewise fascinated and horrified by the exchange of licentious pleasures for business favors.[53] What they found just as unsettling, however, were the drummer's familiar forms of address. A critic writing for a Philadelphia newspaper in 1836, for instance, lamented drummers' inevitable descent into "places of immoral resort," yet saved his sharpest language for their methods, which he compared to a worm infesting a tree trunk: "So the mercantile borer assails, obtrudes himself upon, and insinuates himself into the good graces of a country merchant."[54] Words like *boring, drumming,* and—the *Constellation*'s term—*fastening* emphasized the persistent and adhesive nature of the clerk's face-to-face approach. Even Edwin T. Freedley's popular 1856 *United States Mercantile Guide*—presumably an unbiased description of established commercial institutions and practices— adopted a hyperbolic tone and condemned drumming because it functioned so efficiently, so relentlessly, and so intimately. Drummers hunted for customers "as a cunning animal does for his prey," warned Freedley, by arousing their "appetites and passion" and "captivat[ing] by courtesy."[55] Imagining the viewpoint of a besieged country merchant, Freedley echoed the observations of a British traveler who in 1846 had attacked drummers' unrestrained methods of "surveillance, or vexatious interference" and complained that where "each drummer is at work upon every new comer, the situation of the latter almost becomes intolerable."[56] The worries that all these critics expressed about the loss of individual sovereignty and morality were warnings— aimed at young men who either aspired to or were involved in mercantile careers—of the perils of commercial practice.

However offensive or unnatural the dynamics of drumming may have appeared to critics, Freedley's 1856 designation of them as courtesy accents their customary use within the expanding commercial economy. As historians of the period have shown, the transformation in manners that distinguished antebellum cities was integral to the creation of an urban middle class. Ritualized conduct and dress, as well as the ongoing visual scrutiny of behavior, served to solidify and construct cultural boundaries in a rapidly expanding, increasingly anonymous society. So disorienting were the economic and demographic changes that by the 1830s the confidence man had become one of the most representative figures in the culture—a symbol for the interpersonal skills now necessary to get ahead and a lightning rod for the middle classes' unease about the increasing fluidity of the culture and about their own changeable character. The confidence man represented a new expanse of possibilities, but he also provoked fears—that things were not as they appeared, that seeing was not believing, that sincerity was an instrumental emotion, cultivated to hoodwink, persuade, and captivate naive audiences.[57] As a wheedling persuader in an urban landscape swarming with sharpsters, the drummer prompted similar fears.

But the drummer was not a confidence man—no more than his customer was an easy dupe. Despite the country merchant's fear of sharp dealing and the jobber's fear that poor harvests or a financial panic would prevent the merchant from paying his bills, the drummer and the merchant forged an unstable relationship of mutual advantage whose fixed place in the commercial economy set it apart from both urban confidence games and the "operational aesthetic" that drew consumers to P. T. Barnum's museums for the sheer pleasure of witnessing a spectacular hoax, staged at their own expense.[58] Although critics of drumming were often bent on exposing economic instability and the humbug in the illusive displays of products, they were just as concerned with discovering the logic of a commercial system so heavily invested in misplaced affections—misplaced because sales transactions were made the center of intimacy, warmth, kindliness, and trust. Drummers' interpersonal dynamics turned the sensual attractions of the city to economic purposes and seemed to shift the heart of domesticity to the commercial sphere. More than establishing a correspondence between the drummer as performer and the merchant as audience, drumming created in the commercial realm a refracted image of "hothouse" family dynamics. In the same way that antebellum domestic values were entwined with the market economy, as Gillian Brown has argued, the culture of drumming seemed shaped by home influences.[59] In this sense, not only did drumming represent a threat to the emerging doctrine of separate spheres, but in serving to make customers at home in the marketplace it also appeared to draw affectional power from the reservoirs of domestic sentimentalism.

The appearance of such negative commentary marked the beginning of a tradition of cultural criticism directed at institutionally driven sales practices. Although criticizing economic practice was by no means new to American culture, as Robert Keayne's seventeenth-century "Apologia" for unfair pricing makes clear, and although peddlers, hawkers, and other commercial itinerants had long been the subject of invective here and in England and Europe, the attacks on drumming as a mode of persuasion systematically rooted in face-to-face interaction sounded a new note. Anticipating Arthur Miller's sympathetic excuse for Willy Loman—"Nobody dast blame this man. A salesman is got to dream, boy"—observers criticized drumming as a "system" and "habit" and "long-established practice" that threatened not only "notions of personal and individual freedom" but also the drummer himself.[60] Whereas in New York this criticism was a part of commercial discourse throughout the antebellum period, it was particularly acute during the 1830s and 1840s, that is, the time drumming emerged as a market practice.

The notion that drumming was a commercial practice that systematically drew from some larger cultural matrix is echoed in the fullest fictional treatments of the drummer in the 1830s: Asa Greene's *Perils of Pearl Street* (1834) and Charles Frederick Briggs's *Adventures of Harry Franco* (1839).[61] What each writer attempts, in contrast to the moralists and business commentators, is an encompassing view of drumming within the context of the expanding commercial network. Greene and Briggs dramatize the drummer's improvisational talents in relational and regional terms by insisting on the geographical and cultural tensions that inform face-to-face dynamics. Although these connections may have been hidden from view, their reconstruction in fiction served to both criticize and domesticate the extensive influence of the market.

Both *The Perils of Pearl Street* and *The Adventures of Harry Franco* plot the movement from hinterland to city by tracing the fortunes of country youths who migrate to New York but fail to find success through hard work and steady habits. Greene's hero is not willing to wait for prosperity. He leaves a job with a respectable merchant to pursue great wealth on his own and pays for his impatience by failing as a merchant three times. Duped, swindled, but essentially honest, he refuses to return to his country village without succeeding. When the story ends, he is still in New York, hoping to make a career in politics and planning to pay back his debts. Briggs's fortune seeker, though not committed to a business career, is similarly disappointed in the city. After taking an equally circuitous career path, serving along the way as a sailor and a mercantile clerk, Harry Franco inherits the family estate and returns to his native village. More a retreat than a solution to the chaos that Harry leaves behind in the city—financial speculation has ruined his merchant employer—Franco Ville ironically rests on the profits accrued from an equally expansive venture, a railroad company's decision to run its tracks through the Franco family garden.

In *The Adventures of Harry Franco* and *The Perils of Pearl Street* drumming appears as an emergent market practice deserving of sharper criticism. Writing in the 1830s, Charles Frederick Briggs and especially Asa Greene viewed the drummers' improvisations in terms of the economic upheavals of the decade. Briggs subtitled his 1839 novel "A Tale of the Great Panic," and *The Perils of Pearl Street,* though written before the Panic of 1837, is laced with financial failure. The problem with drumming, as Briggs and Greene see it, has less to do with large-scale economic imbalances or even market speculation than with its inevitable tendency toward misrepresentation. In varying degrees, the drummers in both of these works subordinate self-representation to profit making. For Greene, the more comprehensive of the two, the willingness to become "all things to all men, in order to gain some," to be "orthodox with the orthodox, and heterodox with the heterodox," is a "Protean faculty" that leads inevitably to financial failure.[62] The irony, implicit in Greene's pun, is that in an economy based on credit the heedless pursuit of customers, especially bad ones, augurs disaster, for when nobody pays, the market collapses.

In both texts, the contribution of drumming to financial disaster revolves around face-to-face dynamics. For Briggs, as for Greene, these dynamics are vitally concerned with the persuasive powers of visual presentation. When Briggs's dandified drummer, Jack Lummocks, accosts Harry Franco at a tavern after their stagecoach has stopped, Lummocks mistakes the fortune-seeking youth for a country merchant and, tapping him on the shoulder with an ebony cane, interrupts Franco's "intense curiosity at the grotesque figure of the clown" that he sees printed on a "monstrous circus handbill." Not only does the episode dramatize Franco's anticipation of the urban scene, but the handbill (an advertisement for itinerant exotics) and Lummocks (himself an exotic itinerant, traveling to collect bills and drum up customers) implicate his migratory desire in commercial modes of persuasion. Later, when Lummocks gives Franco his card, Briggs stresses the power of this appeal in visual terms by printing the business card across a page of the novel. The card, like the handbill, gains Franco's attention and, combined with the drummer's own words, his urban finery, and a free drink, persuade him that his trip to New York City has begun with "a very favorable omen, that I should in the very outset of my career, gain the friendship of so fine a gentleman."[63]

These improvisations do not bode well for Lummocks's future. The conclusion of *The Adventures of Harry Franco* underscores Franco's initial naïveté and confirms the dangers of drumming. Having become the trusted clerk of an honest import merchant, Briggs's hero travels to New Orleans, where he learns of the crash of the market and meets his old acquaintance Jack Lummocks. The reprobate drummer has followed a predilection for the fast life to its logical end and gambled away thousands of dollars gained from his southern "collecting and drumming tour." But in losing the company money, he gains a new occupation. "It was the most natural change in the world," Briggs's hero declares. "His habits as a jobber's drummer, exactly qualified him for a gambler's croupier."[64] This judgment justifies Franco's rise. Once the object of Lummocks's ensnaring techniques, the country youth can now speak with righteousness about the flashy, damning habits of drumming and banish them beyond the pale of moral economy. Side by side, however, the degeneration of the drummer and the collapse of the financial markets dramatize a link between personal and impersonal economies that neither Franco nor his author can quite resolve. In sending the youth back home to Franco Ville, Briggs acknowledges the pervasive influence of a corrupt marketplace. In the end, the novel has no place left to go with its moral critique—not even back to the sanctity of a country home, for that place, too, rests on speculative earnings.

Asa Greene makes this point even more plainly in *The Perils of Pearl Street* when, at the end of what can only be called an anti-success story, he refuses to send his protagonist, William Hazard, back to the country village of Spreadaway—to home and possibly to marriage—for redemption. Mercantile success and financial reward so preoccupy Hazard that he cannot imagine returning to the provinces empty-handed and taking a job with the local merchant or, worse still, pursuing his father's occupation as a carpenter. Although he longs to see the girl whom he secretly loved and misses his parents and friends, he will not face the scorn that he knows his neighbors will have for one of their own who, rejecting village life but failing in the city, comes back for sustenance. Here the road to Pearl Street leads only one way.

The life story told in *The Perils of Pearl Street* well describes the social and economic transformations that reconstituted antebellum commercial life. William Hazard's migration from a rural, producer-oriented culture and a home still established along familial lines of authority toward a transient, urban entrepôt and a mercantile career based principally on aggressive self-promotion figures in the novel as a reallocation of cultural energy. The home—or the lack of one—that Hazard finds in New York is a career dedicated not to hearth and family but to commercial and individual success. As if to epitomize this movement away from a stable homelife, Hazard first finds work on Pearl Street as a drummer. And although he despises the work and is fired for ineffectiveness, he does not give up his dream of mercantile fortune. Significantly, at two junctures in the novel he thrives within a more economically traditional jobbing house and even joins the Mercantile Library Association to improve his character, but he finally quits the firm and the association because he cannot wait to achieve success in traditional terms. His imagination, like that of the other figures whom Greene describes—auctioneers, brokers, and hostelers—remains bent on booming the market economy and achieving self-success in "hazardous" ways.

The tropes in the novel, particularly the economic puns, signify the market's lack of substance and its volatility. Greene's satiric perspective concedes the creative possibilities of the shifting economy—for market participants as well as writers—yet expresses an unease about its increasing instability. Hazard's loathing of economic greed and his refusal to embrace commercial practices reflect Greene's Whiggish republicanism—Greene himself was a native of western Massachusetts and a migrant to New York City—and the function of his novel as cultural criticism. Still, like his hero, Greene seems ultimately resigned to the change in the economy; he cannot imagine an outcome that would reoccupy the hinterland that Hazard has left or reinforce the conservative New York mercantile culture that he has rejected. In this sense, Hazard's business failures are the author's own. So are his thoughts at the end of the novel when he surveys his career options and thinks of teaching penmanship but gives up the idea because a "certain famous gentleman" had already advertised to do so. Here, Greene suggests that writing, too, is subject to the hazards of the marketplace.[65]

Drumming epitomizes the systematic deception and commercial fraud that Greene associated with Pearl Street. Indeed, *The Perils of Pearl Street* appears to have developed out of a series of sketches that Greene published in the *New York Constellation* beginning in May 1832.[66] The first extended treatment of mercantile drumming to appear in the United States, the sketches exemplify Greene's view of the precarious, often chaotic mercantile culture of the 1830s, which he knew as a frequent writer and editor for the New York penny press. The initial piece, like the two that soon followed, moves forward "by way of dialogue" in the "S(p)itting Room" of a hotel. Nearly identical to the dramatic conversations that Greene included in *The Perils of Pearl Street,* these dialogues humorously trace the attempts of Spuggins, Juggins, Swinkum, and Inkum—drummers from "Bustle-street" —to gain the custom of the country merchants Vanderspogle, Lookabout, and Johnson. Greene pokes fun at "the very efficient" wholesale houses whose drummers mistake fellow salesmen for merchants and try to push "monkies and paroquets" and "China-ware bedsteads" on naive rural customers. Proving just as sharp as the drummers, however, the country traders collect free theater tickets and champagne without promising to buy. One merchant innocently asks a drummer if by selling monkeys and parakeets he means to get rid of all the members of his firm.[67]

The perils of Pearl Street refer to the pitfalls generated by the gap between real and apparent value in the New York mercantile community. Greene's Pearl Street thrives on the appearance of prosperity. Janus Fairface appears to offer first-rate accommodations at his Superb Hotel but provides only straw mattresses. Wholesale houses appear to rest on solid capital, yet the owners own nothing and must depend on reciprocal credit endorsements to stay in business. "Thus," Greene's narrator writes, "empty-handed as we were on both sides, we were to help fill each other's pockets." Amid the detritus of Pearl Street, merchants meet loans at the last hour by "shinning," that is, running to borrow money and plowing into "wheelbarrows, boxes, barrels, piles of bricks, and other obstacles . . . with [their] shins, the bark whereof is apt to be grievously battered off by the contact."[68]

In Greene's novel even the visual signs of prosperity lack foundation. "Peter Funk"—the elusive, magical figure responsible for bidding up values at New York auctions—lurks everywhere in Pearl Street.[69] A "very Proteus," the epitome of "ubiquity," Peter Funk simultaneously buys goods at auction, stands at storefronts "with a quill behind each ear," and appears "in the shape of a box . . . making a show of merchandize where all was emptiness behind." Funk's "show without substance" exemplifies the excesses and speculations that made Pearl Street precarious for country merchants and would-be jobbers. And when Greene's hero, William Hazard, resists his overtures by kicking him out a window, Funk bounces off, unhurt and indestructible.[70]

The drummer occupies center stage in this show of commercial trickery. Business proceeds when a drummer discovers in a country merchant "the right material to be moulded into the proper shape." Shaped, lured, cajoled, and drummed into the account books of an ambitious, barely solvent jobber, the country merchant becomes like so many boxes on the shelf—apparently substantial. Usually the merchant cannot pay his bills. The "slippery merchant" and his cheaper class of goods draw retail traders of the same ilk, either younger country merchants without much capital or older failures whose poor credit excludes them from better Pearl Street houses. So the drummer perpetuates the insolvency that makes him, trading his "share of discrimination" and "a tongue that will flatter" for "apparent business."[71]

Although William Hazard calls drumming a "contemptible" procedure and claims that it is not his intention to "enumerate all the circumstances which may render a man fit for a drumming operation," he acknowledges that the occupation "requires some little ingenuity and tact" and grants that a man's "countenance, his manners, and his language" have something to do with his success. What Greene, through Hazard, grudgingly makes clear is the codification of drumming. And what he condemns in the way of mental and moral laxness—evidenced by "a neck that will bow, a back that will bend, a tongue that will flatter"—are habits that could not be separated from the selling relationship or the market system that sustained those habits.[72] When in the *Constellation* Greene claims that drumming "consists of fastening" onto presumptive country merchants, and when other critics highlighted the immorality of drumming, they described behavior that, for all its shifting drama, was itself becoming fixed to the marketplace.

But how, given the apparent immorality of drumming, was this fastening of talents and people even able to take place? One obvious answer is that despite the cross fire of republican discourse warning of urban dangers and condemning market disorder, antebellum New York City was a fiercely commercial society determined to develop its economy. Although during the early nineteenth century New Yorkers may have been less confident than during the previous century that the cultural stability of the city depended on trade, boosters of the economy were nonetheless apt to regard the union of economic artifice and natural forces as second nature—a logical consequence of geographical, economic, and natural destiny and therefore deserving of nurture.[73] Another answer, closely related to the first, is that merchants themselves, in particular, country storekeepers, willingly participated in the emerging market system and indeed helped create it. Viewed in this way, antebellum New York was as much a place of freedom and opportunity as it was a city of perils and anxieties.

New York newspapers, for instance, promoted the connection between city and hinterland with pride and solicitude, knowing that the arrival of outsiders in New York—to buy goods and spend money—confirmed and assured the prosperity of the city. In 1833 a writer in the *Journal of Commerce* solemnly observed the arrival of potential customers, declaring that "merchants from all parts of the country are beginning to come in to make their purchases for the coming season." The popular press described crowded markets with downright glee, noting, as a writer for the *Transcript* did in the spring of 1835, that "the stores and warehouses of industrious tradesmen literally swarm with customers from almost every region and district of the Union."[74] When country merchants crowded "respectable" hotels and boardinghouses, journalists did not necessarily worry whether swarms were good things. In fact, they occasionally marveled at the western merchant as if his "way of going, arms akimbo, through the crowd, nothing mindful of his neighbors ribs," presented some new form of life worth preserving.[75]

Throughout the 1830s and 1840s the need to maintain these market relations seemed all the more urgent in light of their fragility and tenuousness. Well aware that the physical dimensions of the marketplace stretched beyond Manhattan, newspaper editors in New York anxiously focused on connections with the hinterland, even reporting the weather and travel conditions elsewhere. For instance, they informed readers when a stage line operating between Albany and Utica added sixteen extra coaches to cope with the tremendous increase of traffic down the Hudson.[76] And they worried about western merchants who had to travel long journeys over poor roads and undependable waterways.[77] Rather than brave "the fatigues of travel in an inclement season," those merchants could order essential goods by letter, particularly if they trusted the supplier, and "await the opening of navigation" when the journey presented more "agreeable recreation." Or—and New York jobbers shuddered at the possibility—western merchants could forgo the wide selection of goods in New York and choose instead to buy in Baltimore or Philadelphia; as one trader noted, "The charges for transportation thence are not so high."[78]

Yet when wholesalers worried about losing trade to Baltimore or Philadelphia, they could take solace in the superior forms of recreation in New York. Although in 1820 New York was still very much like a village, by the 1830s it was well on its way to becoming the most distinctive urban landscape in the United States: busy, anonymous, disorienting, yet exciting. Philadelphia had "steadiness," but it lacked "bustle," and New Yorkers belittled the Quaker city with faint praise. "There is in the streets," a *New York Sun* writer said in 1833, "an air of quiet regularity, where every one seems to go quietly and leisurely about his business."[79] New York promised business—and more: theaters, restaurants, and museums filled with outlandish amusements. The reputation of the city as an entertainment mecca blossomed during the 1830s and 1840s as entrepreneurs like P. T. Barnum and A. T. Stewart catered to the tastes of a rapidly expanding population of working and middle classes. In visiting New York, merchants could count on exploring a city known as the Elephant, an exotic realm of mystery and pleasure, which, boosters admitted, furnished "a poor soil for the growth of morality."[80] According to advice manuals published in the 1830s, 1840s, and 1850s, New York threatened various kinds of moral degradation—drunkenness, profligacy, crime, poverty, various breaches in personal "confidence"—which critics were especially anxious to communicate to rural migrants.[81]

Although literature offering advice about the city occasionally targeted visiting merchants, storekeepers stood in a decidedly different relation to city tensions than full-time residents and rural migrants did.[82] Especially when commercial transactions were concerned, visiting merchants shared in the uneasiness that pervaded the antebellum urban scene. But seasonal acquaintance placed urban pitfalls in a geographical and cultural perspective; what an anxious, emergent middle class feared as a threat to republican selfhood, storekeepers could view as a temporary inconvenience or even an exotic relief from provincial tedium. The trader John Beauchamp Jones, for instance, warned of auctioneers who sold fine gold watches to the highest bidders, then passed off cheaper brass versions.[83] Yet as an inland merchant himself—and well acquainted with the West's own species of "shiftiness"—Jones wrote less out of moral shock than out of a recognition of urban ways and a desire to communicate them.

Not surprisingly, the New York press frequently reflected a similar acceptance of urban realities when it simultaneously welcomed merchants to the big city and tried to protect their interests. In 1835 the *New York Sun,* for example, carried a warning to Western traders to beware of pickpockets while implicitly promoting city entertainments: "If any of you attend the theatre, be sure and leave your pocket books behind."[84] Newspapers like the *Sun* tended to take urban perils for granted, and, to the extent that they catered to an out-of-town audience whose financial well-being reinforced civic prosperity, they provided quick lessons in how to survive—and enjoy—New York. Furthermore, the assumed audience for such admonitions may well have been merchants in search of erotic entertainment. Throughout the 1830s and 1840s many touted "sights" were explicitly for men. When visitors to the city walked into saloons presenting "tableaux vivants," they could expect to see naked women striking poses taken from classical art and literature, and when they attended the theater, they could count on finding prostitutes for hire in the third tier. The sex trade was a central feature of the street life and commerce, notorious enough that country merchants who came to New York knew that they would find opportunities for entertainment unrivaled in any other American city.[85]

In this respect, the dramas of duplicity that appeared throughout the 1830s and 1840s deserve reading not simply as warnings to country greenhorns but as part of a discourse of urban peril that country merchants learned—and loved—to master. For every moral tract concerned with maintaining sincere interpersonal relations, there was a play or novel that celebrated the thrills of visiting the big city and the challenges of turning the world of confidence upside down. Benjamin Baker's popular 1848 play, *A Glance at New York,* in which a bumpkin from "up the river" loses his savings by repeatedly falling victim to two confidence men, gave audiences a chance to laugh at urban scams.[86] So, too, did *The Adventures of Harry Franco* and Herman Melville's *Redburn,* both of whose provincial heroes comically lose in the transactions that they make soon after their arrival in New York.[87]

Such works offered readers and audiences the opportunity to laugh at the betrayals that moralists like Henry Ward Beecher found so disturbing. Comedy gave the middle class a way of diffusing cultural anxiety, a way of laughing away concerns about demographic change and economic volatility. Yet what made a play like *A Glance at New York* funny and popular was not necessarily its making light of the crisis in confidence but its inclusion of a vital working-class perspective in the figure of the Bowery B'hoy Mose, whose ability to see through the shams of the metropolis encouraged street-savvy, working-class males to laugh at—and scorn—the anxieties that preoccupied upwardly mobile urbanites. Mose's national notoriety was also partially due to his guardianship of the wayward greenhorn in the play, a gesture of confidence that no doubt endeared him to hinterland audiences by softening apparent differences between city and country.[88] Although Baker did not stress this rural perspective, it received stronger treatment in the many "Yankee" plays and stories that emerged during the 1830s, 1840s, and 1850s.[89] Following Royall Tyler's 1787 play, *The Contrast,* Yankee plots depended on the urban-rural dichotomy for much of their dramatic force and humor, assumed a natural intercourse between city and country, and, for all their satiric glances at urban culture, often depicted Yankee heroes curiously at home in the big city. Like the Bowery B'hoy Mose, the Yankee Jonathans in these plays negotiate the perils of the city with remarkable ease and confidence.

To suggest that country merchants viewed the urban scene with similar aplomb would be to trivialize the significant efforts and risks involved in undertaking seasonal trips to Pearl Street. After all, merchants came to New York to do business, and considering the resources they had invested in this enterprise—money, character, and even family—no merchant could be too wary. Still, the heroic and comic twists that playwrights and novelists brought to their plots suggest that the urban landscape allowed a sense of freedom and room for interpretive play. When moralists envisioned corrupted youths—victims of false representation—they poked fun at gullible greenhorns or found heroes shrewd enough to see through urban con games. But country traders were not necessarily green and in fact may have had more in common with Yankee and B'howery heroes than commercial earnestness would suggest. At least they shared a recognition of the shifting perils of the city, an understanding that could lead to skepticism and wariness on the one hand or to wonder and enthusiastic participation on the other—a posture that resembled the attitudes of subsequent rural or small-town visitors to the big city. Ultimately, it was the country traders' dependency on the economic resources of New York that brought them inside the city and made them partners in the creation of a transregional marketplace and a commercial culture that transcended urban boundaries. And it was being in the market and not merely subject to the effects of an increasingly market-oriented culture that distinguished them (and other commercial actors) from Yankee heroes, Bowery B'hoys, and middle-class urbanites—even those like Melville's recalcitrant clerk Bartleby whose jobs depended on the market.[90]

Benjamin Shillaber's 1851 play *The Drummer; or, New York Clerks and Country Merchants* collapses the Yankee theater plot into a story of commercial duplicity to emphasize the interconnectedness of town and country.[91] When two criminals try to fleece a New York wholesale house by impersonating retail merchants, a shrewd countryman named Ike Slack and a witty journalist called Mrs. Partington team up to foil them and recover a young woman whom they have kidnapped. As the hero in this farce and an "acting 'Drummer,'" Ike Slack succeeds where the jobber's own drummers fail and, exposing the true nature of the false merchants, sends them to prison for "the balance of the season." In rescuing the woman—his "country produce"—from a New York pleasure den, which the drummers visit, Slack turns conventional wisdom inside out and makes the city drummers look "green."[92]

Here, as in Greene's and Briggs's tales, it would seem that the difference between country and city is the negative influence of the urban marketplace on character. Warning of city perils, Shillaber's representation of a corrupt and hapless business culture that precludes the possibility of success through good works seems like yet another advice manual designed to instruct young men on the make. The resemblance deserves qualification, however, for beyond Shillaber's emphasis on Ike Slack's rural heroism lies a recognition that the market—and its perils—may no longer be contained within the city. More explicitly than either Greene or Briggs (writing more than a decade earlier), Shillaber makes this point near the outset of the play when one of the jobber's clerks, referring to the power of New York credit agencies, boasts: "Every merchant's standing in the whole country is as well-known to us as it is to himself. An institution has been reared whose heart is in New York, and whose veins and arteries reach into every merchant's counting room within the boundaries of our Union."[93] To be sure, Shillaber makes a joke of this declaration when the drummers mistake the villains for the actual country merchants whose identities and credit ratings they have assumed. Still, the plot and much of the humor of the play turn on the ubiquity of business institutions, systems, and rhetoric.

Although the language of the play is drawn from various social worlds, commercial rhetoric rules by dint of the capacity of the market to make connections—locally, nationally, even internationally—a phenomenon that

Shillaber was in a better position to imagine at mid-century. This is particularly true within the countinghouse. After reminding his clerks "to walk in the paths of sobriety," the senior partner turns to his mail. "Fourteen hundred dollars from Wisconsin," he exclaims upon opening a letter. "Invoice of goods shipped from Liverpool per Steamer Atlantic," he says unwrapping a package. "Hallo! a protest! for $1000.00, laid over in Ohio! That is bad.—Ohio's crops are all right. If the man is honest, he will redeem his credit. If he is dishonest, $1000.00 will be carried to profit and loss." Imparting order to this network of commercial transactions, the merchant authoritatively shuffles his papers, directs his employees, pauses to buy the New York *Herald* and *Tribune* from a newsboy hawking papers in the jobbing house, and tells a customer, "Our capital gives us command of the market."[94]

Business capital does command in Shillaber's play, but chiefly in rhetorical and cultural terms. Its strength and fluidity make possible the villains' impersonation of country merchants. "We must drop all Battery slang and use nothing but commercial phrases and Wall Street parlance," one reminds the other.[95] The puns that follow this resolve dramatize their chicanery; their linguistic deceptions, like their disguises, are made possible by a mobile economic culture that brings the distant into contact with the local and takes risks with far-flung connections. Here, as on Pearl Street itself, the drummer serves as the middleman who effects the customer's movement into the counting room. At four in the morning in a fashionable Broadway saloon, the drummers in the play sing:

> We "rub-a-dub-dub" from the morn's reveille,
> Till our Merchants "up town" take flight—
> Till the "cars" and the "steamers" our "sales" bear away,
> For to them we are bound to "drum" through the day,
> And ourselves bound to "train" through the night.[96]

The refrain finds drummers working around the clock in late-night resorts and at the intersection of the expanding national transportation network as Shillaber emphasizes just how much their place in the urban economy depends on far-flung commercial connections. The drummer is as ubiquitous as commercial parlance; both he and the creative powers of the marketplace that he embodies exist throughout the mercantile city and beyond. Even Ike Slack, who seems positioned in the drama to stand for provincialism, is a creature of omnipresent economic forces. Describing his passage by rail from upstate New York, Ike sounds more like the acting drummer whose authority he has usurped than a Vermont-born Yankee: "My hull passage from Cayuga county is a streak of wonderment not to be beat by the one hundred and one nights of the magnificent Eastern tales, nor the indefinite number of Knights of the sublime order of the one thousand and one. Railroads—steamboats—and Morse's telegraph! Hail, Yankee nation, you can't be beat."[97]

The upshot of these movements in and around an expanding transportation network is to minimize regional difference and establish an economy for the play that all participants share. Hence, the customs of drumming, which make a fraternity of jobbing clerks, a home of the mercantile city, and a marketplace of geographically dispersed businesses, also serve as the instrument of the villains' trickery. In what might be construed as an empowering gloss on the country merchant's own position in the market, Shillaber makes the drummer's accommodating ways the tool of the customer. The portrayal bears at least passing resemblance to how a Missouri merchant described his own reaction to being drummed. What critics like Henry Ward Beecher and James Alexander called servile dependence, he deemed good business. He appreciated the drummer's effort to display goods, which "I need, and which I can make money on." Dismissing the complaints of "poor weak fools," the trader insisted that "the man who has not the resolution to say no, when an article he does not want is offered him, had better keep away from the city, and pay some one else who can, to buy his goods for him." As for the litany of "professions and promises" that drummers frequently recited in hotel lobbies, the Missouri merchant enjoyed listening. "I believe just as much as I please."[98]

Implicit in this and in Shillaber's view of drumming is the notion that merchant and drummer alike had the capacity to suspend disbelief, to see truth in relative terms, as a value shaped by the contingencies of the commercial moment. Although not all visiting merchants could so easily accept (or reject) drummers' muddling with the truth, there is no doubt but that the developing sales culture encouraged "onstage" and "offstage" behavior—for both parties—and that buyer and seller alike learned to take the other's profession with a grain of salt.[99] Shillaber treats such prevarications humorously, acknowledging, on the one hand, that drummers are at heart good fellows while suggesting, on the other, that their selling methods resemble the villains' impersonations. The drummers describe the credit agency as a "humbug" but nonetheless rely on its "A1" rating and carouse with their customers before delivering them to their associates in the countinghouse. One of Shillaber's drummers tells his customer that "[I] would feel proud to secure your trade" and that "I am interested in the house whose card I handed you." Apart from this pretense of collegiality and sincerity, what he does not tell him is how he has scanned the hotel register for potential customers and asked the hotel clerk not to tell the "other boys" about the merchant's arrival. He remains confident, although he does not tell his customers, that he can put them "through on" some "traps."[100]

What, in broad terms, did this harnessing of improvisational energies mean for the increasingly commercial culture of the Republic? How did drumming fit into what one historian has recently termed the "collective repression" of the market revolution, its transformation of instinctual freedoms into aggressive self-control and calculating economic thinking?[101] While there is little denying that drumming was part of an increasingly rationalized effort to expand the market system, it would be a mistake to assume that the resulting commercial practices were entirely repressed. On the contrary, antebellum drumming exemplifies the critical importance of such improvisational freedoms to a commercial culture determined to win customers and sell goods. By 1851, as Shillaber's play makes clear, these improvisations were already part of a commercial system. The evolution of drumming in the decades to come, not as a marginal or residual market practice, but as an enterprise absolutely necessary for the growth of a national market economy extended these improvisations beyond the antebellum mercantile city and made the commercial traveler even freer than his antebellum predecessor. Yet both figures derived their self-reliance and authority from institutions that sustained them. In this sense, the perils of Pearl Street referred to the price that people paid for the powers of commercial representation. *The Drummer; or, New York Clerks and Country Merchants* offers a glimpse of such costs when, during a night of drunken revelry, one drummer comments: "This occupation will be the death of me."[102] As Shillaber sensed, if only by way of a joke, and as the succeeding efforts of traveling salesmen would show, being a drummer took all that its practitioners could give.

Without the expansive economy of the 1830s and 1840s the emergence of this improvisational self would not have been possible. Extensive commercial growth, which brought country merchants into the orbit of wholesale jobbers, and intensive urban growth, which made the city as a whole an exotic backdrop for market relations, created a sales context that was never simply economic in nature and nearly always framed by regional and cultural tensions. To succeed in this world as a drummer demanded special talents. Gaining the confidence of countrymen who valued upright appearances but were sometimes willing—and hoping—to relax their guard in the city required both a knowledge of urban pleasures and a shrewdness about rural ways. Offering a look or just a circumspect peek at what could not be seen back home involved not only the promise of theater tickets, oyster dinners, champagne, and city tours but also the appearance of sobriety and restraint.

In a commercial world populated almost entirely by intermediaries, the drummer proved the quintessential middleman. On the one hand, he represented his employer's interests in the marketplace, and, on the other, he served as the country merchant's guide to the city. The upshot was the establishment of the all-male sales culture still prevalent today. Country merchant in tow, the drummer skirted the boundaries of Victorian morality and provided an escape from mundane routine into the carnivalesque underside of the nineteenth-century city. The way back, however, led through the wholesaler's showroom and perhaps to a sale. Like the rural fairs of early modern Europe and England, drumming thus "turned the world inside out," not upside down, reinforcing rather than disrupting the status quo. In the antebellum mercantile city, selling became a ritual whose rotations away from everyday strictures ultimately operated in the service of established commercial interests.[103] By the twentieth century the integration of the transgressive and conventional in salesmanship seemed almost a fact of American culture, a reminder in the hands of such critics as Sinclair Lewis that the riotous sales convention and the debauched wanderings of an Elmer Gantry or a George Babbitt were vital components of modern business enterprise.

2 But One Country

I have enjoyed life at the rate of nine knots an hour since I left you and if I had no *wife* or *warren* to think of, to love, and to care for, the itinerancy would be the *life for me.*
–John Kirk to his wife, Susan Kirk, March 3, 1853

I will start you into buisiness. As I don't think you will ever want to ware your life out braking those clay clodds in the summer & freasing in the winter. I have maid plenty of money since I've bin off the farm & don't have to work half so hard. . . . Come out and see the World.
–William Hutton to his brother Lineus, October 11, 1884

Separated in time by thirty years, in history by the Civil War, and in personal circumstances by marriage and debt, John Kirk and William Hutton discovered the pleasures of traveling from place to place with speed and freedom and getting paid for it. In the emerging commercial network of the nineteenth century both men perceived the same world. Kirk gently confessed its lures to his mother and soberly if somewhat wistfully backed away. "I should like travelling through the country much. I enjoy it well. But I cannot keep myself so busy, but what a father's cares, and a father's responsibilities flash upon my mind." To his employer he also acknowledged the pleasures of travel, but the "idea of being away from my family ten months in the year," he complained, "is murder in the first degree." For Kirk, a reflective and religious man, commercial itinerancy proved unsettling. Selling goods by sample to retail merchants reminded him of the creditors and the family that he left at home. Constant awareness of domestic and financial responsibility dulled the thrill of discovering the country outside stage or train windows.[1]

In the fall of 1858 Kirk agreed to direct the Chicago branch agency of the Pittsburgh iron manufacturer that he had represented and, for the time, stopped traveling. Reflecting on his seven years of travel, Kirk calculated that he had covered by "steam and by state, seventy nine thousand four hundred and thirty seven miles, a longer distance than to travel three times round the world." To his mother he marveled that for all this mileage and the many railway accidents "yet not a hair of my head has been hurt." Only God could be such a deliverer. And in the Episcopal Prayer Book, Kirk found a "very appropriate" response to his safe voyage back from "the perils and dangers of a seven years journey"—the sailor's prayer of thanksgiving. In imagining a map for a new world of speed, Kirk followed older, familiar tracings.[2]

The years separating Kirk's travels from Hutton's brought a world of change to the United States, but William Hutton imagined that life at his former Indiana farm home continued as it always had—grimly. Describing a hard rural world, much like the midwestern landscapes envisioned by such regional writers as E. W. Howe and Joseph Kirkland, Hutton alternately goaded and encouraged his brother to forsake agricultural life for a more exciting career as a traveling salesman. Whether selling furniture, clocks, or

Singer sewing machines, Hutton portrayed himself as a man of a larger, expansive world. In 1887 he chafed Lineus for forgetting the agreement that they had made years earlier. "I havent forgoten the time we went buggy riding and the bottom fell out . . . we had to walk long the fence . . . and when the horse got stuck in the mud we'd clime the fince and give him a lift—and iff you remember we vowed we were going to leave Indiana, and go West, the coming spring and shuck hands on it. Wel I stuck to it & I ainent sorry of it either—for, I have one consolation I never get stuck in the mud any more."[3]

Hutton's business travels took him to California, Washington, Arkansas, Mississippi, and Louisiana. He longed "to see Floridy and explore its beautiful oring groves." Open and free, the West especially struck Hutton as the place where a young man could "get a hold of a fine piece of land that will gain in value." But leaving home meant more to Hutton than casting aside tedious farmwork and a harsh climate. It brought special status. In sloppy, ragged prose, Hutton eagerly told his brother of the places that he discovered. "You ask me what country I liked best of the different countries I have bin in. . . . I am pretty well acquainted with this country now," he reported from Natchez, "but better acquainted with the girls."[4] For Hutton the word *country* still took James Hall's 1828 meaning. Echoing the antebellum literary figure and businessman, Hutton referred not to separate nations or continents but to particular sections of land "frequently of indefinite extent," each with its peculiar features.[5] Travel focused this definition. Acquaintance sharpened the difference between Indiana and other countries, giving home all the more poignancy. As for John Kirk, the idea of home shaped Hutton's vision of life on the road, made it exotic and thrilling. If the picture of home invited Kirk to return, it only compelled Hutton to scrape the mud from his boots, confine the "old frog pond" to memory, and seek new worlds.[6]

From a late twentieth-century perspective, it is William Hutton who seems most like the traveling salesman of ribald jokes and popular culture. Broken grammar and all, Hutton's portrait reveals a conscious self-stylist, a man of the road anxious to impress his hayseed brother. By contrast, John Kirk's ambivalence about travel and his pietistic longing for home seem anachronistic and, ironically, more in line with the moral critique of sales culture than the improvisational practices themselves. Yet both perspectives, indeed both forms of self-representation, were part of the culture made by commercial traveling. Home and adventure competed equally for sway. What evolved from the tug-of-war between the two was a profession constantly struggling to domesticate its economic goals, social relationships, modes of persuasion, and public image. The anxieties of leaving home, the hardships of travel, the demands of employers, the pressures of selling—all cut away at the glamor of the job, its purported romance and adventure. But whatever traveling men lost by way of diminished expectations, they stood to regain by way of professional accomplishment, through envisioning the road as an expansive, commercial space—a territory to be conquered, cultivated, and rationalized.

By 1900 the historical-minded salesman could justly claim that his profession deserved much of the credit for realizing the antebellum wholesaler's dream of a united market economy. Continuing the work begun by city drummers, late nineteenth-century salesmen paced the growth of an increasingly centralized market: they deepened urban-rural connections, tightened relationships between manufacturers and retailers, and promoted national brands. One indication of the traveling salesman's importance to this expansion was the phenomenal increase in the profession, which outstripped the rate of growth for nearly all other occupations.[7] In 1870—the first time the occupational class "commercial traveler" appeared on the census—the government listed 7,262 commercial travelers working in the United States; by 1900 the total exceeded 90,000.[8] Partisan sources calculated much more generously. The Society of Commercial Travellers estimated in 1869 that 50,000 salesmen were "constantly travelling by night and by day over all the threads of the immense network of railroads of this vast country."[9] In 1883 the *Commercial Travelers Magazine* gave an estimate that 200,000 traveling salesmen were working "at an average cost to their employers of $3,000 each, including salaries and road expenses, or an aggregate of $600,000,000."[10] At the turn of the century, according to testimony given by the president of the Commercial Travelers' National League before the Industrial Commission on Trusts and Combinations, 350,000 commercial travelers did business in the United States.[11] And even then, as traveling men saw their relative commercial significance diminished by the emergence of mail-order houses, chain stores, and national advertising, they continued to bring human scale to the market, whether as representatives of wholesalers or corporate manufacturers, or both.

Another sign of the importance of commercial traveling was the opposition that it provoked. In promoting the goods of an expanding consumer culture, traveling salesmen often filled their self-designated role as ambassadors of commerce; however, the turn of phrase reflected their ongoing efforts to negotiate conflict. Selling was itself aimed at overcoming resistance, and life on the road provided daily impediments, yet such occupational friction grew faint in comparison to the ambivalent, even hostile reaction to the commercial traveler—as an economic type or middleman—that pervaded late nineteenth-century social institutions and popular culture. On one level, the scores of licensing laws that sprang from state and local legislatures and that taxed the salesman's movements from place to place, indicated a broad-based effort to come to terms with the dynamics of a new market economy, a revolution in commerce that treated all states as "but one country"—to quote from the opinion supporting the 1887 Supreme Court decision prohibiting "drummer laws." On another level, the salesman's individual representation of larger commercial interests, particularly his manifestation of systematic economic power through intimate, human-scaled forms of persuasion reached beyond larger structural transformations to issues of selfhood. Questions about the traveling man's representativeness—What kind of man might he be? Was he an honorable businessman? A confidence man? A good husband?—were in the mouths of critics and salesmen alike during the decades following the Civil War. The questions pointed to a generic occupational character, an integration of personal and professional identities that grew out of the traveling man's dialectical self-fashioning—dialectical because saleswork hinged on face-to-face interaction and because commercial traveling continually brought salesmen into the public eye.

That the drummer's place in American life became the subject of widespread, frequently acrimonious debate (even more so than during the early nineteenth century) only confirmed the broader cultural issues at stake. At bottom, the extensive and distributive role of commercial traveling brought an essentially urban-based market culture into small-town, rural America, threatening well-established notions of economic self-rule and domestic ideology. Relationships between antebellum wholesalers and storekeepers laid the foundation for this urban-rural thoroughfare but hardly prepared other Americans for the appearance—some might say intrusion—of whole armies of traveling salesmen. Nor were traveling salesmen themselves fully prepared to accommodate this dramatic change of custom; they, too, struggled toward a way to address their paradoxical roles as commercial middlemen. That the salesmen won the debate over their place in the commercial landscape when the Supreme Court provided an abstract rationale for their right to travel did not ameliorate the identity problem so much as it dramatized the extent to which salesmen's individual power belonged not to themselves but to the larger economic interests they represented.

In the effort to rationalize and domesticate their place on the commercial landscape, traveling men exemplified their uneasy relations with the spheres so vital to middle-class interests. By mid-century, the doctrine of separate spheres supported two mutually dependent realms: one allowing middle-class men to become self-made successes outside the home and the other sanctioning their spouses' pursuit of true womanhood within it. So long as the self-making man returned home to the moral influence of his spouse, he ensured this delicate balance; otherwise, the pursuit of business or other kinds of work could be a perilous enterprise. Honesty, prudence, temperance, and self-control—traits nurtured in childhood by conscientious mothers—regulated the movement back and forth between the private and public spheres, helping antebellum men succeed in terms that safeguarded home and family. As early as the 1830s the social reproduction of such values, as Mary Ryan has argued, enabled the development of the middle-class personality, creating what Burton Bledstein has called a culture of professionalism that "emancipated the active ego of a sovereign person as he performed organized activities within comprehensive spaces."[12] Literally and figuratively, the specialized skills, disciplinary authority, and occupational independence that characterized nineteenth-century professional culture developed in the spaces made possible by a putatively separate sphere of domestic work.

It was perhaps the singular achievement of commercial traveling that by claiming an ambiguous public space that seemed beyond the reach of domestic influences it simultaneously reinforced the ideology of separate spheres even as it threatened to turn it upside down. In many respects, the profession epitomized the benefits that upwardly mobile men hoped to gain from a career in business. Traveling men enjoyed a great deal of independence, they had good opportunities for advancement (especially, as the century drew to a close, within larger selling organizations), and they were well paid.[13] Between 1870 and 1900 salesmen earned an average income of $1,200 to $1,800 per year and, where earnings depended on commissions, could triple those amounts.[14] When he began selling hats for a New York firm in 1872, the Iowa salesman Kendrick Brown made $75.00 a month, plus a 5 percent commission on sales that during the course of a single season (about three months) exceeded $6,000. During the 1870s and 1880s at Marshall Field and Company, where salaries often hinged on performance, the better salesmen averaged $2,000 a year, and the very best made as much as $6,000.[15] In 1889, according to one estimate, successful jewelry and drug salesmen earned about $2,500 a year, and the very best salesmen in dry goods, boots and shoes, and groceries could make anywhere between $6,000 and $10,000 a year.[16] By comparison, in 1890 an insurance clerk could expect to bring home about $1,800; a lawyer in a small firm, roughly $4,000; and a skilled worker, between $500 and $800 a year.[17] In terms of potential earnings, then, commercial traveling fell well within the range of middle-class work.

Despite this winning profile, traveling salesmen often remained outside the mainstream of middle-class respectability. And among the various reasons for the salesman's ambiguous status, none was more important than his apparently unregulated movement outside the home. Precisely because of its ideological firepower and capacity to invoke the social practices that traveling men did not follow, home was a key concept for the profession. As sentimental novelists might see it, the traveling salesman's responsibilities carried him into a marketplace that was competitive, exploitive, selfish, and immoral.[18] Although not all late nineteenth-century representations of commercial travelers were negative, names—*drummer, runner, bummer,* and *guerilla*—joined with licensing laws and popular culture to emphasize the traveling man's aggressive threat to home influences. Even among friends, traveling salesmen could feel the stigma of their profession. For instance, in 1889, when a Denver hardware salesman drove his buggy and sample trunk to a dinner party, his host "twitted" him for "carrying samples around to the trade in this very plebeian manner." Although the salesman made more money than his acquaintance, who was a banker, and even though he "was practically as free as the air" and his friend worked "under a boss," these amenities hardly mattered, since the profession seemed to encourage its practitioners to enter a genteel home (this was the rub) as they might greet their customers.[19]

Not surprisingly, the view of the salesman in society at large influenced how he saw himself. Whether or not it was accurate hardly mattered: as a member of a profession necessarily in the public eye, a commercial traveler could not ignore the cultural representations of his own character. As the nineteenth century drew to a close and the salesman's iconographic status thickened, this dynamic interplay allowed business to imitate art, and salesmen to follow in the footsteps of mythic constructions. For the profession as a whole, however, the most important consequence of social judgments was an acute occupational self-consciousness, an almost defensive turning inward for justification and definition that fostered group identity. Even the most negative stereotypes gave salesmen a common ground. From general prejudice to pointed attacks, resistance to commercial traveling accentuated the isolation that many salesmen already felt away from home and created a sense of insurgency that galvanized and united the profession.

Although commercial traveling was the logical extension of antebellum business practices, its market-changing impact stemmed from the revolution in transportation and information systems that took place after the Civil War. As Alfred Chandler, Jr., has shown, the consolidation of a national railroad network, together with a telegraph system, brought heretofore unknown "speed and regularity" to commercial transactions, significantly altering the world of the antebellum jobber. By 1870 railroad companies had built 70,000 miles of track across the nation, the essential framework of a system that encompassed 200,000 miles by 1900. The new efficiency enabled jobbers to receive orders and ship goods more quickly and in much greater volume than ever before. Swifter turnaround then allowed more merchants to take title to the goods that they sold; in the postwar era practically all wholesalers who marketed consumer goods were jobbers. The transportation system also accelerated industrial production and made buying from manufacturers easier. Whereas the old Pearl Street jobber had purchased his goods at auction or from importers, postbellum jobbers increasingly purchased directly from domestic manufacturers and developed "multiunit" organizations for distributing consumer goods to retailers. Finally, wholesale centers expanded. No longer the dominant purveyors of goods to retail merchants, jobbers from New York, Philadelphia, and Baltimore shared the task with western, midwestern, and southern merchants.[20]

Until the end of the century, wholesalers distributed the majority of products that Americans used on a daily basis: hardware, hand tools, furniture, groceries, clothing, and other dry goods. Although manufacturers of agricultural equipment, steel and iron, and such specialized items as spectacles and pens frequently developed their own selling organizations, the independent wholesaler offering a wide range of products continued to dominate the retail market.[21] In the 1860s, according to one estimate, jobbers of dry goods distributed at least 80 percent of the goods sold by U.S. retailers, much of it going to the large number of general stores and retail outlets that emerged as part of the postwar economic boom.[22] By 1890 the wholesaler's position of authority had begun to erode—chipped away by department stores and mail-order houses that eliminated the wholesaler from their marketing chains, and overshadowed by manufacturers of standardized products who either integrated forward and created their own sales forces or, as was more commonly the case, continued to depend on the wholesaler's distribution channels but coordinated the actual marketing themselves.[23] After the turn of the century, it was increasingly the manufacturer's market to control. The integration of mass production and mass distribution, combined with aggressive national advertising, made brand names like Ivory Soap and Quaker Oats household words, dramatically altering the commercial landscape. By 1930 wholesalers still distributed 30 percent of the products destined for retail stores but in a market "designed"—to use Susan Strasser's apt phrase—by manufacturers with national and multinational scope.[24] To be sure, wholesalers and manufacturers fought for control of the marketing channels in the first decades of the twentieth century, and in circumstances that, as Glenn Porter and Harold C. Livesay argue, militated against corporate dominance; in "diffuse," out-of-the-way markets involving generic products in the drug, grocery, hardware, and dry-goods trades, wholesalers continued to oversee the distribution of consumer goods, employing 1,200,000 people in 1919 compared to 170,000 in 1869.[25] But on the whole, the shape of the twentieth-century consumer economy was determined by the marketing strategies of corporate oligopolies. The result was an "abstract" marketplace so pervaded by efforts to create and sell new products and so amorphous in its dimensions and boundaries that "the term [market] might well be applied to nearly anything."[26]

Between this and the more decentralized economy of the nineteenth century there were certainly great differences. Yet there were also important continuities—easily missed by focusing too much on corporate power—not the least of which was the ongoing creation of a commercial thoroughfare between urban and rural America. Indeed, it was wholesalers, not corporate manufacturers, who brought country and town together in a seemingly organic web of financial and commercial relations. The point is brought home in William Cronon's analysis of how late nineteenth-century Chicago came to be "nature's metropolis"—an entrepôt for western livestock and agricultural produce and the hub to a "hybrid system" of towns, villages, farms, and commercial institutions "at least as artificial as it was natural." Chicago wholesalers were essential movers in this developing ecosystem of "island communities" ranged around a central city. By distributing the products of the new age and extending credit to retail merchants, they not only assured the reciprocal flow of capital back to the hinterland but also introduced rural Americans to urban ways, to the modernity implicit in purchasing "newness."[27]

Here the commercial traveler's role proved vital, for it was the salesman who served as the metropolitan connection. At bottom, economic expansion owed as much to human capital as it did to the inanimate forces—financial, manufacturing, and ecological—that historians have tended to stress. Both a creature of urban power and its progenitor, the salesman was the wholesaler's proxy—there to structure commercial transactions—as well as a metaphor for the evolving synthesis of urban and rural cultures. In this respect, Don Marquis's speculation that the old-time drummer operated as a precursor to radio, advertising, and film is highly suggestive. As Neil Harris has suggested for mass media, commercial traveling promised to break down the differences between urban and rural and create a "new amalgam of its own."[28]

To the extent that such an amalgam did exist in late nineteenth-century America, it hovered about the salesman like a spirit, extending a metropolitan discourse along commercial lines and highlighting the flux of modernity.

A salesman, George Von Brown, poses with the tools of his trade—packaged food products, sample case, and order book—around 1910. (Minnesota Historical Society.)

The occupation rationalized notions of rootlessness and transitoriness and, through its emphasis on face-to-face mediations, made personal communication skills an intangible cultural capital. As nineteenth-century market structures gave way to large-scale corporate enterprise, the salesman's mediating role remained basically the same—an ironic reminder that the market was still the product of human enterprise even as it appeared to contravene the human capital involved in its creation.

Immediately after the Civil War commercial travelers representing eastern wholesalers, who were closer to established manufacturers and importers, dominated this enterprise. Then, as throughout the nineteenth century, the great majority of traveling men represented wholesale houses. Just as in the antebellum period, New York jobbers led the way, in the late 1860s employing twice the number of salesmen sent out by Chicago, Cincinnati, and Saint Louis firms combined.[29] Competition, traveling men later maintained, was practically nonexistent. "The mode of selling in these days was simple and direct," recalled Edward P. Briggs, a New York hardware salesman. "There were comparatively few salesmen on the road and they only stopped in the cities and large towns." A salesman "had only to call upon the merchant and announce that he was willing to sell him and show him his samples to receive an order." Kendrick W. Brown likewise claimed to have "seldom met a competitor" when he traveled for a New York hat wholesaler in his home state of Iowa during the early 1870s. To sell goods to a merchant all he had to do "was to get to him."[30]

By the late 1870s, however, as the market expanded geographically and competition among rival cities and within product lines escalated, there was little doubt that the dominion of New York as a wholesale center was ebbing. In Boston alone, according to an October 1876 report in the *Commercial Bulletin,* an average of 130 traveling men left the city each morning for tours throughout New England, the South, and the West. Twenty years earlier, Boston wholesalers had questioned the ethics of drumming and rarely sent men on the road, and then only to collect bills. Now in competition with Chicago and New York merchants for trade outside New England, they not only conceded the necessity of commercial travelers but—feeling the brunt of travel expenses for over one thousand salesmen—began collective negotiations with railroad companies to obtain discounts on telegraph rates and freight charges for sample trunks.[31] In the South market conditions also stiffened. Traveling men from Cincinnati and Louisville (which had the advantage of superior railroad connections) competed for the retail trade and built on relationships established at the end of the Civil War, when wholesalers began to invite rural storekeepers to notorious commercial conventions—held in border cities and, continuing the Pearl Street tradition, replete with urban pleasures—as a way of selling goods.[32] Ranging out from such small cities as Milwaukee, Wisconsin, and large towns like Galveston, Texas, wholesalers established "hierarchical" commercial relations that led first to regional markets and, over time, enabled the creation of a national market economy.[33]

Perhaps the most telling sign that East Coast wholesalers, particularly New Yorkers, no longer dominated the channels of distribution was the emergence of Chicago as an economic power. Even before the Great Fire of 1871 Chicago had established itself as a preeminent wholesaling center. But it was chiefly after a decade of industrial and commercial rebuilding, amid the continued expansion of the railroad network (in which Chicago was the key hub), that the city became—in Theodore Dreiser's famous words—a "giant magnet" to whose "vast wholesale and shopping district" the "uninformed seeker for work usually drifted." By the 1880s wholesalers working out of Chicago had established trade connections to the East and the West that rivaled those of New York in commercial scope and made Chicago drummers famous throughout the land. The rapid growth of Chicago as a commercial hub is clear from census figures, which for 1900 show 3,385 wholesale merchants established in the city—nearly ten times the number reported in 1860.[34]

Marshall Field and Company's battle in 1876 with the powerful New York dry-goods firm A. T. Stewart, and later with the H. F. Claflin Company and the Philadelphia firm John Wanamaker, exemplified the increased competition for new markets and dramatized the growing commercial power of Chicago. Marshall Field withstood A. T. Stewart's efforts to hire away his salesmen and H. F. Claflin's price-cutting, but not without learning a valuable lesson. Shortly after his conflict with Stewart ended, Field increased traveling expenditures in his firm and its reliance on salesmen. Traveling men who visited isolated towns and villages throughout the Midwest offered country merchants not just the famous Marshall Field name but service and valuable advice as well.[35] The commercial traveler who informed retailers on the latest fashions and counseled quick turnaround improved customer relations and reinforced the Marshall Field and Company's claim on the Midwest.[36]

As Field's victories suggest, sheer numbers were generally not enough to win markets. The commercial traveler's ability to expand his employer's share of the market ultimately depended on the relationships that he established with retail merchants. Because the great majority of traveling men "figured on selling the same customers again," as salesman Virgil Smith put it in 1893, commercial relations broadened beyond the point of sale. For Smith, who claimed to have "never misrepresented an article," and indeed for the profession as a whole, the selling depended on an essentially pragmatic business morality, a code of ethics that reinforced the goal implicitly shared by retailer and wholesaler alike: getting the goods to the consumer. The "golden rule" of business, which prompted such drummers as Charles S. Plummer to demand "consideration" from sharp-dealing retailers, sprang from an awareness of this reciprocal relationship.[37] Even though competition from other wholesale houses complicated the relationship, traveling men sought to guarantee sales by improving the retailer's position in the market. By advising a merchant on his purchases or by organizing his stock, a salesman declared his conscientious, honest nature.[38] Well aware that "new faces and new methods break the confidential connection between the house and the customer," he sought to define selling conditions along mutually beneficial lines.[39] Ideally, the lines of communication extended from the customer through the salesman to the wholesale house—and sometimes even reached the manufacturer. The Cudahy Pharmaceutical Company, for instance, in 1894 urged its travelers to write often: "We would like to know of the way you are received by the profession and trade."[40] As early as 1852, when one of John Kirk's customers declared his purchase not "worth a damn," Kirk wrote his employer and suggested some changes.[41] Twenty years later, by letter and telegraph, P. J. Willis and Brother informed the Du Pont Company that another manufacturer was selling gunpowder at significantly cheaper rates. Business ethics, more than profits, motivated the exchange of letters. Unable to ask retail customers to buy from them at a loss, the Galveston jobbing firm felt "bound to protect" its "trade" and urged Du Pont to lower its prices.[42]

To be sure, not all traveling men could count on names like Marshall Field or Du Pont to solidify their hold on the market. Not all wholesalers could afford to send out two types of salesmen—one a "specialty" man to carry the firm's most expensive items, the other a "general" salesman to sell a variety of the basic items.[43] Nor, it should be stressed, did traveling men have to patronize all their customers; not every retail merchant needed the kind of commercial advice Field's salesmen could give. Still, the most basic truth of the profession was that saleswork centered on meeting the customer face to face and establishing a working relationship. By simultaneously expanding and rationalizing these relationships, the commercial traveler sought to domesticate the selling process and create a cultural space in which he and his customer could comfortably work.

At the center of this process was the product itself, the most concrete evidence of the commercial traveler's modernity. In the late nineteenth century there was an astonishing transformation in the products available to consumers. Ready-made clothing (an upshot of the need for standardized uniforms during the Civil War) and ready-made shoes, mass-produced jewelry and cosmetics, canned meats and condensed milk, as well a wide range of goods made from new, synthetic materials (like plastic)—all contributed to the shift from a producer-oriented society to a culture of consumption, what Thomas Schlereth calls the goods life. By the 1890s, in even the most rural general store, Americans found sophisticated product displays featuring everything from chewing gum to seeds. Increasingly, modernity came in colorful, eye-catching packages as manufacturers and retailers moved away from generic products and cracker-barrel marketing techniques and promoted nationally advertised, brand-name goods. Ivory Soap and Uneeda Biscuit are two famous examples of this trend in production and marketing practices, and in the closing decades of the nineteenth century dozens of other manufacturers were likewise engaged in an effort to create and control markets by establishing product loyalty.[44]

By helping retailers market products, often through in-store promotional campaigns, and by passing on current sales techniques, which storeowners then applied in their own efforts to win consumers—how using Ivory Soap, for instance, would make homes cleaner and healthier—traveling men fostered the growth of the new material culture and helped create a new discourse for selling that culture. But during most of the late nineteenth century the shape that the national market would finally take was not fully clear. Commercial travelers representing wholesalers continued to sell generic goods—frequently commissioned for manufacture by wholesalers as their own "brand"—as well as nationally known, branded products, which they distributed in the absence of, and sometimes even in addition to, a manufacturer's own sales organization. For instance, W. Duke Sons and Company used its own sales force to market its tobacco products and also depended on regionally based wholesalers and their drummers.[45] If a salesman traveled for a full-line, dry-goods jobber and sold regularly to general stores, he was likely to carry a variety of complementary items. So Virgil Wright of Saint Louis, whose trade consisted chiefly of saloon keepers, sold playing cards and glasses. When conditions permitted, particularly during the early years of commercial traveling, salesmen sometimes represented more than one house at a time. For instance, E. Barton Martin, who sold shoes on the Texas frontier for a Galveston dry-goods firm during the 1870s and 1880s, also carried a line of furniture on the side.[46]

Although manufacturers' salesmen were distinguished by such nicknames as the Crisco man—and the commercial power that such identity conferred— wholesalers' drummers had a less distinct affiliation with their employers and, hence, relatively more independence and freedom to enlarge the market on their own terms. It was partly because of these marketing conditions that the generically dubbed traveling man became such an important, familiar figure during the late nineteenth century. On a variegated commercial landscape, filled with increasing numbers of salesmen representing many different wholesale houses (and some manufacturers), large and small, and selling a diversity of products, the traveling man appeared the common denominator and the principal source of the power of the market.

The nature and direction of this power and, more important, the traveling salesman's relation to it, remained uncertain. From a late twentieth-century perspective, the economy seems to have evolved in a straight line, building from decentralized regional markets to an omnipotent national economy; however, the very business of selling obscured this Whiggish view. So painstaking did E. Barton Martin find commercial traveling that in 1877, writing from the Texas frontier, he wondered to his wife if selling goods by sample was "played out."[47] Obviously, it was not. That Martin even wondered highlights both the ambivalent dynamics of commercial growth—as seen within the market—and the unsettling newness of his profession. From the salesman's point of view, the market was often less an object of unremitting economic growth than an enterprise mixed up with promotion and conflict.

Reluctant customers, the haggling over prices, and competition from other salesmen all made commercial traveling an unlikely context for romance and

WHITE SWAN SOAP

ROSIN SOAP Agt.

NB. WHITE SWAN SOAP IS THE BEST & CHEAPEST, FOR ALL USES.

ROCHESTER LITHO. CO.

A popular form of advertising throughout much of the late nineteenth century, trade cards flourished in the parlors and scrapbooks of consumers who collected them from retail merchants. Although commercial travelers were often responsible for distributing such cards to storekeepers, trade cards sometimes featured salesmen as objects of ridicule. Here, the triumph of White Swan Soap over a competing brand becomes the occasion for the rival salesman's expulsion from a store. (Warshaw Collection of Business Americana, Archives Center, National Museum of American History, Smithsonian Institution.)

adventure, even when the quest developed along strictly commercial lines. Pricing was perhaps the most frequent source of friction. Storeowners, wholesalers, and salesmen alike deplored the lack of consistency in prices. Retail merchants pointed to discrepancies among comparable products—sold by competing salesmen—and complained when traveling men sold the same item to another storeowner at a lower price. For their part, wholesalers blamed traveling men for cutting prices just to make a sale. Salesmen were caught in the middle—charged by employers to establish commercial relationships and left to entertain customers' claims that they could get the same products elsewhere at cheaper prices. Placed on the spot, usually without immediate recourse to their houses, salesmen negotiated solutions to such conflicts, perhaps by lowering prices, and answered to their employers later.[48]

Effective commercial travelers not only closed sales but also kept their eye on the complex weave of factors that went toward the profitability of those sales: the wholesaler's product costs, the customer's stock needs, the customer's ability to pay, and prevailing economic conditions, both local and general. The oft-repeated advice—in this instance, an 1887 reminder in the *Pottery and Glassware Reporter*—was to know the customer's "traits of character;

his business habits; how he treats his trade, the line of goods he has the most frequent call for; whether he sells close or with a profit, and judge his man accordingly."[49] Such knowledge redounded to the advantage of the salesman: he could structure a sale according to circumstances, vary prices in the context of a larger, commercial matrix. Hardware salesmen, for instance, worked harder to sell their specialty lines, where profits (and commissions) were much higher, than to sell staple items like nails.[50] So the salesman endeavored to create markets by introducing products profitable to wholesalers and—so the pitch went—to storeowners as well, a project that demanded an understanding of customers and markets and that for some products could take years to launch.

Conflict was an unseen constant in this selling process, a necessary adjunct to the microcosmic labor of rejection and success that the cumulative, macrocosmic development of the market obscured. Such conflict, moreover, reflected the larger tensions that constituted the growth of industrial capitalism. At the point of sale, the commercial traveler worked hand in hand with material "progress" to sell the convenience of new products to the American public, create new needs where none existed before, and ameliorate the consequences of overproduction where consumer needs had already been satisfied. Persuasion, negotiation, improvisation, and assumed familiarity were the methods that salesmen used to blunt conflict, distinguishing them from other business types who rose to prominence in the late nineteenth century. Yet salesmen had difficulty pinning down their role in the market economy: they lacked the vocabulary necessary for theorizing the meaning of commercial traveling for the individual salesman.

Beginning in the 1860s and continuing into the twentieth century the conflicted boosterism peculiar to commercial traveling surfaced in texts that announced the benefits of sales enterprise in the course of defending—and defining—the profession. An early example is *The System of Commercial Travelling in Europe and the United States: Its History, Customs, and Laws,* published in 1869 by the Society of Commercial Travellers as a "Memorial" to traveling salesmen. The pamphlet begins with a recital of the importance of commerce in world history, then moves on to condemn licensing laws and the "narrowmindedness and commercial bigotry that would, if possible, prevent the free communication of useful and indispensable knowledge." The rhetoric is typically edgy and defensive. Although sales proponents preached mostly to the converted (with a missionary spirit that resembled the efforts of admen to outline the objectives of modern advertising), their ebullience was often framed by righteous insecurity—an awareness of the commercial traveler's precarious relation to entrenched social norms. Ironically, the society assumed the second-class status of the occupation even as it asserted the salesman's commercial rights. The grounds for assimilation or naturalization into what the society understood as "honorable" citizenry were ultimately bound up with the commercial traveler's uncitizenlike removal from the honors of settled life.[51]

Subsequent representations of the character of salesmen that dealt directly with their mobility found answers in comforting images of progress and unity. The "modern Knight errant" described in Henry Horn's *Drumming as a Fine Art* (1882), for example, confronts a "wilderness of possible customers" with "one eye upon his Railway Guide and the other upon his sample chest."[52] A romantic figure to say the least, Horn's salesman eschews the puerile adventurism of self-oriented travel for the equally inflated prospect of trailblazing the commercial wilderness. Rather than deny the hardships of his profession, Horn affirmed and ennobled them, recasting the mundane conflicts of the road as the marks of a higher calling. Sometimes such thinking gave way to visions of national prosperity and cultural rejuvenation. According to Alexander Belcher, the author of *What I Know About Commercial Travelling* (1883), commercial travelers were pioneers who swept across the continent in trains, stages, steamboats, and wagons. He predicted that visitors to the "the remotest part of our civilization," where "villages spring up as if by magic," would find the traveling man with his samples "pushing for an order."[53]

In trade literature, the urge to see traveling salesmen as agents of cultural progress was irresistible. Into the twentieth century, spokesmen for the profession routinely traced its lineage to prehistoric times and the Old Testament, asserting that as ambassadors of commerce, salesmen had always played a crucial role in "the formation of social neighborhoods."[54] Like the author of the *Official Souvenir* of the 1896 Commercial Travelers' Fair, they frequently sounded a nationalistic note, maintaining that commercial travelers knit "the bonds which unite a patriotic, loyal and liberty loving people."[55]

Compared to representations of the Pearl Street drummer, these late nineteenth-century portrayals by occupational insiders present the union of individual agency and commercial power in glowing terms. Viewed as part of an economically manifest destiny, the salesman appears less an aberration of the moral economy than an extension of it through travel. As Linus P. Brockett emphasized in his 1871 manual *The Commercial Traveller's Guide Book,* the "system" of commercial traveling integrated three elements—railroad, product, and customer—and allowed "the farmer boy on the plains" and "the miner in the Rocky Mountains" to "suggest as important improvements in the form, patterns, or styles of goods, as the more practised artist in the city, for they commune oftener than he with nature, the great source of inspiration in art."[56] This was drumming re-envisioned—not as an immoral business practice nor even as a revolutionary system of distribution but as a synthesis of consumer and salesman founded in production-oriented values. Brockett's rhetoric suggests a providential unity of commerce and democracy that was fundamentally at odds with the transience of the modern era. Still, as both William Cronon and Ross Miller have argued in another context, it was exactly this kind of faith that enabled the development of modern economic and urban structures.[57] Although commercial visionaries generally failed to characterize the emerging commercial system in innovative terms, and although

The optimism of visionaries like Brockett and Belcher was also subject to satire. Both the "savage" Indian and the "pioneering" tobacco drummer become targets of humor in this trade card about commercial expansion. (Warshaw Collection of Business Americana, Archives Center, National Museum of American History, Smithsonian Institution.)

their belief in manifest economic progress may have been a hedge against the chaos of modernity, their thinking proved a vital component of historical change.

Thus boosters of commercial traveling promoted the positive impact of the occupation on the national culture and struggled to articulate its modernity. The wished-for vocabulary, derived from what might be called distribution-oriented values, would provide a conceptual framework that explained the salesman's circular movement through a world of suppliers and buyers. The problem hung on the commercial traveler's paradoxical nature (itself the product of modern economy): how to express the relation between the individual salesman's concrete, apparently isolated presence on the road and the larger economic structures (as well as the collective endeavors of other salesmen) to which that presence was linked. As Howard Horwitz has argued, a similar linkage characterized the "sublimation" by the Standard Oil Trust of individual agency into an Emersonian vision of transcendental power. Horwitz's top-down view of how corporate entities worked to limit market fluctuations by figuring their efforts to control the economy as the effects of a financial system "naturally" seeking harmony exemplifies the ironic representation of individual power through both the effacement of the self and the consolidation of selves (or corporations) in larger bodies (trusts), a "logic," Horwitz stresses, that was a product of the great transformations of the late nineteenth century.[58]

Though likewise constituted—and limited—by broad economic forces, the salesman worked from the ground up; he was only an agent, without claims to ownership or property. If captains of business denied self-agency in the search for greater individual power, traveling men rarely escaped their role as middlemen and, discovering their volitional power in mere agency, thus worked at the intersection of freedom and authority extended to them by absent business interests through a transcendent system of travel. The moment-to-moment, place-by-place dynamics that described the salesman's effort at commercial unification resisted easy description, however; and although by 1900 commercial travelers—like early twentieth-century advertisers—seemed sure of their modernity, the first generations of salesmen (from the late 1860s to about 1890) could appear both shallow and clumsy in their struggle to identify the unique modernity of their occupation. Understandably so. While admen endeavored to adapt the residual power of personal sales appeal to mass communication—from the top down—commercial travelers were faced with the ground-level task of developing sales practices for a market network whose potential significance they sensed but could hardly see.[59]

Nevertheless, the thrust of the profession was to naturalize life on the road in order to profit by it. Maps and guidebooks, credit agencies and professional associations, in promising guidance through unknown territory, offered both theoretical understanding and comfortable reassurance of the system that constituted commercial traveling. Although there could be no adequate substitute for the familiar spaces left behind, the effort to domesticate the road was the consequence of an occupation that collapsed the home into economic work. Emerging voluntary organizations such as the Commercial Travelers National Association of New York emphasized the "Advantages, Privileges and Franchises" of the occupation and promised members discount railway fares, reduced telegraph rates, accident insurance, and savings plans.[60] On the other hand, R. G. Dun and Company placed the system within traveling men's grasp. Until the 1850s Dun stored evaluations in huge, bound ledgers, organized by state and then again by county, and provided credit information on demand to subscribers. The expanding commercial network brought changes in this rating system. In 1859, responding to another agency's innovation and, more generally, to national commercial growth, Dun began transferring its recommendations to a published reference book, which gave subscribers access to the credit ratings of merchants in all the counties surveyed. Confidential information, once passed around by hand in Dun's New York offices, was now abbreviated and rationalized. Users discovered the potential customer's "estimated pecuniary strength" and the rating—"A1" being the highest—with the help of an explanatory key.[61] By 1880 the reference book contained population estimates of towns and information on railroad travel, in addition to the individual ratings. Responding to "the need of ready reference to the immediate locality of places and their geographical location" (and now relying on ten thousand credit investigators and sixty-nine branch offices), R. G. Dun had the traveling man's interests in mind.[62]

In turn, traveling men acknowledged the help that Dun's credit system gave them in evaluating a customer's ability to pay.[63] Moreover, by implicitly promising a marketplace distinguished by stability and order, trust and honesty, Dun's rationalized credit system itself inspired confidence. So much so, in fact, that in 1874, when a young lightning-rod salesman discovered a copy of *Dun's Commercial Book of Credits for the South* left by a drummer in a Baltimore hotel room, he decided to become a commercial traveler. "I am going from house to house selling something that I can never sell again," he wrote. "I tell them good-bye and never see them again. I want a business that will enable me to sell to a customer something that he will continue to use as long as he lives."[64] In this instance, by providing proof of the ongoing business relationships that defined the culture of commercial traveling, Dun's *Book of Credits* marginalized saleswork that thrived outside mainstream economic channels. Just as important, it encouraged a metaphoric vision of a united commercial network. Given the promise, on paper, of speed and efficiency, of future business contacts, traveling men had all the more reason to think themselves part of a system and to work within it. By internalizing the market system whose objective reality they simultaneously helped create, traveling men steered a course between plotted action on the one hand and improvisational freedom on the other.

As William Maher suggested in his 1888 book, *A Man of Samples,* the life within this commercial system frequently lacked adventure. "In a traveling man's experience, no two days are exactly alike, and yet there is a monotony in the story of a trip because the history of one day is so much like the history of every day."[65] Maher's characterization is not necessarily inconsistent with more glamorous descriptions of commercial traveling. Rather, the view of life on the road is from the inside; actions that from one perspective inspire celebration are seen here as rationalized routines. Maher allows for diversity of experience on an ad hoc basis, but the monotonous narrative that unites them apparently has no real possibility as a story—or adventure—for the object of each trip and is always the same: to sell. "Lamentations of the Traveling Man," a poem written in the 1880s, drives home a similar point.

> Our employers expect us to sell lots of goods,
> In towns that are lonely and far in the woods,
> We travel on freight trains, we drive in a hurry,
> Expenses foot up and we get in a flurry;
>
> Our samples are heavy, the charges are high,
> We have no redress, the money must fly,

> An itemized expense account they always expect,
> And if it runs light, they're sure it's correct.[66]

The realistic literature of commercial traveling stripped away illusions even as it earned salesmen the right to celebrate their profession. Even before the salesman began to sell goods, he had expended much of his energy. Returning to Cincinnati after a trip to Kentucky in the spring of 1875, the drug salesman William White disabused his brother of any romantic notions that he might have had about life on the road. "This traveling business is awful hard work," he complained. "One is obliged to work all the time. Get into a town at 7 o'clock in the evening and have to go round and see customers and talk with them all the evening in order to prepare the way for the morrow."[67] White's reaction to his first days on the road—in a buggy—echoes the feelings of traveling men who rejected the idea that "seeing the country, viewing magnificent cities," and "speeding along at sixty miles an hour over the rails" made their lives enviable. "Everything becomes insipid," Virgil Wright warned his friends, "except the desire to be at home with your family and friends."[68] As regularly as the seasons, work made demands of traveling men and, "disregarding whatever ties of affection or trust" they had, required them to "resume their business relations" when they least wanted to.[69]

The notion that commercial traveling was just plain hard work often emerged in contrast to visions of home. In this sense, the tedium attested to by Maher, Wright, and other salesmen stemmed from frustrated expectations. It was as if salesmen longed for release from domestic life, hence answered the call to travel, but yearned for the sanctity of home once on the road and faced with the imperatives of the job. Henry Horn, who was as ebullient as any salesman in his characterization of commercial traveling, nonetheless acknowledged the relentlessness with which the occupation exacted a bond of loyalty that superseded and in some circumstances supplanted domestic ties. Such loyalty, however, had an obvious price. One salesman, when he was working, saw his family every other Sunday. Although he enjoyed his job and took pride in his increasing sales, he did not agree with his boss's compliment that "I love to work and work because I love it." Rather, he wrote his parents, "I love to work because I am paid for it."[70]

The grounds for allegiance to home and work divided along occupational lines made possible by railroad travel. Telegrams, letters, and trains linked the salesman to the office, bringing him close enough to receive orders and send them. Enterprising salesmen made connections, switched jobs, and changed locations. To travel from place to place and sell by sample, a drummer did not need a permanent home, at least not in the traditional sense. A commercial traveler could be with his family one day and wonder the next that he was two hundred miles away selling goods. The railroad enabled traveling men to grasp employment opportunities far from home and even, like E. W. Howe's characters in *A Man Story,* to represent firms in cities not their own.[71] In this respect, the 1870 census report is especially suggestive: whereas eastern wholesalers dominated U.S. markets in 1870, the greatest number of commercial travelers resided in Illinois and Ohio.[72] Although many of these salesmen were certainly working out of branch offices of large eastern firms, many may have temporarily relocated, shuttling back and forth between their territory and homes in the East. The dynamics of the profession encouraged such arrangements, but such commuting was more likely to occur on a smaller, regional scale. Thus Joseph W. Babcock, later a congressman from Wisconsin, traveled during the 1870s for a Dubuque, Iowa, lumber firm while his family lived in Cedar Falls with relatives.[73] In Texas, E. Barton Martin worked out of a dry-goods house in Galveston—over two hundred miles from his home in San Marcos. Like Babcock, Martin often had the "blues," whether he was on the road selling goods or at a boardinghouse in Galveston and going to an office every day. "Kiss the children and sister Minnie for me," Martin wrote his wife from San Antonio in the spring of 1877. "And tell her whatever she does, never to marry a traveling man, they are the most unhappy men on earth."[74]

Besides the vicissitudes of travel, the anxieties of being away from home, and competition from other salesmen, traveling men faced governmental regulations in the form of state and municipal licensing laws. Connecticut, Delaware, Georgia, Illinois, Indiana, Iowa, Kentucky, Louisiana, Maine, Maryland, Michigan, Montana, Nevada, North Carolina, Oregon, Rhode Island, Texas, Virginia, and West Virginia all passed drummer laws of some sort during the nineteenth century. So, too, did the cities of Chicago, Detroit, Louisville, Philadelphia, Richmond, Saint Louis, and Washington, D.C., among others.[75] By requiring traveling men to purchase licenses before doing business, legislators in effect taxed commercial traffic. In Georgia during the 1870s, for example, itinerant merchants—whether they sold "by sample or otherwise"—were required to pay $50.00 to work in each county they entered. In Montana the fee was $25.00 per county, while in Kentucky, the General Statutes of 1867 stipulated that traveling salesmen be assessed $10.00 for every one hundred eligible voters in each county they entered.[76] In urban areas, where markets were more concentrated, license costs tended to be higher. During the early 1870s an annual license cost $50.00 in Washington, D.C., and $100.00 in Richmond; in Saint Louis the same privilege—but for only six months—cost $150.00.[77] In Baltimore, out-of-state traveling men selling "either by card, sample, or other specimen, or by written or printed trade list or catalogue," paid $300.00 for a license that lasted one year. Those who did not pay and were caught paid $400.00.[78] Although such legislation was not always strongly enforced, when it was, it presented the most concrete obstacle that a salesman could face—but also the most easily challenged.[79] Negative jokes, fiction, and cartoons offered a kind of resistance to commercial traveling, but they remained, in effect, closed to rebuttal. State and federal courts, however, provided a forum in which commercial travelers could press their cases and possibly even shape the legal discourse concerning their role in American society.

As Morton Keller has argued, regulatory legislation of this sort grew out of

A salesman for Rockford Silverplate Company poses on the railroad trestles in Lanesboro, Minnesota, around 1900. Photograph by Gilbert Ellestad. (Minnesota Historical Society.)

a general conflict between local government and the national economy. By exercising "police power"—in Keller's words, "the right (and duty) of the American commonwealths to protect the health, morals, and safety of their citizens"—local governments sought to control the effects of an increasingly pervasive market economy. Loosely defined by the Supreme Court in the first half of the century as an instrument for safeguarding domestic and communal values, police power became in the late nineteenth century a device for regulating pervasive economic activity, interstate commerce, for instance. The use of police power exemplified the local struggle to understand a rapidly transforming economy—but in an outmoded cultural discourse.[80]

Simply put, the motive for licensing legislation was protectionism—both economic and moral. More complicated, however, were the questions of how these two motives interrelated and how, as legislators exercised their local police powers, state and federal courts interpreted the effects of the laws and conceptualized the dynamics of the new market economy. The central issue for legislators and jurists alike, however, was the same system of commercial traveling celebrated by boosters, its features now turned inside out to expose its disadvantages.

As critics and legislators saw them, the moral shortcomings of drumming were never far from its strengths. Just how far may be seen in a 1874 sermon that William H. Baldwin, a Boston minister, gave before an audience of potential traveling men at the Boston Young Men's Christian Union. Echoing advocates of commercial traveling, Baldwin acknowledged the revolutionary potential of faster travel and telegraphed transactions. Because the nation had "conquered time," a storekeeper was now able to stay at one place "busily attending" to customers and just as "busily attempting to check off the long list of polite friends from the several commercial centres"—that is, traveling salesmen—who arrived "fully prepared to save him the long and tiresome journeys to which the buyers of former years were subjected." But as the title of the sermon made clear—*Travelling Salesmen: Their Opportunities and Their Dangers*—the new efficiency held moral peril for salesmen who, in taking advantage of the freedom of the road, would "kill time" and fall prey to drink or gambling. So Baldwin encouraged his audience to stand firm, cultivate sound habits, and resist temptation. In conclusion, Baldwin compared the beginning salesman to the country boy who, in leaving the "old homestead" for a "new city life," also confronted moral peril.[81] Giving the moral of his sermon a familiar frame, Baldwin thus repeated the rhetoric of moral suasion that surrounded the Pearl Street drummer.

In drummer laws that appeared throughout the nineteenth and even into the twentieth century, the argument took one turn further as traveling salesmen, apparently influenced by the forces that Baldwin warned of, became agents of moral corruption themselves. During the early 1870s licensing laws in Georgia and Maine required salesmen to give evidence of "good character"—indeed, in Maine, "good moral character"—as well as proof of having been a U.S. citizen for at least five years.[82] In safeguarding the well-being of their citizens, some cities targeted drummers without seeming to understand their legitimate commercial functions. To "improve morals," the government of Hot Springs, Arkansas, made drumming a misdemeanor in 1875. "It is well-known," the lawmakers stated, "that persons who run, drum, and solicit patronage for physicians and quacks, boarding-houses, bath-houses and gambling dens, cause great inconvenience to this resort . . . and greatly injure the morals [of the citizens]." Eventually the Arkansas courts recognized this discrepancy and ruled that the law could not apply to those engaged in "lawful and useful occupations."[83] Moral reasoning may also have played a role in the prosecution of commercial travelers under existing peddler laws, which ante-bellum legislators fashioned to protect rural economies and which late nineteenth-century lawmakers either stretched to suit the occasion or revised to accommodate the emerging distribution system.[84] Significantly, however, in places like Stanford, Kentucky, in 1870 and Kansas City, Missouri, in 1885, where commercial travelers were successfully prosecuted for operating with-out a peddler's license, higher courts ultimately overturned the verdicts, pointing out that because drumming differed from peddling, the licensing laws did not apply to the commercial travelers.[85]

The importance of such reversals lay not only in the courts' recognition of misapplied peddler laws but also in their increasing understanding that com-mercial traveling was a marketing innovation that required different treat-ment under the law. But the perception that selling goods by sample was something new did not automatically exempt salesmen from regulation. In fact, many licensing laws seemed motivated by that very perception—and by blatant commercial self-interest. Pressed by local merchants, in particular small wholesalers who felt threatened by larger, out-of-state firms, legislators in many places used their police powers to protect the home economy.[86] Code writers revealed their intentions when they indexed licensing laws under the subject headings Revenue or Taxation and designated the presumptive target—usually out-of-state salesmen. In the twenty-five years following the Civil War exceptions to licensing laws abounded. Georgia, Indiana, Kentucky, Maine, Maryland, Missouri, Virginia, and West Virginia all had laws that exempted residents or merchants of home manufactures from paying licens-ing fees.[87] Georgia, one of the first states to recognize and tax drummers by law in 1859, repealed the act a year later, but only for "citizens of the slave-holding States of the United States."[88]

To the extent that licensing laws sprang from commercial self-interest rather than moral anxiety—from a desire to advance one wholesaler's drum-mer at the expense of another's—they evinced local support for the expand-ing market economy. Still, the laws tell only part of the story. Not all merchants lobbied legislative representatives for protective assistance; indeed, through-out the 1870s and 1880s, in an emerging show of support for interstate commerce, merchant groups petitioned the U.S. Congress to pass federal legislation that would repeal drummer laws. Even at the local level, as the genesis of the 1868 license law of Maryland makes clear, there was disagree-ment over protectionism. Controversy surrounded the Maryland bill even before the state legislature passed it.

In January 1868, James W. Owens, a Baltimore commissions merchant, wrote H. Tillard Smith, a member of the Maryland House of Delegates, to urge the adoption of a license bill that would shelter Baltimore from the incursions of "peddlers" from New York, Boston, and Philadelphia. Owens resented traveling men who rented offices and sold by sample but paid no more than he did for a license to do business. "What I think of this," he complained to his representative, "is that no such person should be allowed a license for such purpose at rates similar to those charged to our home merchants." Owens proposed that the law "discriminate" between foreign and domestic merchants and that clerks issuing licenses ask "such questions under oath as would discover the real character of the applicant."[89] Just what Owens meant by character he did not say; but his use of the word with all its moral implications in an argument devoted to commercial self-interest suggests how fluidly economic discourse overlapped and mixed with moral rhetoric.

Baltimore retailers, however, disagreed with Owens. Representing the General Dry Goods merchants of the city, Robert H. Dryden and Son wrote Smith to object to the proposed bill. A special nonresident license promised to help Dry Goods Commission Merchants, but to the "detriment and disadvantage" of dry-goods retail merchants. The "increase proposed for Non-Residents will undoubtedly cause *very many* to relinquish the Licenses they have been accustomed to take out."[90] For Baltimore commissions merchants the disappearance of nonresident salesmen may have meant a greater share of the market, but for Dryden and Son and other retailers it constricted the market and diminished the choice of wholesale products. Despite such protests, the proposed bill became law, and until the Supreme Court struck it down, out-of-state commercial travelers paid three hundred dollars for their licenses—and resident salesmen nothing at all.

So conflict proved a vital component of market expansion—both within and without commercial culture. Notwithstanding the anxiety over domestic values that prompted lawmakers in some locales to draft licensing laws aimed at restricting immoral behavior, legislative foes of commercial traveling could also be partisans of limited state or regional markets, supporters, that is, of certain, but not all, drummers. What at first glance signified resistance to marketplace culture was sometimes just a part of the competition. For traveling men who knew only the effects of license laws, the latent history mattered little. Even if, as one salesman claimed, "every man who has traveled on the road has probably had more or less trouble about license[s]," few commercial travelers accepted trouble calmly.[91] Licensing laws angered traveling men, most of all when they targeted nonresidents. Southern city fathers especially seemed to conspire against out-of-state salesmen. In Baltimore, Washington, and Richmond, for example, not only were unlicensed traveling men fined up to five hundred dollars, but half the amount was paid to spotters of the crime.[92]

Throughout the 1870s and 1880s the trade literature denounced the "commercial bigotry" and "invidious legislation" that stifled trade so that local industries might be "coddled."[93] Categorically rejecting the idea that business communities benefited from such protection, defenders condemned the "epidemic" of protective legislation and showed little or no sympathy for "infected" communities. They saw only "scheme[s]" which, in addition to hampering their sales, raised prices for retailers and consumers.[94] As the Dryden and Son letter demonstrates, license fees also increased the cost of entering the market, potentially reducing the number of salesmen and the amount of merchandise (and the prices) that retailers had to choose from. Where local authorities recognized these disadvantages, they often refused to enforce existing license laws or, better yet from the commercial traveler's point of view, repealed them altogether.[95]

Commercial travelers fought back against license laws. As early as 1869 the Society of Commercial Travellers provided a list of offending license laws and, citing a *New York Herald* editorial condemning the laws, called upon Congress to encourage interstate commerce. Continuing the protest in the 1880s, the *Commercial Travelers Magazine* alerted readers to the states that taxed traveling men; so did the 1882 edition of *Bradstreet's Pocket Atlas of the United States*. Professional associations like the Travelers' Protective Association made their primary objective "the repeal of all Municipal, County, State or Territorial laws imposing or enforcing a license tax on Commercial Travelers."[96] By the early twentieth century a wide range of companies published legal handbooks advising traveling salesmen how to proceed should they encounter restrictive licensing laws.[97] Firms instructed agents not to pay license fees but to contest them, for as one manual stressed, "Up to the time this book is published no case has been lost in trial by any of the Company's salesmen."[98] Through the adversarial give-and-take of adjudication, commercial traveling gained professional legitimacy while the romance of the road receded in significance.

In court opinions and state codes, "selling goods by sample" became a familiar, embattled phrase as jurists struggled to define the legal, economic, and social ramifications of commercial traveling. Not all courts agreed that "the railroad, the steamboat, and the telegraph are followed by new legal questions" and a "new body of law."[99] Ruling on a Vicksburg occupational tax, for instance, one federal judge, U. M. Young, compared traveling men to store clerks, not to merchants or peddlers ("they are quite like neither"). Although "for many years a very large part of the commerce of the State had been transacted by them," they were "mere solicitors of orders for others." Vicksburg's city charter did not recognize them as taxable, nor would Young. He freed the drummer but offered him little respect.[100]

Young's portrayal of the commercial traffic in a southern city illuminates some of the obstacles that traveling men had to overcome in 1880. Admitting the commercial necessity of drumming, Young saw the salesman as moving through the established business community, not as part of it. Without an economic or legal stake in the community, the commercial traveler lacked "authority" and "power." He did not own the goods that he sold, and left town after concluding his business. The commercial traveler's special mobility did not impress the Mississippi judge. The drummer did not drive a buggy or ride a horse through Vicksburg, nor did he hire a wagon or take some public conveyance. To Young, he seemed like a man without property, a "mere solicitor" who, walking "about the city" and "beyond its limits," hardly deserved a place among men of substance, let alone a legal foothold.[101] Such a place, Young insinuated, belonged not to commercial travelers but to the men who sent them.

Commercial travelers gained a foothold in an 1887 Supreme Court ruling.

Young's opinion of the salesman's character, like others', reflected a parochial economic view that denied the already fluid, transregional nature of American commerce. In *Robbins v. Shelby County Taxing District* the Court cast aside commercial provincialism and, affirming the dormant yet active power of the commerce clause, rejected the notion that taxing commercial travelers "passing through the state" constituted a legitimate exercise of police power. In language that reverberated in succeeding opinions, Justice Bradley declared "that in the matter of interstate commerce the United States are but one country, and are and must be subject to one system of regulations, and not to a multitude of systems."[102] Acknowledging what traveling men had always proclaimed—that the United States was indeed one market—the Court effectively protected and even nurtured the system of commercial traveling.

Bradley gave notice of the position he took in *Robbins v. Shelby County* when, in a separate opinion, he concurred with the 1870 decision that overturned the Baltimore license act of 1868. Maryland legislators discriminated against nonresident merchants, the Court decided in *Ward v. Maryland,* and thus violated "the privileges and immunities" guaranteed to all citizens by the Constitution. Bradley agreed but was "of the further opinion" that the Court did not affirm strongly enough the sole right of Congress to regulate interstate commerce. He objected to all taxes on interstate merchants, even those that affected residents and nonresidents equally.[103]

More than any previous judicial decision, the Robbins case vitalized the legal rights of traveling men while it asserted the arrival of an expansive commercial system. American ways of transacting business had changed, and Bradley recognized those changes, confirming that Robbins, a Cincinnati drummer selling stationery in Memphis, had the right to pursue customers beyond the boundaries of Ohio. How else, Bradley asked, "is a manufacturer, or a merchant, of one state, to sell his goods in another state, without, in some way, obtaining orders therefor?" A merchant might establish warehouses or branches in other states, but those are matters "of convenience, and not of compulsion." He could solicit customers through the mail; still, he would be subject to state regulations. Inconvenient and inefficient, these alternatives hardly seemed "practicable" when a merchant could obtain orders "by personal application." The Court encouraged these face-to-face transactions, finding that "the negotiation of sales of goods, for the purpose of introducing them into the state in which the negotiation is made, is interstate commerce."[104]

In the Robbins decision the Supreme Court made interstate commerce an area of national concern, not a "privilege" bequeathed through state legislation. To the extent that the judgment promised the reversal of lower court decisions and the revision of many state and local ordinances, it speeded the expansion of the national commercial network. To commercial travelers the Court sent a more concrete message, recognizing their right to commercial movement—not as mere solicitors but, they could hope, as individual businessmen worthy of respect.

Ultimately, *Robbins v. Shelby County* confirmed the salesman's right to participate in interstate commerce, legitimating what the development of the profession had already made clear: that commercial travelers drew power from the economic system that nurtured them. About the traveling salesman's rights as a free individual the Court said nothing; Bradley's opinion went toward the affirmation of an abstract principle that the salesman symbolized in his role as the wholesaler's agent. In this way, the Court rationalized the salesman's representative status, ironically reinforcing the dynamics that both placed salesmen on the road and constituted their vulnerable in-between status in the culture. But to regard this qualified confirmation of the commercial traveler's individual rights as further evidence of what Alan Trachtenberg has called incorporation would be a mistake. Strictly speaking, the majority of late nineteenth-century wholesale firms were unincorporated businesses run by two or three partners, often from the same extended family.[105] The *Robbins v. Shelby County* decision concerned a process that began in antebellum mercantile cities and accelerated after the Civil War, when drummers continued to function as they did well before corporate business practices appeared—as agents of merchant capitalism. That the forces of incorporation—for instance, railroads and industrial manufacturing—speeded the growth of commercial traveling does not change the origin of the sales culture in the decentralized urban market of the early nineteenth century.

The conflicts that led to *Robbins v. Shelby County* did not end there. Well into the twentieth century, local communities continued to justify restrictive legislation by invoking the right to police power. Advocates still insisted that their ordinances had nothing to do with interstate commerce, but rather were aimed at the questionable "character and conduct" of salesmen who remained safely "hidden behind the provisions of the federal Constitution."[106] Despite the Court's persistent defense of the national commercial system, bitter partisans held fast to their belief that "there can be no doubt about the advantages to be gained in any community by the prohibition of peddling and canvassing."[107] In regulating the marketplace such advocates sought to protect the moral character of their homes.

By 1890, however, there could be no doubt that commercial traveling meant business. The rationalization of business practices continued apace, undermining the serendipitous pleasures of the road and bringing sales practices under the reign of efficiency, speed, and organization. Indeed, William Hutton's return to Indiana in 1892 is somehow poignant. Although he bragged to his brother about his promotion and offered him a sales position, he stopped talking of beautiful orange groves or the chances of going west. As manager of a Singer Company branch office, he reveled in being boss, even if it meant a return to the muddy Midwest. Hutton no longer explored exotic countries of indefinite extent but watched over a company territory in his home state. In again urging his brother to work with him, he revised the story that he had told years earlier. "We have the nicest wagons here," he tempted Lineus. "Your red wagon is ready."[108]

3 A Grip on the Land

In their role as middlemen in the market economy, traveling salesmen inhabited a highly visual and tactile world—sometimes, in places far from urban amenities, literally a landscape in the making. To be a traveling salesman in late nineteenth-century America meant mastering the physical contingencies of road life and the props of the trade: cumbersome baggage, product samples, and catalogs. It required both a practical imagination and a knack for persuasive, sometimes histrionic self-presentation. Joined together on a landscape of railroad depots, Main Streets, and retail stores, traveling and selling were crucially linked in the same relentless effort to establish commercial territory. The key to the traveling man's luminous, if ambivalent, role in folklore and his persistence in the memories of onlookers such as Sherwood Anderson lay in this aggressive, improvisational ethos—a way of thinking and acting that made salesmen fluid, self-creating creatures of an expansive commercial landscape.

Accurate or not, the image of the commercial traveler that gained popularity in the late nineteenth century—the man wearing flashy suits, importing urban news, telling dirty jokes, mashing young women—spoke of his creative presence in modern transitory culture. Recalling the first drummer whom he saw as a child in his nineteenth-century country village, Earl Denham described the cultural savvy that eventually persuaded him to become a traveling salesman himself. "He wore a derby, spats, fancy vest, striped trousers, nose glasses, patent leather shoes, and carried a cane which he kept twirling around his finger all the time he was seated." Surrounded by boys, clerks, and loafers, the traveling man made the general store his headquarters while he dispensed jokes and wisdom from the world outside. "He seemed to know all the news of the day, and was the first really conversant man I had ever come in contact with."[1]

While it is doubtful that all late nineteenth-century drummers consciously viewed their craft as the manipulative, self-creating performance that Denham and others described, the combination of constant travel and changing selling conditions did encourage traveling men to discover the commercial value of role-playing. Just as the urban landscape became the defining context for the antebellum drummer's sales efforts, so the road framed the traveling salesman's commercial relationships by granting him a particular cultural knowledge: a familiarity with life in and between urban and rural America. More than ever the traveling salesman played the role of middleman in a business and cultural sense, but now his understanding of the world extended beyond the symbolic zones of the city. Mobile, transitory, and—as observers frequently noted—ubiquitous, he extended the reach of urban business interests while helping to create a commercial culture that, on the one hand, transcended regional differences but, on the other, depended on those very differences. Traveling salesmen universalized the local in that their assimilation and transmission of knowledge particular to a specific place or culture— for instance, news of crops in another part of the state or descriptions of city amusements—contributed, in a larger sense, to the creation of a mass culture.

Their impact resembled that of the modern advertisement—the crucial difference being that the salesman's appeal was personal and hence far more likely to be adapted to local circumstances, to his customer's particular needs and even character. Life on the road, like life in twentieth-century mass culture, made "I"—which, in nineteenth-century terms, was seen as stable and unshakable—subject to the contingencies of the moment. At bottom, commercial traveling demanded a flexibility of purpose that presaged a more modern conception of self, what cultural historian Warren Susman has called personality.

Yet for traveling men the need for flexibility seemed less like a historical shift in consciousness than simply part of the job. At least it did for William White, who made his first selling trip in 1875. In representing his Cincinnati firm, White reckoned that he had done well. He had sold two bills unexpectedly in Kentucky, one to a merchant who gave him the order because White "did not bore him and could talk about something besides business." So White gave up talking about samples and orders. "I have made several customers by not bothering them too much," he wrote his brother, "and find it the better way." After meeting "lots of different men," White concluded that "one is obliged to judge human nature pretty well to know how to take them."[2]

The implications of White's lesson—that the canny salesman could alter his demeanor, depending on the customer—were extended even further, and much less prosaically, in William H. Maher's 1876 account, *On the Road to Riches*. In answer to the question "What are the requisites of a traveling salesman?" Maher echoed Asa Greene's description of the urban drummer's task: "He must be 'all things to all men.'" Maher conceded that his advice was "delightfully indefinite" yet argued that its ambiguity would help travelers gain not only "the good will of customers" but also their trade. Stressing the importance of "adapting yourself to your company," he warned aspiring salesmen that if "you cannot read faces stay at home."

> You will be laughed at before your first day is over. You go into a store, the proprietor of which is an entire stranger to you. You hope he is a "good fellow," but you must "trust to luck." You look up and down the counter until one face strikes you, and you go towards it. It belongs to the proprietor. Instead of finding the man popularly called a "good fellow," you see that he is a stern man who "wants no nonsense" and "talks business." In a flash you are that kind of man yourself. You comprise your remarks into short, telling sentences, and watch him narrowly. When he says he wants nothing in your line today you know he means it. You will probably sell him the next trip, because you took him as he is.[3]

Maher's realization that to sell goods a salesman must become the customer's kind of man reveals the extent to which even nineteenth-century drummers learned to see the self as capital. But it also illuminates the long-term considerations that inevitably governed these improvisations. For the commercial traveler typically dealt only with the trade—with retailers, not consumers. More so than the peddler, the patent-medicine seller, and other commercial itinerants, he was likely to return to a customer.

Maher's instructions demonstrate an attentiveness to and seriousness about professional methods and structures missing in antebellum descriptions of drumming. Still, they lack the highly stylized, self-conscious air that distinguishes later descriptions of modern, scientific salesmanship. Educated, experienced, and gentlemanly, Maher's sharp-eyed traveling man relies on a fund of knowledge, which, however effective, remains unnamed. Whether his persuasive talents refer to his own experience, established or emerging commercial practices, or general cultural knowledge, they do not proclaim an organized system of expertise. The lessons of commercial traveling would remain uncodified until the 1890s. In the 1870s and 1880s traveling men who had something to say about how to succeed typically stressed the importance of experience—as indicated by such titles as *Twenty Years on the Road*—a wisdom that eluded institutional forms of pedagogy and that could be acquired on individual terms. This is not to say that traveling men were unconscious of their methods or unwilling to generalize about their occupation. Indeed, such works as Maher's *On the Road to Riches* may be taken as efforts to epitomize the experience of commercial traveling and specify the necessary abilities. Rooted still in nineteenth-century notions of character but pulled toward a more fluid notion of self by demands of the profession, seasoned traveling men—among whom Maher was perhaps the most eloquent—lacked a specialized language for describing the dynamics of face-to-face sales. Consequently they stressed—as Seymour Eaton did in his 1891 *How to Succeed as a Drummer*—the need for culturally honored, though highly general, attributes like "clear perceptions, common-sense, and probity."[4] Or, rather than boiling the profession down to essential qualities, they described the various sales types in behavioral terms—the Aggressive Drummer, the Persuasive Drummer, the Friendly Drummer, and so forth.[5]

The difficulty of codifying sales practices and conceptualizing job skills was not simply the result of the relative immaturity of the profession. Because commercial traveling involved such a wide variety of duties only the broadest of characterizations adequately designated the skills necessary for success. The sense that traveling men had to be experienced generalists—able to travel, balance accounts, and meet people—was particularly acute in matters of human nature. More than any other skill, gauging human character and acting accordingly made commercial travelers effective salesmen. Even during the twentieth century, when traveling men increasingly hewed to modern business practices, veteran drummers distinguished themselves from common people by emphasizing their ability to perceive and intuit—an ability that sharpened with experience. "You cannot fool the drummers," Wilbur Castelow maintained in *Only a Drummer* (1903), for "they are great students of human nature in all its branches." Hotel romances, Pullman car trysts, and other illicit meetings that most people failed to notice—these things rarely escaped Castelow's notice because drummers "lead a sort of railroad life, and have to be educated up to most of all the tricks in it."[6] Education in this sense is the product of exposure. Its lessons, as Castelow's tongue-in-cheek portrayal of road life reveals, are neither strictly commercial in nature nor wholly inapplicable to business matters. *Only a Drummer* catches the spirit of learning by serendipity. Always "looking for something new," Castelow's drummer learns the road as he goes along—usually just by looking. Riding the cars at dusk he might look out the Pullman window into a house and see people "in the dress that Nature alone provided for them." Yet "it is quick as a flash—simply a passing look at a living picture. No drummer tries to catch a second look, because he knows the train is going too fast to do so."[7] However titillating, the tale instructs as much as it entertains. Whether inexperienced or distracted, the ogling drummer wasted time when he looked again. As greenhorns hesitated or paused to correct their mistakes, veterans hustled down the road to make another town.

In 1903, surrounded by didactic manuals about scientific selling techniques, Castelow's colorful, self-conscious paean to experiential learning may well have seemed a throwback to earlier ways of apprehending the road. And yet what appeared as residual know-how, even nostalgia, was at the same time a basic element of the occupation, now encrusted with notions of modern business. For nineteenth- and twentieth-century salesmen alike, commercial traveling demanded a creative will to travel and sell—in physical terms, a series of equally purposeful movements that bound the road to the sales encounter. "In making the towns we have laid out," James Eaton's employers, the Chicago cutlery house of Jewett and Butler, wrote him in 1864, "we think you will make them the easiest [by taking] one after the other."[8]

Traveling to sell, drummers did not simply accomplish distances. Among commercial travelers, *making* became a verb form with a specific transitive meaning. Like *canvass*, whose obscure English origins converged with *hawking* —the capture of birds in a canvas net—*to make* anticipated a new status. Whereas *canvassing* means to seek, solicit, and finally to secure a pledge, *making* connotes the commercial conquest of a place and anticipates its new condition—sold.[9] Commercial travelers referred to making towns casually as they described their daily activities. A salesman from Iowa who began traveling in 1872 recalled that "the first town I made was Morrison, Illinois." In 1880, from Georgetown, Texas, E. B. Martin wrote his wife and told her that he had finished his work for the day in time "to make this place as stated." And the 1893 manual *How to Become a Commercial Traveler; or, The Art of Selling Goods* contained a chapter entitled "Making Country Towns." By 1914 the term had gained wider acceptance but without losing its special meaning. Describing his trip to Battle Creek, Michigan, Julian Street reported in *Abroad at Home* that a woman selling newspapers and candy in the depot mistook him for a traveling man. When she asked him what "line" he traveled in and what town he was "making next," Street struggled to convince her that he was really a writer.[10]

More than the actual changes that followed in the drummers' path, the

YOU REALLY SLEEP on Traction Sleepers

You can't help but sleep in the roomy, clean, cool sleepers operated by the

Illinois Traction System
(McKINLEY LINES)

This is the *only railway* offering sleeper service between St.Louis, Springfield and Peoria. Longer berths, windows in uppers, safe deposit vaults, electric fans.

When You Make Illinois

Remember that the Illinois Traction System is a "real" electric railway offering service any hour between

St. Louis, Springfield, Peoria, Decatur Bloomington, Lincoln, Champaign Danville and other Illinois points

Your Way Any Hour Any Day

Traveling men make Illinois in this advertisement for Illinois Traction System. From Order of United Commercial Travelers, Grand Council of Illinois, *Souvenir Program, Grand Council Meeting of Illinois* (1915). (Courtesy of Library of Congress.)

phrase *making towns* refers to how commercial travelers viewed the landscape. It describes the aggressiveness that they brought to the business of selling goods and the improvisational spirit that shaped their movement from place to place. Despite the hardships that accompanied constant travel, even because of them, commercial travelers gained a special understanding of the road and a unique vision of it. It was this view, one created and framed by the vicissitudes of travel, that frequently won the drummer an attentive audience.

At bottom, *making towns* referred less to a codified system of expertise or set of governing rules than to a shared way of seeing and apprehending the world—call it common sense—that, however loosely configured, nonetheless constituted a working social structure and served as the cultural core of the occupation. To use the term of the cultural theorist Pierre Bourdieu, traveling men functioned within a *habitus*, whose ongoing reproduction accommodated improvisatory practices that, however makeshift and spontaneous, resulted in the codification of cultural expressions and forms.[11] For traveling men, improvisation came as mundane, but essential, digressions within generally conceived business plans. Whether in departing from an established sales pitch or plotting a travel route beyond railroad junctions with a pocket atlas, improvisation allowed salesmen to expand the geographical dimensions of the market and develop face-to-face selling techniques without disrupting established conventions. By the early twentieth century the results of this improvisational ethos were found in selling procedures—in scientific salesmanship—that marked not a shift from but rather a culmination of the older, freewheeling era.

When it came to identifying the deeper significance of the profession, traveling men were generally not the most reflective of men. Still, their descriptions of how they worked reveal a remarkably unified occupational perspective. Travel, in particular, fostered a shared "inland imagination." Throughout the late nineteenth and early twentieth centuries, railroad networks shaped itineraries and determined which towns a traveling man visited. Specially designed railway and hotel guides translated this geography of speed and efficiency and assimilated it to the salesman's commercial needs. One touted guide was the *Pocket Companion* (1871) of the Claremont Manufacturing Company: "The Commercial Traveller, by its aid, can tell at a glance not only how to get to any town, but whether it will pay to go there." Brockett's *Commercial Traveller's Guide Book* was a "manual"—an instructional text and kind of cultural map. Brockett identified the best hotels and money order and express offices; included tables on tariffs and stamp duties; and, by naming some of the leading book publishers, even considered his audience's reading tastes. Most important, he provided lists of towns on railroads and those "not on railroads" but "easily accessible from railroad stations." For each entry he identified the distance from station to town, the population of the place, and specific stores and manufacturers. Another guide, L. C. Breyfogle's *Commercial Traveler, Being a Hotel Guide and Gazetteer of the United States* (1881), provided similar assistance and, for a slight fee, offered annual Correction Sheets updating travel information.[12]

Salesmen who lacked a concrete understanding of local geography, as Simon Skidelsky did in 1889 when planning a trip to western Pennsylvania and Ohio, consulted such guides—which, for Skidelsky, proved to be "every folder of every railroad in existence." After compiling a list of towns with the help of the guides, Skidelsky "mapped out" his route.[13] For novices these route plans proved indispensable. One New York employer instructed his new salesman to visit all the "principal cities" on the Hudson River and along the New York Central Railroad to Buffalo and Lockport. "Take a map," he advised, "and write down your list of cities, allowing sufficient time in each to call upon all the dealers whom you think will use our line of goods."[14]

An understanding of commercial geography and the capacity to use it proved important requisites to selling goods by sample. They were also part of the shared knowledge so essential to establishing a work culture—what salesmen understood to be professional common sense. Something of this sense informed the letter that Daniel Groh wrote to his brother in Lebanon County, Pennsylvania, from Jersey City in 1887, stipulating which towns he should make on his trip east. Both Groh brothers represented a Chicago stencil supply firm, and Daniel steered his brother away from towns that he had already canvassed. As Groh felt sure his brother would come the shortest way—through Allentown or Easton—that left two choices: the Central Railroad of New Jersey, or the Delaware, Lackawanna, and Western. "There is also the Lehigh Valley R.R. running from Easton & Phillipsburg to N.Y.," he added, "but by that route there is only one town Flemington Junction 1,851 [the population] between Phillipsburg and Bound Brook." Groh gave his brother a list of towns to canvass and told him what kind of tickets to buy. Rockaway, with a population of 914, "would hardly be worth stopping at but might pay."[15] Acutely sensitive to the particular demands of business travel, Groh accomplished in his detailed letter what the authors of Dun's reference books and other commercial guides did in their lists and maps.

With the disposition to structure came the ability to get from point A to point B by improvising around existing travel opportunities. Sometimes—when the law allowed it or railroad men could be persuaded—traveling men rode on freight trains. In an empty railroad depot in some "much-to-be condemned" town, a traveling man might jolly a conductor or inspector to let him catch the local freight instead of the regular passenger train three hours later.[16] With luck he might find himself in the caboose, finishing a half-written letter, speeding on to his next town.[17] Or if he was covering the Texas frontier in the 1880s, he could join other drummers "lying out on the sidings, doing without meals and exhausting one's patience" waiting for the freight to depart. To pass the time as the yardmen unloaded or switched cars, they would wander off to smoke cigars, shoot craps, or hunt jackrabbits until the conductor blew the whistle to call them back.[18] When a traveling man did reach his destination as planned, he did so at the railway's convenience, often scrambling in the middle of the night to find a hotel and store his sample trunks.[19] Hard travel dramatized and strained the salesman's link to both institutional forces and the material world, requiring a multiplex of talents—men able to do physical as well as mental work.

Where railroads had not been built, persevering salesmen found other ways to make towns and do pioneer work. Howard Peak made his first towns in Texas by horseback in the 1870s, and in 1883 a Chicago salesman, Henry R. Hamilton, endured the discomforts of stagecoach travel in Montana.[20] In 1892, T. H. Young traveled from one Illinois town to another by rail, wagon, and then by sleigh, depending on the weather.[21] While canvassing Connecticut in the late 1860s, Augustus Ayling secured his wagon top to sleigh runners to improve his travel through the snow. Later, when he traveled by rail from Newtown to Winsted, Connecticut, he shipped the wagon before leaving so he could use it upon his arrival.[22]

Sometimes for unexpected reasons a wagon or buggy proved more effective transportation than the railroad. "I have driven across the country a good deal by team," Joseph Babcock wrote his wife from Fayette, Iowa, in 1876. "There has been a man with me selling boots & shoes from Boston and we hire a team together which makes it about as cheap as R.R. fare and pleasanter & quicker."[23] One such alliance "with a man in another line" brought William White unexpected success when he sold some goods in a town that his partner wanted to visit.[24] Long wagon rides together gave drummers an opportunity to discuss customers, hotels, and travel experiences. As Wilbur Castelow joked in *Only a Drummer*, salesmen were often "put wise in their home city by brother drummers" who knew more about the place than they did.[25]

Calling cards like these announced the
impending arrival of the traveling
salesman on his rounds.

(Warshaw Collection of Business
Americana, Archives Center, National
Museum of American History,
Smithsonian Institution.)

(Courtesy of Strong Museum, Rochester, N.Y.)

Yet if chance seemed to direct a traveling man's education, throwing his way the benefits of a Pullman car conversation or a temporary travel arrangement, job objectives reminded him that the circumstances of road life did not arise fortuitously. "I am put on the road to fight for territory, to win territory and to hold it," a drummer declared in 1908. "I am seen to be an evolved pedler," a "modern specialist" whose "function" is "to sell continuously in a defined area."[26]

Although salesmen at work in the 1860s, 1870s, and 1880s experienced less "direction" in their travels, they still answered to employers. James Eaton's foray into Illinois, made by wagon in the spring of 1864, exemplifies the conflicts under which salesmen continually traveled. Although he moved from place to place in apparent freedom, no traveling man rode for free. Informing Eaton that he had been seen driving the horses too hard, his home office angrily asked, "How is this?—You must remember that if you abuse those horses you abuse the owner."[27] By the early twentieth century such directives were most often issued by a manager whose modern perspective of a sales territory included "maps and tacks and geographically arranged card files with significant colors for the cards."[28]

According to the *Oxford English Dictionary,* the term *territory* originated in the United States around 1900. However, its appearance in E. Caldwell's 1893 book *How to Become a Commercial Traveler* suggests that it was part of business vocabulary in the early 1890s and probably before.[29] *Territory* followed *making towns.* Both terms gave linguistic currency to emerging sales practices; together they designated and circumscribed the nature and scope of the salesman's commercial powers. If *making towns* connoted the traveling man's creative energies and the discipline necessary to implement them, then the territories established by employers placed limits on the traveler's geographical freedom. The responsibilities implicit in covering a territory, moreover, focused the meaning of making towns, sometimes in a negative way. Indeed, as Caldwell pointed out, drummers who bragged of making only the big towns on one side of the Mississippi contributed to the lore of commercial traveling at the risk of losing their jobs.[30] The open road offered ambitious salesmen the opportunity to succeed—within certain boundaries. Traveling men learned by experience and improvised as circumstances demanded, but commercial necessity determined the time and the place of their education and, if it occurred, their good fortune.

This dynamic interplay of energy and space brought traveling men a special understanding of the landscape. For wholesaler, manufacturer, and salesman alike, selling merchandise meant an enlarged market and more customers, but to the traveling man a territory denoted more than his selling region. It signified his working world, an area that over the years, through seasonal trips and repeated sales, became a home of sorts. Familiarity made a single personal landscape of diverse features and regional differences. Even when he returned to his home office—to organize bills, pack samples, or write customers—the time spent traveling from place to place, meeting people, and staying in the same hotels gave shape to a distinct vision, to a territory that existed as much in the imagination as it did in fact. Customers, competitors, and acquaintances blended with topography and human-made structures, becoming landmarks in their own right and enabling an intimate understanding of the road.

Repeated trips over the same ground distinguished veteran salesmen from novices looking at their territories for the first time. In 1892 T. H. Young, a Chicago clothing salesman, described his first visits to several places in Iowa and Illinois in sequence but without any regard for the overall unity of the trip. Unacquainted with particular towns, Young did what his more experienced partner told him to do and looked around on his own for a while.[31] More an adventure in discovery than a seasoned run through a territory, Young's descriptions suggest that time and practice gave selling routes identities, and salesmen the ability to see disparate elements as one piece.

As a knight of the grip, the salesman had an intimate, specific knowledge of labor that linked him to an older, traditional world of work and separated him from more sedentary occupations, in particular the office work required of urban, white-collar personnel, which was just emerging during the 1880s. Whether hauling trunks off a wagon bed, hurrying through a railroad depot, or gesturing as he displayed his wares to a merchant, the salesman was surrounded by things that, if he wished to succeed, he learned to master and manipulate. Although he relied on telegraph operators and express trunk lines, the drummer who made towns in the 1890s still profited from knowing how to drive a team of horses or handle a hitching weight. Indeed, as late as 1917 the National Salesmen's Training Association advised traveling men to hire a livery team when making smaller towns and to share the expense with another salesman.[32] Thus, with an irony characteristic of so many historical transformations, even though commercial traveling enabled the creation of a modern mass market, the work of traveling and selling frequently rested on residual kinds of knowledge and practice.

In poems like "The Drummer and His Grip" and "Ode to an Old Grip Sack," traveling men characterized their daily relations with the physical world and celebrated the comfort that familiar things brought during hard times.[33] Indeed, the title of N. R. Streeter's 1889 compilation, *Gems from an Old Drummer's Grip,* refers to more than poetry. It describes order forms, stationery, clothing, toiletries, and the few personal items that evoked the surroundings of home. Invariably salesmen joked about the unlikely combination of Bible, flask, and family picture that accompanied them in their travels, but such banter only confirmed their emotional attachment to small, portable things and their struggle to make a home in shabby hotels on the frontier or in small, poor towns, where they ate stale food on dirty plates and shared beds and roller towels.[34]

Little wonder the trade literature frequently defined the commercial traveler's relation to his baggage in solemn, historical terms. Baggage held a traveling man's stock in trade: catalogs, circulars, and samples. In 1893 a writer for the *Commercial Travelers Home Monthly Magazine* compared the difference in power between the locomotive and the horse to the difference in size between the "colossal sample trunk" and the saddlebags carried on horseback by eighteenth-century commercial travelers. Similar reasoning prompted another writer in 1883 to explain the origin of the word *baggage* in terms of the "bag-man's" transition from horse to gig. Now driving a vehicle, the traveling salesman "was compelled to economize space" and had to "gage" his "bag" according to the available room.[35]

The commercial traveler's dependence on his baggage can hardly be overestimated. Nothing could replace the goods themselves—except samples, which salesmen carried from place to place. Traveling men continually emphasized the importance of persuading merchants to look at samples, particularly because recalcitrant customers often decided to buy after viewing them.[36] A complete knowledge of the product line gave salesmen something to talk about, yet even the most eloquent speeches could fail without a visual presentation of the wares. As one traveler urged in his imagined sales pitch, "You must get this merchant started"—by showing him the goods. Drummers understood that the "careful traveller who keeps his samples in good order makes the best salesman," and they frequently spent long hours packing and arranging samples before going on the road.[37] Some firms even set aside special rooms and employed clerks to help organize samples.[38] When making towns, a traveling man often worried as much about the handling of his baggage as he did about his own safety.

Throughout the late nineteenth and early twentieth centuries salesmen condemned the rough handling of their sample trunks, protested excess baggage charges, and agitated for changes. Railroads had "no excuse for piling the largest and heaviest trunks on top, and carefully stowing traveling-bags, sample cases, and valises where they are morally certain to be crushed in transit or on removal," complained one salesman in 1883. To railroad companies, samples merely represented goods destined for future delivery—not actual freight—and carriers treated salesmen's baggage as personal property, refusing to give it special status. According to commercial travelers, however, this refusal ignored their voluminous contribution to railroad business.[39]

In 1910 the Congress intervened to regulate the movement of freight from one state to another. The Mann-Elkins Act recognized the peculiar importance of samples and required railroads to create a system of rates to govern their conveyance, but the ambiguity of the law prompted a writer for the *Commercial Travelers Magazine* to lament that "where there is so much of uncertainty as to the status of so important a commodity as sample baggage, there naturally must be great uncertainty as to the standing of a claim for loss of time due to the failure to properly handle this commodity."[40] Although the effort to correct vague baggage regulations led to numerous Interstate Commerce Commission investigations and committees, traveling men faced the same problems on trains in the 1910s that they had in the 1880s. Now carriers recognized the special status of sample trunks but complained that the trunks have "continued to grow in size and be built in shapes which made it difficult to handle them and impossible to store them to advantage."[41] Even after legal wrangling and federal regulation, the physical problems of baggage remained.

For instance, in 1872, when Kendrick Brown took over a New York clothing salesman's Iowa territory, he inherited two large sample trunks, which he called white elephants. Although trunks improved in design and construction, many late nineteenth-century salesmen struggled daily—and often alone—with heavy, cumbersome loads. Typically "bound and clamped with iron," trunks like Brown's were "specially constructed for the protection of contents" and, when filled, weighed twice as much as ordinary trunks. No wonder T. H. Young felt some resentment in 1892 when his partner hopped a train in Washington, Iowa, leaving him to drive a farmer's wagon and eight sample trunks to Delta by himself.[42] Still, even heavy sample trunks granted traveling men some freedom. A drummer could invite a customer back to his hotel to view a wide variety of styles displayed in a "sample room"—the temporary showroom provided by hostlers for commercial travelers—without lugging his baggage from store to store.

In some product lines, traveling men carried their samples by hand. Increased mobility, quick and easy display, and shorter meetings with merchants made this approach especially attractive in cities where salesmen could take advantage of dense business districts. Drummers who sold stationery, jewelry, men's furnishings, photographic supplies, or any goods that could be

Even as late as the 1900s commercial traveling could require hard, physical labor. Here the salesman William Baehr is shown hauling his sample cases. From the *Crescent and Grip* (March 1906). (Courtesy of Library of Congress.)

packed and carried in a leather satchel or wooden case commonly greeted the trade with "two immense bags, each weighing about fifty or sixty pounds."[43] Hardware salesmen and travelers selling bulky items displayed catalogs or advertising circulars instead of a full line of samples. In the 1860s and 1870s the shoe salesman Harry T. Nisbet toted "large black grain leather bags" containing men's boots, women's shoes, and children's slippers—all "mixed together in almost endless confusion."[44] By the mid-twentieth century, however, when many traveling salesmen drove automobiles and luggage became more compact, any one of Nisbet's successors could lift from the car trunk a single sample case, rather like a large rectangular box with a handle on top, carry it into a store, and show to his customer a case lined on both sides with two dozen or more left-foot shoes.[45]

Nowhere were commercial travelers' material requirements more apparent than in the creation of sample rooms, places reserved for salesmen to show samples and meet customers. Sample rooms became common features in many hotels throughout late nineteenth-century America, but they were by no means standard. As early as 1876 the Fayette House in Fayette, Iowa, promised free bus transportation to and from the depot, a local stage line, livery services, comfortable accommodations—and Good Sample Rooms.[46] Galveston's Giardin House likewise provided "suitable sample rooms," while in Mount Sterling, Kentucky, the proprietor of Reese's Commercial Rooms claimed to have "especially adapted" his establishment "for showing samples."[47] And in large cities like Chicago, whose Palmer House boasted four hundred sample rooms and hosted giant product fairs in the 1880s, standardization—and modernization—seemed the rule.[48]

But not all towns were Chicago or even Fayette. Sometimes a traveling man could find no place to display his wares and greet customers. In places like

Advertisement, *Commercial Travelers Magazine* (September 1883). (Courtesy of Library of Congress.)

Increased Business Bringing Sample Cases and Bags

A few leaders shown. Catalog and folders describe more than one hundred other styles, sizes, etc. Will gladly ship anything from regular stock on approval.

Send samples or specifications and let us design and submit sketch and prices of one or more cases, bags, etc., absolutely free and without putting yourself under any obligation to us whatsoever.

KNICKERBOCKER CASE CO.
Knickerbocker Bldg., Fulton and Clinton Sts., Chicago, Ill.

WM. SCHWEITZER, President   Established 1900   H. H. LABADIE, Sec'y-Treas.

Specialists and Original Designers Cases, Bags, Etc.

No. 97—SINGLE TIER CASE.

Waterproof covered. Five trays, 14x3½x1; base 2 inches deep. Wood or aluminum trays.

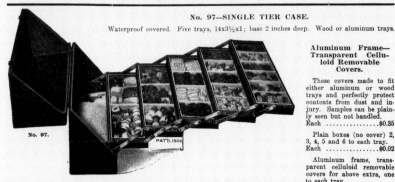

No. 97.

PAT'D. 1909

Aluminum Frame—Transparent Celluloid Removable Covers.

These covers made to fit either aluminum or wood trays and perfectly protect contents from dust and injury. Samples can be plainly seen but not handled.
Each $0.35

Plain boxes (no cover) 2, 3, 4, 5 and 6 to each tray.
Each $0.02

Aluminum frame, transparent celluloid removable covers for above extra, one to each tray.
Each $0.35

Price each:
No. 97—Wood Trays $3.50
No. 97—Aluminum Trays 5.00

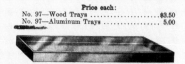

"Made Right" Sample Cases are Traveling Show Cases

Irrespective of line, there is positively no surer, quicker or more satisfactory means of selling goods. Every time the Trays shoot out they bring down an order.

No. 106—Cabin Bag Sample Case.

Black cowhide leather, otherwise like our No. 1 combined Bag and Case, except with greater capacity in top independent compartment.

These cases help the salesman sell goods or we wouldn't sell the cases.

Ten trays 14x3½x1 inches; base 2 inches deep. Also furnished with box in bottom instead of trays 15x 7⅜x7⅛. (See No. 52 in catalog.) Or with loose trays like our No 54. Either wood or aluminum trays.
Wood trays, each...........$19.00
Aluminum trays, each....... 22.00
With box, each............. 14.50
Loose wood trays, each...... 16.75

No. 106.   PAT'D 1908

Advertisement, Knickerbocker Case Company, around 1910. (Division of Rare and Manuscript Collections, Cornell University Library, Ithaca, N.Y.)

Combined Display Counter and Sample Case

A Startling Novelty In Itself.

Closed

Cover Removed

By one simple, quick operation all trays are extended in almost a vertical position and automatically locked, though as easily released for closing. Samples of any line cannot possibly otherwise be so effectively or more advantageously displayed.

Made to order any size; scope or case style.

Patent Applied for

Trays Extended

No. 1 — Combined Sample Case and Bag.

Smooth black cowhide leather, with 10 wood trays, 14″x3½″x1″, and base 2″ deep. Independent compartment in top for large samples, order book, stationery, etc.
Price, each $16.00

COVER REMOVED, TRAYS EXTENDED, FOLDED UP AND COVER REPLACED IN 5 SECONDS.

COVER REMOVED AND TRAYS EXTENDED EXPOSING ALL SAMPLES IN 3 SECONDS

SHOWS ALL KINDS OF GOODS Q U I C K L Y AND ATTRACTIVELY.

No. 11—Combined Sample Case and Bag.

Identical to No. 1, except with 10 aluminum instead of wood trays.
Price, each $19.00

No. 104—Double Tier Case.

Suitcase style. Black grain leather covered. Outside 19½x13x6. Contains nine trays, as follows: 7 trays 18x5x1 outside; 1 tray 18x5x1½ outside; 1 tray 18x5x1⅛ outside. Base 2 inches deep. With wood or aluminum trays.
Wood Trays, each..................$16.00
Aluminum Trays, each.............. 20.00

ANY SIZE OR STYLE OF CASE, BAG, OR COMBINATION MADE TO ORDER.

No. 104.

All Prices F. O. B. Chicago

Grocery salesman holding sample case, around 1910. (Courtesy of Strong Museum, Rochester, N.Y.)

Plattville, the setting for Booth Tarkington's 1899 novel *The Gentleman from Indiana,* "transient trade was light": only "occasional commercial travelers" stopped there. A "rickety omnibus that lingered" by the station took an hour to get to the town's only hotel, a gathering spot for locals but empty of visitors most of the time.[49] In such places, salesmen often improvised, as Victor Jacobs once did in a small Texas town. Clearing out a space in front of the general store, he hauled out a couple of flour barrels and a shutter to create a counter.

Hotels catering to traveling men appealed to their need for convenience, sample rooms, and proximity to a railroad depot. (Warshaw Collection of Business Americana, Archives Center, National Museum of American History, Smithsonian Institution.)

In making the road their home, traveling men became familiar figures in hotel lobbies.

Salesmen gather at the Pullman Exchange in the Portland Hotel, Cripple Creek, Colorado, 1895. (Denver Public Library, Western History Department.)

American House, Denver. (Denver Public Library, Western History Department.)

Brown Palace, Denver. (Denver Public Library, Western History Department.)

"Then," he wrote, "I proceeded to open my trunks and to show my samples in this improvised open-air sample room, and, after an hour's work, was the lucky possessor of an order."[50] Where improvisation led to improvements, and sample rooms or other services appeared, the commercial traveler seemed a progenitor of change. But some traveling men avoided the Platt-villes, where improvements failed to appear and modernity illuminated the drawbacks; they headed instead for "electric-light towns" with comfortable hotels and better services.[51] From making towns, traveling men learned that

Hotel lobby, Winona, Minnesota, 1926. (Minnesota Historical Society.)

the built environment changed unevenly—quickly in some places, slowly in others, and in many not at all.

Over time, salesmen increasingly expected sample rooms to be standard features in the commercial landscape. Certainly traveling men making small, out-of-the-way places during the 1870s and 1880s welcomed the efforts of hotel proprietors who turned parlors into sample rooms or, as one landlord did, met a salesman at the railroad depot and carted his two-hundred-pound trunk back to the hotel in a wheelbarrow.[52] In circulars like one the Boston Merchants Association distributed in 1876, wholesalers and salesmen demonstrated their appreciation for the services that better equipped hostlers extended, and praised hotels throughout the East and Midwest for their discount rates, baggage service, and showrooms.[53] But by 1900 traveling men complained when such amenities were not routine services. And whereas salesmen had once bristled at hotels advertising "Single meals, 20 cents. Day Board, $3.00 Per Week. Drummers, $2.00 Per Day," they now considered the absence of sample rooms and unreasonable rates as an unprofessional disregard for the commercial public.[54] In a 1905 article for the *Crescent and Grip,* a trade journal published in Saint Paul, Minnesota, an angry salesman denounced hotels for charging extra for sample rooms. Reminding readers that

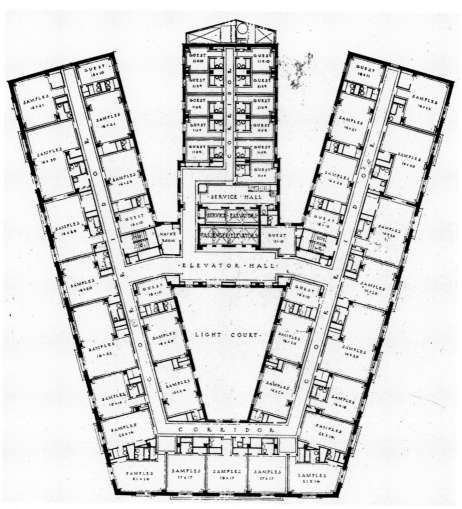

Large commercial hotels such as the Statler in Detroit set aside space for sample rooms. From the *Architectural Record* (May–June 1915). (Courtesy of Newberry Library, Chicago.)

the country hotel had been "a stench in the nostrils of decency" until traveling men "revolutionized these conditions" and sped the development of modern conveniences, the author claimed that "we are as justly entitled to the use of the sample room as we are to the use of the toilet room." Writing for the *Sample Case*, another turn-of-the-century salesman argued that hotels should "create a standard for sample rooms, with rules governing the[ir] care." In many towns "there are no sample rooms," or "if the landlord does have one," it

After meeting a customer, a shoe salesman presents his stock in a hotel sample room. From *System* (March 1906). (Courtesy of Cleveland Public Library.)

"will be filled up with all the old refuse about the place" and even "filthy with disease and animal life."[55] But if neglected sample rooms spoke of small towns that once thrived or aspired to commercial prosperity, traveling men left such failures unexplained. Nor, for their part, did managers of country hotels dwell on the neglect. Accepting the need for sample rooms, they, too, concentrated on the growth of their profession and, in trade journals like the *Hotel Monthly,* debated whether they should charge traveling men an extra fifty cents for the use of one.[56]

At the high end of the economic infrastructure lay the modern hotel, which commercial traveling was partially responsible for developing. A leader in modern hotel construction, Ellsworth Statler had by 1915 promoted design innovations chiefly by catering to commercial travelers. The "Statler idea in hotel planning" meant whole floors given over to sample rooms, specially located freight elevators, and, within the rooms themselves, Murphy beds to save salesmen "the inconvenience of engaging two rooms."[57] These and other features—like private bathrooms, cold running water, thermostats, and individual telephones—brought innovative engineering and distinctly modern design concepts to hotel life. And they expressed, as one of Statler's architects stressed in a 1918 article for the *Architectural Forum*, a simplified, standardized "idea of *service*."[58] Extending the commercial landscape beyond the storefronts of local merchants, such services exemplify the impact of the traveling fraternity on the built environment. Although commercial travelers did not appear to make this landscape, any more than they seemed to make the products they sold, the thousands of salesmen circulating through towns and stores served as the catalyst for material change.

Hotel sample rooms, advertising displays and circulars, the samples themselves—all constituted a visual landscape whose capacity to elicit desire and persuade merchants to buy hinged on the salesman's effectiveness at presenting its component parts and becoming part of the spectacle himself. Like an advertisement or the sensuous environment of the department store, the salesman's powers of persuasion relied on the dynamics of reception—how well the message played to his audience. But unlike either ads or department stores, which for any single encounter remained fixed and unchanging (excluding the personal sales efforts and services of the department store), the salesman's face-to-face presentation was relational and changeable. The potential power of the individual approach thus rested on improvisation, on the salesman's ability to adapt the terms of sale to the contingencies of the moment and to the needs and wishes of the customer. As a performer always enacting dramas to spark commercial desire, the salesman had to be ready to alter his script even while the props and scenery remained generally constant. The transitory, makeshift nature of the job accentuated the improvisation, so traveling salesmanship was always a play in the making, an ongoing process that resisted closure and assumed new wrinkles as the commercial context shifted.

Yet beyond acknowledging the fluid, contingent nature of selling, experts struggled to identify the best methods for controlling these personal interactions. In a 1887 article entitled "Travelers' Methods—the Secret of Selling Goods," a writer for the *Pottery and Glassware Reporter* identified two approaches—one a "straightforward" presentation of samples and prices with "no waste of time and words in idle talk or congratulations," the other a slow, indirect assault on the customer's affections, involving "nothing but pleasure for the first day" but ending in a "very incidental manner" with a sale.[59] Eschewing the abstract considerations of technique and human character that would later distinguish discussions of salesmanship, selling methods are described here by way of example rather than underlying principles. The figure of the salesman acting as a persuasive, volitional agent externalizes the mechanics of selling, making them legible parts of the commercial landscape. Of a piece with the aggressive, improvisational ethos of the road, the emphasis on individual agency reinforces the view of late nineteenth-century commercial traveling that emerged in the twentieth. "We had no selling pattern," one traveling man recalled of his methods during the 1880s; "we cut our own pattern."[60]

Such freedom is relative, of course. Commercial traveling during the two decades immediately following the Civil War may well have been characterized by individual accomplishment; nevertheless, salesmen were also striving to distance themselves from other, freewheeling sales agents whose methods they both deplored and shared. Compared to the many peddlers, hucksters, and fakirs at work in the late nineteenth century, traveling men appeared to lack freedom. Selling a wide spectrum of home remedies and novelties, itinerants frequently exploited the public's desire for "something new" and after working a town either adopted a new sales trick or moved on to another place. "When I seemed to have skimmed the cream of one thing," one versatile fakir confided, "I tried something else, falling back on old schemes when it was necessary or profitable."[61] Successful ruses like the "give away" game lured victims with the promise of free merchandise. From his wagon a huckster would pass out gimcrack products, at first giving them away, then demanding a few cents, but always handing back the money and letting the spectators keep the goods. Finally, after giving away scores of worthless novelties, he would raise the viewing fee to a dollar but say nothing about returning the money. Amid cries of outrage, he skedaddled with his sideshow—and the money.[62]

Fakir schemes reinforced public distrust of commercial itinerants and gave legislators ample reason to enact restrictive licensing laws. For their part, commercial travelers generally sought to disassociate themselves from the sleight-of-hand chicanery that marked transient sales and to emphasize the orderliness of their enterprise. Acutely conscious of the poor public image that followed disorderly selling—and determined to control their appearance in the marketplace—A. Schilling and Company told its representatives in 1884 how they did *not* want them to act. Declaring a "rooted dislike" of the drummer who sold goods "by sheer force of pertinacity and impudence," the company urged its salesmen to rely on "sound, logical arguments" rather than "glibness of tongue." By emphasizing the "character" of the product, talking with "spirit and intelligence," and utilizing "the knowledge of the world you possess," a Schilling tea representative could "inspire confidence in the merchant"—and sell goods.[63] Although the negative reference is to a loud, aggressive, or slippery drummer, the bad manners smack of unrestrained, one-time sales efforts, the sort typified by street-corner operators: free agents. In this regard, there was more to the traveling salesman's frequent celebration of the services that he provided retail merchants than a desire to nurture long-term commercial relationships or simply to sell goods. By advising a merchant on his purchases or by organizing his stock, a salesman declared his conscientious, honest nature and his difference from sales agents unwilling to enter into such relationships.[64] Similarly, veterans such as Edward Briggs, in warning that "new faces and new methods break the confidential connection between the house and the customer," stressed the need to maintain well-established business relationships in terms that recall the unacceptable opposite: a marketplace distinguished by constant turnover and lack of trust.[65]

And yet escaping the brush of fakirs, peddlers, and other onetime sales personnel was not always so easy for the simple reason that their methods sometimes resembled commercial travelers'. For instance, J. P. Johnston's 1888 account, *Twenty Years of Hus'ling*, reads like a textbook on sales improvisation.[66] Ignoring the protocol that shaped commercial traveling, Johnston bought jewelry from wholesalers and sold it at retail prices to storekeepers. Proud of his ability to "hustle," he laughed at salaried drummers, who spent so much time "getting acquainted" with merchants before inviting them back to their hotels to look at samples. Toting a sample case from store to store as a drummer would, Johnston outsmarted "this class of salesmen" by pushing ahead of them and quickly throwing open his case for display. "I considered a sale half made when this was accomplished," he bragged. "I never quit talking or quit pushing sales, and always hurried my customer through as fast as possible."[67] Johnston did not worry about establishing long-term relationships with his customers, nor did he discuss credit terms and freight rates as a traveling man would. His profits depended on how many merchants he could hustle in one day, while his approach—quick and dramatic—resembled that of a patent-medicine seller or circus barker. After he dazzled the customer and left waiting drummers to fume and wonder how well he knew the merchant, Johnston took the money and moved on, savoring his triumph over legitimate selling practices.

Much of the literature written by traveling men during the last two decades of the nineteenth century seems a direct condemnation of freewheeling selling methods. Cautions against drinking, the emphasis on correct dress, and even the instructions on how to shake hands—Caldwell's advice was to "grasp firmly and earnestly, but by no means violently, and make him believe that you are, as you say, indeed 'glad to see him'"—stress the importance of business etiquette in creating a well-ordered marketplace.[68] In a business culture guided by Benjamin Franklin's dicta, where character and community reputation influenced credit ratings as much as assets or capital did, businessmen had every reason to attend to appearances. County by county, in judging prospective borrowers, agents for R. G. Dun looked for "good morals, character, and business capacity." For example, E. B. Martin, in his hometown of San Marcos, Texas, sold goods to the Daily brothers, who, according to Dun's credit report, "were raised in this country and enjoy the entire confidence of the community," while one of William White's customers in Kentucky boasted "perfectly good" credit among those who knew him, because they "universally regarded" him as a "high-minded, honorable" man.[69] Not surprisingly, experienced salesmen likewise emphasized the importance of working hard, cultivating independence, and appearing to be of strong character.[70] In their desire to sell goods, traveling men understandably sought to inspire confidence in merchants by maintaining the appearance of sincerity and integrity —hence the importance of manners, which, if specific guidelines were fol-

Scene by scene, these trade cards dramatize a salesman's success on the road and his employer's satisfaction back home. (Warshaw Collection of Business Americana, Archives Center, National Museum of American History, Smithsonian Institution.)

lowed, demonstrated virtue. In *Leaves from a Drummer's Diary* (1889), Charles Plummer advised salesmen to exercise restraint. The circumspect salesman waited until a busy merchant finished his task before presenting his business card, or he left and came back later if another salesman had arrived first.[71] As Henry Horn put it in *Drumming as a Fine Art* (1882), the successful salesman dressed well, but not too well. The W. F. Main Company admonished its travelers to practice "Politeness, Patience, Perseverance" and "proper" manners to distinguish themselves from "swarming drummers" who pressed exasperated merchants.[72] So the merchant-father in George Lorimer's best-

selling *Letters from a Self-Made Merchant to His Son* (1902) tells his son to avoid flashy suits and dress neatly and cleanly.[73] Virtuous habits—scrupulously displayed—paved the way to successful salesmanship.

On the one hand, the streamlined discourse (language and gestures) that came to distinguish traveling salesmanship may be seen as the product of an increasingly rationalized marketplace. On the other hand, the discourse evidenced a more refined form of improvisation, the persistence and evolution of residual forms of persuasion in a new context. Prevailing concerns for orderly business necessarily circumscribed sales practices and kept them from becoming too much like the improvisations of J. P. Johnston and other hustlers. Nonetheless, the commercial traveler's sales pitch was an improvised performance; the sales encounter was the culminating scene to which all salesmen's efforts were directed. Given the apparent self-sufficiency of each sales encounter within a travel schedule that included many such visits, commercial traveling exemplified the paradox of selling personally to a mass market. Although traveling men treated all their customers as "you," giving every one undivided attention, they resumed the road at the conclusion of business and began the cycle of selling again.

The universal "you"—so important to all forms of personal salesmanship—led in the late nineteenth century to traveling men's well-known reputation for geniality.[74] But geniality did not always mean cheerfulness or warmth of disposition, that is, the qualities typically associated with the salesman's glad-handedness. As William H. Maher suggested, it also referred to the salesman's expansiveness and adaptability to his customer's perceived character and needs. This kind of geniality was rooted in the antebellum urban drummer's attempt to be all things to all men. Granted, the development of the genial sales personality in the second half of the century, following the wholesaler's extensive search for markets, took shape under substantially different circumstances, but the dynamics of accommodation and assimilation were similar. Just as the antebellum drummer subordinated the resources of the mercantile city to his sales effort, so the traveling man, drawing from his experience on the road, presented a wider world—or, depending on the customer, selected aspects of it—to small-town merchants.

The reversal of the geographical relationship that once took country merchants to the city but now imported cosmopolitan know-how to the hinterland thus proved critical to the personality constructed by commercial traveling. To speak of a generic commercial self risks simplifying the complicated dynamics of selfhood, but it highlights the specific circumstances that governed the professional behavior of all traveling men. Warren Susman, C. Wright Mills, and Arlie Hochschild have all argued, albeit in different ways, that the sales personality or malleable self who creates and manages emotions in an "instrumental" manner—actually selling the self—in order to succeed at work or in society evolved within the highly modernized structures of twentieth-century commercial culture.[75] That the traveling salesman (and even the urban drummer who preceded him) modeled this behavior well before its conceptualization in societal terms is hardly surprising given the transience of commercial traveling and its emphasis on face-to-face interactions. What is surprising about these interpersonal dynamics is that they evolved in a cultural space that was neither urban nor provincial but a mixture of the two: a distributive culture based simultaneously on upholding and erasing regional differences.

The ongoing publication of joke books specifically associated with commercial traveling shows the link between the salesman's improvisational self and this evolving transregional market culture. Cheap pamphlets like *Drum-*

mer's Yarns (1886), *The Kansas Man Abroad. Tales of the Plains. By a Traveling Man* (1889), *That Reminds Me* (1894), *A Drummer's Parlor Tales* (1898), *Drummers' Samples: A Series of Short Stories Told on the Rails* (1903), *On a Slow Train Through Arkansaw* (1903), and *A Drummer's Diary Containing Twenty-Five Stories as Told by a Traveling Man* (1906) sold a brand of humor that publishers believed only a travel-wise salesman could deliver.[76] Taken together, however, the titles imply less a sense of individual ownership or authorship than the drummer's unique ability to circulate the humor of the culture through face-to-face business relationships. Joking was thus a form of verbal capital resembling the rhetoric distributed by earlier role-playing itinerants—for instance, the Yankee peddler and the blackface minstrel—and belonged to a national comic tradition explicitly tied to mobility.[77] Yet the salesman's position as business representative (within a modernized oral tradition made possible by technologies of speed) also distinguished him from these figures and hence made his notoriety for crude humor—what one observer called his robust profanity— somewhat puzzling.[78] Given the business community's stated concern for sobriety and restraint, the popular image of the salesman as purveyor of drinks and teller of jokes appears out of step with prevailing conventions. Views of road culture—like that of *The Kansas Man Abroad,* featuring a mysterious traveler who follows a group of convivial drummers from one town to another and listens as they spin yarns, only to tell a tall tale better than any

Thomas Carey's jest books featured the drummer as a consummate joke teller and entertainer.

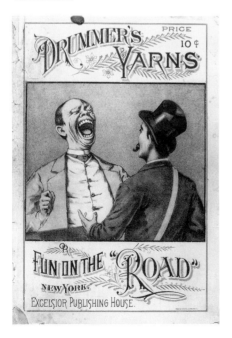

Cover, *Drummer's Yarns* (1886). (Warshaw Collection of Business Americana, Archives Center, National Museum of American History, Smithsonian Institution.)

Cover, *That Reminds Me!* (1894). (Courtesy of Library of Congress.)

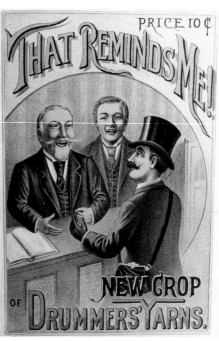

Cover, *Drummer's Yarns: Fifteenth Crop* (1900?). (Courtesy of Library of Congress.)

salesman's—would seem to be pure projection, the wish fulfillments of a citizenry restrained by convention.[79]

So perhaps they were. But drinking and raucous joking were not merely cultural fictions. As salesmen lamented, they were a part of sales culture, more than most representatives of the culture cared to admit—at least in public. And those who did acknowledge their role in selling goods did so with self-conscious humor, owning such deviations from sober respectability as further proof of a drummer's improvisational talents and even making them part of another story of the road. George M. Hayes's 1884 account, coyly dubbed *Twenty Years on the Road; or, The Trials and Tribulations of a Commercial Traveler by One of Them*, is a case in point. In describing the beginning of his career as a wholesaler's representative, Hayes notes his employer's admonition: "Any general advice I consider useless; you must learn by experience; but one point I want to press particularly on your mind: In making a new customer, try and read him through and through, but don't let him read you. Follow this rule, and act honestly and conscientiously. . . . Sell your goods on their merits, never misrepresent, and make the acquaintance of as few drummers as possible. Keep sober, be polite, economical, and you will succeed." In the subsequent twenty years, Hayes succeeds by following these instructions, simultaneously exploiting their elasticity and improvising within an ambiguous cultural space bounded by Victorian-era proprieties. For Hayes, the stipulations "learn by experience" and "read" the customer lead to commercial opportunities seemingly barred by the so-called rules of mercantile exchange. Hayes remains sober but does not refrain from drinking; nor does he stand in the way of his customer's good time. In fact—as he suggests in explaining how he outsmarted two Chicago customers who plotted to get him drunk for previously bringing them home "half full" and selling them more goods than they needed—liquor is a customary component in his sales routine, one part of business entertainment among many, including dinner, billiards, and socializing. Hayes succeeds by secretly drinking tea while they again drink too much whisky—a victory that his customers later concede when, hung over and acquiescent, they give Hayes two of his best orders of the season.[80]

Sales methods like these, one might say, were a throwback to the world of the antebellum drummer. Yet their carnivalesque appeal, which seems so at odds with the rationalizing tendencies that powered the nineteenth-century market revolution, may well have been more the custom than some salesmen were willing to admit. According to Edward P. Briggs, the custom of treating retail merchants to drinks was so common in the years between 1865 and 1885 that "it was a necessary preliminary in order to get acquainted with a new party upon whom you called."[81] It was precisely this anomalous recourse to undisciplined human expression that, with discipline and ritualization, the traveling salesman turned to commercial advantage. Salesmen like Hayes preserved the scabrous elements of face-to-face relationships and harnessed them to an emerging market system; they enabled the transformation of older selling practices into modern modes of persuasion. The traveling man's infamous joke-telling epitomizes the subordination of human desire to commercial purposes. Telling jokes, particularly dirty jokes, brought salesmen face to face with customers and established a masculine context for laughing about titillating material—and ultimately selling goods. Although the jokes may have been about potentially disruptive actions, and although their illicit contents implicated the salesman as man of the world—not only for telling the most recent yarns but also for presumably knowing something about the subject matter—the implicit and most important meaning of the jokes was the establishment of a shared sales culture.[82] Like so many other aspects of commercial traveling, joking was a form of improvisation that aimed finally at gaining and controlling the customer's attention.

The eventual historical effect of this ongoing effort to win customers was the codification of selling techniques. A new word for a new era, *salesmanship*, signaled the traveling man's unique relation to the commercial landscape and caught the improvisational spirit implicit in his wide-ranging path through sample rooms and railroad depots. Entering the language in the 1880s, when the expansion of American commercial and industrial activity began to make selling a specialized technique, *salesmanship* described a new kind of work. In usage since the early sixteenth century, *salesman* joined the suffix 250 years after a similar compound word—*craftsmanship*—appeared in print. Like the ending *scape* of *landscape,* the suffix *-ship* confers a "skill or power of accomplishment" and derives its meaning from the Old Teutonic word *skap,* "to create or to *shape*"—another word whose development proceeded from similar roots.[83] However tangled or obscure, the etymologies of these words illuminate the motive power of salesmanship, the intentions of its practitioners. If in making towns the traveling man exemplified his mastery of the landscape and his ability to move from place to place, through salesmanship the modern commercial traveler evinced his skill in face-to-face transactions, where, through language, gesture, and display, he sought to create favorable selling conditions.

By 1900 salesmanship had become a concept and a method described in books, trade journals, and commercial colleges. Shaped by psychological theory, by attention to what one expert called "the instincts of imitation, rivalry, acquisitiveness," salesmanship marked the internalization of selling methods and a closing down of the broader, cultural landscape that throughout the late nineteenth century had always seemed the drummer's natural territory.[84] Rooted in everyday selling practices and evolved over time, salesmanship still owed something to traditional hucksterism. Quick wits and an occasional sleight of hand still sold goods, though such improvisation was now viewed as a science. In the opening decades of the twentieth century the traveling man still presented the world as his own and, in inland villages, spoke knowingly of electrically lit hotels or reported familiarly on nearby towns and the upcoming harvest. And still he built commercial confidence by gauging his audience's reactions as he gestured and talked. But as the marketplace became even more competitive, and selling methods more sophisticated, the salesman had less time for onlookers and restless boys. As he earnestly presented his goods to retail merchants, he appeared less the creature of an unbounded world than the representative of modern business enterprise.

4 Only a Drummer

By 1890, if Americans could picture a drummer without having seen one, it was because the tremendous explosion in print media had brought him into the parlor—in magazines and books, on chromolithographs and trade cards. For journalists, illustrators, travelers, and writers of fiction the traveling salesman became a stock representation of the commercial spirit of the Gilded Age, but in terms utterly unlike those used to describe the most noted business figure: the tycoon. Scale and setting describe the difference in type. The tycoon—consider Christopher Newman in James's *The American* or Howells's hero in *The Rise of Silas Lapham*—had the physical stature and social power that (however incomplete) confer a sense of control, of economic and cultural forces, missing in portrayals of the traveling man. In fact, the drummer's relative lack of such qualities makes him a figure still worth noting. The traveling salesman was rarely a hero and barely a character but most often a caricature of the economic interests that he represented and never owned, hardly worth noticing yet frequently and vividly portrayed, though seldom in well-defined commercial terms. In retrospect, he may best be viewed as both the target of criticism for a society struggling to understood the human face of a systematic commercial economy and an emergent type whose circulation in the literary and cultural marketplaces ironically served to domesticate and mythologize that face.

An 1885 painting, *The Drummer's Latest Yarn,* is a case in point. Archibald M. Willard is best known for his patriotic representation of a revolutionary war fife-and-drum corps, which he completed in time for the U.S. centenary—it is alternatively entitled *Yankee Doodle* and *The Spirit of '76*—but during the course of his career he illustrated scores of quintessential American scenes, many of them comically drawn. *The Drummer's Latest Yarn* is a more complicated example of Willard's appeal to the funny bone, for the artist makes humor itself the subject of his painting. In a crowded railroad car, a group of travelers watch as a portly, well-dressed man rears back in his seat to laugh. The laughing man is the visual focus of the painting. Not only is he positioned at the middle of the image, but the gazes of the passengers show him to be the center and instigator of the scene: the drummer and yarn teller referred to in the title. Reactions are mixed. The older man facing the drummer remains detached, impassively looking on, while the young boy leans across the aisle in rapt attention. The response of the younger man seated next to him is familiar, almost intimate. As the salesman lifts an arm to counterbalance and accentuate his laughter, his companion grasps his shoulder with one hand and stretches out the other—acknowledging the humorous effect of the joke and establishing a context for masculine fellowship. Meanwhile, behind the two men, out of the drummer's immediate circle of companions, a middle-aged woman looks on in disgust. The painting reveals a range of competing reactions, from distaste to admiration, roughly representative, according to gender and age, of a cross section of the population.

The Drummer's Latest Yarn affords a glimpse of the theatrics that occasioned the traveling salesman's emergence as a cultural type. Image and title together

The Drummer's Latest Yarn. Painting by Archibald M. Willard. (Courtesy of Charles J. Cella.)

locate the drummer beyond the commercial sphere and within the metropolitan corridor of the railroad, where he becomes a ubiquitous object of interest for onlookers situated inside and outside the frame. By implicitly including the viewer in the drummer's circle, the painting reenacts the interior drama and extends the salesman's improvisational powers beyond the canvas. Yet if the painting coyly invites its viewers to take part in the yarn's telling, it also reconstitutes several perspectives in a single image to be seen in a single gaze, thereby alluding to the interplay of perception and aesthetic production that went toward creating the drummer's mythic status. Simultaneously the subject and the object of the painting, the drummer creates his own audience while the viewer—in becoming both participant and observer—learns something of the crucial link between the salesman's self-making role in the social landscape and his equally dramatic presence as a represented figure in literature and popular culture.

What *The Drummer's Latest Yarn* tells of this link, however, involves more than meets the eye. The topic of the painting apparently stemmed from a death that Willard witnessed while traveling on the Lake Shore railroad in Ohio. According to a 1891 report, Willard watched as a drummer told a funny story to a "very appreciative man" who started to laugh, then "became hysterical and could not stop"; he "struggled, strangled and died on the car." But

114

given the drummer's central position in the painting, Willard must have revised the incident, in which case the salesman becomes the victim of *The Drummer's Latest Yarn,* a man who dies from laughing too hard at his own joke. The change in the title of the painting over the past half-century—to *Drummer's Last Yarn*—bears out this view, illuminating a darker, more tragic salesman than the image itself might first suggest, and an interpretation more in keeping with twentieth-century sensibilities.[1]

The alleged death in Willard's painting and the apparently actual one behind it describe a culture preoccupied with the dynamics of commercial selfhood. Reflected in the drummer's genial surfaces was a fluid, volatile self, distinguished not so much by depth of character as by a destructive attention to the opportunities and limitations of the market. Although this vision of the deconstructing self—literally, the death of the salesman—may be familiar to late twentieth-century Americans, the problem for late nineteenth-century observers concerned a lack of vocabulary, for how, in the absence of concepts like "personality," should this figure be described? For many critics the traveling salesman was "only a drummer"—to use Wilbur Castelow's phrase—a man whose efforts at making a living scarcely warranted symbolic analysis. The "only" (as Castelow sensed) referred simultaneously to the salesman's diminished social standing and to an apparently incomplete self: by making his living and his home on the road the salesman divided his loyalties to family and community. What made the salesman good to think—and portray—was this flawed self and its seemingly intimate connection to social changes, whose causes were beyond sight and understanding. Yet in noting this connection, critics also diminished the salesman's capacity to effect change—and hence his status as a man—by exposing his assumption of power as unearned and pretentious. If only a drummer, the salesman was merely a representative for forces larger than himself.

While the bulk of writing about traveling salesmen thus seems vivid and shallow, there were good reasons why. Like Willard, late nineteenth-century writers and analysts acknowledged the link between direct observation and discourse by engaging the drummer where he was usually seen—in public: in railroad cars, on Main Streets, in small towns. But realism reinforced rather than clarified the questions that surrounded the salesman's ubiquity. Although by sharp, ethnographic descriptions of dress and speech, commentators caught the salesman's visual and sensual powers, they had difficulty accounting for their presence. What they glimpsed of the relation between the drummer's improvisations and the expanding market they revealed piecemeal, refracting an image of a strangely detached figure whose apparent lack of any stable referents—to home, community, and established place of business—was part of a broadly felt breakdown in traditional meanings and associations.[2]

The sensory details that characterized late nineteenth-century representations of drummers did not simply reflect the visual show that real salesmen brought to commercial practice; more often than not, they constituted the starting point for cultural criticism. Middle- and upper-class anxiety over expansive market practices continued to shape criticism, as it had of the antebellum urban drummer, but added to the discourse were enough new perspectives to indicate that the opposition was crucially tied to regional tensions and caused by the extensive geographical and cultural reach of the economy. In structure, the link between wholesaler and retailer remained much the same, but the change of custom that now placed the salesman under the gaze of small-town eyes made him a symbol of the "ruthlessly disruptive incursions of capitalist enterprise," which, as Warner Berthoff has argued, were the principal motives behind the development of literary realism.[3] In this way, literature was of a piece with the licensing laws aimed at limiting the commercial traveler's purview. Again and again, writers addressed the complex relations between hinterland and city by condemning drummers for their undermining of domestic harmony, for their sexual aggression, local interference, commercial misrepresentation, and more. But the structure of feeling that emerged around the salesman was not entirely negative. Alternatively evoking the lure of the city, the power of commerce, and the romance of travel, the salesman spoke of a cultural transformation that, on one level, threatened the integrity of small-town life yet, on another, invited relief from the hemmed-in world of Main Street. The demographic shift from small town to city that twentieth-century critics—thinking mainly of aspiring writers— would characterize as "the revolt from the village" was thus augured by the drummer's presence on Main Street and refracted in regional and local-color fiction.[4]

It is tempting to think of the commercial traveler's meaning in the terms that historians have used to characterize the impact of twentieth-century advertising: as constitutive of a new symbolic order that threatened to erode established ways of seeing. There is little doubt, for instance, that the traveling salesman's transitory appeals to commercial desire, as well as the cumulative effect of the entire profession's movement from place to place (resulting in the drummer's generic ubiquity), prefigured modern advertisers' similarly (and seemingly) decentralized efforts to win buyers. Moreover, the visual impact of commercial traveling, combined with the sum total of the salesman's represented parts in literature and illustration, appeared to anticipate modernism by generating through the interplay between market forces and aesthetic production a dramatic field that was both depthless and fragmented.[5] Yet despite the cumulative effect of the drummer's presence in the culture, nineteenth-century analysts were more apt to view the salesman in individual terms, as a problem in self-governance. Unlike an advertisement, the salesman was not a textual abstraction. His appeal was immediate and concrete, and it was his recourse to commercial improvisation as personal self that drove the ambivalent, sometimes downright negative, reactions to his place in public. As the ambiguous interpretive history of Willard's painting suggests, improvisation was truly Janus-faced, containing threats to both the salesman's audience and himself. Although the meaning of *Drummer's Last Yarn* may indeed be a twentieth-century product, the envisioned death of a salesman, made so familiar to late twentieth-century sensibilities by Arthur Miller, refers to the loss of self already implicit in the dynamics of commercial traveling even though nineteenth-century observers rarely faced this loss head on. In general, however, the erosion of selfhood mandated by the drummer's own will to improvise or sell himself—the creation of what was later called personality—increasingly claimed the attention of analysts as the century drew to a close and the dynamics of salesmanship evolved.

One of the great ironies attending the drummer's rise to prominence is that this improvisational self became the property of the culture that represented it. In noting the love of imitative, lifelike representations in late nineteenth-century America, Miles Orvell has argued that the tendency in popular culture was "to enclose reality in manageable forms, to contain it within a theatrical space" in order to "offer the illusion of mastery and comprehension" in a transforming society that seemed otherwise chaotic. To view the traveling salesman in this way is to place him within the consumer culture of a middle class simultaneously fascinated by the exotic and determined to circumscribe it. Here again the history of Willard's painting is instructive, not only for what the image reveals of the drummer but also for how it appeared to viewers. Like much of Willard's work, the painting was reprinted, copyrighted, and sold—probably as a chromolithograph—by James F. Ryder, an innovative Cleveland photographer who was vital in promoting Willard's career. The chromo's likely resting place on some parlor or office wall epitomizes the drummer's gradual domestication as a figure of local color suitable for a mass audience and suggests that by claiming the salesman's improvisational self as its own, the middle class helped mythologize it.[6]

The same could be said of the salesman's appearance on the trade cards that retail merchants distributed to consumers. Prized for their colorful, at times humorous, depictions of American scenes, trade cards, like chromos, became part of the domestic landscape and were frequently collected and pasted in albums. Literally millions of these cards were produced between 1850 and 1890, prompting the highly successful lithographer Louis Prang to observe that "hardly a business man in the country has not at one time or another made use of such cards to advertize his wares."[7] Many such businessmen were commercial travelers (who distributed the cards to retailers), and such cards even featured negative portrayals of drummers—facts that highlight the salesman's domestication in ironic, though by no means idiosyncratic, terms. As scholars have made increasingly clear, aesthetic production was no less subject to the expansive marketplace of the post–Civil War era than any other economic practice. And what figure was better able to represent the complicity of business and self, or, for that matter, art and commerce, than the traveling salesman?

From late nineteenth-century writers and artists came no real answer to this kind of question. The drummer was rarely a full-fledged subject or character suitable for exploring the relation between salesmanship and art or

Trade card, 1880. (Courtesy of Strong Museum, Rochester, N.Y.)

In late nineteenth-century popular culture—in trade cards as well as literary sources—the drummer's antics and improvisations appeared beyond the pale of middle-class respectability and made him a highly recognizable, somewhat unsavory social type.

writing, for his improvisational practices and his role as middleman were at odds with the producer-oriented values so crucially tied to aesthetic practice. Although writers, for instance, were acutely aware that they labored in an industrialized marketplace of literary commodities, many also held to a preindustrial or artisanal conception of their work.[8] In this sense, the salesman's domestication in late nineteenth-century culture had little to do with any artist's or writer's in-depth engagement with the traveling man; rather, quite the opposite was the case. Critics stayed their distance and with shallow, negative treatments of the drummer reinscribed qualities that over time became part of familiar cultural stereotypes. Insofar as such representations objectified the salesman and presented him as other, they functioned as a sort of racial and ethnic stereotyping. To the extent, however, that they constituted fluid surface descriptions, their components were easily borrowed, reshaped, and adapted to suit other purposes and genres. Whereas in one text a salesman's commercial aggressiveness may connote a frightening lack of gentility,

Trade card, around 1890. (Courtesy of Strong Museum, Rochester, N.Y.)

Trade card. (Warshaw Collection of Business Americana, Archives Center, National Museum of American History, Smithsonian Institution.)

in another—for instance, a dime novel—the aggressiveness may become the basis for heroic action. This was perhaps the other great irony of the salesman's rise to cultural prominence: although the majority of late nineteenth-century texts represented the traveling salesman in negative terms, the dynamics of the market, indeed the salesman's presence in an astonishing number of texts, worked toward establishing him in the public eye as a figure whose significance transcended any single or several portraits.

One of the earliest, most widely circulated representations of the commercial traveler was Charles Follen Adams's poem "Der Drummer." Printed in newspapers and on trade cards and collected in an 1877 edition called *Leedle Yawcob Strauss and Other Poems*, "Der Drummer" is a touchstone for the ambivalent cluster of characteristics that made up the traveling salesman's image in popular culture. Adams begins his poem by recording in dialect a German-American storekeeper's impression of the traveling man.

> Who vas it gomes indo mine schtore,
> Drows down his pundles on der vloor,
> Und nefer schtops to shut der door?
>   Der Drummer.

> Who dakes me py der handt, und say,
> "Hans Pfeiffer, how you vas to-day?"
> Und goes for peesness rightdt away?
>   Der Drummer.

Stanza by stanza, Adams's narrator describes how the drummer cheats him on goods, "gomes around ven I ben oudt," drinks his beer, and even kisses his daughter, and predicts that "ven he gomes again dis vay" the salesman will "mit a plack eye goes avay."[9] The accompanying woodcuts, however, make light of these transgressions. Whereas the dapper drummer appears a good-natured rogue with a twinkling eye, Hans Pfeiffer is a short, fat, bespectacled—and duped—merchant. Given the opportunity, Adams seems to ask, what drummer could resist tricking old Hans? Yet if the illustrations and the poem effectively caricature the German, they also take for granted the salesman's commercial and sexual aggressiveness, as well as his dishonesty and false geniality. Adams's humor cuts two ways, targeting the immigrant storekeeper as a fit object for ridicule and presenting the salesman as the most appropriate figure for meting out the abuse. Here and throughout late nineteenth-century popular culture, the salesman appears as an aggressive middleman through whom jokes and ethnic stereotypes are passed and reproduced.

Assuming the perspectives of small-town midwesterners, Robert J. Burdette and George W. Peck likewise treated the salesman's "mashing" and slick volubility as humorous set pieces. Burdette referred knowingly in the 1870s to the traveling man whose "breath is nearly as bad as his morals, who wants to tell you all about the daughter of a wealthy merchant who was 'just dead gone' on him the last time he went over this road," while Peck gave his readers a

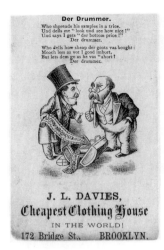

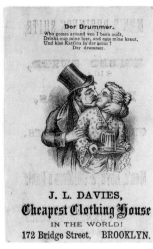

Trade cards added to the popularity of Adams's poem. (Warshaw Collection of Business Americana, Archives Center, National Museum of American History, Smithsonian Institution.)

drummer who would "sell you bean coffee with one hand and point to the golden streets of Jerusalem with the other."[10] Comic sketches like these feature the salesman's jaded, worldly perspective and his up-to-date slang as distinctly urban traits, which the narrator seems to have gathered with the authority of a Main Street reporter who sees all.

Even when Burdette moved away from the pungent sketches that distinguished his writing at the Iowa *Hawkeye* and wrote prose that was closer to fiction, he stuck closely to his inland imagination. "The Legend of the Good Drummuh," for instance, anthologized in *Chimes from a Jester's Bells* (1897), tells of a heroic traveling man called Abou Ben Evrawhair making "the city of Mhrahaha in the land of Ohoho" during "the reign of the good Caliph." Abou endures all the hardships of a seedy hotel—a surly clerk, a rough bed, and an uncooperative porter named Rhumul em Uhp—but succeeds because he went into the merchants' booths in the bazaar and "filled" the storekeepers "to overflowing with new stories and marvelous incidents by flood and field, and he wrote down orders which they gave not while they laughed, and got upon them the cinch of the good salesman."[11] Words and phrases like "hustler," "he wrote down orders," and "got upon them the cinch of the good salesman" add a commercial voice to the formal, biblical prose, suggesting the salesman's own punctuation of the rhythms of small-town life.

The shifting narrative eye in this story demonstrates the sketch writer's indebtedness to the culture of travel made possible by the expanding transportation system. In an essay written in 1920, John Dewey reasoned that transience had led to an American literature written for people "who are going from one place and haven't as yet arrived at another. They cannot have depth or thickness—nothing but movement. . . . The result is of necessity a crackling surface."[12] The jokes, sketches, and short fiction that concerned life

George Ade's "four-flush drummer."
(Collection of the author.)

on the rail moved toward these conditions. In "The Legend of the Good Drummuh" Burdette all but adopted the traveling salesman's mobile perspective as his own; in another sketch he even praised their knowledge of the road and repeated their jokes.[13] Still, the upshot of Burdette's using the salesman and setting the tale somewhere between Iowa and the East is to prohibit the narrative and the audience from attaining any penetrating realism or depth. Rendered exotic and familiar at the same time, the drummer becomes a safe (domesticated) object for entertainment.

George Ade also exploited the expressive possibilities offered by the salesman's comic voice while at the same time honoring his middle-class audience's tastes. The pungent slang of the "fables" he wrote for the *Chicago News* during the late 1890s gave Ade the voice of a wisecracking city man who, having left his midwestern village, could speak with authority and humor about small-town mores. For a city populated by fellow migrants Ade wrote prose that captured the banter once heard in general stores, hotel lobbies, and railroad depots.

Even more frequently than Burdette, Ade made use of the traveling man. To dramatize feigned intelligence, he referred to the "same old line" of "four-flush" drummers who (lacking a fifth card in the same suit) bluffed their way through conversations. To illustrate male camaraderie, he "bunched" a group of husbands on a porch "listening to a Story that a Traveling Man had just brought to town."[14] In *Doc' Horne,* a novel describing the social life at a Chicago hotel during the 1890s, he had his hero claim to have been an important Civil War strategist masquerading as a commercial traveler. And for his 1903 play, *The County Chairman,* Ade cast a drummer as a backslapping ladies' man.

But if Ade appropriated the traveling man's comic voice, he also shaped and transformed it. Cut loose from its commercial context, the improvisational mask becomes an artistic or stylistic device, a way of connoting the drummer's worldly perspective without having to adopt it wholly. Thus, in "The Fable of the Brash Drummer and the Peach Who Learned That There Were Others," Ade limits the influence that a drummer has on the ambitious daughter of a small-town "Mortgage Shark." Gleaning fashion hints from trade catalogs and etiquette tips from "the Questions and Answers Department of an Agricultural Monthly," the daughter longs to "make a Showing" but lacks a guide—until she meets a traveling man. Ade describes how.

> Now it happened that there came to this Town every Thirty Days a brash Drummer, who represented a Tobacco House. He was a Gabby Young Man, and he could Articulate at all Times, whether he had anything to Say or not. One night, at a Lawn Fête given by the Ladies of the Methodist Congregation, he met Daughter. She noticed that his Trousers did not bag at the Knees; also that he wore a superb Ring. They strolled under the Maples, and he talked what is technically known as Hot Air. He made an Impression considerably deeper than himself. She promised to Correspond.

By the end of the tale, Ade has cleverly reversed their positions so that they do "correspond." Having acquired an eastern education, the daughter now apes the drummer's vacuous posturing but mistakes him for a citizen of the town, explaining that "I meet so many People traveling about . . . I cahn't remember all of them, you know."[15]

Ade's pun on *correspondence* owes something to his understanding of sales improvisation. The brash drummer's inability to make his words and actions correspond with any internal substance or meaning—he can Articulate but his words are Hot Air—derives, Ade suggests, from his job: he represents not himself but other interests. In "The Fable of How the Canny Commercial Salesman Guessed the Combination," Ade addresses the dynamics of representation more explicitly and describes a drummer who, trying to sell a bill to a country merchant, puts on a "copyrighted smile," moves through a series of "Cold Propositions," tells "two of the Latest," switches and tries "the Sympathetic Dodge," until finally he succeeds by claiming to believe in religious predestination.[16]

Compact and muscular, Ade's swiftly told fables read like sales pitches and advertising copy. The capitalized nouns and verbs capture the heightened emphasis that Ade's salesmen give their gestures and propositions. More important perhaps, they suggest the larger-than-life effect of an urban voice in a small town, alluding not only to the traveling man's perspective, which, Ade suggests, is one-dimensional and limiting, but also to a wider, cosmopolitan view of American culture. This later view, as "The Fable of the Brash Drummer and the Peach Who Learned That There Were Others" makes clear, in turn brought proportion to Ade's depiction of the drummer. It gave the brash drummer the improvisational power to make the Mortgage Shark's daughter, but no more, and it established a pattern that Theodore Dreiser would follow in his portrait of Drouet, a commercial traveler who likewise makes a small-town woman—although Carrie is a "daisy," not a peach—only to discover that his influence has limits.

Better than fiction or even journalistic sketching, travel writing was able to reveal how the traveling salesman's entry into popular culture began with his relation to the surfaces of American life. At the very least, travel writing shows just how important perception and setting were to constructing the salesman's image. Given its express use of direct observation, travel writing generally indicates an accuracy or objectivity, which may finally seem as subjective as any fiction writer's view of reality. For travel writers who documented the salesman's place on the landscape, the gray area of interpretation concerned the salesman's ubiquity—a fact of quantity that analysts accounted for in terms of individual behavior. That is, travelers not only remarked on the great numbers of traveling men they saw; they also found the seeds for such abundance in the drummer's personal character, or his lack of one. "He is at home everywhere," a journalist noted, "in perfect keeping with the surroundings."[17] For practically all observers, the drummer's most salient feature was his adaptability, a trait that both defined and perpetuated his status as a cultural type. Yet the sense that the salesman seemed literally part of the American scene through which he traveled, made the related question—how did he get there?—more difficult to answer. Throughout the 1870s and 1880s analysts tried to answer the question by stressing the drummer's ready assumption of the public domain, identifying the attitudes and personal qualities that lay behind his ongoing annexation, and educing from experience a typical commercial traveler.

As Almon Gunnison observed in his 1883 book, *Rambles Overland,* the "commercial-traveller genus abounds in these Western States." On station platforms, in the shade of water tanks, in hotel lobbies, and in the railroad cars, Gunnison spotted the "omnipresent drummer" and examined him. "In the seat just ahead is an ideal specimen of the fraternity. He is arrayed in wonderful expanse of linen, and has that air of proprietorship which belongs to the average over-fed young man." Gunnison looked even closer to "admire the soft folds of his pulpy neck, really envying his rare capacity for looking wise." When the corpulent drummer discovers that he has boarded the wrong train and tries to catch another, Gunnison described the anticipated conclusion with glee. "We encourage him with mirthful words, make suggestions as to styles of locomotion; but, despite this help, he fails," and "alone upon the track, with samples dropped and pulpy fists shaking east and west at the retreating trains, we leave him with his meditations and his samples."[18]

Not all travelers so scornfully dismissed the salesman's efforts to make the road his home. On assignment for an 1882 study of the South, the *Atlantic* correspondent noted that this "extremely hospitable" class of businessmen was one of the "chief features" of the region; a year later the *Century* included a "gentlemanly" drummer among the "non-descripts" whom its traveling reporter discovered on a Mississippi river boat; and a writer in New England when the economy dwindled in the 1890s blended drummers into a picturesque landscape.[19] Although some observers saw harmony, others sided with Almon Gunnison and condemned salesmen for their unctuous, imperial manner. Amid complaints of "well-fed, self-satisfied-looking" drummers looking hungrily at the landscape beyond the railroad-car window or crowding out "picturesque excitement"—which, in the West, meant cowboys and desperadoes—there was general agreement that the commercial traveler's aggressive sales ethic went hand in hand with his proprietal regard for public space.[20] To sell goods, traveling men first had to own the territory, to feel at home in it. During his 1889 tour of the United States, Rudyard Kipling, for instance, blamed the drummer's disregard for economic and social boundaries on Americans' wholehearted embrace of freedom and "versatility." By encouraging unqualified people to take up important tasks, versatility bred "dangerous casualness" and, by fostering the "unlimited exercise of the right of private judgment," spawned "blatant cocksureness." Appalled by one commercial traveler who seemed ready to invite him home without even knowing his name, Kipling cringed to hear another salesman extol the virtues of the Baptist church "with the artless freedom that an American generally exhibits when he is talking about his most sacred private affairs."[21] By abolishing the sacred differences between private and commercial life and shaping public space to suit his business needs, the drummer abandoned his claim to gentility and, for Kipling, proved an apt representative of American culture.

Kipling was a rarity among nineteenth-century travelers in that he sought to explain rather than merely dramatize the drummer's aggressive ease in public. Given a negative turn by Kipling, *versatility* summarized what the commercial traveler himself would have acknowledged to be his most important asset: the ability to be all things to all people. In their continual efforts to make towns, traveling men extended their improvisational powers so that they appeared to be all things to all men—and in all places. This refusal or inability to discriminate between cultural spaces and occasions was perhaps what most bothered Kipling, who like many American critics, had difficulty understanding the drummer's unchecked familiarity, particularly when it led to the collapse of barriers between the domestic and commercial spheres. It was not, then, simply the wheedling attempts at persuasion and potential chicanery that struck critics of salesmen. It was also—as Mark Twain made clear in his condemnation of two "scoundrels" whom he heard bragging on a riverboat—that such salesmen knew no bounds. Significantly, Twain's account of the conversation in *Life on the Mississippi* begins with an acknowledgment of his role as eavesdropper and then goes on to describe how, although they barely knew one another and had no other audience, they quickly "dropped into business" and, over breakfast, regaled each other with stories of their sales success. Scoundrels not only because they sell imitative products—oleomargarine and "cotton-seed olive-oil"—and are committed to making their products ubiquitous, the drummers lose respect in Twain's eyes because they are incapable of imagining their lives in anything other than commercial terms. They were "brisk men," Twain writes, "energetic of movement and speech; their dollar their god, how to get it their religion." Utterly lacking self-consciousness, the drummers anticipate their own ubiquity—in speech, gesture, and space—as the extension of their natural selves.[22]

The critical tone and foreshortened perspective that in travel writing were chalked up to the salesman's own limited vision and narrow commercialism also appear in fiction—but without the tourist's documenting eye to vouchsafe their source in direct observation. Still a figure best seen to be understood, the drummer in late nineteenth-century literature was likewise held to the surfaces of public life—seen everywhere—everywhere, that is, except the home. As a represented figure, the drummer's place was thus constrained by the same limitations that bound the travel writer. Ironically, despite the freedom of being able to build on observation, few, if any, fiction writers were willing to follow drummers into their homes and examine—or imagine—the domestic inflections of their versatility. In a peculiar way, the conventions of sentimental domestic fiction worked in reverse to confine traveling salesmen to Main Street culture and maintain the integrity of separate spheres. The upshot was to establish a visual vocabulary that confirmed salesmen's expressive role in the public realm but denied them a place in the private world of emotion and depth.

Drummers proliferated in late nineteenth-century literature, often as nothing more than incidental figures in fictional landscapes, but their ubiquity was nonetheless inscribed as a fact of everyday perception. References like this one from a *Munsey's* adventure tale—"A look of disappointment passed from the wealthy flour manufacturer from St. Paul to the hat drummer from Philadelphia, and from the latter to me"—or this one from William H. Bishop's novel *The House of a Merchant Prince* (1883)—"[the wholesale firm] sent out a swarm of ingenious commercial travelers to represent its interests through the length and breadth of the land"—exemplify the salesman's instrumental use by writers to evoke scenes or settings whose association with commercial traveling they assumed their readers would understand.[23] In and of themselves the salesman's appearances in popular literature hardly seem worth noting; taken together, however, their frequency suggests that a pervasive, if superficial, knowledge of the marketplace enabled writers to adapt the traveling man's role as a literary device or convention. By the 1880s readers knew, without any writer having to explain, who the commercial traveler was and what he did. A decade earlier, writers were far more likely to explain their presence in literature as, for instance, William Dean Howells did in his 1871 novel, *Their Wedding Journey*. In noting a drummer's shipboard encounter with two young ladies, Howells assumed little knowledge on the reader's part and explained that "the young man gave himself out as one who, in pursuit of trade for the dry-goods house he represented, had travelled many thousands of miles in all parts of the country."[24]

During the years to follow, distillations gave way to shorthand references and cameo appearances. Writers were also more likely to allude to the salesman's cultural and economic impact.[25] Smartly dressed drummers became a visual index of urban fashion and influence, ranging from portrayals of the "trigly coated" to detailed descriptions of masculine accessories: "linen cuffs of the same pattern, fastened with large, gold plate buttons" and "lavender striped shirt-sleeves, with a black silk handkerchief."[26] Playing off this image allowed writers to undermine expectations shared by characters and readers alike. At the beginning of Hamlin Garland's story "Up the Coule" (1891), for instance, a successful actor returns home to rural Wisconsin after an absence of many years, and the town loafers, disdainfully eyeing his handmade suit and cravat ring, assume that he is a traveling salesman.[27] The presumption that any well-dressed outsider must be a drummer functions negatively here as the first sign that Howard McLane's attempt to bridge the gap between his new life in the city and his old existence will be painful and unsuccessful. Even where miscues cast the salesman in a more positive light (he "looked so faultlessly elegant," one of the three Miss Merritts confides to another in a *Ladies' Home Journal* story of 1895. "A drummer," the sister mistakenly responds. "They always dress handsomely"), they connoted a transient figure who could not be assimilated to mainstream small-town life.[28]

Local colorists in particular, musing elegiacally and ambiguously over the demographic and economic shifts that left many small towns isolated, liked to refer to the "occasional" drummer whose visits accentuated the backwater rhythms of places like Penniville, the setting for a 1892 short story by Margaret Deland. "The village was small, forty houses, perhaps, besides the tavern—called by those who 'put on airs' the hotel—for the occasional drummers that visited the place with sewing machines or gum boots; and for the travelling photographer, with his enlarged crayon head; and the dentist, who came twice a year."[29] Ostensibly this description has nothing to do with the plot of "A Fourth-Class Appointment," which concerns a postmistress who after losing her job marries the out-of-town political appointee brought in to replace her. But Deland's story is finally about Penniville's conflicted relation with cultural change—figured here as the world outside—and in this respect the drummer's incidental appearance dramatizes the paradoxical dependence of the village on the very forces that threaten its existence. Deland's response, typical of local-color fiction, was to accommodate the forces of change (rather than protest their impact), in this instance by utilizing a marriage plot that unites the outsider and the native. Here and elsewhere the drummer played a limited narrative role, serving to direct the action toward some fictionalized home setting while still representing some realistic shard of extensive economic power. Reconceived in fictional terms, the drummer as middleman signified exchange—the transformation from one landscape to another— but himself was never a broker for those changes.

In the hands of George Washington Cable the salesman's mediating role was stylized to accentuate the rapprochement of northern and southern cultures during the postbellum years. In both *Bonaventure* (1887) and *John March, Southerner* (1894), commercial travelers represent economic interests of the New South, but their personification of progress and modernization is not allowed to interfere with the novelist's primary emphasis on romance.[30] Indeed, the drummers remain unnamed and become the butt of jokes. *Bonaventure,* subtitled a "prose pastoral" but simultaneously concerned with the modernization of the Acadian backcountry, dramatizes this lack in an especially ironic manner when, midway through the novel, Cable calls to mind "a certain wild, dark night in November" and describes a tavern "glowing with hospitable firelight" within which "sat a goodly semicircle of men,—commercial travelers" discussing crops and smoking cigars. The importance of this conversation, however, emerges after Cable playfully names the other guests— two men and two women who begin relationships that by the end of the novel culminate in marriage.[31] One of the men, George W. Tarbox, is a New Hampshire native and the author and salesman of *The Album of Universal Knowledge.* Tarbox is not a drummer but rather "a self-made man" who represents himself and his Yankee wisdom without the support of other economic interests. "You, gentlemen," he tells the gathered company, "all are, what I am not, commercial tourists." Tarbox reads human nature more carefully than the traveling men—and more independently—and thus facetiously praises his audience's perspicacity. "Before you, I must be modest. You, each of you, have been chosen from surrounding hundreds or thousands for your superior ability, natural or acquired, to scan the human face and form and know whereof you see." In deriding the vanity of a profession that, seeing only the surface of human nature, judges too quickly and speaks too soon, Tarbox distinguishes his own powers of observation, his privileged access to universal knowledge, and, in an Emersonian will to power, his possession of himself. If the drummers have been chosen, Tarbox chooses himself, promotes his own history, and so participates in the creation of fiction.[32]

Cable's representation of commercial power, then, draws on the salesman's improvisational talents only to contrast them with a more individualistic— and more legitimate—self-producing economic authority. The commercial tourist's ability to read and respond to human character is at bottom typical of the profession; his ubiquity is finally contained within a domesticated interior. Still, the loose ends to this solution remain, consisting, as they do for all Pennivilles represented in late nineteenth-century local-color writing, in once and future connections to an economic system that simultaneously enables the isolation of a locale and sustains its existence. The traveling salesman proved a most vivid human reminder that the integrity of a place was a function of its perceived dependence on a transregional commercial system. The problem for literature was how to represent this complicity or, put another way, how to avoid representing it. Even by objectifying and condemning the salesman, the problem persisted in the dynamics of representation. Whereas writers distanced salesmen from small-town norms by presenting them as urban outsiders, they had little choice but to acknowledge the drummer's place on Main Street—a tension evident in the sensory nature of their prose.

It is this sense of complicity that informs what is perhaps the most subtle and then again the most revealing occasional use of the traveling salesman in late nineteenth-century American literature: in Stephen Crane's 1898 short story "The Bride Comes to Yellow Sky." Crane's story is simultaneously a parody of western pulp fiction and a dramatization of regional historical change.[33] And it is the drummer's role as a middleman in the story that indicates the volatility of this dual purpose. In telling of Sheriff Jack Potter's marriage and his nervous return to Yellow Sky in a gleaming Pullman car with his bride, Crane insinuates the death of the Old West, a demise symbolized by Scratchy Wilson's refusal to engage Potter in their familiar, ritualistic play of guns. Now bound to the "environment of their new estate," a life of middle-class comfort anticipated and epitomized by the interior of their parlor car— "dazzling fittings," "sea-green figured velvet," "wood that gleamed as darkly brilliant as the surface of a pool of oil"—Potter has given over the roughness of western bachelor living for domesticity and hence is unsuitable for combat. Through his portrayal of Potter and the westward-traveling railroad, Crane suggests that Yellow Sky has been domesticated not simply by civilized eastern values but also by an all-pervasive market system. The importance of railroad time in pacing the action and providing the characters with a shared schedule—the Potters and the townspeople alike anticipate the 3:42 P.M. arrival of the train—points to Crane's interest in portraying the standardization of frontier life. The Pullman car, which helped standardize railroad track size and middle-class notions of domestic comfort, likewise represents this trend toward systemization, and Scratchy Wilson's shirt, manufactured on the lower East Side in New York, and his boots, also worn by boys in New England, suggest that Yellow Sky is well on its way toward becoming part of a national market economy and diminishes the sense that the Potters's arrival signifies dramatic, cultural change. Even the appearance of the town, in particular the "vivid green grass-plots" that stand across from the town saloon, shows the emergence of material well-being and middle-class respectability. Potter's marriage, which, like a business deal, is a finished "transaction," may be more a product of Yellow Sky than its tough-and-tumble western heritage suggests.[34]

The drummer, a talkative "foreigner" shown regaling a group of townsmen in the Weary Gentleman Saloon, sets the stage for the confrontation between Potter and Wilson. As the drummer learns of the feud between Wilson and Potter so does the reader—and the suspense builds.[35] The drummer effects more than a narrative bridge, however; his place in the middle of the story represents the point of transition between Wilson's older, western style and Potter's newly minted, bourgeois estate. That Wilson's attire already signifies commercial involvement implies that this exchange has been ongoing—that the drummer's presence in Yellow Sky is in fact familiar. Crane calls the drummer a "new-comer" and explains that he "leaned gracefully upon the bar, and recited many tales with the confidence of a bard who has come on a new field," yet the repetition of the word *new* suggests the same kind of parodic irony that attends Scratchy's western getup, Potter's new estate, Yellow Sky's economic boosterism, or, for that matter, the status of the story as a western adventure tale—none are wholly new, for they manifest and extend prior commercial efforts and patterns. Although this traveling man may be new to town, his yarn telling is a familiar, tedious refrain (certainly his graceful pose against the bar indicates that he has performed this role many times

The drummer holding forth in Crane's short story "The Bride Comes to Yellow Sky." From *McClure's Magazine* (February 1898). (Courtesy of Newberry Library.)

before); except for his immediate companions, the rest of the town "was dozing."[36] True to his stereotypic role in the culture, however, the drummer assumes that he has come upon a new field and, despite the weariness of the saloon, gives his old stories fresh energy (as saleswork requires).

Here, Crane may well have employed the drummer's ubiquity to reflect comically and perhaps subversively on the writer's place in the literary marketplace. By comparing the drummer to a bard, Crane implies that the analogy may work the other way—that the writer working in an established genre, as Crane does in "The Bride Comes to Yellow Sky," shares the salesman's problem of making his work new and grabbing the attention of an audience who has seen it all before. On the other hand, the crucial difference between the two, as Crane also indicates, resides in the author's capacity to treat his unoriginality in an ironic fashion. Crane's literary perspective affords a self-consciousness of method and material that is finally unavailable to the salesman, who must win his listeners' confidence by persuading them of the originality and sincerity of his appeal. To be sure, the sincere appeal may rest on a cynical understanding of the work that has gone before it, but Crane suggests that the drummer—"innocent and jocular"—lacks both self-awareness and an understanding of Yellow Sky.[37] Unlike his companions he hides in fright when he hears of the conflict between Wilson and Potter, taking seriously what Crane is at pains to poke fun at. Significantly, Jack Potter also fears the impending confrontation. He, like the drummer, is a middleman (albeit a consumer) caught up in and enabling a historical transformation that he cannot see. In this respect, "The Bride Comes to Yellow Sky" reflects an existential condition common in Crane's fiction: human beings with limited agency performing acts for purposes they scarcely understand. The drummer in this story focuses the commercial forces that give shape to this condition, which points once again to the observer's complicity in a market culture that seemed to both demand and resist criticism.

The drummer's limited fictional role especially exemplified his covert importance for writers entangled with the problem of how to represent the diminishing autonomy of small-town life. Less ambivalent critics framed the problem starkly. For them the drummer represented an expansive urban commercial system set to colonize the hinterland culturally as well economically, hence the populist stance adopted by critics like Hamlin Garland. In general, Garland depicted traveling salesmen as rough examples of manhood who "swore cordially," "snarled," and, when confronted with an unattached woman, could become like animals. In "Fair Exile," one of several stories collected in *Other Main-Travelled Roads* (1892), when a group of drummers see an attractive, well-dressed woman seated alone in a railroad car the "tip" is "passed along from lip to lip." They "were like wild beasts roused by the presence of prey. Their eyes gleamed with relentless lust. They eyed the little creature with ravening lust. Her helplessness was their opportunity." The image of the salesman courting the girls on Main Street or mashing unaccompanied women on trains was common in late nineteenth-century popular fiction, but Garland offers something more. The hybrid prose, which fuses commercial argot to expressions of instinctual desire—female helplessness becomes like business opportunity, while "lip" is conjoined to "tip"—establishes a naturalized foundation for the salesmen's rapacity and Garland's cultural criticism.[38] The view promoted here of unfettered masculine power threatening the feminine is more pointedly treated in *Rose of Dutcher's Coolly* (1895), where in describing a drummer's gaze of "breathless admiration" at the brilliant, small-town heroine, Garland implies that to return this gaze is also to give in to a larger social desire to abandon home.[39] The salesman becomes a touchstone of hinterland anxiety about urban influence. Rose does eventually leave for Chicago, however (and, like Howard McLane, becomes involved in the arts), which goes to show just how tenuous this defense of indigenous values could be. As Garland himself knew, the road leading from small towns to cities was fluid; the dichotomy between hinterland and urban center was possible only because the two had always been commercially linked. Garland's own struggle over the conflicting claims of his native hinterland, the Middle Border, and the urban, literary career that he pursued suggest a personal investment in his ambivalent representation of drummers.[40] His coy portrayal of Howard McLane as would-be drummer (and guilty prodigal son) suggests his own identification with commercial traveling and the disengagement from native, domestic bonds that such a life entailed. At bottom, however, the resemblance was only passing; Howard McLane is not really a drummer, and Rose of Dutcher's Coolly finally leaves for Chicago to realize deep-seated literary talents, not in response to cheap, dining-room glances.

Thus the distance between critics and the traveling man whom they represented was vast; indeed, the figure scarcely seemed to deserve notice—and yet there the drummer was, playing a vivid if minor role in fictional landscapes. To amuse an urban audience, a 1884 *Judge* cartoon entitled "A Drummer's Experience in a Country Village" (see fig.) had the effect of caricaturing both the traveling salesman and the rural citizenry, who gawk at his arrival and then make his stay in the village miserable. Images like these make clear how important hinterland imagery was to urban critics who, in denying the drummer's metropolitan origins, were concerned with asserting their cosmopolitan and class interests against a commercial type who had abandoned all claims to gentility. The same genteel standards pertain to Owen Wister's denigrating portrait twenty years later—both the town and the drummer are slovenly—as Wister idealized a picturesque frontier and the virtues of the strenuous life in the face of a debilitating, intrusive commercialism.

The opening scenes of *The Virginian: A Horseman of the Plains* (1902) contrast the "squalor" of Medicine Bow with the natural beauty of the surrounding plains, and Wister's genteel eastern narrator gives these two landscapes representative men. Amid the "false front" houses and dingy stores,

"A Drummer's Experience in a Country Village," *Judge* (June 14, 1884). (Courtesy of Library of Congress.)

the four drummers who have come to make the town—"two Jews handling cigars, one American with killer consumption, and a Dutchman with jew'lry"—are perfectly at ease. Filth "was nothing to them." Wister links the drummer's "leering stories" and "celluloid good fellowship" to the shabby frontier town, paralleling its pretensions to communal respectability with the drummers' sullied manhood; both are essentially false and unnatural.[41] On the other hand, Wister's Virginian, is one of the "sons of the sagebrush . . . who live nearer nature, and they know better." He is everything the drummers are not: quiet, clean, and strong. No "dinginess of travel" can "tarnish" the Virginian's splendor, and whereas he requests—and receives—a fresh towel, the drummers are content to dry their faces with a "degraded" roller towel. And when one of the drummers (the American one) claims to recognize the Virginian, saying that he remembers seeing him around the Chicago stockyards, Wister's hero dismisses the possibility, thereby distancing himself from the salesman and from the implication that he was employed as a middleman, delivering beef to the market.[42]

Wister's representation of the drummer, among the most negative in American literature, was by no means a fictional contrivance. Wister drew the material for his novel from his own trip west during the late 1880s, a venture into the strenuous life designed to restore his health following a nervous breakdown. In the journal that Wister kept of this trip, he condemned the "damned drummers" whom he frequently encountered and for whom he was sometimes mistaken. "There is no escaping these fetid commercial bores," Wister complained. "Their song is always the same—booms in Kansas City, dead times in Omaha, skinned Yankees in the South, capital moving to Denver—and outside these facts that nobody but a fellow brother of the spawn cares to hear, their minds are a howling wilderness." More important, Wister continued, "these people produce nothing, improve nothing, and help nothing, except when they help themselves to somebody else's money by menacing—cheap juggling on the one hand, and silly credulity on the other."[43] Wister's condemnation rested on a cross section of prejudices, ranging from xenophobia (and anti-Semitism) to classism to a disdain for petty commercialism, that describes the drummer's dramatic otherness in fiction: an uncleanness, or (in Wister's words) a "hateful taint," that made the profession taboo.

And yet Wister condemned only some commercial practices. Indeed, by the end of the novel, the Virginian has become a powerful businessman who owns coal-rich land and has a "strong grip on many various enterprises." Wister's celebration of this kind of man pays tribute not only to the "vanished" West of the 1870s and 1880s but also to the myth of the self-made man. In the Virginian, the cowboy and the businessman come together in a union that the tenderfoot narrator (or Wister) foreshadows in the first scene of the novel, when through a Pullman window, he watches a cowboy expertly rope a pony. The narrator calls the cowboy's movements "the undulations of a tiger, smooth and easy," while another passenger comments: "That man knows his business."[44] Broad and powerful, the movements of this kind of businessman —a producer and mover of wealth rather than a parasitic middleman— fascinated Wister while the smaller, degraded gestures, and even the language, of commercial travelers repulsed him. The coalescence of Wister's anxiety about hyphenated Americans (at a time when immigrants from southern and eastern Europe were transforming the appearance of American culture) with this deeply entrenched distaste for trade assured the drummer's status as an alien on the landscape.

Nearly always, then, the drummer was an object of ambivalent feelings, if not scorn, in late nineteenth-century representations, a type whose perceived limitations of character were frequently joined to broader anxieties about the emergence of a national marketplace. Sometimes the traveling salesmen figured as a subject and principal character in literature, but then only in domesticated form, without the commercial aspects of self that made him so objectionable to critics. Edward Everett Hale's 1877 novel, *G.T.T.; or, The Wonderful Adventures of a Pullman*, features a pharmaceutical salesman in a principal role but has little to do with commercial traveling or any issues related to the marketplace.[45] In other literature where traveling men occupy prominent positions, the same strictures apply; the narratives serve as genteel travel romances, and the drummers as convenient plot devices.[46] In the title to his 1884 novel *A Commercial Trip with an Uncommercial Ending*, George H. Bartlett humorously speaks of the difficulties of making commercial traveling the basis for popular fiction. The story concerns the partner of a New York mercantile firm who temporarily replaces one of his traveling salesmen only to discover that "all the good rules relating to eating and sleeping could not be followed by a commercial traveler" and yearns for his normal routine as a "gentleman of leisure."[47] By the end, he has renounced commercial traveling, fallen in love, and returned to his former existence, but not without comically dramatizing some of the customs of the road—and his inability to follow them.

The sales self's unsuitability for conventional popular fiction was likewise made clear in at least half a dozen adventure stories that feature drummers as heroes, but in roles only marginally related to commercial traveling. Novels such as *The Drummer Detective; or, The Dead Straight Trail* and *The Get-There Sharp; or, Grip Sack Sid at Rocky Comfort,* published in 1888 and 1890, replicate Deadwood Dicks, launching slick salesmen into Wild West towns to perform heroic deeds.[48] The veteran dime novelist Joseph Badger describes Gripsack Sid Harper, a detective from Chicago who masquerades as a drummer, mixing the images and language of two worlds. Sid's "neat 'grip-sack' of alligator leather which hung against his left hip" evokes the pose of a gunslinging cowboy while his "easy, glib conversation" marks him "as one of that nearly ubiquitous class known as 'drummers.'"[49] In two tongues, western and com-

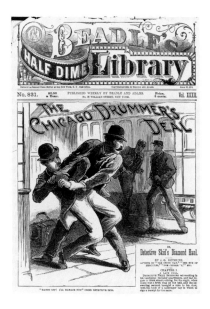

Such dime novels as *The Chicago Drummer's Deal* (1893) offered a heroic view of the drummer. (Chicago Historical Society.)

mercial slang, Sid asks, "What do you think of this for a sample, pardner?"[50] Multivoiced and multi-imaged, the salesman that evolved within the dime novel showed readers a broad-gauged hero at work in a familiar dramatic setting; they saw, in short, a wholesale revision of the drummer's commercial improvisations that had nothing to do with the expanding market system or the misgivings that people had of the ubiquitous salesman.

The drummer's marketability as a hero or principal character in popular entertainment forms required the rejection or domestication of the very traits that constituted his place in the marketplace. As the object of humor and criticism, the traveling man might appear as many onlookers found him: as a disruptive, even threatening presence on the American scene. To command the sympathy and attention of readers and audiences, to be a central figure in fiction or drama, however, the salesman was depicted at a distance from his place as a middleman. To be a central figure in fiction or drama—and to appeal to a buying public—the drummer had to be something other than his commonly represented self.

More than any single sketch or story written between 1880 and 1900, George Jessop's play *Sam'l of Posen; or, The Commercial Drummer* dramatizes the tensions involved in foregrounding the salesman as hero. First produced in New York on May 16, 1881, *Sam'l of Posen* played to appreciative audiences throughout the 1880s and became a career-launching venture for the lead actor, M. B. Curtis. In 1883, Curtis purchased the copyright from Jessop, and well into the 1890s continued to revise and repackage both the play and its lead character, Samuel Plastrick.[51] Curtis's efforts were so successful that in 1885 a correspondent for *Frank Leslie's Illustrated Newspaper* could claim that Americans' knowledge of the traveling man derived from three sources: direct observation, newspaper humor, and "Mr. M. B. Curtis's broad but clever sketch of 'Sam'l of Posen.'"[52]

Sam'l of Posen is a comic melodrama. Clever, brave, well-dressed, determined, and witty, Jessop's drummer turns his improvisational talents to good works and saves a jewelry store from catastrophe by exposing a villainous nephew's plot to claim the firm. Although Plastrick never pauses in his efforts to sell something or make a profit, his honesty and good heart distance his acts from purely commercial motives. To the extent that Samuel is, as he declares, "always open for business," Jessop's play strives to incorporate the improvisational practices of drumming.[53] But as one reviewer shrewdly noted after a 1894 production of the play, Plastrick was not true to life. Essentially a comic type, his "unctuous speech, his quick comprehensive glance, and his free use of the peripatetic vernacular which drummers are supposed to use to excess" made him something of a caricature. He was not an accurate representation of "anything seen in the respectable or fairly honest commercial line," nor was he a fair depiction of a German-Jewish immigrant; rather, the reviewer went on to say, he was a cultural type, a character whose "supposed" features, though not realistic, made him a familiar figure.[54]

Jessop's dialogue confirms the impression that Plastrick is an enlarged, somewhat revised version of the humorous figure already described by Charles Follen Adams and others. Early in the play, Jessop demonstrates his intentions to make selling the occasion for verbal and physical humor.

> **Samuel:** You want to buy some shoulder-braces? Three for a dollar.
> **Fitzurse:** No, sir. I don't care for them.
> **Samuel:** Well, everybody knows his business best. If you want to buy any Boston garters, two pair for a quarter. They have brass buckles and attach at both ends. They never break to pieces. You want to buy?

Rebuffed but persistent, Samuel tries to sell other products.

> **Samuel:** Well, everybody know his business best. Would you like some rolled plate collar buttons? I'll sell you three for ten cents.
> **Fitzurse:** No. I don't wear them.
> **Samuel:** Don't wear them? How do you keep your shirt on without collar buttons?
> **Fitzurse:** You are a horrid fellow.

The drummer "stick[s] it to him" until he makes the sale, thus emphasizing the unifying, comically rendered message of the play: everybody's business belongs to the traveling man.[55]

Although Jessop's drummer is indeed a type and is thus limited in scope, there is little doubting his difference from other humorously cast salesman. For one thing, he is not briefly seen; he is the primary character and hero. For another, Jessop gives the drummer wider volitional scope, though, to be sure, this involvement mainly serves melodramatic ends. Finally and most important, as an 1894 reviewer recognized, *Sam'l of Posen* was a commercial success because it embellished and refigured an already established cultural type. Curtis's presentation of the drummer, in this sense, was both a self-conscious supplement to Jessop's original 1881 script and a market-driven revision made possible by the steady accretion of cultural materials related to the commercial traveler. The title of Curtis's 1894 production was *Sam'l of Posen, the Drummer Up to Date*—and for a good reason.[56] Curtis apparently made every effort to evoke the drummer's cultural image but did not want to call to mind the salesman's more threatening qualities.

The surviving playbill from Curtis's production is a multilayered presentation of the traveling salesman's cultural image. On the front of the program is a picture of Samuel Plastrick, drawn to accentuate the salesman's stereotypic ethnic characteristics (swarthy features, hooked nose) and illustrate his physical role as a traveling man (holding his sample cases). On the back is printed Charles Follen (mistakenly, Francis) Adams's poem "Der Drummer." Inside the program is a Drummer's Balance Sheet, humorously listing the salesman's vital statistics—for instance, number of cigars smoked in a day, number of

Cover and detail from *Sam'l of Posen* playbill. (Warshaw Collection of Business Americana, Archives Center, National Museum of American History, Smithsonian Institution.)

THE COMMERCIAL DRUMMER.

DRUMMER'S BALANCE SHEET.

Miles travelled	2,250	Suits of clothes made	2
Number of trunks	2	Goods sold for other	
Shown samples	61	firms	$5,600
Sold goods	34	Commissions from	
Been asked the news	56	rival firms	280
Told the news	3	Salary $6 per day for	
Lied	33	forty days	240
Didn't know	20	Saved from daily ex-	
Been asked to drink	11	penses	120
Drank	11	Money put in savings	
Changed politics	17	bank	500
Changed religion	3	Cash on hand	70
Daily expenses allow-		Got drunk	11
ed by house	$9	Badly broken up	2
Daily expenses actual	6	Slipped out on hotel	
Been to church	0	keepers	4
Accompanied girls		Cigars smoked	200
from church home	17	Cigars given away	3
Girls flirted with	42	Number days actual	
Agreed to marry	2	work	32
Expected trouble with	1	Number days charged	
Kicked out of the		firm	40
house	2	Light wagons stove up	2
Left by back door	3	Attended horse races	11
Dodged fare on rail-		Made on bets	89
road	5	Lost on bets	55
Number of persons		My actual profit for	
cheated	34	forty days	640
Tried to cheat	61	Firm's actual profit	
Hats ordered	3	for forty days	610

Hast du Geschn,
SAM'L OF POSEN.

customers cheated—together with a thumbnail sketch of the typical drummer's life. "He is usually slung to a satchel," and when joined by other drummers, they "swap lies about the big bills of goods they have sold in the last town, and exhibit to each other the photographs of the last girls they made impressions on." Nonetheless, the salesman is an "energetic and genial cuss" representing the "growth of this fast age"—a figure, that is, which the producers assumed, and made the sure that, their audience recognized.[57]

What this collage of details finally says about the substance of self is less important than how the self is represented. Here, as was so often the case in the late nineteenth century, the traveling salesman proved inaccessible from any one perspective; his representative quality truly resided in the notion of growth and speed—always moving, always elusive. And yet as a figure whose constituent parts formed some kind of whole, it seems fair to say that viewers had the traveling salesman where they wanted him, where the accumulation of images had been leading: framed within some theatrical or linguistic space

Trade cards that drew from Jessop's play promoted the salesman's rakish reputation and circulated anti-Semitic images.

"DER DRUMMER IS DER MOST INNOCENT MAN IN THE WORLD."

TICKETS

G. A. WEED & CO ,

CLOTHING, HATS & CAPS

Eingham·on, N. Y.

Trade card. (Warshaw Collection of Business Americana, Archives Center, National Museum of American History, Smithsonian Institution.)

that provided visual evidence of an imaginative process that made the salesman larger than life. Like the foreign-born factory workers or the poor, who were reclaimed by middle-class reformers, the traveling man was thus Americanized and domesticated to meet prevailing cultural tastes. Especially during the 1890s and into the early twentieth century, anxieties about ethnic identity helped motivate representations of drummers. Beyond concerns about ethnicity, however, lay deep-rooted reservations about the salesman's role as an economic middleman. Since the emergence of the drummer in the antebellum mercantile city, critics had struggled along similar lines to understand this new species of economic man. Only now, more than ever before, the criticism spread outward from urban centers, helping make the traveling man a national icon. The importance of such mythmaking lay not only in its obfuscation of the actual business accomplished by salesman or in the over-

Trade card, around 1885. (Courtesy of Strong Museum, Rochester, N.Y.)

Trade cards dramatizing scenes from *Sam'l of Posen*. (Warshaw Collection of Business Americana, Archives Center, National Museum of American History, Smithsonian Institution.)

blown image, whether absolutely negative or fuzzily ambivalent, that it brought to Americans but also in the impact that it had on commercial traveling itself. If, in the long run, popular culture accentuated the vision of a profession exempt from domestic and community norms, traveling men had the task of correcting it.

5 For the Good of the Order

First in the crowded car is he to offer—
This traveling man, unhonored and unsung—
The seat he paid for, to some woman, young
Or old and wrinkled. He is the first to proffer
Something—a trifle from his samples, may be—
To please the fancy of a crying baby.
He lifts the window and drops the curtain
For unaccustomed hands. He lends his "case"
To make a bolster for a child, not certain
But its mamma will frown him in the face;
So anxiously some women seek for danger
In every courteous act of a stranger.
Well versed is he in all the ways conducive
To comfort where least comfort can be found.
His little deeds of thoughtfulness abound.
He turns the seat unasked, yet unobtrusive,
Is glad to please you, or to have you please him,
Yet takes it very calmly if you freeze him.
He smooths the Jove-like frown of the official
By paying the fare of one who cannot pay.
True modesty he knows from artificial;
Will flirt, of course, if you're inclined that way,
And if you are, be sure that he detects you;
And if you're not, be sure that he respects you.
The sorrows of the traveling world distress him;
He never fails to lend what aid he can.
A thousand hearts to-day have cause to bless him,
This much-abused, misused "commercial man."
I do not seek to cast a halo 'round him,
But speak precisely as I've found him.
—Ella Wheeler Wilcox, "The Commercial Traveler" (1901)

The illustrations to George M. Hayes's 1884 account of commercial traveling, *Twenty Years on the Road,* present two different views of masculine work culture. The first, seen on the cover, shows a cigar-smoking drummer balancing his sample cases (see fig.). It points to a colorful life of pleasure consistent with the drummer's notoriety in popular culture. The second, contained within this portrait of worldly freedom, is a picture of the author holding a baby, and erroneously taken, Hayes humorously points out, for a "foundling asylum." Among traveling men the image was a tongue-in-check reminder of the profession's reputation, for more than any other working man, the drummer epitomized—and attenuated—the movement away from home. On the road or with customers, commercial travelers were either traveling men or boys, members of a distinctly masculine business culture whose fraternal practices

Cover, *Twenty Years on the Road* (1884), by George M. Hayes. (Courtesy of Library of Congress.)

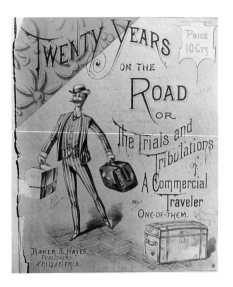

From George M. Hayes, *Twenty Years on the Road* (1884). (Courtesy of Library of Congress.)

—dirty-joke telling, drinking, and womanizing—appeared exempt from domestic or feminine influences. Although more women than men worked in retail sales, men dominated commercial traveling; throughout the nineteenth century women accounted for only 1 percent of the national force of commercial travelers, and by 1910 their participation totaled just 2 percent.[1] From this perspective, even to suggest that salesmen were tied to the domestic sphere would seem ludicrous.

Yet if for some salesmen the union of home and road provoked laughter, the profession itself came to take the conjunction seriously—as a business proposition. Indeed, between 1870 and 1900 in trade journals like the *Sample Case* and the *Traveling Man,* such professional organizations as the United Order of Commercial Travelers offered advice on business ethics and sales techniques and promoted what can only be called a sentimental or domesticated work culture. In spite of the apparent absence of home values from commercial traveling—and often because of it—concerned salesmen declared their commitment to family and home and called for the influence of domestic values in business relationships. Aware not only of the scurrilous reputation that followed them on the road but also that this reputation was in some cases well deserved, traveling men strove during the late nineteenth century and well into the twentieth to refashion their professional image and distance themselves from "unprofessional" sales practices—like drinking and joke telling. In refining their sales techniques and distinguishing them from more vernacular modes of persuasion—those practiced by peddlers, street-corner fakirs, and patent-medicine vendors—traveling men simultaneously professionalized their occupation and helped to domesticate commercial practices. By the early twentieth century, sales reformers eschewed the moniker *drummer,* preferring instead to think of themselves as modern salesmen whose methods and techniques were consistent with modern business enterprise. Reform of the profession took place alongside and in reaction to the growth and rationalization of the American economy, which gathered momentum in the closing years of the nineteenth century.

But the infusion of domestic values into the culture of commercial traveling had a significance that reached beyond business methods per se. Negotiating the boundaries between spheres was commercial travelers' most pressing dilemma, a problem that, transcending product lines and business differences, went straight to the salesman's status as a respectable member of society and the occupational struggle to fashion a professional identity. By his dislocation from the most sacred of all American institutions—the home—the commercial traveler inevitably triggered distrust and, through drummer laws and various literary and cultural expressions that cast him as a tawdry character, achieved a separate life as the object of cultural representation. To see the traveling salesman as solely the object of domestic ideology, a marginalized figure, however, is to miss his importance as the subject of the dominant cultural idiom. To be sure, traveling men felt the limits of their power in the ambivalence that they often aroused. But as members of an ascendant busi-

Cover, *Commercial Travelers Magazine* (September 1883), the first trade journal to address the professional interests of traveling salesmen. (Courtesy of Library of Congress.)

ness class who grasped the rhetoric of domesticity as their own and made it a natural part of their professional discourse and identity, they proved volitional actors in their own behalf. In this sense, traveling men denied any strict division between home and work—even as they sought to overcome those differences—and capitalized on the fluid, discursive nature of domestic ideology, drawing power from what Linda Kerber has called the "metaphor" of "separate spheres."[2] Thus salesmen participated in the wider cultural debate over the relation between the increasing presence of the market economy and the long-standing cultural commitment to home and hearth. Literally and figuratively, they struggled to make the road their home and asserted domestic identifications to stabilize and consolidate the place of their profession in the American scene.[3]

While the institutional effort to domesticate sales culture may seem to have grown from purely instrumental, if not cynical, motives, a complex blending of gender- and work-related roles made the attempt more than a public relations effort. Both the product of rapid market expansion and a response to its effects, the impulse to create a home sprang from the everyday rhythms of the work, from the atmosphere of transience and dislocation. Along the railroad corridors and Main Streets, in depots, hotels, and stores, thrown together by shared business customs and common work patterns, traveling men derived comfort and strength from makeshift social gatherings and fostered a collective identity not unlike the solidarity that working-class men derived from their job experiences. Separation from home life, from wives, families, and loved ones, accentuated the need for community. Male business culture—what salesmen frequently called fellowship or fraternity or brotherhood—helped fill the gap, posing an alternative and even a potential threat to sedentary home life. But to the extent that fraternal relationships presented a substitute for absent domestic structures and, according to nineteenth-century conceptions of manhood, encouraged sobriety, restraint, and self-control, they actually reinforced home values. Seen in this way, the man on the road—even as he physically moved away from his loved ones, even while he cultivated a culture of some intimacy among his peers—had little choice but to acknowledge the power of domestic virtue.

Regarding this issue of masculine consciousness, the traveling salesman was stuck in the middle: drawn forward and back between an all-male world of business and travel and a domestic sphere of family and nurture. This bifurcated image is a metaphorical figure for a fluid, emotional matrix, which the salesman had always to negotiate. The salesman's domesticity (or, for that matter, his commercial spirit) was not an essentialized or easily isolated attribute. Rather, it was a potent force that compelled him to honor its code in a occupation that was simultaneously pulling him away from the physical origins of home. Insofar as any culturally shaped emotion may be considered natural, the traveling man's attachment to domestic values was exactly that: real and authentic. Socialized in "the cradle" of middle-class values, as Mary Ryan has put it, a good many traveling men had every right to think of themselves as natural defenders of domestic values even after they left home.[4]

Thus the idea of home could have a powerful, albeit frustrating, impact on how salesmen experienced their work. Edward Clark, whose work selling books by subscription during the early 1880s technically placed him outside commercial traveling but who nonetheless referred to himself as an irrepressible drummer, described these frustrations well. Writing to his brother from Lawrence, Kansas, Clark complained about traveling back and forth over the midwestern landscape without being able to behold its expected beauty. Wistfully imagining that "three months from now the eyes of the traveller as he speeds across these broad plains will be greeted by magnificent fields of golden grain stretching on either side as far as the eye can reach," Clark was careful to distance himself from this hypothetical traveler, for he knew that three months thence he would have business elsewhere. Instead, he settled for a more realistic anticipation, the knowledge that by Sunday he would be at home with his family. His stay there would be short, for he expected to begin a trip the following week to Illinois, "and by the time I have completed that, I must needs repeat the one which I am now about completing." For Clark, the ironies of road life consisted not only in having to downplay the pleasures of seeing the world at sixty miles an hour but also in being constantly aware of the home he had left behind. Home was not an abandoned site that periodically returned in memory as a sentimental object of affection but an internal structure that needed constant emotional maintenance, which the salesman earnestly, if somewhat anxiously, supplied. Traveling over two thousand miles in one month, visiting thirty-two towns in four states, and staying up five nights in ten caused Clark to complain to his brother that "the same routine will be repeated as the months roll on. You can well imagine that when I occasionally get a day to spend with my family I make the most of it."[5] For Clark, as for John Kirk, homesickness was a constant condition that shaped the patterns of work. Traveling to sell was as much an exploration of duties, shaped and restrained by an internal domestic landscape, as it was an outward journey into commercial territory.

The records that E. Barton Martin left of his travels through the district of Austin and the interior of eastern Texas during the 1870s and 1880s epitomize the tension between home and work that many commercial travelers struggled to negotiate.[6] Frontier travel conditions and Martin's absence from home made road life a pioneer effort. "I don't know if I ever was so miserable before," he wrote his wife, Julia, in 1876. "I work, work, work, and try to drown my troubles by constant employment but that tearful face I left on the sofa is ever before me."[7] At times melodramatic, Martin's attempts to assuage his wife's loneliness and care for her uncertain health—all at a distance—magnify the daily anxieties that traveling men felt when they left home.

To cut short the distance that separated them, Martin wrote his wife frequently and performed domestic chores on the road. The location of the Martin home in San Marcos, just north of Austin, made this effort to maintain domestic ties easier. Because his territory included San Marcos—an arrangement that satisfied his Galveston employer, the dry-goods house P. J. Willis and Brother—Martin knew the area and the people and could make his home a departure point for selling trips into the interior. Moreover, as he told his father-in-law, he got to see more of his family "than I would if they were in Galveston."[8] When he traveled, he compensated for his absence by passing on the regards of friends, shopping for furniture, and even arranging for his wife to borrow money from one of his San Marcos customers.[9]

Striving to maintain a natural marital relationship even as he traveled from place to place, Martin understood that the letters he wrote his wife took the place of the everyday face-to-face conversations they would have had across a dinner table had he been home. "I never think of what I am going to write to you when I commence a letter to you," he promised, "but just write ahead as if I was having a 'chat' with you."[10] Whether from a small hotel in the Texas interior or from his rooms in Galveston, Martin wrote earnestly of his social and business affairs. He described his reactions when a customer ran out on a bill, confessed to "having the blues" when he could not sell shoes, bragged when the firm accepted his idea for an advertising circular, and gloated when he became P. J. Willis and Brother's most successful salesman.[11] Inevitably, Julia Martin knew her husband's business. And whether or not she wanted to help, he enlisted her support, asking her once, in fact, to persuade a merchant to wait for him and not buy from another salesman.[12]

Thus Julia Martin became an active presence in her husband's territory. When Martin was gone, he wrote her in detail about his travel plans, creating a verbal map that Julia could trace at home while he followed it on the road. "My trip is already made out," Martin informed her when he described his "regular spring boot and shoe trip" of 1880. "I first stop at *Hockly* then *Homestead, Chappel Hill & Brenham.*" From Brenham "I have to take a team and go to *Caldwell, Lexington, Ellee* and *Krohm's P. O.*, striking the R.R. again at *Burton*, then *Ledbetter, Giddings, McDade, Manor, & Austin*, from there I run out to see you, and back to *Round Rock*, and regularly around my frontier trip." By underlining his destinations and explaining how long he would take to make each town, Martin endeavored to bring home that much closer to work. Later that spring, lonely and estranged, he wrote to Julia from Bagdad that "if you will notice on the map you will find this place is much nearer you than you would suppose on noticing it so far along on my list."[13]

Although not all traveling men professed this sort of commitment to home and family and although very few wives made so concrete a contribution to their husband's business as Julia Martin did, there is no doubt that the link between home and work served as the unseen professional ballast. On the one hand, these ties could be as solid as the letters that wives sent to their husbands—written reminders of the life left behind that provided emotional support and practical advice. On the other hand, domesticity asserted its power elusively and subtly, as a force capable of ordering experience and constituting selfhood. Beyond their declaration of faith, domestic-minded salesmen placed their loyalty to home at the center of consciousness. In "A Drummer's Constancy," a poem written in the late 1880s, the salesman John Dewitt maintained that "Though he's obliged to roam, / The "drummer" loves his home, / And worships his own wife's attractive face." Challenging readers to "peep into some traveller's watch-case," he promised that where you will find a picture hid; / I guarantee 'twill be his wife's sweet face." An 1884 song entitled "The Traveling Man; or, What Are the Little Ones Doing at Home?" contains a similar declaration of faith. In defending domestic solidarity, Thomas S. Quincy, a member of the Northwestern Traveling Men's Association, promised: "Faithful I'll be though temptors assail me. Home, Honor and Love ever first in my pride."[14] The illustration to Quincy's sheet music dramatizes commercial traveling as a movement into the world—indeed, the marketplace—that internalizes domestic morality (see fig.). The four-part tableau juxtaposes the landscape of travel to the domestic treasures left behind—wife, children, piano, and toys—but with the effect of integrating them and fixing home permanently in the salesman's mind. Whereas the road leading from home is figured here in allegorical terms, as a place of temptation, the salesman inhabits a different imaginative space, a work culture in which the differences between home and marketplace have blurred, where, as Quincy would have it, a salesman's order book—depicted at the center of the illustration—continually prompts the question "What are the little ones doing at home?"

Sheet music for Thomas S. Quincy's 1884 song about a homesick traveling man. (Minnesota Historical Society.)

Traveling men frequently gravitated to this sort of spatial metaphor when representing the relation between home and the road. Husbands writing their wives would refer to the picture or memento that they brought with them and displayed in their hotel rooms. "I am sitting and writing you with a nice little set of pictures before me," George Hood wrote to his wife in 1862. "So you see I have my little family before me although away so far from you."

Men who treasured photographs from home imagined them as people and missed the images when they were gone. William White lamented the absence of his tabletop companion and, writing to his sister, asked her to "please return the picture soon—it travels with me." Traveling men describing their days on the road, as Howard Peak did in his memoir *A Ranger of Commerce; or, Fifty-Two Years on the Road,* remembered the Bibles that they carried in their gripsacks—perhaps next to a flask of whisky.[15] Tongue-in-cheek alternatives to earnest defenses of domestic piety even found their way into the marketplace—as in an advertisement for Drummers Pride cigars reproduced here (see fig.).

By such close juxtapositions, of Bibles to whisky or babies to cigars, traveling men pointed to the slippery texture of life on the road, an existence in which domestic values were both a wedge against all that was transient, temporary, and possibly immoral and the basis for commercial reform. There were, of course, good business reasons for avoiding liquor and gambling: physical and financial dissipation threatened economic solvency. Nevertheless, such practices were a part of sales culture—for customers as well as salesmen—and had been since the antebellum period, when country merchants visiting New

York and other mercantile cities were treated to urban pleasures by whole-salers' drummers. As leisure activities, they seemed peculiarly suited to the rhythms of road life. In describing the "advent of Sabbath" in Maltoon, Indiana, one weekend in 1881, Edward Clark shrewdly identified the source of temptation. "Sunday is usually a day of uneasiness to the average traveling man," wrote Clark, "and I am sorry to say in many cases an unfortunate day—especially to the younger portion of them. Feeling the need of recreation, they seek for it, alas, as the sequel invariably proves, where it does not exist, namely in the social glass and the gambling table, and Monday morning frequently finds them utterly unfitted both in body & mind for that which they are employed and paid—and oftentimes disgraced by having appropriated that which was not their own to unlawful uses."[16] Though couched in the language of moral reform, Clark's description of the perils of commercial traveling moves away from the objectifying rhetoric of critics like Henry Ward Beecher and toward a subjective engagement with sales culture itself. Clark objects to drinking and gambling for practical as well as moral reasons: both spoil salesmen for work and, even worse, tempt salesmen to draw from their expense accounts to pay debts and, in essence, steal from their employers. The assessment is reminiscent of antebellum anxiety over urban drummers, except that Clark assumes the importance of the job and sympathetically acknowledges its inherent pitfalls. By his attention to the wayward younger portion, Clark also suggests that gambling and drinking are potential occupational hazards, which may be bested with maturity and experience. Sunday's uneasiness becomes densely freighted, a reference not simply to immoral pursuits or to Clark's anxiety about Sabbath breaking but, first and perhaps foremost, to work patterns of commercial travelers. So accustomed is the average traveling man to the consuming pace of his job that a break in the rhythm turns a day of leisure into a time of unease. Here, idle hands indeed do the work of the devil, but the sins have more to do with the work culture itself than any moral framework.

Clark's discernment of the implicit dangers of the road went to the heart of the occupation's vexed identity. Indeed, something like his diagnosis figured as the starting point for the widespread effort within the profession to discipline the social movements of commercial travelers and create a shared business culture. Compared to the hierarchy, formality, and ritual that governed commercial travelers in Victorian England, American salesmen did appear to lack order. The commercial room reserved for traveling salesmen in British hotels, for instance, was a forum for strictly regulated behavior. There, under the leadership of the President (the longest resident in the hotel) and the Vice President (the most recent resident), travelers drank to the health of their colleagues, made sure to wish the entire room good morning and good night, and took care not to appear at breakfast in their bedroom slippers.[17] The absence of such a regimen in the United States goes a long way to explaining why traveling salesmen in this nation were, and perhaps still are, envied for their freedom and autonomy. It also points up the comparatively new, seemingly boundless, apparently democratic nature of the nineteenth-century market. In such an economy, face-to-face capitalism could easily look like American exceptionalism—liberated and unrestrained.

But the challenge of creating order among a mobile population of commercial travelers and finding a cure for the ills that Edward Clark identified had less to do with combating recalcitrant salesmen than with highlighting and nurturing components of a discourse that already existed. The salesman's independence was, after all, relative; it signified everything that traveling men appeared to escape: sedentary work patterns, domestic responsibilities, and so forth. The freedom of the road and the settled order of home reflected one another; imagining one called the other to mind. That drummers called themselves boys even while they expressed their devotion to home and family—that is, while accomplishing the work of men—reveals their difficulties in regarding the road as a wholly separate sphere. As E. Anthony Rotundo has argued, nineteenth-century "boy culture" paved the way to manhood by separating young males from direct adult supervision—in particular, the gentle, moralizing influence of mothers—and by establishing an intermediary proving ground for self-reliance and aggressive, spontaneous behavior. Being a man, however, also meant assimilating values learned in the home from the mother—sobriety, responsibility, cooperation, and restraint—that is, accommodating boy culture to the regulations of middle-class life. Business culture especially demanded this paradoxical hybrid of attributes; correct commercial conduct was the consolidation of behavior learned both within the maternal orbit and outside it—with other boys.[18]

When traveling salesmen talked of becoming boys, whether by trading stories, talking business, or drinking, they staked out a cultural space apart from domesticity and affirmed the difference of their occupation from others. Yet pursuing boyhood as an adult (figuratively returning to their youth) was hardly the same thing as participating in boy culture as a child. Not surprisingly, then, salesmen frequently referred to the oppositional character of their boyish transition into male fellowship with some irony, implicitly conceding that in the adult world of business there were limits to the free play of boyish qualities. Self-reliance, assertiveness, improvisational thinking, and mastery of the physical world were, to be sure, crucial to commercial traveling, more so perhaps than to other business professions. When carried beyond the bounds of sobriety and restraint, even during leisure time, however, boyish conduct had the potential to harm business interests, damage the civic image of the profession, and threaten masculine ideals. Thus while fascinated novelists, admiring observers, and traveling men themselves thrilled to the possibility that the boys on the road rotated beyond the bounds of ordinary existence, most salesmen knew better.

Sales reformers knew better still and insisted, by way of addressing the temptations of the road, that commercial travelers recall their responsibilities as businessmen, discipline boyish enthusiasm, and honor their commitment to home and profession. As traveling men and observers alike suggested, the high road to the male sales culture was thus an idealized, domesticated view of professional unity, best typified by fraternal rather than filial imagery. "Brethren, did I say. Yes, Brethren!" declared Charles N. Crewdson in *Tales of the Road,* his 1905 paean to fraternal relationships. "To the man on the road, every one he meets is his brother—no more, no less. He feels that he is as good as the governor, that he is no better than the boy who shines his shoes. The traveling man, if he succeeds, soon becomes a member of the Great Fraternity —the Brotherhood of Man." Even so ebullient a supporter had to admit that not all traveling men were "angels"; still, he argued that "in their black wings are stuck more white feathers than they are given credit for" and in general praised the moral fiber that enabled the majority of salesmen to avoid profligacy and dissipation, assuring his readers of the ethicality of the profession—and its solidarity.[19] Other traveling men used similarly effusive language. In an 1893 how-to book, one salesman called the social meetings of his fellow travelers a "feast of reason and flow of soul," and the same year Virgil Wright claimed in *Ten Years on the Road* that whether business was good or not, traveling men always enjoyed "a hearty shake of hands."[20]

In the same vein, the counter to negative representations of sales sociability were poems like Ella Wheeler Wilcox's "Commercial Traveler," quoted in the epigraph to this chapter, and James Whitcomb Riley's "Traveling Man" (1881), both of which promoted the commercial traveler's domestic values in terms that not only sentimentalized the separation from home but cast the salesman as an unsung hero. Although Wilcox's defense of the "much-abused" salesman—which features the train-traveling drummer not as a masher, as George Ade had him, but as a help with crying babies and distressed women—is the more obvious and, because it was written later, the more self-conscious attempt to reverse the critical discourse, Riley's poem also offers a revision of the salesman's image. In "The Traveling Man" Riley imagines an Olympian banquet where, amid the jokes and laughter of the traveling fraternity, the poet would "pour out the nectar the gods only can" and drink a toast to the salesman's success and "the house represented by him," as well as to the drummer's sweetheart or the family whom he leaves behind.[21] The visit by Riley's bard presupposes an intimate gathering of salesmen whose dedication to family any onlooker would recognize and whose good times on the road were only an extension of harmonious relationships at home. Echoing Riley's poem, a drawing published in a November 1885 issue of *Frank Leslie's Illustrated Newspaper,* entitled "The Commercial Drummer's Thanksgiving," likewise suggested that fraternal relationships were finally a surrogate form of domesticity. In an effort to capture a "bright spot in the commercial traveler's hurried, lightning-express kind of life," *Leslie's* artist depicted a group of five traveling men arranged around a blazing hearth in a snug Virginia inn.[22] Cigars in hand, sample trunks piled behind them, the drummers have yielded to the domestic comforts of the house. With knickknacks cast across the mantel and a buck's head hanging on the wall, one drummer spins his yarn while the others chuckle. As the waiter leaves the room to replenish drinks, he turns

Drummers trading sales tips in Crewdson's *Tales of the Road* (1905). (Collection of the author.)

around to share the joke. Together the salesmen appear to have forgotten the commercial world outside and absent families and, at least for the moment, established their own home on the road.

For the dozens of professional organizations that emerged after the Civil War, these peculiarly domestic scenes and, more important, the good-hearted men who occupied them, became the centerpiece of a fifty-year struggle to bring stability and respectability to commercial traveling. By providing mutual aid to traveling salesmen, fraternal organizations objectified the powerful, if ambiguous, relations between job and home. Both the product of social relationships established on the road and a force for occupational unity, these organizations protested discriminatory licensing laws, fought for discount travel rates, agitated for better hotel service, and gave salesmen a venue for discussing common business interests. Most of all, they offered members a "fraternal plan of home protection"—that is, life and accident insurance—which, from the perspective of the road, dramatized anxieties about domestic responsibilities as it worked to alleviate them.[23]

Commercial travelers addressed the need for group protection in the early 1870s while striving to promote their fledgling occupation. For instance, L. P. Brockett proposed establishing a "commercial travellers' mutual association,

At home on the road in "The Commercial Drummer's Thanksgiving," *Frank Leslie's Illustrated Weekly,* November 28, 1885. (Courtesy of Harvard College Library.)

organized not for the benefit of individuals or companies, but for the general good of the members of the profession." Managed by traveling men alone—"not by outsiders"—the association would have "no aim or object except their benefit in all possible ways." Brockett hoped in particular that commercial travelers would underwrite their own accident and life insurance—the risks of travel being "so great" that no salesman was "justified" in working without a policy—at rates lower than those available through public corporations.[24]

In 1871 this kind of insurance plan was still a relatively new idea, at least in the United States. Although fraternal organizations had flourished during the eighteenth and early nineteenth centuries, the first society to assess fees and pay claims—the Ancient Order of American Workmen—was not established until 1868. Unlike fraternal secret orders, which were primarily social and ritualistic in purpose, fraternal insurance associations, or mutual aid societies, as they were also called, promised tangible benefits. Similar in function to the ancient burial societies of Greece, the medieval guilds of Europe, and the friendly societies of England, the fraternal benefit associations that thrived in late nineteenth- and early twentieth-century America provided economic assistance to the dependents of members who died or suffered accidental injuries. Although life insurance companies assessed their policyholders on a regular basis, fraternal insurance societies typically charged members after a death. And although this method often proved actuarially unsound, societies typically resisted "graded-assessment plans" and "mortality charts." To adopt these methods meant treating poor risks differently and hence undermining the sense of equality that brought members together.[25] So fraternal benefit societies continued to cleave to their social and spiritual foundations and their "ritualistic form of work"—the sometimes elaborate ceremonies that dramatized solidarity—even when their "practical" plans to insure their members lacked the financial common sense that distinguished profit-oriented, commercial insurance companies.[26] In practice and in spirit, fraternal benefit societies throve on the principle of mutual assistance, of support ministered from within. And so, too, Brockett suggested, could traveling salesmen.

The appearance of two New York groups, first the Commercial Travelers National Association in 1870 and then the Commercial Travelers' Protective Association in 1875, seemed to answer Brockett's call. Through "the power of cohesion" on the one hand and "organization, combination, and cooperation" on the other, both groups vowed to cut salesmen's travel expenses and defray business costs. But neither organization pursued the idea of mutual benefit much beyond the promise of cheaper railroad fares and reduced hotel rates. Although the Protective Association hoped "to induce all travelers to get into the habit of regularly securing an 'accident policy'" and the National Association looked "forward to establishing a system of mutual benefits," neither one satisfied the need for an association managed solely from within —by commercial travelers. In essence, their propositions resembled investment opportunities, third-party proposals extended to merchants and commercial travelers alike. Eventually these organizations failed.[27]

Others survived and even flourished. Between 1880 and 1905, in cities and regions throughout the country, traveling salesmen established dozens of fraternal associations. Some remained purely fraternal and, like the Commercial Travelers Club of New York, sought to promote "social intercourse, good fellowship and benevolence" among its members.[28] Most, however, functioned as mutual benefit societies and not only declared their commitment to fraternal unity but also vowed to lend financial support to needy associates. Thus, while the Rochester Commercial Travelers' Mutual Benefit Association promised in its 1899 constitution "to bring about a more social and intimate acquaintance among the commercial travelers of this city" and to pay "proper respect" to deceased members, it likewise emphasized that "in case of the death of any one of our members, a sum not exceeding $50.00 shall be paid to the proper beneficiary."[29] Besides declaring allegiance to each other and to their homes, the Rochester commercial travelers also lent economic support to the structures of fellowship.

By 1899 such plans became familiar fixtures in the lives of commercial travelers. Beginning in the 1870s and continuing through the late nineteenth century, traveling salesmen established new fraternal insurance associations and swelled the ranks of existing ones. The first of these organizations, the Commercial Travelers' Association of the State of New York, which appeared

Cover, "Directory of the Albany Commercial Travelers' Club" (1891). (Courtesy of Library of Congress.)

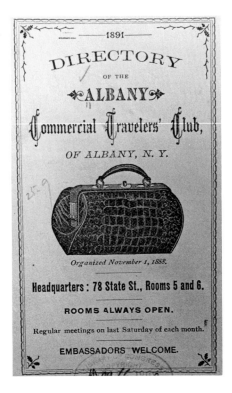

in 1872, set an example that other associations followed. According to an 1883 *Commercial Travelers Magazine* account, the association grew out of a spontaneous meeting among three New York traveling men who determined to "push things" beyond social organization and provide "mutual aid and relief for the families of deceased members." Subsequent organizations—the Northwestern Traveling Men's Association (1875) and the Western Commercial Travelers' Association (1878)—remained true to this "noble example" and, with an "answering echo," developed similar mutual aid programs.[30] On local, state, and regional levels others followed: the Iowa State Traveling Men's Association (1880), the Toledo Traveling Men's Association (1882), the Utica Commercial Travelers' Mutual Accident Association (1883), the Cape Cod Commercial Travelers' Association (1887), the Pacific Coast Commercial Travelers Association (1890), and more. Finally, there were larger, national organizations, like the Order of United Commercial Travelers of America (1888) and the Travelers' Protective Association of America (1890), whose national lodge systems with divisions by state, posts, and subposts exemplified the rapid growth of the occupation in a culture obsessed with the link between home and work.[31] Over time, fraternal organizations institutionalized the shifting language of domestic values and moral danger and used it to dramatize the need for home protection, fraternal unity, and professional reform.

The success of these associations based on the fraternal plan of home protection marked the maturity of the profession.[32] As the outgrowth of shared business practices and common problems, the mutual benefit society epitomized traveling men's increased awareness of their collective needs and identity. Camaraderie and professional self-consciousness were not, by themselves, enough to guarantee the future of a association, however. Its long-term health depended as much on organizational ability and business acumen as on the sentiments that shaped its founding—despite tales of how the Commercial Travelers' Association of the State of New York and the Northwestern Traveling Men's Association flourished by virtue of spontaneous meetings on trains or in hotels. Successful fraternal associations operated as effective business organizations; they reflected financial competence and independence and offered members substantial savings on insurance plans. Whereas commercial enterprises like the Travelers Insurance Company of Hartford charged traveling men twenty-five dollars a year in 1886 for accident and life insurance, mutual benefit societies assessed members less than five dollars for similar coverage.[33] "Think of it!" crowed Henry Pixley, the president of the Commercial Travelers' Mutual Accident Association of America in his 1888 annual report—"five years insurance in case of accident causing disability; giving to the insured all the benefits covered by its policies, the constitution and by-laws, for the small sum of $23, or less than $5 a year." To Pixley, those five years of growth hardly represented the results of a "lottery scheme" or the efforts of a "bragging, boasting, big advertising Association" trying to get rich. Rather, the measured growth of the association from its inception in 1883 exemplified the policies of "a Fraternal, a Mutual, a Benevolent Association" managed "for the sole benefit of its members."[34] And as the association expanded to serve nearly six thousand members in 1890 and close to sixty thousand in 1910, it continued to provide "mutual protection against the accidents which may occur at any minute in the life of a commercial traveler."[35]

Terms like *indemnity fund* and *death assessment* referred technically and graphically to the protection that commercial travelers sought from the hazards of the road. Claims lists described more honestly still the chief purpose of the mutual benefit society. Hotel fires, railroad collisions, broken sample trunks, and slippery marble floors provided the basis for just some of the more than four hundred claims presented to the Commercial Travelers' Mutual Accident Association in 1891. On death claims there were three in 1890— the association paid $5,000. For loss of limb—two men lost arms—it paid $2,500. For minor injuries, which accounted for the great majority of claims, the association paid members weekly indemnities of no more than $25.00.[36] A similar range of benefits prevailed among other fraternal insurance associations that offered accident coverage. And as late as 1920 the Travelers' Protective Association of America paid on the same scale—$5,000 for death claims and no more than $25.00 for weekly indemnities.[37]

In appealing to prospective members through the pages of trade journals,

From *Salesmanship* (June 1906). (Courtesy of Library of Congress.)

Beginning in the late nineteenth century, advertisements urging salesmen to join fraternal organizations and acquire accident insurance filled trade journals.

fraternal associations tugged on domestic heart strings, insisting that insurance was both a familial necessity and a professional duty. "Accidents will happen to you," warned the Iowa State Traveling Men's Association in a full-page, illustrated advertisement that appeared in a 1902 issue of the *Sample Case*. "What about your family in case you meet with accidental death or are disabled so that your earning power stops?" The answer to such questions resided in the advertisement itself—a picture of a group of traveling men holding hands—an image, that is, of domestic intimacy transforming the road (see fig.). That same year the Order of United Commercial Travelers published an equally stern warning: "Inform yourself as to your Duties and Privileges." The depiction of a mother and her children on one side of the

Advertisement for Iowa State Traveling Men's Association. From *Sample Case* (October 1902). (Courtesy of Library of Congress.)

page and a sketch of a traveling man and his sample case on the other made the duties obvious.[38] Traveling salesmen were to seek protection for their families through organized fellowship.

The hard sell persisted even in fiction written by and for commercial travelers. The hero of a 1912 story, "When Chapin Changed His Mind," published by the *Commercial Travelers Magazine,* remains indifferent to accident insurance until a fellow traveling man dies on the road. Shocked, Chapin obtains insurance. Later, when he has an accident and his wife falls ill, he has little doubt of its necessity. Another more humorous testimony to the value of accident insurance appears in "Mary Jane's Traveling Man," a tale featured in the *First Annual Announcement of the National Association of Traveling Men,* published in 1912. Convinced that traveling men follow a dissipated, dangerous life, Mother Kearns objects to her daughter's wish to marry a commercial traveler and urges her to find "a good steady fellow that stays at home and isn't running under them autobileys and getting himself burned and scalded in railroad accidents and leaving you a widow." But, Mary Jane points out, traveling men usually carry large insurance policies. Mother Kearns changes her opinion and agrees to the marriage.[39]

The lessons implicit in such fictional decision-making stress more than the value of accident insurance. Indeed, the emphasis on domestic morality represented an effort by fraternal insurance associations to circumscribe an ethical professional identity for commercial travelers.[40] As much as this attempt smacked of sentimentalism, it marked a critical point in the genealogy of the

American salesman. Bearing little resemblance to the flashy drummer, the crafty peddler, the scheming patent-medicine seller, or other sharp-trading dealers in folklore, the traveling man described in fraternal publications promised to make selling a profession worthy of respect. Charitable and dedicated to home and hearth, this salesman appeared less a liminal figure than a citizen intent on preserving mainstream values. By insisting and indeed presuming that most commercial travelers remained devoted to these values, fraternal organizations sought to move the salesman from the margins of culture—where writers and critics so often placed him—and construct a virtuous professional image.

To move from insurance advertisements to visions of business morality, salesmen did not have far to go. In the *Sample Case,* the *Commercial Travelers Magazine,* the *Crescent and the Grip,* and the *Traveling Man,* both discussions took place on the same page; both sprang from a discourse rooted in evangelical Protestantism and domestic piety. The man who insured his family from harm was also a man who attended church when he traveled, abstained from drinking, treated his customers and competitors as neighbors, and, like a good Samaritan, helped those in distress. For the man who was not all these things there was always the possibility of change, a transition that arbiters of fellowship characteristically represented in religious terms.

To effect widespread change was not simply a matter of purging the profession of "unscrupulous" men with "unfixed habits and without business training" and retaining the "bright, intelligent, honorable and upright men of good address," as one critic suggested in 1882. Indeed, fraternal organiza-

Cover, *The Traveling Man* (February 1908). (Courtesy of Library of Congress.)

tions barely addressed the call to "separate the goats from the sheep," not because they lacked the mechanism to do so—in fact, their membership policies frequently stressed the importance of upstanding character—or because the idea seemed repugnant to them.[41] Rather, the occupation as a whole, which the fraternal organizations did not wholly represent, was beyond their control. Wholesalers and corporations had the final say about the salesmen whom they hired. All that fraternal organizations could do was adopt a rhetoric of moral suasion and try to convert unscrupulous salesmen to their way of thinking and persuade them that their unfixed methods—even if they sold goods—were ultimately counterproductive to the profession. Reformers were likewise hedged in by their own reluctance to denigrate the profession; too much castigation of salesmen who treated for drinks and pursued immoral activities, too much acknowledgment, in short, of the potentially liberating qualities of the road, would only prevent them from extolling the salesmen's contributions to American society. Hence, magazines like the *Sample Case*, the journal published by the Order of United Commercial Travelers, struck an optimistic, evangelical tone. Brothers writing for other brothers assumed a like-minded audience and described a world of business that they had all helped make better. Writers scourged the immoral, unprofessional drummer, but chiefly to highlight the moral strengths and conscientious deeds of the majority of traveling men. Fellow salesmen lamented the pitfalls and temptations of commercial traveling yet stressed the improvements that their profession brought to the road. "For the good of the order"—to use the reform motto of one trade journal—traveling men simultaneously boosted the accomplishments of commercial traveling and celebrated their role as virtuous businessmen.[42]

Dedicated to reform from within, members of fraternal organizations described efforts to improve their profession in the idiom that they inherited from religiously inspired nineteenth-century reform movements—the discourse of Protestant evangelicalism. The Order of United Commercial Travelers acknowledged this debt in an acrostic gloss on its abbreviated name UCT—Unity, Charity, and Temperance.[43] Fraternal-minded writers stressed these standards—and the evangelical ethos of Protestantism—when they castigated intemperate salesmen and described the history of commercial traveling as if it were a version of *Pilgrim's Progress*. That pleas for stabilization and reform of the profession emerged from the structures of fellowship and came in rhetoric that smacked of domestic idealism was hardly a surprise. To be sure, male business culture could be an alternative and even a threat to domestic values. But fraternal relationships also worked to fill the gap left by absent domestic structures and, to the extent that salesmen honored church and family on the road, reinforced their strength. For pietistic salesmen moving from the home and to the road, ascendant Protestantism was as portable as a flask of whisky and its discourse as natural as the longing for release from domesticity.

When filtered through domestic morality, evangelical Protestantism gave sales reformers a powerful idiom for reimagining and justifying the objectives of commercial traveling. In fiction, writers sympathetic to sales reform demonstrated how evangelical reform could make fellowship Christian and banish temptation from the commercial sphere. The boys in George H. Briscoe's 1891 novel *Angels of Commerce; or, Thirty Days with the Drummers of Arkansas,* attend church on Sundays, assist helpless widows, and "hurry away" from their hotel dinners "to write wife, mother, or sweetheart, and later on congregate in the parlor, where experiences are exchanged, interspersed with incidents of road life." Eschewing commercial truculence and remaining loyal to the domestic world they left behind, Briscoe's drummers make the road a home and hence combine domestic and commercial values. Fittingly, the novel ends when "the queen of the realm" escorts two returning salesmen "toward the house, grips and top-coats are deposited in the hall, the door closes, and so—good night."[44] In *Angels of Commerce,* this domestic scene—more than any hotel or smoking-car gathering—proves the bright spot in a commercial traveler's hurried life. John Dewitt's "I'll Meet You in the Morning," one of several "true tales" published by the *Commercial Travelers' "Home" Monthly Magazine* during the 1890s, likewise illustrates the regenerating effect of home, this time through the conversion of a traveling man who, after the death of his son, becomes a "changed man, going about on the trains, in business, active in church work[,] ever ready to give a testimony wherever possible." In bringing the home—where the conversion takes place and "a woman's touch could be seen at every turn"—ever closer to the road, where this "good natured skeptic" once believed "men had more important things to think of" than religion, DeWitt adumbrated the concerns of nineteenth-century sentimentalist writers and affirmed the goals set forth by fraternal insurance associations.[45]

Other stories published in the *Commercial Travelers' "Home" Monthly Magazine* dramatize the reform of the road. "Sam," an 1893 tale, tells how Samuel Isaacs, a diminutive Jewish salesman, saved a violent, intemperate drummer named Bulldozer from a hotel fire and became his friend for life. "The Hypocrite," a story set in Great Britain, describes a self-righteous commercial traveler's career as an evangelical preacher and his eventual fall from grace after embezzling funds. And "The Orphans Story," also published in 1893 but set in 1903, highlights the good fortune of a mother and her young daughter who, left stranded and penniless when the father—a commercial traveler—dies in a railroad accident, finally discover a membership certificate to a fraternal insurance association in one of his coat pockets and claim the benefits.[46]

These benefits, lodgings in a home for traveling salesmen and a place in the home school, highlight the larger didactic purpose of "The Orphans Story": to champion the objectives of the parent organization of the *"Home" Monthly Magazine.* In short, the Commercial Travelers' Home Association of Syracuse, New York, intended to institutionalize domestic harmony. A charter, published in the first issue, underscored the goal of building a "Home" for indigent members and widows, a hospital for the sick and disabled, and a school for orphan children. In language that echoed the professed intentions of countless mutual aid societies the association vowed to "furnish other aid and assistance to members and their families, as may be provided, from time to time." For its part in this venture, the *Commercial Travelers' "Home" Monthly Magazine* solicited new members, explained the purpose of the association, and, more importantly, "disseminate[d] thoroughly the Home gospel."[47]

Stories like "I'll Meet You in the Morning" and "Sam" did disseminate a home gospel but not simply by celebrating the sovereign virtues of nineteenth-century domesticity. What these tales affirm is less a litany of moral prescriptions than a mechanism for making them stick. Conversion proves the turning point for characters mired in the crises described. The hero of Alwyn M. Thurber's 1896 novel, *Quaint Crippen, Commercial Traveler*, gains piety by steps. At the outset, Thurber's sharp-witted, Boston salesman leaves home "with that dexterous air and beaming countenance customary with a drummer who has been out before." But this genial self fades when, after rescuing a stranded Mrs. Thorne and her child from a railroad depot, Quaint falls in love. Then his "old habit of now and then an opera, story-telling, and laughter at the hotel, or strolling with some drummer up and down the business streets—any of these seemed too much like his old self,—the self which existed before the light of another creature's eyes." While visiting the widow's estate in Connecticut, Quaint gives up talk of "the lacka-daisical storekeeper" and "good indorsed paper"—despite being "very largely himself when talking about business"—and becomes earnest and sen-timental. Transformed, Quaint appears honorable—"quaint" rather than typical—for failing to live up to a drummer's notorious reputation, signified by Thurber's none-too-subtle caricature of the mashing Lem Gabbetz, a "squatty" Jewish drummer with "roguish eyes" and "sly glances." So Thur-ber's story resembles a conversion narrative, framed by the sins of sales cul-ture. By the end of the novel, Quaint is engaged to marry the widow whose spiritual faith chastened his own aggressive commercial spirit. Now saved from the temptations of the road, Quaint promises to try "home missions for a time" and thus make business the provenance of sympathy and reform.[48]

Conversion likewise proved the evangelical strategy on which organiza-tions like the Commercial Travelers' Home Association depended to gain members and to define an ethical identity for commercial travelers. Even where a Christian ethos was absent, in fiction like "Sam," where the drunken drummer casts aside his reprehensible habits but without acknowledging di-vine power, the structures of conversion persisted in a secular form to order and reform the customs of commercial traveling. Religious or not, conversion as a mode of persuasion shaped the development of salesmanship and the contours of fellowship. With roots deep in the social and evangelical history of the United States, conversion offered fraternal associations an idiom broad enough—and flexible enough—to embrace professional pitfalls and suggest possible safeguards.

Nowhere was this idiom of conversion more dramatically exemplified than in the goals and activities undertaken by the Gideons, the Christian Commercial Travelers' Association of America. Known chiefly for placing Gideon Bibles in hotel rooms across the country, the Gideons sprang to life as other fraternal associations claimed to have done—spontaneously and unexpectedly. But for the Gideons this creation story had a special significance: it revealed the hand of God. Indeed, the order traced its evangelical roots to Janesville, Wisconsin, where one night during 1898 two traveling men who found "no room in the inn" ended up in a room together and, discovering that they shared a devotion to Christianity, resolved to establish a fraternal organization for devout salesmen.[49] "The object of the Gideons," this resolution finally read in the *Gideon Quarterly,* "will be to recognize the Christian traveling men of the world with cordial fellowship, to encourage one another in the Master's work," and, the charter continued, emphasizing the evangelical nature of the group's mission, "to improve every opportunity for the betterment of the lives of our fellow-travelers, business men and others, with whom we may come in contact; scattering the seeds all along the pathway for Christ."[50] Unlike fraternal insurance associations, the Gideons concentrated on the social, evangelical spirit of fellowship. But this evangelism also had a practical purpose. In walking with God, the Gideons hoped to convert—and reshape—the commercial world.

According to one Gideon, hotels, railroad cars, and stores "are not places that would be chosen by the majority of Christian workers; but in these fields the Gideon finds his best opportunities." Encouraging one another to take advantage of such opportunities and condemn the sins of commercial traveling, Gideons called for the elimination of drinking, gambling, dirty jokes, Sunday trading, and other "forms of temptation peculiar to traveling men."[51] Nor did Gideons confine their criticisms to commercial travelers. Reforming the road meant abolishing all noxious, immoral habits, even those belonging to customers. In fact, a "word of disapproval dropped against the use of profanity or vulgarity, to the merchant with whom [the Gideon] is dealing, is often kindly taken and is of profit."[52] Aware that business customs grow out of social relationships—that, for instance, it takes more than one man to tell a story or treat for drinks—Gideons worked to convert both sides of the counter.

Nonetheless, Gideons made the "winning of traveling men for Christ" their main "business."[53] In a sermon given on the Gideons' first anniversary, July 1, 1900, the Reverend L. C. Smith reminded his audience that the commercial man traveled "alone," "unprotected," "away from home and home influences." For all his freedom and independence, the traveling man remained at risk. "No one knows him and no one will know where he is or what he does," he warned. Even though road life brought temptation, Smith revised the essentially bleak conclusion reached by the Reverend William H. Baldwin nearly thirty years earlier in his sermon *Travelling Salesmen: Their Opportunities and Their Dangers.* Focusing on the opportunities for conversion, rather than the

Bringing evangelical piety to the road, Gideon brothers assemble in their Chapel Car en route to the Fifth Annual Convention at Minneapolis in 1904. From *Gideon* (September 1904). Photograph by George R. Lawrence. (State Historical Society of Wisconsin, WHi [×3] 46119.)

possibilities of sin, Smith took as his text the parable of the Good Samaritan and urged Gideons to extend the benefits of "Christian companionship." Even the "most self-reliant man has his hour of need," he declared. "Now is the time to tell him of the better way."[54]

This better way opened a path for a better traveling man, who "makes a business of his religion" and "puts religion into his business."[55] Gideons who echoed Smith described a moral commercial world where salesmen "carry the grip for Christ," represent the "greatest house on earth . . . selling boots and shoes as a side line to make expenses," and stay only at temperance hotels.[56] If such language indicated the impact that evangelical Protestantism had on business practices, the influence also worked the other way, showing in the peculiar interplay of commercial and religious elements how God could be sold. After all, one Gideon pointed out, "those methods that are so successful in the selling of merchandise by a commercial salesman can be equally successful if adopted in the work of our Master." Winning souls on the road seemed perfectly logical to Gideons, who looked upon life and business as part of the same "journey of discovery" toward Christ. To the Gideon who wrote "Traveling Men of the Bible" and singled out Jesus Christ as "the noblest example" (more than twenty years before Bruce Barton depicted him as an advertising man in *The Man Nobody Knows*), the nexus between commerce and spirit appeared blessed.[57]

So Gideons struggled to infuse salesmanship with the evangelical spirit of Christianity and, in combing railroad cars for fellow drummers and possible converts to wear the blue button that symbolized their order, presented to early twentieth-century Americans a new sort of salesman. Associated chiefly with the 1920s and the satiric—and adulatory—portraits conceived by Sinclair Lewis and Bruce Barton, this vision of the salesman-as-hero, the businessman as profitmaker and seeker of souls, originated at the turn of the century and even earlier in those fraternal associations determined to fuse commercial values and domestic piety.[58] To be sure, the Gideons counted for very few of the commercial travelers working in 1902—there were 1,900 of them, even after the order broadened its membership qualifications to include traveling insurance salesmen, buyers, and freight agents.[59] But the Gideons were not the only fraternal association to stress the commercial traveler's need for Christian guidelines. In similar pietistic rhetoric, the Order of United Commercial Travelers, for instance, proposed a "better way" of selling goods and molding character. And unlike the Gideons, in 1902 the UCT boasted almost 20,000 members—all commercial travelers.[60]

Better than any other fraternal association, the Order of United Commercial Travelers spelled out the significance of fellowship and its relation to business practices. In the *Sample Case*, its national organ, UCT brothers affirmed their devotion to unity, charity, and temperance. The "initial, fundamental principle," however, was fraternalism. And fraternalism, as Charles G. Daniel, the supreme secretary, explained in 1903, was not simply an artifact of organization; it sprang from the very nature of commercial traveling, which separated its members from "the pleasures of their homes and the society and companionship of home friends." Consequently, traveling men grouped together on the road so that "on trains, in the stores, while waiting possibly for the same customer, in the hotel reading-room or office after the arduous duties of the day are over, you will see the wearers of the Grip and Crescent [button] enjoying each other's society, meeting on common ground, with an assurance of confidence reposed and accepted that is, in a great measure, foreign to those outside the profession." Although fraternalism "may not admit the relinquishing of an order to a competitor," Daniel argued that it should "incline one to be less selfish, to throw off the feeling of jealousness and covetousness which creeps in where a competitor has been successful."[61] Thus fraternalism—properly conceived—promised to banish aggressive male behavior from the commercial realm and supplant it with a version of masculine etiquette shaped by domestic, pietistic virtues.[62] More than did the material benefits of the organization—its accident insurance and fund for widows—this standard became the basis for promoting the UCT advantages.

In spite of such efforts to annex a virtuous commercial sphere in the name

On such jewelry members of the Order of United Commercial Travelers proudly displayed their commitment to unity, charity, and temperance. From *Sample Case* (January 1903). (Courtesy of Library of Congress.)

of fraternity, ambiguities nagged even the most hopeful traveling men. UCT loyalists complained that too many members cared only about the insurance features and consequently neglected "the social and fraternal teachings" of the order.[63] Throughout the early years of the twentieth century continual reminders that the jolly drummer and his "unsavory reputation" belonged to the past suggested that perhaps he was not yet gone.[64] In a 1908 letter in the *Traveling Man,* one angry salesman protested the frequent depiction of the traveling salesman as "a sort of low comedian." The "kind of traveling man who figures in joke books, if there are such freaks, wouldn't hold a job fifteen minutes with any firm in this country." Business competition had become "keen and ruthless" and "strenuous," he declared, and commercial travelers had little time to pursue unprofessional activities.[65]

Here and elsewhere, the promotion of domestic values was simultaneously a self-conscious repudiation of the traveling man's negative image—as fashioned within popular culture—and an equally self-conscious effort to reform sales culture itself. The objective was not the wholesale rejection of improvisational sales techniques, a denial of visual and verbal modes of persuasion, but rather—as demonstrated by the rising tide of salesmanship manuals during the early twentieth century—their rationalization and domestication within the context of an increasingly commercial society.

Ironically, though not surprisingly, sales reformers did not necessarily show charity when considering wayward traveling men. "In some flocks a black sheep may live, and thrive indefinitely," a salesman wrote in a 1912 issue of the *Commercial Travelers Magazine,* "but among our fraternity it is woe unto him at an early date. He will find that nine out of the ten boys are 'agin him.'" If he drinks to excess, cheats at cards, or acts immorally, the writer continued, "the glad hand" is "withheld." If he "is always well behaved and a good fellow," then "he soon makes his standing sure" and becomes part of "a fraternity that, while it has no secret signs, passwords or grips; is yet more fraternal, more cohesive, and more strongly banded together than almost any secret society."[66] Operating beyond the bounds of any particular fraternal organization, as part of the culture itself, fellowship thus promised to enforce efficiency, order, and conformity within the commercial landscape.

Yet in some cases the politics of fellowship served to disqualify would-be members for reasons that had nothing to do with moral qualifications. Whereas the UCT invited "the Protestant, the Catholic, the Gentile, the Jew, without discrimination or preference" to join and promised "to break down all the barriers of birth, race or environment," it made no mention of including nonwhites in its association. Other organizations, like the Travelers' Protective Association, also declared that "fraternity" means loving "thy neighbor" "of every race, sex, color, occupation . . . as thyself," yet included only "white" male persons of "good moral character."[67]

Such contradictions illuminate the limitations of organized brotherhood and the exclusionary distinctions of the larger culture. They also suggest the assimilating power of fellowship in a commercial world dominated by native-born whites. Statistically this domination was significant. According to the 1900 census, nearly 65 percent of commercial travelers claimed native white parents, 22 percent had native white foreign parents, and about 13 percent were born to foreign white parents. Less than two hundred of the 93,000 traveling men were black.

Culturally this domination proves more difficult to assess. Throughout the late nineteenth-century ethnic jokes and trade cards, particularly anti-Semitic caricatures of salesmen, seemed to confine foreign-speaking and Jewish traveling men to the margins of the commercial landscape.[68] As Abraham Cahan showed in his portrayal of commercial traveling during the 1890s, the possibility of becoming one of the boys and succeeding as a salesmen hinged on the dynamics of exclusion and assimilation. For the hero of *The Rise of David Levinsky*, the road is more than "a great school of business and life"; it functions as a rite of passage. While traveling and selling, Levinsky struggles to slough off his Russian Jewish identity and become more "American." On a railroad car filled with one other Jew and three Gentiles—all traveling men, Cahan suggests—Levinsky talks excitedly of national politics and Spencerian notions of business competition, "so conscious of the whole performance that I did not know what I was talking about." Yet the price of this performance, as Levinsky acknowledges when the other Jew ridicules his "Talmud gesticulations," is his cultural heritage. "I laughed with the others," he recalls, "but I felt like a cripple who is forced to make fun of his own deformity."[69] Speeding along the commercial corridor, basking in the bright glow of a well-appointed dining car, and listening to smutty jokes, Levinsky affirms his Americanness through the gestures and customs of business fellowship. Cahan's description also hints at what Sinclair Lewis later critiqued in his representations of Elmer Gantry and George Babbitt—that although Main Street moralizing might have a leveling or sanitizing effect on business, it could provide a safe haven or home to the salesman, inevitably returning from his necessary flirtations with transgressive behavior, whether dirty-joke telling, drinking, or sexual dalliance.

By 1920 the ironic consequences of the fraternal movement were clear. Now in articles explaining the relationship between employer and employee, fellowship connoted "efficiency," "cooperation," and "organization." According to one explanation, fellowship constituted a corporate "science" of "Human Engineering," offering benefits to customers, stockholders, and the public.[70] As if transformed by long commercial usage, the original impulse to protect home and family became part of the marketplace itself. Although vestiges of evangelical piety lingered in the glad hand and the genial backslap, the traveling fraternity appeared a self-sufficient business culture whose customs barely evoked Christian devotion.

In one sense, this transformation reflected the "search for order" and the great scientific and bureaucratic organization of knowledge that reshaped American culture during the late nineteenth and early twentieth centuries. Presenting an ever more rational, ever more secular face to the world, the twentieth-century United States became ever more modern; inevitably, as the profession established its own organizations and journals, the customs of commercial traveling did, too.[71] Once standardized, the attributes of fraternal solidarity—geniality, generosity, goodwill—often seemed conventions of the marketplace, learned strategies that prevented competition from disrupting the smooth operation of business. Charles Edmund Barker, in a 1902 *Sample Case* story, "The Youngster," describes how a college-educated greenhorn undergoes a "great change," relinquishing a busy social life and adopting a "commercial traveler's ethics." Demanding hard work, "true grit," and more "business-like apparel," these ethics finally have very little to do with spiritual life.[72] Thus even the idiom of conversion lost its evangelical edge to a commercial rite of passage.

Although the triumph of rational fellowship was by no means absolute and although twentieth-century commentators continued to examine the traveling man's ambiguous relation to home, family, and God, there was no question but that the marketplace was now domesticated and that the salesman's craft in many ways belonged to all.

6 *Sister Carrie* and the Logic of Salesmanship

Early in Theodore Dreiser's turn-of-the-century novel *Sister Carrie*, the traveling salesman Charles Drouet gives Carrie "two soft, green, handsome ten-dollar bills." Unemployed, ill, and "utterly subdued in spirit," Carrie is considering going home to Wisconsin; Drouet's gift, however, allows her to stay in Chicago—with him. The episode is a turning point in the narrative, but not simply because it pushes a melodramatic plot. As Ellen Moers and Walter Benn Michaels have demonstrated, the exchange of cash directs us to one of Dreiser's most important themes: the powerful blending of sexual instinct and economic desire. In Michaels's analysis of the "popular economy" in the text, the scene is especially important because it implicates Carrie—and Dreiser—in a never-ending, never-satisfied quest for money and power.[1]

To Dreiser's representation of these apparently institutionalized desires might be added a third, equally naturalized desire—the longing for home. Ironically, Dreiser associates this longing with Drouet, a homeless figure, to say the least, and a character whose motivations seem fairly obvious. Dreiser describes Drouet as a thoroughgoing, unconscious sensualist who "loved to make advances to women, to have them succumb to his charms, not because he was a cold-blooded, dark scheming villain, but because his inborn desire urged him to that as a chief delight." As his desire for women appears unsatiable, what else could this "pig," this "child," this "merry, unthinking moth of the lamp," have in mind but the sexual conquest of Carrie?[2]

Yet the salesman's "inborn desire" deserves further scrutiny. As Dreiser would have it, Drouet is not simply a profligate. To Carrie, "and indeed to all the world, he was a nice good-hearted man. . . . He gave her the money out of a good heart—out of a realisation of her want. He would not have given the same amount to a poor young man, but we must not forget that a poor young man could not, in the nature of things, have appealed to him like a poor young girl. Femininity affected his feelings. He was the creature of an inborn desire. Yet no beggar could have caught his eye and said, 'My God, mister, I'm starving,' but he would gladly have handed out what was considered the proper portion to give beggars and thought no more about it." Later in the novel, Dreiser dramatizes this peculiarly sentimentalized, humanitarian reflex. Walking out of the theater together, Drouet, Carrie, and Hurstwood pass a homeless man who begs for "the price of a bed." Drouet, Dreiser emphasizes, "was the first to see [the man]. He handed over a dime with an upwelling feeling of pity in his heart. Hurstwood scarcely noticed the incident. Carrie quickly forgot."[3]

This exchange of money, the instinctive outpouring of Drouet's good heart, suggests a softened, even domesticated view of the drummer. There is a great deal of difference between twenty dollars and ten cents, but as the subsequent representation of the Captain and his street-corner collection for indigent men makes clear, even pocket change has a place in the (less visible) moral economy of the novel. Like the Captain's plea for money, Drouet's small donation goes toward restoring a man to his home. His impulse to help, I might further argue, springs from the acculturated, if not inborn, power of nineteenth-century domestic ideology. Viewed in this way, Drouet is not only a masher attracted to any available woman but also a good-hearted man whose feelings have been affected by the culture of femininity. Consider, for example, Drouet's domestic possibilities: his role as homemaker in providing Carrie a place to stay in Chicago; his influence as fashion guide in dressing Carrie in the right clothes and guiding her deportment; and his pose as husband—false, to be sure, but no less sincere than George Hurstwood's attempt at conjugal attachment.

Given Drouet's oft-hinted-at promiscuity and the traveling salesman's notorious reputation in late nineteenth-century culture, this act of generosity appears laughably ironic. Yet given the opening chapter of *Sister Carrie*, where Dreiser urges his readers to view the drummer as a recognizable, social type, the irony begs for some broader cultural explanation. What is at stake in Dreiser's representation of the traveling salesman? What is behind this peculiar conjunction of domestic and commercial values?

These questions become even more pointed in light of Drouet's relative neglect by Dreiser critics, who typically focus on Carrie and Hurstwood. Although Drouet appears briefly in the last two chapters, his disappearance halfway through the novel seems to signal Dreiser's primary narrative concerns: charting the rise of Carrie and the fall of Hurstwood. Readers have tended to value Drouet accordingly, affirming from a variety of perspectives his "necessity to the plot," as Charles Shapiro put it, but leaving his narrative role unexamined. Shapiro, for instance, saw Drouet "unconsciously" assuming the crude, materialistic values of the Gilded Age; F. O. Matthiessen argued that Drouet's perspective, like Carrie's, is Dreiser's own; and Ellen Moers, noting Dreiser's plagiarism of George Ade, concluded that behind the borrowing "lay a memory of his own Drouet"; but none of them fleshed out their observations.[4] More recent critical efforts to recover the historicized realism of *Sister Carrie* have likewise glossed over Drouet's role in the narrative, an omission all the more puzzling given their detailed attention to the dynamics of the marketplace. Two of the latest, most influential readers, Walter Benn Michaels and Philip Fisher show the impact of urban consumer culture on the trajectory and texture of the narrative but pay less attention to the distinctive roles that Dreiser's characters play in the economy. Hence, as Michaels argues, Carrie's relationship with Drouet breaks down according to the logic of desire that naturalizes the Dreiserian world; she must move on and up or else fall and become worse. Why Drouet remains at equilibrium, why at the end of the novel he is, in Dreiser's words, "as light on the wing as ever," Michaels does not say. Fisher, who is more sensitive to what he calls the hierarchy of work at play in the novel, implies that Drouet's ability to survive is due to his "naively present" self, which is "in balance with the objects it sells and separates from itself in the act of selling"—a provocative, if somewhat vague, characterization of a figure whom Dreiser never shows working (unlike Carrie and Hurstwood). Fisher recognizes Drouet's privileged relation to urban commercial power and hence his allure to Carrie, but because his principal concern in his essay is to show the significance of Chicago as a "mediating term" and consciousness-shaping environment, he is less interested in pursuing the implications of Drouet's role as a middleman within a transregional market system.[5]

And yet it was Dreiser's singular achievement not only to dramatize and amplify the drummer's position as sales improviser and cultural middleman but also to acknowledge self-consciously the salesman's imaginative reconstruction as a popular cultural type—all within the frame of a historically conscious, retrospective view. Dreiser's point of embarkation for his narrative, August 1889, is a moment of emergence for both the home-leaving Carrie and the urban marketplace to which she is bound. It is also the drummer's moment. But as Dreiser suggests in a grandiloquent gesture to historical transformation—"Lest this order or individual should permanently pass"—Drouet is a type whose moment has passed and whose importance in the 1880s consisted in linking hinterland and city, in giving economic exchanges cultural meaning on the interpersonal level. Written in 1899, after several of Dreiser's own urban journeys, the novel may be the first nostalgic meditation on the drummer's mediating role from the perspective of a small-town migrant. If, as Amy Kaplan has argued, *Sister Carrie* works to recontextualize the sentimental—understood here as the emotional attachment to home—and give it new life in the "aesthetics of consumption," then Dreiser makes Drouet the pivot of this change, locating in his improvisational powers what might be called the aesthetics of distribution.[6] In this opening chapter and throughout the first half of the novel, Drouet functions as an all-important middleman, guiding Carrie into the marketplace, preparing her for success, and reconstituting her yearning for home in a new domestic setting. Focusing on Drouet's role in this geographical, historical, and cultural passage complicates the division between city and hinterland and foregrounds the traveling salesman's limited, but nonetheless crucial, agency in Dreiser's novel of commercial drama.

In this sense, Dreiser's departure from the elusive, fragmentary depiction of traveling men that characterized most late nineteenth-century literature marked an unprecedented, even sympathetic engagement with the sensual, everyday rhythms of the new commercial culture. Although Gilded Age novelists frequently turned to the figure of the businessman as a way of examining and criticizing the excesses of American commercial life, their failed search for a "capitalist hero" generally targeted financiers and entrepreneurs. A string of books beginning with Mark Twain and Charles Dudley Warner's *Gilded Age* and including *A Connecticut Yankee in King Arthur's Court*, as well as the work of William Dean Howells and Henry Blake Fuller, created what amounted to a subgenre of realistic novels devoted to business enterprise; but as Henry Nash Smith observed, the writers knew very little about what was happening in the economy.[7] The more important point, however, is these novelists' almost exclusive focus on the issue of economic power as it relates to ownership and production. Even so varied a novel as *A Connecticut Yankee in*

King Arthur's Court, which satirizes late nineteenth-century sales schemes and advertising ventures, is principally concerned with Hank Morgan's role as a big businessman. The major writers of the late nineteenth century were not as concerned with middle- or low-ranking figures in the business hierarchy.

Although the frequent appearance of drummers in fiction suggests that many writers were drawn despite themselves to the mundane spectacles of commerce, domestic plot conventions blended with unease over emergent market practices to rule salesmen out of the realistic narratives in which we would most expect to find them. William Dean Howells's 1885 novel, *The Rise of Silas Lapham,* is a good example. Howells says enough about Lapham's paint business to indicate his reliance on brand-name packaging and advertising (on fences, bridges, barns, and rocks), yet says nothing about how the paint is actually sold, relying instead on broadly conceived market dynamics to account for its fate. Howells's lack of interest in this kind of economic drama surfaces obliquely when Lapham's future son-in-law, Tom Corey, offers to invest his thirty-thousand-dollar inheritance in the struggling paint company. Knowing how determined Silas is to maintain full control of the company yet "believing" in the paint himself (as he tells his own father), Corey assures Silas that he regards this proposed infusion of funds as an "investment," not a step toward partnership, and explains his desire to become more financially involved in negative terms. "I should like to feel," he tells Lapham, "that I had more than a drummer's interest in the venture." Consistent with the thrust of the novel, this comment serves to distance mere commercial representation from the more substantial responsibilities of ownership and production and, in the context of Corey's developing relationship with Penelope, to make honor in business equivalent to sincerity in love. The novel's moral economy requires this inextricable link between business and romance.[8] To be an upright businessman and successful suitor, Tom must profess his financial interests and express his feelings sincerely, just as Silas must acknowledge his familial relationships and origins and deal honestly with his business problems—an equation successfully completed at the end of the novel when Silas returns to Vermont and Corey, newly married, assumes responsibility for directing the newly organized paint company's interests in Mexico and Central America.

Given Tom Corey's crucial position in *The Rise of Silas Lapham* as the balancing point between old and new Boston, between inherited and self-made wealth, and between a defunct and reorganized business, it is all but impossible to imagine him taking a drummer's interest. Indeed, Howells's occasional jabs at sales puffery suggest an unease with commercial modes of persuasion and a moral concern over the middleman's lack of responsibility. If a drummer did not have to represent himself and own up to his interests, then how was he to be held accountable? Certainly, he could not be assimilated into a successful marriage plot. The fate of Bartley Hubbard, the unscrupulous journalist who appears briefly in *Silas Lapham* and more prominently in *A Modern Instance,* has the makings of the kind of self-promoting middleman whom Howells held up for censure. More than a type, however, even Hubbard is granted a space that Howells denies the traveling salesman mentioned in *The Day of Their Wedding*. In that 1896 novel, in which he examines a Shaker couple's quest for earthly love and their flight from the utopian community (where they are not allowed to marry) to the "world-outside" (where they discover that they have to pay for "pretty much everything"), Howells uses the wife of a traveling man (who loves to shop) to dramatize the self-centered, shallow attractions of American consumer culture, as well as the base social relationships that it encourages. When, for instance, the wife of the drummer describes how (after being engaged three times) she met her husband through a flirtation on a railroad car (Howells deploys the classic mashing scene), the idealistic heroine starts to lose faith in her feelings, fearing that her own love may be the consequence of short-lived "looks"—mere sensual inducements.[9] Even without introducing the drummer himself, Howells insinuates his influence, which is strong enough to send the Shakers back to their original home to live without the bliss—such as it appears to be—of married life. However comically, Howells introduces the absent salesman and his consumer wife to highlight the pervasive and troubling union of superficial affect and commercial modes of persuasion. As critics have made clear, Howells as a realist was dead set against all forms of sentimentalism, literary and otherwise.[10] What is worth emphasizing about *The Day of Their Wedding*, however, is how tightly Howells ties emotional "effectism" to commercial culture and how firmly he opposes its union to honest representations of emotion and ideal domestic conditions.[11]

Four years later, Dreiser's treatment of this triangular relationship began where Howells stopped, figuring domesticity, commercial persuasion, and sexual desire not as competing fields of value but as closely allied forces. *Sister Carrie* initiates in novelistic form Dreiser's lifelong fascination with a wide variety of American business types and stands as perhaps his most complete engagement with mundane commercial desire. Certainly Dreiser addressed these themes in nearly all his writings. Besides devoting his "trilogy of desire" to the machinations of the financier Frank Cowperwood and *Jennie Gerhardt* to the intrigues of the scion Lester Kane, Dreiser wrote frequently and obsessively about the successes and failures of striving or middling characters like Clyde Griffiths in *American Tragedy*. Even figures less likely to be associated with profit making—Culhane, the Solid Man; De Maupassant, Junior; W.L.S., the artist; and Dreiser's songwriting brother, Paul Dresser—all described in *Twelve Men*—show Dreiser's engrossment with a culture in which any talent can be bought and sold and where commercial transactions are the locus of power and desire.

The attention to social conflict that often distinguishes Dreiser's commercial dramas suggests a kind of sympathy for characters struggling—or, to use one of Dreiser's favorite words, "longing"—for success. Such sympathy is curiously at odds with his celebration of the desires and spectacles that determine their fates. Dreiser's attachment to the romance of determinism, while characteristic of naturalistic writers, seems especially problematic in the context of his apparently objective, Balzacian style of realism. In *Sister Carrie*, however, where desire is always a market force, the gap between sentiment and object frequently narrows. The department store products that speak "tenderly" to Carrie and the Chicago mansions that invite with a "siren voice . . . whispering in her ear" do not expose the differences between commercial melodrama and hard reality, or between romance and realism, so much as they collapse differences. Indeed, as Alan Trachtenberg has argued, the novel may speak in several tones, but the voice is always the same and its effect is always aimed at one end: Carrie's gradual "awakening" to a world that constantly prompts but cannot satisfy her desires.[12] Given this goal, what does it mean that Charles Drouet is the first person to speak in the novel?

On the one hand, Drouet's appearance at the beginning of the novel bespeaks the small-town migrant's passage to the urban netherworld of confidence men and painted women and of the well-grooved literary tradition, scored in the United States by Charles Brockden Brown and Nathaniel Hawthorne and in Europe by Honoré de Balzac, whom Dreiser had by this time read. Dreiser evokes the dark reputation of the city when he explains by way of general maxim that when a girl leaves home she either "falls into saving hands and becomes better, or she rapidly assumes the cosmopolitan standard of virtue and becomes worse."[13] Drouet's disembodied voice in her ear proves this maxim; he is the first tempter—in Kaplan's words, a "serpent" echoing "her desires." The drummer does appear the conventional evil seducer. On the other hand, Dreiser turns this stock scene inside out—both here and in subsequent passages—just as he does for his maxim (Carrie's material rise being equivalent to her moral fall)—by suggesting that the drummer's appearance has less to do with urban influence per se, especially anything evil, than with the commercial traveler's ubiquity. Kaplan touches on this ubiquity when, in characterizing Drouet's "air," she compares his effect to an advertisement's.[14] But Drouet is not an advertisement; although his role as a drummer in the 1880s prefigures more abstract selling strategies, it nonetheless overshadows the nascent power of advertising. This, indeed, is Dreiser's point in the first chapter. In describing the endangered type, Dreiser is at pains to emphasize Drouet's identity as a salesman and give solidity to his appeal—in clothing, shoes, voice, and so forth. The distinction is subtle but crucial for considering Dreiser's representation of face-to-face improvisations and understanding the difference between Drouet's whisper here and whisperings later in the novel.

In Drouet, contemporaneous reviewers saw a "living, breathing and talking" drummer, a "representative" character, and "a self-seeking, moralless young business man of a type becoming too common in the world"—in short, a familiar social type. Even the one reviewer who astutely noted that Dreiser had lifted "a page entire" from Ade's *Fables in Slang*, attributed the theft to his all-absorbing realism.[15]

For his part Dreiser learned of the traveling man's role at a close second hand. As a teenager, he worked for a Chicago hardware jobber, watched the drummers come and go, and listened to the clerks boast of becoming road salesmen. Although Dreiser did not share their ambitions—"To go from town to town and try to persuade people to buy things—how could one do that?"—he envied the drummer's freedom, writing in his autobiographies of his youthful longing to embark on "journeys far and wide." To a young man raised in small towns and eager to find success, drummers appeared "among the most fortunate of men, high up in the world as positions go, able to steer straight and profitable courses for themselves."[16] This valorized, somewhat romantic view of the salesman's freedom and opportunity stayed with Dreiser as a token of his own impoverished upbringing in places like Terre Haute, where it seemed that he might never break loose from constricting circumstances. If by succeeding in song writing and returning home with stories of urban glamor, his older brother, Paul, gave some hope of escape and personalized it, then traveling salesmen objectified the passage out, belonging, as Dreiser put it in *Jennie Gerhardt*, to a "raft of indescribables who, coming and going, make up the glow and stir" of the "kaleidoscope world." In his travel narrative *Hoosier Holiday* (1916), Dreiser again comments on this landscape of shifting perspectives when, in a Sandusky hotel ("Jennie's world to the life"), he encounters large plate-glass windows and a line of armchairs that he imagines would "naturally" be occupied by village loafers, idling politicians—and traveling salesmen.[17]

These provocatively fuzzy descriptions speak to F. O. Matthiessen's claim that in writing the opening chapter to *Sister Carrie*, Dreiser identified with both Drouet and Carrie. As an observer drawn to this raft of indescribables, Dreiser seems, like Carrie, to be mesmerized by the unspecified glow of commercial flux, and as a writer, he seems to be concerned to keep this flux at a distance, to diffuse the salesman's influence into a broader cultural matrix. Yet Dreiser singles out the traveling salesman (substituting kaleidoscope with telescope) as one of several privileged participants in this glow and stir. The salesmen in Sandusky are observers of the flux of life, but they are also exempt from the dreary working world that they watch through the cinema-style hotel windows. The question raised here is, To what extent do these figures surpass their participant-observer status and become creators of atmosphere? Stated another way, given Dreiser's simultaneous identification with Carrie and Drouet, what difference do these two perspectives describe? Is Drouet, like his counterpart, more "carried" by circumstances or more an actor within them? Or is he, as a fanciful reading of his name might suggest, able to "draw" Carrie and hence exercise some control over the ambient cultural forces?

By dramatizing qualified answers to these questions, *Sister Carrie* adumbrates the general cultural history of commercial traveling. Just as his real-life counterparts did, Drouet improvises within a space circumscribed and vitalized by a larger economic structures. Significantly, however, Dreiser's representation of this role, though rooted in an acute awareness of the business applications of selling, takes shape outside the business arena. Dreiser is principally concerned with the drummer's cultural impact, his peculiarly personal mediation between small-town landscapes and the ineffable, pressing allurement of the outside world. This view was not simply his own but also grew from his understanding of the salesman as a cultural type, which was enhanced as Dreiser sought to see this type through others' eyes. Consider, for instance, how he renders, in his autobiography *Dawn* (1931), his sister's description of walking into downtown Sullivan, Indiana, to buy a pair of slippers and meeting a drummer.

> In the first shoe store I went into, there was a young drummer standing about, only I didn't know he was a drummer. The clerk was out, and after looking me over, this man came over and said he would wait on me. "How much did you want to pay for the slippers?" he asked. "I just have a dollar," I replied. "Look at these," he said, and opened a bag or small trunk in which he carried his samples. I was enraptured. There were eight or ten styles, and they seemed to me beautiful. "How much are these?" I asked. "Well, if any of them fit you, you can have them. They're worth four dollars, but I won't charge you anything." He leaned toward me and smiled. Besides, I thought he was handsome. I began to like him."[18]

In fact, she agreed to run away with him. But the plan failed when the station agent found her stepping on the train and sent her home. As other small-town women had, Dreiser's sister sensed in the shine of new goods a sample of the world outside. Together, the products and the salesman become the focus of her desire while she becomes the object of the drummer's improvisational skills.

The collapse of family history into literature is as conspicuous here as in the story of Hurstwood's theft and flight to New York, which Dreiser based on another sister's experience with an absconding architect. In this instance, the fictional sister completes what Dreiser's actual sister began and, following the corridor south from her Wisconsin village to the "mysterious city" of Chicago, dreams of "some vague, far-off supremacy which should make it prey and subject, the proper penitent, grovelling at a woman's slipper."[19] Throughout *Sister Carrie,* the objective correlative for anticipated prosperity is often a new shoe, and its negative analogue is the opposite. In fact, Robert Elias's account of Dreiser's impoverished childhood begins with a discussion of the baby Theodore's earliest visual memory: his mother's worn-out shoe sole.[20] Not surprisingly, Carrie's fantasies of success focus on shoes: the "dainty slippers" that she longs to own, Drouet's "heavy-soled tan shoes, highly polished," which she admires, and Hurstwood's shoes "of soft, black calf, polished only to a dull shine," which she admires even more. Nice shoes make Carrie feel "the worn state of her shoes" and inspire a longing for material prosperity that leads her to quit her job in a shoe factory.[21] Dreiser's recollection of his sister's temptation by a shoe drummer may perhaps be apocryphal; true or not, it

A turn-of-the-century shoe salesman. From *System* (March 1906). (Courtesy of Cleveland Public Library.)

suggests a fetishized spectacle of desire—and a range of urges—staged on Main Street and orchestrated by a salesman.

Dreiser's references to commercial pretext in *Sister Carrie* deserve close attention. The first sentence of the novel suggests that Carrie's consumer instincts and her yearning for urban experience were whetted well before her departure. Her "cheap imitation alligator-skin satchel" and "a yellow-leather snap purse," like her ticket, the four dollars, a small trunk, and the scrap of paper with her sister's address, signify portability and transience; they all point away from home. Yet the concern for fashion that informs Carrie's "total outfit" is linked to her small-town shopping experiences. When Drouet tells her that he knows "quite a number of people in your town. Morgenroth the clothier and Gibson the dry goods man," Carrie interrupts him, "aroused by memories of longing their show windows had cost her." The exchange charac-

terizes the dual nature of Carrie's desire to consume—an instinctual, spontaneous longing and a redoubled desire, borne of memory. The second, residual form of arousal blends ironically with Carrie's wistful regret at leaving
home and establishes an originating base for her developing desire: the economy of Main Street. By visible signs that designate Carrie's love of clothes and
her impulse to imitate, Dreiser shows just how far Carrie's education has
proceeded—by urban standards she is already a "half-equipped little knight"
whose "daring and magnetism," "past experiences and triumphs," have prepared her for leaving—and by working inward, linking these physical details
to her emotions, he indicates that Carrie's sense of inferiority when she observes Drouet derives from influences at home. In noticing "the worn state of
her shoes" or the "shabby" condition of her dress, in becoming "conscious" of
her "inequality" with Drouet, she simultaneously draws on acculturated feelings and (half) knowledge. Although in this respect Dreiser's naturalizing
tendencies—for instance, his generalized sense that a (that is, any) "woman
should some day write the complete philosophy of clothes"—seem at odds
with the few details that he offers of Carrie's development, the overall effect is
to tug this urban novel and its city-bound heroine back to their small-town
origins.[22]

The very name that Dreiser gives Carrie's hometown contributes to the
sense that island towns and metropolitan centers are now fluidly joined. Columbia City confers newness and connotes the boosterism that gave small
towns hope that some day they would be the next Chicago, but the allusion to
Chicago's 1893 Columbian Exposition suggests a temporary, imitative status
that invidiously links the existence of the town to larger urban forces. To reach
the real city, although she has dimly known it all along, Carrie must leave
home and, invoking the essence of the name Columbia City, hope for safe
passage to a new world.[23] Simply by sending Carrie on this journey, Dreiser
gives the lie to readers who would find represented in *Sister Carrie* the totaliz-
ing impact of consumer culture. To be sure, Carrie's longing for urban commercial culture begins at home, but she cannot find satisfaction there. In
reflecting on the gap between Columbia City and Chicago, Dreiser asks,
"What, pray, is a few hours—a few hundred miles?" The distance, he implies,
is too much to be measured.[24]

More than any detail, however, Drouet's presence in the opening chapter
frames Carrie's passage from her old to her new home in commercial terms.
Where Carrie is half-equipped, Drouet is "a knight of today," that is, a knight
of the grip—a comparison that derives its sense of difference from their
shared identities as transient seekers of success.[25] From the start, Carrie and
Drouet are joined by their polar connections to the commercial system that
links city to hinterland—she as consumer, he as a middleman to retailers. The
familiarity that this connection creates between them, the sense that they have
something in common, is enabled as much by Carrie's interruption as it is by
his calculated effort to place their encounter on equal footing by recalling his
customers' names. But their incipient relationship is hardly one of equality;

rather, following the hierarchy that governs the urban-hinterland system, Drouet appears as a powerful, larger-than-life figure, and Columbia City as another town that he regularly makes. For her part, Carrie recognizes and honors Drouet's status by her willing answers to his questions. The crucial role that Drouet plays in Carrie's transition to the city, then, rests on commercial and cultural work which his type has already done, and in putting down "some of the most striking characteristics of his most successful manner and method," Dreiser takes pains to explain the drummer's power over Carrie in terms a small-town American, urban migrant, or reader of journalistic humor and local-color fiction would understand.[26] Carrie is also able to read Drouet's character as being somehow connected with his typicality, so that "whatever he had to recommend him"—and he is "attractive," as far as his "order of intellect" is concerned—"you may be sure was not lost upon Carrie, in this, her first glance."[27]

Dreiser stresses Drouet's typicality in several ways. He uses contemporaneous slang, circumscribing *drummer* and *masher* with quotation marks. He gives Drouet the distinguishing marks of his profession—flashy clothes and the "secret insignia" of the Order of the Elks, membership that separates Drouet from other travelers while binding him to a commercial brotherhood. The visual and sensory details that distinguish this portrait, from Drouet's gray fedora to his polished tan shoes, likewise establish his presence in the railroad car as he might have been seen on Main Street and as he was depicted in popular culture.

Dreiser's self-conscious reconstruction of a common cultural grammar is nowhere so apparent as in his appropriation of George Ade's fable "The Two Mandolin Players and the Willing Performer."[28] Dreiser plagiarizes Ade when cataloguing Drouet's method of meeting women in department stores and parlor cars; the result is a taxonomic description of the masher (Drouet's name is not even mentioned) that highlights the "type" of an "order" and illustrates its "characteristics."[29] In a sense, Dreiser's theft is absolutely consistent with the typicality of Drouet's portrait; what the text logically sacrifices in the way of artistic originality it regains in cultural authenticity by acknowledging the commercial, social, and literary practices that created this type. Furthermore, Dreiser's use of Ade only accentuates the reader's awareness that Drouet's techniques, as well as his features, are not unique; rather—like the details of an ethnographic text—they are the product of a culture.

All these details, taken together, resemble nothing so much as a composite figure drawn from a half-century of cultural history. And they all lay the groundwork for Carrie's forthcoming relationship with Drouet and her eventual commercial success. Indeed, what Drouet "makes" of Carrie in the opening chapters is what the novel as a whole takes as its subject: the ongoing transformation of Dreiser's drifting heroine by market forces. Although, as Philip Fisher has noted, Chicago is the central staging area in the novel, a renovative setting in which newcomers anticipate their future selves, it is Drouet who, in helping Carrie to a meal, "contributed the warmth of his spirit

Late nineteenth-century Americans experienced something of the glamor evoked by Charles Drouet when they played the McLoughlin Brothers' 1890 Game of Commercial Traveler and mapped their own routes through the territory. (Courtesy of Pamela Walker Laird.)

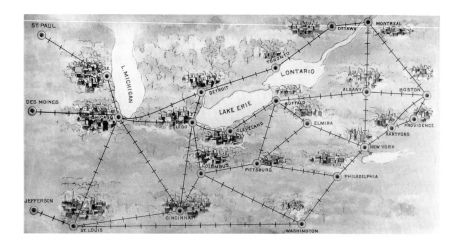

to her body until she was a new girl." He introduces Carrie to this transforming world, gives her the money to buy clothes, advises her in their purchase, presents her with a home, and, when she takes up acting, gives her a new name and the "ginger" to get the job done. If acting is the central metaphor in the novel and if Carrie learns to act in this city of commodities, thus translating her desires into material reality, who else but Drouet provides the best instruction?[30]

At bottom, Dreiser's choice of a traveling salesman to mediate between Carrie's old home in Wisconsin and her new one in Chicago makes *Sister Carrie* more than a naturalistic urban novel. Whereas Drouet is of the city and takes pride in representing the Chicago dry-goods house Bartlett, Caryoe and Company, his power stems less from the urban setting as such than from his role as a middleman within a commercial system vested in city-hinterland relations. Drouet's movement from place to place represents the transience in the novel—a flow of commercial forces that lifts up Carrie and pushes characters from one setting to another. Drouet's chief trait—"geniality"— announces this movement in social terms, imbuing his face-to-face improvisations with a psychic energy that simultaneously enwraps and outstrips its object. His success as a salesman, Dreiser points out, derives principally from this geniality. Hurstwood warms to Drouet's "genial nature," and Carrie bathes in an "irresistible flood" of it. By the end of *Sister Carrie*, the "but slightly changed" Drouet is still as light on the wing as ever, still exuberant and overflowing with warm feelings.[31]

As ubiquitous as it is magnetic, such nimble geniality epitomizes both the drummer's need to be all things to all people and its integration into an increasingly abstract market system. Because Drouet is at home everywhere, he can survive, and indeed thrives by, the dislocation of place that dooms Hurstwood's move to New York. Where Hurstwood's work as saloon manager proves place specific and socially discriminating, Drouet's is placeless and relatively undiscriminating. Thus figured, the drummer's personality is unbounded and adaptable, which is to say that Drouet's outer-directed sympathies and appetites assert their power with equal force. The same sensitivity to physical comfort that impels Drouet to offer a beggar money—when Hurstwood and Carrie hardly notice him—also instructs his sexual practices. Drouet's desire is described as an "unhindered passion," and his frequent examination of pretty women as a "habit" that not even his attachment to Carrie abates.[32] In the initial draft of *Sister Carrie*, Dreiser links these desires to commercial traveling when he explains that on "his trade pilgrimages" Drouet "was like to forget Carrie entirely" and go "merrily forward, pursuing the routine of his satisfactory employment" while he "stinted himself nothing in the way of flirtation and observation" and "seldom failed to respond" when friends "called him out to this or that sortie upon the susceptibilities of the fair sex."[33] Here, satisfactory employment gives a common context to trade and sex. In making towns, Drouet makes women, too, for as Dreiser maintains in both texts, to succeed with many women a man must be "all in all to each." Although the improvisational arts shared by salesmanship and mashing provide a system for intimacy, they preclude exclusivity in any one encounter or relationship. Dreiser implies as much when he says of Drouet that he "carried the doom of all enduring relationships in his own lightsome and unstable fancy." For her part, Carrie comes to understand the "logic" of Drouet's pervasive desires from listening to him expound the merits of other women, by which the drummer "went on educating and wounding" his "pupil and victim," compounding a paradox peculiar to his type.[34]

Drouet's failure to understand the logic of such actions dramatizes his lack of imagination and intellect, as well as his inability to live outside his emotions—all shortcomings that Dreiser attributes to his role as drummer, all failings that could doom him. Dreiser's observation that Drouet could just as easily be "hornswaggled" by a "deeply-dyed villain" as flatter "a pretty shop girl" shrewdly turns the salesman's role inside out by making him the potential victim of his own good nature and confidence. But Drouet does not fail. In fact, the narrative emphasizes Drouet's "enlivening" effects and his role as Carrie's maker and teacher. In an expanding consumer culture where spectacle and self-promotion go hand in hand, Drouet's commercial acumen as clothing salesman and connoisseur of women proves invaluable, and under his tutelage Carrie improves in a "material way."[35] The original text illuminates Drouet's part in this education even more clearly than the revised version. He writes:

> With Drouet's experience and opinion for a guide she had learned to select colors and shades which had value in relation to her complexion. Her dresses draped her becomingly, for she wore excellent corsets and laced herself with care. Her hair had grown out even more luxuriantly, and she knew considerable concerning dressing it. She had always been of cleanly instincts and now that opportunity afforded, she kept her body sweet. Her teeth were white, her nails rosy, her hair always done up clear of her forehead. She had some color in her cheeks, a large soft eye, a plump, dainty chin and a round, full neck. Altogether, and at all times, she was pleasing to look upon.[36]

Now able to bring fashion ever closer to her physical attributes, Carrie benefits from Drouet's commercial experience to discover her better self.[37] Carrie appears here as the object of both fashion know-how and male sexual desire, of both domestic and economic work, for Drouet reconstitutes her body along the most intimate lines and prepares her for public view. This improved self assumes its role before an audience of a general, nondescript character. Carrie knows considerable about hair care, but how? She keeps her body sweet, but for whom? Dreiser does not say. Leaving the source of Carrie's consuming expertise hidden and mysterious, he presents her as she might appear in public: a self-possessed object of desire.

The source remains hidden to Carrie as well. Although she learns to present and see herself as others do, she remains a "mirror of the active world," perfectly suited to the stage, only slightly better able to penetrate her self's reflection than Drouet. Yet it is Drouet who helps Carrie discover this histrionic self by encouraging her in role as Laura in *Under the Gaslight*. By boosting her confidence with his "ardent good nature" on the night of the Elks club performance, Drouet effects Carrie's transfer of identities; he enables her to assume another self.[38] Drouet's ability to sell Carrie on her own acting talents is particularly interesting in its qualification of the notion that the salesman is always selling himself. Here, perhaps more than in the earlier refashioning of Carrie, Drouet aids in a self-transformation—one that results in Carrie's movement out of the dressing room (and home), away from him, and onto the stage. In effect, Drouet sells Carrie's self to herself and brokers her successful rise in the culture. Little changed since his appearance on the Chicago-bound train or, before that, his implied presence on the Main Street of Columbia City, his role continues to be that of cultural middleman.

In this sense, Drouet loses Carrie the moment he sells himself to her on the train and awakens in her a longing to better herself. By accomplishing what all salesmen claim to do—that is, giving the customer what she wants—Drouet encourages the movement and forgetfulness that drive Dreiser's cycle of commercial desire. An important consequence of Carrie's improvement is that she is now able to initiate the cycle herself—and sell herself. Indeed, as Carrie literally arrives at each new stage in her life, she sloughs off a previous self (or name) and assumes a new one, thereby reflecting, if not assuming, the work of the traveling salesman.

Mobility, indeed travel, thus becomes an important context for self-making and future accomplishments. When, for instance, Carrie gets ready for her dramatic performance at the Elks club, the "painfully anticipated matter of make-up which was to transform her" is reduced in importance, and she relaxes in the comfortable atmosphere of "travel and display" and feels encouraged to go through the "open door" to scenes of wealth and fame. The "kindly" and encouraging voice that she seems to hear, more down to earth than the voices emanating from "far-removed" city scenes of wealth, sounds free of "illusion."[39] Reminiscent of Drouet's introduction on the train, the flaring gas jets and open trunks are familiar to Carrie, not only because as a small-town girl she may have longed to escape or because the passage from hinterland to city has made possible her present opportunities but also because life with Drouet has habituated her to this world. "He took her about a great deal," Dreiser says of their relationship, "spent money upon her, and when he travelled, he took her with him."[40] This subtle shift of focus returns the novel to its original frame and, evoking a commercial culture of travel and display, reveals that preparation that readied Carrie for her movement on the stage.

The source of this dual fascination with self-transformation and movement was, of course, Dreiser's own small-town background and his fierce yet ambivalent effort to wrest himself free from poverty and find success in an urban literary marketplace. Carrie's longing for success was surely his own, as was her inability to let go of the past completely. Immediately following her flight with Hurstwood to Montreal, Dreiser addresses this ambivalence. As if to explain why Carrie could possibly have given into Hurstwood's deception, Dreiser explains that "to the untravelled, territory other than their own familiar heath is invariably fascinating. Next to love, it is the one thing which solaces and delights. Things new are too important to be neglected, and mind, which is a mere reflection of sensory impressions, succumbs to the flood of objects. Thus lovers are forgotten, sorrows laid aside, death hidden from view. There is a world of accumulated feeling back of the trite dramatic expression—'I am going away.'" By this account, travel plays a deterministic role in creating a new, expansive present behind which the past and all memories of home wither. Carrie looks out upon the landscape and feels that "her life had just begun"; she is "saved," Dreiser explains, because she is "hopeful." Yet as Thomas P. Riggio has argued, this hope is in part based on a desire for a better home than the present one, which she is perpetually in flight from.[41] Whereas Carrie lacks "excellent home principles" and the novel as a whole dramatizes one false home after another—from the apartment that Drouet and Carrie occupy to the Hurstwoods' heartless family residence to the anonymous New York apartment to Carrie's final hotel residence—Dreiser continually evokes the ideal of home and its attendant warmth and security as a possible, if utopian, goal. This paradoxical relation to home accounts for Carrie's ongoing "blues." It also helps explain the appeal of Drouet, who, in giving Sister Carrie twenty dollars, becomes a "brotherly sort of creature in his demeanor" and effects an exchange that vouchsafes Carrie's acceptance of another domestic situation.[42]

What Dreiser called the curse of all American fiction, the necessarily happy ending, hardly afflicts *Sister Carrie*.[43] Eschewing the dictates of more traditional plotting, which would lead to some restoration of domestic order, Dreiser sets his characters adrift in a commercial culture to discover their own market value and to populate a novel whose primary vehicle—mobility—both anticipates and undermines the possibility of some final resting place. Given this state of unease, it is not surprising that Frank Doubleday expressed reservations about publishing *Sister Carrie*.[44] Nor is it surprising that Drouet should be so much at ease in the novelistic economy; the drummer's happy reappearance in the concluding chapters underscores not only the ubiquity of sales discourse but also the salesman's exchange value in society as Americans moved from small island communities and insular home principles toward urban mass culture.

As Dreiser saw it, the diffusion of domestic values into an abstract, placeless market was well under way at the turn of the century. By setting *Sister Carrie* in the 1880s, Dreiser was able to catch Chicago—and the national market economy—in the formative stages, when sidewalks were half finished, solitary houses stood just outside the city, and drummers like Charles Drouet, cut loose from traditional ties and free to make the road their home, were still a novelty. Yet in adopting this retrospective view, Dreiser also sounded an elegiac note for a moment he knew would soon disappear. One mark of this nostalgia is his portrait of Drouet, whose manner and method he painstakingly describes in the first chapter "lest" they pass from memory. Drouet's return in chapter 46—in his new position as sales manager—suggests that the drummer has disappeared from the cultural landscape. Dreiser's representation of this transition—from one "species" of businessman to another "type"—may be taken as a sign of the organizational developments that brought face-to-face sales methods into modern business enterprise. Yet in personal terms Drouet has barely changed. Still genial and good-hearted, Drouet appears last in the lobby of the Imperial hotel, driven "home" by bad weather, his "desire" still "stirred" for "those pleasures which shut out the snow and gloom of life."[45] Although the snug domestic circle that this vision of dreamed-for shelter evokes is not available to Drouet and although he finds satisfaction in the transient spectacle of modern consumer culture, the vision nonetheless remains the object of his inborn desire. While Carrie remains unsatisfied in her persistent longing for a better place, Drouet is content, if unreflective, in his homelessness, sensing that in a culture governed by commercial desire, home is only where the heart is, and domestic bliss, like any sale, may be part of just another stop along the road.

Reflecting Dreiser's general investment of human desire and sentiment in market forces, the simultaneous reappearance and disappearance of Drouet suggests that the death of the salesman is a result of the improvisational skills that facilitated his commercial success. Although Drouet survives and indeed thrives as a business actor, his absorption into the urban landscape at the end of the novel describes the waning of his power as a cultural type and the

The relationship between salesman and sales manager is represented in this 1908 advertisement for the National Salesmen's Training Association. (Warshaw Collection of Business Americana, Archives Center, National Museum of American History, Smithsonian Institution.)

assimilation of his personal magnetism by the marketplace that spawned him. The genial voice of the drummer heard in the first chapter becomes the disembodied siren call of consumer culture, and the sales pitch gives way to more pervasive modes of persuasion—a transformation not unlike what modern advertisers caused by adapting intimate modes of address (moving from "one" to "you") to an impersonal medium.

Some sense of this exchange emerges almost halfway through the novel when Drouet returns home unexpectedly one morning and, discovering that Carrie has gone out, begins a flirtation with the chambermaid.

> "Let me show you something," he said, affably, coming over and taking out of his pocket a little lithographed card which had been issued by a wholesale tobacco company. On this was printed a picture of a pretty little girl, holding a striped parasol, the colours of which could be changed by means of a revolving disk in the back, which showed red, yellow, green, and blue through little interstices made in the ground occupied by the umbrella top.
>
> "Isn't that clever?" he said, handing it to her and showing her how it worked. "You never saw anything like that before."
>
> "Isn't it nice?" she answered.
>
> "You can have it if you want it," he remarked.
>
> "That's a pretty ring you have," he said, touching a commonplace setting which adorned the hand holding the card he had given her.
>
> "That's right," he answered, making use of a pretence at examination to secure her finger. "That's fine."
>
> The ice being thus broken, he launched into further observation, pretending to forget that her fingers were still retained by his. She soon withdrew them, however, and retreated a few feet to rest against the window sill.

Here Drouet assumes the familiar role of masher while the chambermaid willingly plays the coquette. Still, there is more to this encounter than physical desire. At the heart of the drummer's proposition lies an understanding of the chambermaid's deepest longings—her desire for change and for novelty. By manipulating the trade card, Drouet commands the maid's attention. Her response to Drouet's geniality—"I wish I could travel"—evinces the same longing that so often overtakes Carrie, a subjunctive mood or desire for self-transformation that Dreiser ties to the fluid possibilities of the market.[46] Dreiser underscores the drummer's individual role in eliciting desire, but not without demonstrating that his personal agency is also reliant on other modes of persuasion. Although by the 1890s the trade card was obsolete, other forms of print advertising having taken its place, its presence in this scene looks forward to the future of modern advertising. On the other hand, Drouet's face-to-face improvisations reveal the human element without which the later emergence of modern advertising as a pervasive cultural power would not have been possible. Carrie, in moving from her role as Main Street consumer to actor depicted life-size on a Broadway theater poster, drifts toward a consumer culture whose persuasive powers, however naturalized, seem largely impersonal. Lest the human face in this cultural exchange go unnoticed, Dreiser remembered the traveling salesman.

7 The Mechanics of Consumption

As well as anyone, Thorstein Veblen characterized the transformation that reshaped American business practices during the early twentieth century. "Local color," he noted in 1904, "is falling into abeyance in modern life, and where it is still found it tends to assert itself in units of the standard gauge." Not surprisingly, Veblen attributed the decline of local color to the leveling influence of a machine-driven market economy. The "comprehensive mechanical processes of industry" exerted their influence nationwide: dictating consumption, rationalizing distribution, and shaping consciousness. Consumers who longed for the latest products, store clerks who sold goods at fixed prices, even lawyers and bankers "whose business is in a peculiar degree remote . . . from the oversight of mechanical processes" but who reasoned in "pecuniary" terms, now "habitually" evinced a standardized, "mechanical" way of thinking. Although the "mechanics of consumption" brushed practically all Americans, they pierced traveling men to the quick, transforming the drummer's inborn desire into the dynamics of modern salesmanship.[1]

But from the large-scale economies that haunt Veblen's view of modern America commercial travelers remain strangely absent. In abeyance, expunged, or simply not considered, the traveling salesman suffers from the logic that, according to Veblen, ruled American business enterprise. He drops from sight, and with him the "mitigating effect which personal contact may have in dealings between man and man is therefore in great measure eliminated."[2] So the salesman becomes a faceless, assembly-line entity. Absolutely free from the local color that made *The Theory of the Leisure Class* a popular success in 1899, Veblen's analysis in *The Theory of Business Enterprise,* written five years later, thus catches the mood of a new era. In modern America, at least in Veblen's corporate America, there were no walking sticks, no liveried servants, no treasured pets, and certainly no ubiquitous drummers. They belonged to an earlier era.

Yet traveling salesmen remained significant, if changed, participants in the commercial culture. For the many transformations that followed from and sustained the maturity of the corporation during the early twentieth century —large-scale manufacturing, integrated marketing structures, and national advertising—the modern salesman proved vital.[3] Indeed, traveling salesmen occupied the pivotal points in a series of exchanges that linked corporations, retail stores, and consumers. More than advertising, which, after all, was salesmanship on paper, the salesman gave the mechanics of consumption a human or natural countenance.

As in the years after the Civil War, when drummers took to the road, so, too, in 1900–1920 came a reorientation of the traveling man's methods and perceived importance.[4] A modern salesman rather than a drummer or order taker, the twentieth-century traveling man continued to make towns and carry a grip, but, eschewing loud suits and smutty jokes, he moved systematically through his territory and followed a path of advertising circulars and teaser letters that his house laid out before him. When he closed a sale, he had more than his own good nature to thank. He had an entire organization, a

Illustration for *Ginger Talks* (1905), by Worthington C. Holman. (Warshaw Collection of Business Americana, Archives Center, National Museum of American History, Smithsonian Institution.)

No. 3.

SALES GINGER

Published by
SALESMANSHIP
The Magazine for Business Getters
Williams Building, Chicago

system of selling goods, that enabled, and in fact demanded, his success. Ideally, if not actually, he disowned the improvisations of his nineteenth-century predecessors and, erasing local color from his sales pitch, embraced the principles of scientific salesmanship and efficient management. Such, at least, were the guidelines that sales "experts" and commercial travelers advanced in the sales manuals, trade journals, advertising ephemera, and instructional literature that flooded the market after 1900.

By the early twentieth century salesmanship was a formal discipline taught in business colleges and corporate training programs. Nor did salesmanship flourish solely within institutional boundaries. Beyond specialized journals—like the *Commercial Travelers Magazine* or Frank Dukesmith's *Salesmanship*—how-to articles and salesmen's success stories abounded in the *Saturday Evening Post* and *Collier's*. For a generation of ambitious young men intent on success and willing to take a correspondence course or read a book, salesmanship became a cultural touchstone.

By 1915, whether aspiring salesmen read Worthington C. Holman's *Ginger Talks* or James W. Elliot's *Salesmanship: An Artistic Science,* they had an expanding array of titles from which to choose. Consider, for example, the number of books that the Library of Congress catalogued under the heading "salesman-ship." In 1925, according to Edward K. Strong's contemporaneous study, *The Psychology of Selling and Advertising*, the library listed only 10 books on the subject published before 1900; nearly 40 published between 1900 and 1910; over 200 published between 1910 and 1920; and 150 published during the following three years alone.[5] Neatly paralleling the growth of salesmanship first as a term, then as a concept, and finally as a taught discipline, Strong's informal publishing history dramatizes the rise of salesmanship as an impor-tant commercial and cultural practice.

The hyperbole of twentieth-century sales enthusiasts notwithstanding, the modern salesman and his scientific selling techniques sprang from at least a century of commercial practice and development. The growth of fraternal organizations, the confirmation of the drummer's legal right to interstate commerce, the ongoing exchange of selling methods among commercial trav-elers and within their respective business houses—in short, the history of the profession—provided the basis, or the prehistory, for modern sales princi-ples. Besides "salesmanship," other subject headings and other books show this prehistory and trace the origins of modern selling not only to nineteenth-century drummers but also to peddlers and book agents. Accounts like Wil-liam H. Maher's *On the Road to Riches* (1876) and Virgil Wright's *Ten Years on the Road* (1893) make clear that aggressive, self-conscious selling techniques bloomed well before the advent of modern business enterprise. Canvassing instructions for door-to-door agents, such as the 1885 pamphlet *How to Intro-duce the Personal Memoirs of U. S. Grant* and the 1883 *Instruction Book of the Southwestern Publishing House*, reveal the strength of these techniques away from Main Streets and crowded cities along byways and back roads.

No salesman plied his trade without some precedent or guide. "I did not write this book," said Maxwell Droke in his *Making a Success of Salesmanship* (1922). "It was written for me by dozens of salesmen in as many lines; men who have told me their stories."[6] The selling stories retold in Droke's book—and retold again in countless other instructional manuals of the period—evince a vernacular tradition and a fund of accumulated knowledge, which all sales-men shared but which none could claim for his very own. As much as any factor, the repetitiveness that characterizes this literature of salesmanship affirms the debt that all salesmen owed to mercantile know-how. For salesmen, there was no genuine Ur-text, only a wide range of advice manuals and com-mercial textbooks whose similarities—or intertextuality—reflected actual business practices. Whether originating with a peddler, a French commis voyageur, an English bagman, a Scotch draper, or even a confidence man, the knowledge that guided the most scientific of twentieth-century salesmen evolved out of a widely practiced, historically shaped, and often unrecorded tradition of selling.

Yet for sales experts who heralded twentieth-century salesmanship as largely a new phenomenon, modern selling methods appeared to be con-nected to the transformed manufacturing economy. Using publishing figures as a springboard, Edward Strong called his readers to "witness the growing interest in salesmanship" and, more important, behold the radically changed industrial capacities that made those sales techniques essential. Once, national economic problems had hinged on production; now, Strong claimed, they turned on distribution. Hugh Chalmers, a former salesman for National Cash Register Company who eventually presided over his own automobile company, agreed. In a 1910 *Collier's* article he argued that the problems of production that plagued primitive societies had disappeared; now "it is easier to make than to sell, easier to supply demand than to create a want." So the salesman—"backed by advertising"—was now "the most perfect factor" in solving the "world's greatest problem [of production]." Echoed in the introductions to various instructional manuals, this view of the salesman as the perfect answer to the national distribution problems was the perfect pretext for scientific selling.[7]

This view also made selling part of the dilemma that Karl Marx had diagnosed years earlier: how to create demand, overcome competition, and still make a profit in an economy committed to overproduction. Indeed, there was little denying that "profits have been narrowed, and salesmanship is on a basis of strict business logic," as James H. Collins wrote in a 1907 article for the *Saturday Evening Post.* Nor did Walter D. Moody dispute these conditions in *Men Who Sell Things,* which appeared the same year. "The enormous pressure of new business and the constant tightening of competition seem to crush out the hope and energy of a large proportion of salesmen," Moody lamented. "The great problem of modern business progress to the salesmen is how to deal with this tendency,—how to prevent being crushed out and shoved to one side in the mad commercial whirl for conquest."[8] If the modern salesman survived this maelstrom of commercial activity after being squeezed, bullied, and threatened, how could he possibly muster the strength to conquer the distribution problem?

To a business generation familiar with Edward Bellamy, populist platforms, and various utopian alternatives, such questions assumed alarming urgency. Throughout the late nineteenth and early twentieth centuries critics denounced the middleman and attacked the inefficient, costly distribution system of which he was a part. Not merely a defense of the producer ethic but also a response to the current volatile economic instability, these attacks often evinced a longing for an efficient, centralized market—like the one that Bellamy depicted in his immensely popular 1888 novel, *Looking Backward.* In some utopian novels, like Henry Olerich's *Cityless and Countryless World,* published in 1893, traveling salesmen had no place, and consumers were "rid of that extra burden." In *The World a Department Store,* a tract written in 1900, Bradford Peck jabbed at the "vast army of traveling salesmen" whose expenses wring out "another grist from the producer." Disillusioned perhaps with his own business relationships, or, like his hero, "continually pestered by hundreds of drummers," Peck, a failed merchant from Maine, imagined a society where business advanced according to cooperative Christian ideals.[9]

If utopian proposals worried salesmen, the very real, fast-growing mail-order houses frightened them. More so than the many idealists and cranks who surfaced during the late nineteenth century, companies such as Montgomery Ward and, in particular, Sears, Roebuck and Company, profited from the economic and political unrest.[10] Indeed, something like Bellamy's dream of direct shopping, of "transmitting" tubes extending from "sample stores" into homes, made catalog shoppers of countless Americans and turned Sears into a very rich man. But while country folk delighted in circumventing traditional channels and anticipating something new in the mail, traveling men loathed Sears, who, according to one angry salesman had "the instincts of a peddler."[11] Mail-order shopping threatened the existing distribution channels, so jobbers and retail merchants, as well as commercial travelers, condemned the practice. Not surprisingly, opposition peaked in 1912, when Congress debated the merits of renewing and extending parcel post service. Voting to continue it, Congress thereby reinforced the efficiency and popularity of mail-order houses.[12]

From mail-order advertisements, Americans learned that traveling men spelled waste. As early as 1879, B. and A. Galland, manufacturers of ladies' undergarments, turned the popular aphorism *Caveat emptor* against the middleman. In presenting its catalog to the trade, the firm encouraged merchants to "make your selections with as much ease as if you had a line of samples before you, and dispense with the suasive eloquence of the traveling salesman, who will use his best efforts to sell you more goods than you want." Shrewdly, twentieth-century copywriters brought such protests into the new era by evoking streamlined utopias and describing a consumer's paradise—a world without middlemen. "The Last Middleman now CUT OUT," exclaimed Lincoln, Leonard and Company in a brochure. "No Jobbers—No Salesmen—No Agents—No Dealers." We are "Now Selling Direct to the User." Reaching out through the mails to consumers and retail merchants alike, catalog houses promised reduced costs to people (like Bradford Peck) who resented traveling salesmen and the unnecessary expenses that they incurred. "I prophesy the complete abandonment of the traveling salesman." "Our only salesman is our catalogue." "No goods sold through traveling salesmen." The "only means that I employ is the U.S. mail service." "We employ no salesmen."[13] And the barrage continued. Aimed at a familiar target but in keeping with the new era and its gospel of efficiency, turn-of-the-century criticism of the commercial traveler stressed his drag on the market rather than his ability to hoodwink or seduce the customer.

On the other hand, proponents of modern salesmanship denied that the commercial traveler had outlived his usefulness; instead, they championed his new-found strength. The "well-rounded salesman," Walter Moody affirmed, "will find methods to preserve his talent and energy from decay." The "efficient salesman" will realize "that professional salesmanship must supersede the old school of unorganized ways and methods." The "old-time 'minstrel' travelling man," however, "is a thing of the past, and with him have gone the days of getting business by means of circus tricks, chicanery, and sleight-of-hand performances in tact."[14] Traveling men, sales managers, and business observers supported Moody's claims. To survive the commercial traveler had to evolve, and to evolve he had to adopt the business principles of the new era. And so by 1900, nearly twenty years after *salesmanship* entered the American vocabulary, selling became scientific, and *drummer,* a crude moniker.

Although traveling salesmen had always resisted the slangy designation *drummer*—preferring instead the more professional-sounding *commercial traveler*—during the early twentieth century their resistance grew more historically conscious. From a Darwinian perspective, Charles Munn Clark, editor of the *Commercial Travelers Magazine,* argued that "the inflexible law of evolution" had made the "old time drummer" and his "sporty" ways obsolete. Speaking for a new era in salesmanship, one writer claimed in 1913 that the "age is past and gone, never to return, when the main requirements for successful salesmanship are 'gab' and clever story telling." The "change has not been wrought through any great spasm of virtue," he continued, "but rather because the well bred, polished knight of the road has demonstrated his ability to accomplish more than his coarser brother of former years."[15] By the 1900s, according to self-described modern salesmen, this coarser brother had disappeared—or was about to—and commercial travelers were delivering eulogies that distanced their modern methods from older, inferior business practices. As early as 1895 commercial travelers announced that "business methods have changed" and that the "old drummer has gone."[16] But he was slow in passing. In 1903, J. H. A. Lacher complained to his fellow United Commercial Travelers that the old-time drummer's tawdry reputation unfairly followed modern commercial travelers and sullied the profession. Traces of the past thus lingered. "The traveling men of those early days are gone, but they have left their successors a heritage of injustice and wrong, for tradition has preserved the reputation of the former and conferred it upon the latter. With all due respect to those pioneer drummers, when compared with the traveling salesmen of the present, they are like an unorganized multitude compared with a disciplined army. Discipline, progress and competition have wrought the change. There is no dilly-dallying on the road today; the race is for the sober and swift and not the gambler and the debauched."[17] Ambivalence colors this modern salesman's view of history. Yet by stressing the progressive development of business practices, an inevitable law of evolution that rewards only the fit, Lacher resolves this ambivalence. Although in name traveling men bore the burden of the old-time drummer's indiscretions, in substance those in the profession had evolved beyond primitive—unorganized—behavior to become like a new species of businessman.

So modern salesmen divided commercial practices into successive, increasingly superior ages and, naturalizing the transition from one to another, wrote their own romantic brand of history. Seen historically, commercial traveling became an evolving, organic process, and the modern salesman, the beneficiary of naturally developing selling practices.[18] Economic history wore a human face; more important, twentieth-century salesmen appeared part of a steadily improving commercial culture. Providential history this was not, but for traveling salesmen beset by tremendous commercial change, Darwinian succession augured unity, progress, and comfort. Evolutionary principles pulled twentieth-century salesmen closer to modern, specialized business practices. Words like *generation, evolve, successors,* and *brothers* enabled twentieth-century commercial travelers to preserve the line of descent and still condemn the unprofessional business practices of their predecessors. They evince, moreover, the metaphoric power that naturalism exerted not just on literature but on commercial culture as well.

Whether traveling men remained entangled in work, ignorant of trade literature, or simply did not care—or notice—they wrote nothing about the ironies implicit in the historical designations that in 1900 made any commercial traveler who had been working for longer than ten years an old-time drummer. Adapting to "progress" banished fears of obsolescence and made the 1880s seem a time long past, even to forty-year-olds. But not even the prospect of modernity obviated the frustration and conflict that attended economic change. Indeed, not all commercial travelers viewed the advent of modern business enterprise as natural growth.

Certainly P. E. Dowe did not. In 1899, as president of the Commercial Travelers' National League, he appeared before a congressional commission on trusts and industrial combinations and denounced prevailing commercial tactics. When urged to describe the impact of trusts on traveling salesmen, Dowe testified that "thousands of travelers have been dispensed with and thousands reduced in salary." When asked, moreover, if these job losses might be temporary, he assured the commission that the combinations "will throw out permanently some of them who are old, who have been in their special lines so long that they know only those lines." These veteran traveling men would find it "difficult to adapt themselves" to other businesses. "To-day," Dowe continued, "the merchants, jobbers, and manufacturers want the very best men, the most experienced men that they can get." As for what *experienced* meant or implied about the impact of modern business practices on veteran salesmen, he said little, except to deride the representatives of the baking-powder trust who went from dealer to dealer like "dummies," merely taking orders.[19]

From Dowe's perspective, the integration, price fixing, cooperation, and structural rationalization that distinguished the trust movement and contributed in part to the maturity of the modern corporation corrupted the natural economic order. Dowe rejected claims that trusts streamlined operations, reduced costs, and gave consumers cheaper products. No group "better appreciates the significance of the 'survival of the fittest'" than commercial travelers, he declared. But "to be forced to the wall by a species of speculative conspiracy and the centralization of capital does not sit well upon their digestive apparatus." The trusts were an "accursed thing that stalks" the land "falsely garbed as scientific economy."[20] Adapting to this mutation, no matter how evolved it appeared, struck Dowe as a suicidal act.

Outraged and confused, Dowe attacked the trusts as many late nineteenth-century Americans did: for their offense against democracy and nature.[21] Lacking the detached wit of Veblen, who wryly called these monstrosities "large-scale economies" and their methods "modern business enterprise," Dowe hewed to the views of Louis Brandeis and other critics who struggled to preserve smaller establishments. His tribute to the "poor boys who became great men, beginning at splitting rails, tanning hides, driving canal horses, etc.," rehearsed widely held beliefs about individualism, independence, and small-scale business. All self-made, Dowe's heroes achieved success by creating their own destinies. The emergence of industrial combinations, however, threatened this tradition. "The trusts have come," he warned, "as a curse for this generation and a barrier to individual enterprise."[22] Far from punning on the word *generation,* Dowe turned to it as instinctively as he did to other natural images. It represented an organic entity in time, a historical construct whose traditions, precepts, and rhetoric he both assumed and defended against large, self-generating organizations.

In retrospect, Dowe's 1899 defense of beleaguered commercial travelers sharpens in significance, and not just for the insight that it offers into the breakdown of small, independent wholesalers. To be sure, in lamenting the loss of sales jobs and decrying the tactics of salesmen employed by trusts, Dowe described, even if unknowingly, an important transition in the history of the corporation; he portrayed the impact of vertically integrated organizations, that is, industrial combinations that extracted, manufactured, and sold their products. But beyond these structural changes, he dramatized another crucial, albeit perceptual and rhetorical, shift: the moment prior to the emergence of progressive sales methods when commercial travelers could not imagine being naturally part of a falsely garbed scientific economy. Later spokesmen thought differently; certainly, they spoke differently. In assuming the language historically associated with the producer ethic, they seemed to adapt to the changed economy. In the equation that they now imagined and described, commercial travelers no longer operated as independent factors; they were not the pioneers of commerce that their nineteenth-century predecessors bragged of being. Instead, they accepted as a natural fact, or at least as a rhetorical given, their identity within a larger corporate body. The older language survived, but offered a different guise. Naturalism reinforced the commercial traveler's role in the new market economy.

So Dowe's testimony throws into relief commercial habits and customs that thereafter changed—gradually, to be sure, but not as naturally as some salesmen claimed. Spokesmen like J. H. A. Lacher denied their own volitional role when they characterized the traveling man's transition from sloppy drummer to efficient salesman as a gradual evolution. But salesmen intent on change proved instrumental in the development of progressive business techniques when they consciously promoted themselves as improved, modern salesmen. They became reform-minded. They marketed more than goods; they sold their new image or role in the marketplace. In embracing this new image and rejecting the older one, commercial travelers refined earlier efforts to convert profligate drummers to the ethical standards of the fraternal order. The culmination of long-standing efforts to reform the profession from within, modern business techniques thus appeared to spring naturally from commercial culture. New but not unfamiliar, progressive yet tied to the past, modern sales techniques emerged from a long line of descent. For Lacher and others, maintaining this genealogy—and emphasizing the sense of tradition that it conferred—was the first step in reforming it.

Nothing better dramatized this apparently natural transition from one commercial era to another than the spate of father-to-son books published between 1904 and 1925. Of these epistolary novels, George Horace Lorimer's are certainly the best known. But his *Letters from a Self-Made Merchant to His Son* and *Old-Gorgon Graham: More Letters from a Self-Made Merchant to His Son,* which the *Saturday Evening Post* published serially in the early years of the century, were only the first of several books that described changing business principles as a generational transition. In many of these works—Frank Tinelli's *"Pointers" to Commercial Travelers* (1906), Joseph Austrian's *"We Need The Business,"* R. L. James's *Letters from an Old Time Salesman to His Son* (1922), and even a monthly news bulletin, *"—Like the Message to Garcia,"* published by the Chicago advertising agency Henri, Hurst, and MacDonald—letters of advice from the paternal salesman or executive to his rising salesman-son pass on years of accrued experience and authorize modern commercial practices, sometimes through folksy humor and good old common sense. Thus Lorimer's self-made merchant urges his son to avoid telling jokes while doing business, and Tinelli's father reminds his charge that the "day of the Drummer is a thing of the past" and that the modern commercial traveler "is strictly business and entirely effective."[23] With such lessons these fictional fathers smoothed the transition from old to new and suggested that selling had become a young man's profession.

Others addressed this transition more bluntly. "Young men are to be preferred as recruits," it was stated in the Alexander Hamilton Institute textbook for sales managers in 1918. "They have greater possibilities for improvement and development than older men, whose habits of thought and action have become fixed. The money invested in training a man twenty-seven years old, is much better spent than the same amount would be in training a man fifty years old, who could turn in the same amount of business." Besides, the institute writer reminded readers, "there is always the danger that an applicant who has not made a good connection before he is thirty or thirty-five years of age, may have some characteristics that will tend to make him a disloyal salesman or a drifter." Like other instruction manuals, the textbook left little doubt of the youthful salesman's relation to his parent organization. Managers should pick men "whose futures are before them and who are willing to cast their lots with the house."[24] Sustained by hard work, systematic efficiency, and an organizational loyalty resembling filial piety, the traveling man assured the prospects of his house as he advanced his own. Although the house trained and shaped the salesman, their interests proved indistinguishable: both struggled to vouchsafe a future for progressive business methods. Careless improvisations and drifting, old-time ways had no place in this new generation of business methods or in the generation to come.

Images, as well as rhetoric, made this exclusion seem perfectly natural. As depicted by early twentieth-century illustrators, whether the commercial traveler strode past billowing smokestacks on the cover of Worthington C. Holman's 1905 *Ginger Talks* or attentively faced a sales manager in advertisements for the National Salesman's Training Association, he dramatized the apparent, if not inherent, advantages of youth, vitality, and power.[25] As drawn by J. C. Leyendecker for a 1903 *Success* magazine article entitled "The Necessity of Correct Dress in Business," the traveling man was young, sleek, serious, and without the whiskers so popular during the late nineteenth century—the epitome of modern business efficiency (see fig.). As presented in *Letters from a Self-Made Merchant to His Son* and sketched by F. R. Cruger and B. Martin Justice, he likewise embodied smooth-shaven, youthful power. Unlike the old-time salesman, whose "capital-in-trade consisted of a flashy appearance," the salesman now resembled a "well educated, neatly dressed gentleman who knows all about the goods he sells." Principally addressed to the "young man entering business today," C. M. Connolly's article—"The Necessity of Correct Dress in Business," from which this adjuration is taken—and Leyendecker's illustration, like much contemporaneous business literature, located in youthful power the future of modern salesmanship.[26]

So progressive sales advocates contributed to the youth cult that increasingly dominated twentieth-century culture. In idealizing, purifying, and regenerating business practices, they departed from earlier conceptions of authority and power—which upheld age, maturity, and tradition—and offered the image of youthful power that Americans beheld at sporting events and movie theaters across the nation.[27] Yet the urge to make things new—and youthful—struck American business even before it seized the film industry. Traveling men had always been boys, and by 1900, with the effort to expunge the old-time drummer, reform-minded businessmen were striving to revitalize commercial culture. In perpetuating the new image, reformers sped the reorientation of American culture—a shift in habits and attitudes that reflected the ever-quickening pace of modern life. Irrational and even antimodern, images of power, youth, determination, and vigor spoke to a broadly felt need for natural forces in a secular, commodified culture. But if the prescriptive measures to which turn-of-the-century bourgeois Americans turned—camping, bicycling, romantic fiction—promised relief from the demands of a rational industrial world, they likewise eased the transition to modernity. Similarly, business reformers promoted an image of sales success

"Here's your sample case; there's your territory; get the orders."

Exemplifying the sense of efficiency and power implicit in modern business enterprise, advertisements like this one for the Sheldon School of Salesmanship addressed readers through the directives of a sales manager. From *Salesmanship* (May 1907). (Courtesy of Library of Congress.)

that romanticized the mechanics of consumption yet simultaneously encouraged its growth.[28]

Juxtaposing youth, power, and salesmanship, progressive sales avatars struggled both to revitalize and systematize business practices. And although the traits they encouraged in salesmen—confidence, resolve, martial vigor—resonated with the youthful spirit implicit in salesmanship, the characteristics, rather than youth itself, served as the standard for modern salesmanship. In urging the individual salesman to "preserve his talent and energy from decay," for example, Walter Moody stressed the modern salesman's "husbanded" strength and his ability to develop those "newer, better, and quicker methods" that "the over-anxious, the old-timer and all other types of negative salesmen" lacked. Distinguishing salesmen by type instead of age illuminated the power of salesmanship as a natural force whose "roots," according to James Knox, author of several books on selling and founder of the Knox School of Salesmanship and Business Efficiency, "permeate every avenue of the factory and go clear back and are deeply embedded in the subsoil of the producer."[29] Yoked together, the persuasiveness of the salesman and the

The traveling man

Groomed for success, J. C. Leyendecker's traveling man is youthful,
clean-shaven, and neatly dressed.
From *Success* (May 1903). (Courtesy of
Harvard College Library.)

organicism of the market offered a potent, if paradoxical, union of industrial
and natural power on which all salesmen who persevered could depend.

Salesmanship thus rested on attributes that resided within the individual.
More than the Emersonian notion of self-reliance, however, salesmanship
proved a science and a system that made individual sovereignty and personal
experience the occasions for an education in business efficiency. In reciting a
variety of aphorisms—that salesmanship requires "character-building," that
"personality is capital," that "we can mold ourselves"—writers hammered
home the truth underlying all attempts to define salesmanship: that salesmen
are made, not born. By "careful training," wrote Adolph Johnson in his 1911
Hints on Salesmanship, "you can make yourself what you will."[30] Others agreed.
In 1912 the International Correspondence Schools of Scranton, Pennsylvania, dismissed the "old remark" that "salesmen are born, not made." The
author of *The Salesman's Handbook* instead preached "the doctrine of made
men as well as that of born men" and implicitly assured students they had
spent their money well. "It is not an easy matter to gauge accurately just what

one inherits. Some seem, from early childhood, to possess marked qualities, but results show that the great plan of nature provides that, by proper application, almost any man can attain reasonable proficiency in many different arts. . . . Almost any one of fair intelligence can, with a little observation and experience, learn something of the art of selling; considerable aptitude and experience should result in more than ordinary ability, even though the science of selling is not studied in an orderly manner."[31] Bringing a vocabulary and educational outlook derived from nineteenth-century concepts of Christian nurture and even older, Puritan notions of spiritual preparation into the commercial sphere, pedagogues of salesmanship urged students to improve nature—literally, to cultivate qualities best suited for selling. Like Benjamin Franklin's pious, but secular, plans for self-improvement, preparing for commercial success depended on systematically assimilating proven techniques and methods. Just as important, the techniques themselves constituted a system or network of commercial customs, which objectified and institutionalized the salesman's business identity. Without this system, experts emphasized, no modern salesman succeeded. The salesman who ignored this system or, in James Knox's words, "who must work out his own salvation on the field of Salesmanship" risked losing business and job.[32] Traveling men no longer merely pushed, hustled, and improvised to make towns on their own. In the modern commercial system, which they helped make and which made them, traveling men adopted and applied the techniques of an expanded consumer culture.

Modern business methods reshaped commercial traveling in two related areas, first, by rationalizing face-to-face selling methods and, second, by changing the salesman's relationship with his employer. Together, the methods of scientific salesmanship and the principles of modern sales management streamlined the entire selling process and changed the customs of traveling salesmanship. As traveling men hewed to the changes, they experienced some of the same transformations in work culture that factory workers, office employees, and retail sales clerks did.[33]

No word better describes these transformations than *system*. From 1900 to 1920 the notion that every salesman is constitutionally linked to a greater whole assumed increasing urgency. To businessmen of all types, but particularly traveling men, *system* denoted efficiency, accountability, and organization. Like the title of the widely read business periodical *System*, it connoted techniques that not only tightened the salesman's relationship with his employer but also made business a theoretical enterprise.

As P. W. Searles observed in his 1904 article "The Handling of Salesmen," the advent of system represented a historical change in sales management. Just "a few years" earlier the salesman traveled as "his own boss." Independently, he evaluated customers, "dictated his seasons of travel," and "made the towns which suited his fancy." But now "that exacting master of detail . . . has made it possible for the employer to know more about his business and management of his affairs." Searles's master system required each traveling sales-

Proponents of modern business enterprise used even cartoons to stress the value of systematic sales practices. From *Salesmanship* (May 1906). (Courtesy of Library of Congress.)

DON'T SKIP THE SMALL DEALER

man to mail back a report card for every town visited. His route planned in advance, a list of customers approved before he left, the commercial traveler routinely recorded the results of all sales calls and dutifully kept the house informed about his trip. Searles explained that not only does such a system apprise the house of "the exact whereabouts of a salesman any day in the week," but a particular card "will show whether the customers of the house have been visited and will also show if any new customers have been secured in addition to those listed to the salesman before starting out on his trip." Like other sales managers who thrilled to the prospect of monitoring and controlling their salesmen's progress, Searles made sure his readers understood in detail just how his system "revolutionized" commercial customs.[34]

Other systems abounded. There were files for follow-up letters and advertising circulars, loose-leaf binders for customer ratings and product prices, forms for expense accounts and product evaluation, and maps for outlining routes and diagnosing territories.[35] One organized salesman, promoting the value of his system, even urged other traveling men to take an office on the road in his specially designed trunk. He boasted: "I have a complete sales kit, latest bulletins for special cases, a typewriter for reports, correspondence and for writing quotations or proposals. I have tools for repairs, rating books for credit, house organs for ginger, and an agreeable occupation for a lonesome night in a dull town."[36] Not even William F. Milburn's traveling office could wholly revolutionize commercial traveling, but, taken together, the many attempts to improve efficiency and boost profits could and did reshape business practices and relationships.

In promising managers increased control over salesmen and their territories, system objectified early twentieth-century faith in efficiency and exemplified the impact of scientific methods on marketing structures. It extended

For the traveling man who "took the office along," the bureaucratic and organizational innovations of the new era not only augmented business efficiency but also created new tasks. From *System* (February 1917). (Courtesy of Harvard College Library.)

Frederick Winslow Taylor's management principles beyond the industrial process so that the salesman's "initiative" (his "hard work," "good-will," and "ingenuity"), like the worker's, became part of a system of "absolute uniformity." System offered complete standardization. Thus sales managers might assume, as Taylor's shop managers do in his 1911 *Principles of Scientific Management*, "the burden of gathering together all of the traditional knowledge which in the past has been possessed by the workmen and then of classifying, tabulating, and reducing this knowledge to rules, laws, and formulae."[37] Ideally, scientific sales management banished idiosyncratic selling methods and, by screening out local color from business organizations, sped the development of the mechanics of consumption.

Based directly on Taylorism, Charles W. Hoyt's 1912 *Scientific Sales Management* begins as so many commercial works of this period do: the author distinguishes between old and new salesmen. More specifically than other sales experts, however, Hoyt described the differences in organizational terms. A "'big me' species," bluff, hearty, and inefficient, the old salesman considered his own interests first. Typically, he imagined his customers and his territory as his very own, rather than belonging to his house. The new salesman, on the other hand, "works for the house and the house works for him." His "territory by cities, towns, and by individual customers is laid out for him. He expects it, and he co-operates with those who do the planning at headquarters so as to make the results of this work better and more efficient." Without drawing attention to himself or his interests, he plays the part of "missionary" and always emphasizes the needs of his organization first. He even considers the sales manager "his best friend."[38]

In one sense, *Scientific Sales Management* and books similar to it offer a compelling illustration of the commercial traveler's diminished independence. Now viewed as one of several factors in a determined, organizational effort to decrease "cost-to-sale" ratios and eliminate "rule of thumb" selling methods, the salesman seems a scaled-down version of his bigger, self-centered predecessor.[39] Compared to the sales manager, the figure of chief importance in many selling accounts, the modern salesman lacked stature and authority. Indeed, from the manager's point of view, the commercial traveler was often only one of several or many salesmen. When he participated in sales meetings or cooperated in advertising campaigns, he became, as one writer observed in a 1904 article for *Salesmanship* magazine, "a cog in the machinery of the house's organization." According to another expert, the "old idea" that "salesmanship is a thing apart from office management" had given way to a new one. "Now, the manager is considered just as much—indeed more—of a salesman than the men under him."[40] By correctly matching salesmen with territories, coordinating their movements in the field, overseeing their communications with the home office, and occasionally joining them on the road, sales managers used their authority to squeeze profits from a competitive market.[41]

Given a salesman's file of report cards, from which a manager could "assemble his whole trade and interview, at glance, each customer," how could the manager deny his own essential role in the selling organization? Armed with a Shaw-Walker routing system, whose drawers pulled out to reveal maps that allowed him to be "in constant touch with all his territory," what manager did not think of himself as a commanding officer in a war of sales?[42] Certainly, Kendall Banning did. In 1905 he wrote an article entitled "A Military System for the Sales Campaign" in which he pointed out that Napoleon had first used the "map-and-tack" system of routing personnel during his European campaigns. Now managers used it in their sales campaigns. And "'sales campaign' is not a misnomer," wrote Banning. "It really is a campaign—a fight for territory, with success dependent upon training and distribution of forces, whose orders come whence all information goes—the office of the sales manager."[43] Writing fiction for *System* magazine, Daniel Louis Hanson (a sales manager himself) and F. J. Selden portrayed managers as commercial generals bucking up their troops. In Hanson's 1907 story "The Salesman Who Lacked Courage," a determined manager arrives on the scene of a "faint-hearted" salesman's big transaction, presumably to show the buyers a united front—and offer a lower price—but ultimately to insist that his salesman make the deal himself, which he does, thus revitalizing his career. Selden's tale "The Crew That Worked Dubuque," published in 1906, highlights a sales manager's ability to motivate salesmen. The manager sweeps down upon a group of brand-new salesmen who, working together and deciding business is "slow," want to move on to the next town. With a "look that cut in his eye" and a "hardness that ground in his jaw," he condemns their laziness, fires one man, and threatens to dismiss the others if they cannot produce.[44] They succeed, just as the manager knows they can; before leaving the home office, he consulted his index system and found Dubuque loaded with customers.

For readers caught up in modern business, these success fables dramatized the importance of order, discipline, and tenacity. Brief and to the point, they offered quick, easy lessons to businessmen whose schedules and attention spans left them little time for more leisurely reading. Stories like Hanson's "Selling Moses Irons" provided five pages of melodramatic business entertainment, a conclusion that sounded the mood and methods of the era—"It is no longer fickle luck that rules, but a man's merit and fitness—and "the first realizing glimpse of that long dream of the ages—the standardization of men."[45] Other views—for instance, cartoons published regularly in *Salesmanship*—sent similar messages, similarly brief. "Use modern arms and ammunition" counseled the title of a 1906 cartoon that showed a uniformed salesman choosing his weapons from a battery of swords and bows, cannons and guns, labeled, appropriately, "antiquated methods" and "up-to-date ideas." Another, appearing a year later, urged salesmen to "climb up on the friendly shoulders" of a giant, for only by tapping the "collective knowledge of many men"—represented by the giant—can a man "see the things that would be 'way outside his horizon if he stood down on the ground alone."[46] Like sales managers whose ginger talks and office correspondence encouraged hard work and cooperation, business writers and artists celebrated the features of an increasingly standardized commercial culture.

Use Modern Arms and Ammunition

Cartoon, *Salesmanship* (April 1906). (Courtesy of Library of Congress.)

CLIMB UP ON THE FRIENDLY SHOULDERS

Cartoon, *Salesmanship* (January–February 1907). (Courtesy of Library of Congress.)

Holman's *Ginger Talks* epitomized the strenuous, martial spirit that promised to reinvigorate commercial culture.[47] The full title, *Ginger Talks: The Talks of a Sales Manager to His Men,* identified the source of Holman's directives; as from a dais erected in his home office, he proclaimed that "selling goods is a battle, and only fighters can win out in it." At other times, he sounds like a football coach, urging his players not to quit in the "pile-up" but to summon "sheer grit, courage, nerve, determination." Although Holman denied that he was "delivering a sermon or a medical treatise" when he encouraged men to cultivate robust health—"I am speaking purely from a business standpoint"—his usual form of address to "you men" and reliance on slang exemplify the way institutional orders frequently appeared as colloquial language. Even while Holman disclosed the benefits of hard work to his "Brother salesman," his role as guide and boss never disappears from sight. Prefaced by an epigraph from Theodore Roosevelt's *Strenuous Life* and dedicated to John H. Patterson, the founder of National Cash Register, *Ginger Talks* spells out the commercial rewards of speaking softly and carrying a big stick. But as much as Holman celebrated the seemingly universal qualities of courage, determination, and power, he never lost sight of the organizing principles that made the human body "a machine" and the selling enterprise a success.[48] He remained committed to those principles.

Before *Ginger Talks* appeared—indeed, before the surge of scientific sales principles—John H. Patterson discovered the advantages of standardizing sales methods. As the founder of "the first school of salesmanship" whose "genius" Holman acknowledged in his dedication, Patterson achieved an almost legendary status among proponents of scientific sales techniques.[49] In view of the product that he marketed, Patterson seems unusually prescient. At first resisted by store owners, restaurateurs, and others, the cash register became a familiar item in stores across the nation and symbolized the accountability that merchants initially feared to impose on their employees. Like Frederick W. Taylor, Patterson understood the need for system and efficiency in the workplace. But he also understood that to sell his revolutionary product he needed a system that linked salesman and customer.

The selling system or sales "primer" that the National Cash Register Company developed during the early 1890s was the first of its kind. A distillation of selling methods culled from company travelers, the primer provided a sales talk that after some revision salesmen had no choice but to follow. Banished were idiosyncratic sales pitches. Banished also were slipshod grooming and illegible handwriting. The company even hired an elocutionist and a writing instructor (Holman) to correct and smooth out salesmen's verbal inadequacies. In 1894 the company established a sales training school at its factory in Dayton, where salesmen, old and new, received an education in how to demonstrate and sell cash registers.[50] By 1901, according to E. D. Gibbs, an instructor at the school and the advertising director of the company, students were learning how to demonstrate their product—and more.

> Green men have been taken and by a systematic course of study are now able to talk intelligently upon all cash register subjects and to demonstrate a machine in an easy, natural and effective manner. To the old salesmen it has also been a benefit. The rough edges of their talk and manners have been smoothed down. . . . Elocutionists have taught us that in talking we must use the fewest possible words, and every word that we do use must be heard. . . . We are too apt to send the words out through the teeth instead of opening the mouth and allowing the words to roll out and just drop down where they belong. The difficulty with most men is that they do not open their mouth wide enough in talking.[51]

At the National Cash Register Company and elsewhere, salesmanship proved a mode of persuasion that depended as much on training, even creating, a presentable salesman as it did on changing the customer's mind.

At the heart of scientific salesmanship lay an increased awareness of the relationship between salesman and customer—and a determination to control that relationship. Much of this effort focused on the psychological laws governing the selling process. Although traveling men continued to handle the physical tasks of their occupation, they grew ever more convinced that the battle for sales and profits took place in an ambiguous, but penetrable, territory of the mind. Short of supplanting the aggressive, improvisational spirit that characterized late nineteenth-century attempts to make towns, the increased attention to psychological dynamics shifted the foundation of commercial creativity and reoriented the salesman's education. As the art of selling became a science, and psychology replaced common sense and probity, salesmen worked systematically to master the mechanics of consumption and improve their appearance, habits, and attitudes. Learning now from books and schools what traveling men once gleaned from the road, aspiring salesmen needed only to adopt the scientific point of view recommended by Adolph Johnson and others to discover that developing "those qualities of body and mind that build up a strong personality which is capable of persuading and controlling the minds of others" constituted the essence of salesmanship.[52]

The image of the conquering personality and even the idea of developing the personality distilled a notion of improvisational selfhood that had long been a part of the marketplace.[53] In 1916, when Orison Swett Marden once again repeated the aphorism, intoned by Asa Greene during the 1830s and William Maher in 1876, that the "tactful salesman is 'all things to all men,'" the strategies for facilitating this face-to-face relationship and the transactions that would follow were all but commercial givens. True now for store clerks, insurance agents, bankers, stock brokers, and high school students enrolled in salesmanship classes, the wisdom of the marketplace had traveled beyond the road to become part of the culture at large.[54] Both a cultural touchstone and a code of commercial practices, salesmanship commanded the attention of popular self-help gurus like Marden, whose book, *Selling Things*, wedded social success to selling ability.[55] Yet even Marden's tract, addressed as it was to all those who "form a part of the world's great system of organized barter," remains rooted in the same commercial tradition that spawned Maher's *On the Road to Riches* and the National Cash Register Company's sales primer. Even his tactful salesman remained capable of improvisation. "Not that he is deceitful or insincere," explained Marden, "but he understands different temperaments, different dispositions, different moods, and readily adapts himself to all." With "his finger on the mental pulse of his prospect," the tactful salesman knows "that the moment a prospect shows signs of being bored" he should end his sales pitch. If not, "the next time he calls this bored suggestion will come to the mind of the prospect, who will refuse to see him."[56] Like Maher's drummer, who knows not to talk nonsense with uninterested customers, Marden's salesman gauges his prospect's character and, safeguarding the incipient relationship, saves his selling talk for later.

But for all the remarkable similarities to the older drummer's account, Marden's advice manual is of a different historical moment. Infused with the language of the new craft—words like *mental pulses* and *suggestion*—Marden's self-conscious description of salesmanship reveals the commercial and cultural context that framed its writing. And it suggests that as traveling salesmen pursued their trade they rarely forgot that their own selling practices, short of being wholly derivative, belonged to an objective, independent system of knowledge. They understood, as Marden did, that it "is scientific salesmanship to-day, and not luck"—or mere experience—"that gets the order."[57]

How could they not understand? Urged by managers, fellow salesmen, and self-proclaimed experts to bring system and efficiency to their professional and even personal lives, early twentieth-century commercial travelers ignored scientific salesmanship at the risk of dismissing the ruling principles of their occupation. "Have a system for everything," advised Stanley Woodworth in his 1912 book, *Success in Salesmanship*. Hardly alone in encouraging salesmen to revamp their lives, Woodworth prescribed techniques that included far more than card indexes for customers. The successful salesman ate regularly, spoke crisply, and observed carefully. Letting his words "be spontaneous" but the "ideas, and phrases that best express them," part "of a definite plan," Woodworth's salesman learned by scrupulous, scientific methods how to "adapt himself to the moods and characters of the many men he calls upon." By mastering the "laws of analysis," set forth in a 1903 *Salesmanship* article, the salesman sought to assess the advantages of his environment and "separate the good and bad points indicated in the varying personalities" involved in business. Such mastery, however, began with the self. "Above all," the author of "How to Study Salesmanship" concluded, "you must study your own personality in its relation to the rest of mankind and learn how to keep yourself in that frame of mind whereby one individual influences another to act."[58] Ironically, commercial adaptability and flexibility followed a rigid system for living. To meet the demands of a competitive marketplace, more important, to respond successfully to the changing marketplace, salesmen naturally assimilated the machinelike habits of modern business enterprise.

In 1905, *Salesmanship* magazine reproduced as the "Greatest Ginger Talk Ever Written," a William James essay on habits. His observation that "at the age of twenty-five you see the professional mannerism settling down on the young commercial traveler" speaks to the peculiar balancing act—between plasticity and rigidity, possibility and finality—that hopeful scientific salesmen inevitably performed. His warning that for "most of us, by the age of thirty, the character has set like plaster, and will never soften again" illuminates the developmental perspective that, in the commercial world especially, favored youth.[59]

So the effort to make salesmanship scientific yet natural paralleled broader attempts to depict the emerging corporate economy as the logical unfolding of an organic process. Writ large, the marriage of systematic economy and natural forces offered a panoramic, romantic view of commercial history.

Portrayed in detail, however, as a close study of successful salesmanship, the union evinced the difficulty of highlighting commercial might in natural, let alone realistic, human terms. Overdeveloped and out of scale, the superhuman salesmen left no doubt of his masculine force. Indeed, there was little room for human frailty among the traits that sales experts instructed readers to cultivate. Developing a strong personality, as Arthur F. Sheldon constantly reminded readers, and students at the Sheldon School of Salesmanship in Chicago, meant eradicating negative qualities and cultivating positive ones. Extravagance, doubt, fretfulness—in fact, many of the attributes historically associated with the "weaker" sex—augured failure. Courage, strength, confidence, and will, on the other hand, enabled the "well-rounded, symmetrical man" to succeed in business and provided the basis for unrelenting, systematic selling. Attaining these traits, according to Marden, Sheldon, Holman, Moody, Knox, and other proponents of sales success, depended on natural development. "The foundation for salesmanship can hardly be laid too early," declared Orison Swett Marden. But failing a start in early childhood, the ambitious man could take Sheldon's sales course or a similar one and, following the "Evolution of Success: A Chart of Character and Health-Building," begin afresh in a culture devoted to progressive business principles.[60]

The hero of Elmer E. Ferris's 1915 tale, *The Business Adventures of Billy Thomas,* undergoes such a transformation. At the outset of the novel, the rough-edged twenty-two-year-old Thomas dreams of becoming a traveling salesman but, lacking "the courage to make the venture," plods on in his job as a shipping clerk for a coffee manufacturer. By the end, twenty-odd years later, he has risen to the top of his field and become a sales manager. The change in Thomas's career comes quickly, naturally, and melodramatically— yet without the lucky break or convenient benefactor so important in Horatio Alger, Jr.'s, nineteenth-century success stories. Billy Thomas determines his own success, first, by reading a self-improvement manual; second, by taking a physical culture class; and finally, after a fight with a coworker, by proving his courage to the company owners. Promoted to road salesman, he appears in the second chapter as a successful commercial traveler, now regaling his former office mates with stories of how a "card index scheme" helps him win customers.[61] System and confidence, methodically developed, bring him success within a selling organization.

Billy Thomas's success not only begins *with* himself; it begins *in* him, in "a thought world of belligerency and victory, a world in which he was the central and triumphant figure" and "a man of aggressive and conquering spirit." Following a "system of mental exercise and autosuggestion" and later a regimen of physical exercise, he becomes a new man. The transformation dramatizes the practical benefits of what, in another Ferris tale, a psychology professor calls the idealism of modern psychology. No man "need be the victim of his temperament," muses Ferris's academic proponent of modern business; even the "undervitalized anaemic" can "work out a new birth" by saturating the subconscious mind with suggestions and plans. "Picturing one's self in his thought as he wishes to be, and insisting that he is that" is a crucial process for the ambitious salesman, but not only because it promises a changed personality.[62] Implicit in Ferris's fictional perspective, yet explicit in practically all salesmanship manuals, is the understanding that selling itself rests on psychological rules. If by a psychological system the salesman shaped the requisite sales persona, by the same inner logic he learned to read and even control the customer's thoughts and desires. If by autosuggestion the salesman created a conquering personality, by suggestion he made a compliant customer. In a commercial landscape governed now by scientific method and psychological law, salesmen brought theory to practice as they sought to make towns and control minds. Whereas youth gave modern salesmanship the appearance of power, psychology enabled salesmen to harness such strength from within.

Although the influence of psychology on modern thinking hardly needs amplification, its impact on business practices, particularly salesmanship, demands closer attention. Indeed, the role of psychological theory in explaining and imagining face-to-face business relationships during the early twentieth century was tremendous. "All business is ultimately the affair of minds," explained Hugo Munsterberg. "It starts from minds, it works through minds, it aims to serve minds."[63] Echoing the conclusion reached by Adolph Johnson in *Hints on Salesmanship*—that "everything affecting the transaction takes place in the mind"—the Harvard psychology professor brought to business literature the authority that his academic status gave him. Yet in making commercial practice an essentially psychological process, neither his *Business Psychology*, which appeared in 1915, nor his *Psychology and Industrial Efficiency*, published in 1913, expanded the spectrum of information already available in dozens of salesmanship manuals. Munsterberg's observation that "the commercial traveler adjusts himself to the wishes, reactions, and replies of the buyer" only repeated the wisdom of Maher, Marden, and others. And his recognition that salesmen addressed those wishes by discovering "whether the psyche of the individual with whom he is dealing can be influenced more strongly by logical arguments or by suggestion" merely reflects the view of selling that routinely accompanied definitions of scientific salesmanship.[64]

Indeed, scientific salesmanship turned out to be a psychological system that allowed salesmen to summon and direct unseen, irrational forces. In 1895, according to J. S. Barcus's *Science of Selling*, salesmanship involved "focusing arguments in favor of the transaction in hand," but by the early twentieth century it had become an expanded mental process consisting of more than "reason why" persuasion.[65] No wonder experts on modern salesmanship frequently compared selling to advertising: both modes of persuasion prepared the customer to buy. "After all is said," one writer concluded, "the advertising writer is just a salesman minus sample case, hotel bills and yarns." At the same time, the salesman functioned as a "walking and talking advertisement" whose personality "is the figurative illustration, type and talk of the printed advertisement. He creates favorable or unfavorable impressions, just as the advertisement does."[66] Consciously exciting interest through oral, rather than textual, presentations, the salesman converted his audience with evangelical fervor and, more tangibly than the advertising writer, established a direct relationship between buyer and seller.

Depending not only on logic but on emotional suggestion, too, the salesman advanced through successive stages: he captured the customer's attention, gained his interest, sparked his desire, and, converting desire to decision, closed the sale.[67] Each step in the transaction, as F. H. Dukesmith emphasized in the first issue of *Salesmanship,* published in 1903, "is absolutely dependent on the other." So it "naturally" followed that to be successful a salesman "must conduct every sale along these lines." Although Dukesmith allowed that "the same methods cannot be successfully adopted by all salespeople," the efforts of his journal—like those of other commercial periodicals and books—to foster a "practical understanding" of the psychological principles underlying salesmanship inevitably contributed to the paling of local color in the selling process.[68]

Although dividing the sale into steps afforded salesmen "a definite working basis—a strategic plan of attack," little sign of conflict accompanied the well-designed attack. Under the efficient, scientific salesman's direction, the sale moved smoothly from start to finish. In a 1908 article for the *Traveling Man,* F. H. Hamilton counseled salesmen to move methodically through the steps of a sale and close as quickly as possible, but never by jeopardizing or ignoring the intervening steps. "You are asking him to change the current of his thoughts," admonished Hamilton, and "to fix them upon yourself and your proposition, to the exclusion of whatever important concerns of his own may be occupying his mind at the moment of your call." Equipped with the sensitivity—and the vocabulary—of the modern psychologist, the perspicacious salesmen took care not to interrupt his prospective customer with the familiar phrases "I represent—can you spare me a few minutes—I want to show—." These, he cautioned readers, are "all about the salesman." Instead, Hamilton encouraged salesmen to exploit the implications of egotism and consider the sale from the customer's point of view. "The surest way to interest him is to talk about his business, his prospects, his opportunity, his expectations of making more money or bettering himself in any way." Holman agreed that arousing the customer's interest begins "by getting over on HIS side of the fence."[69] By presenting the transaction entirely from the customer's perspective, the salesman appeared the natural ally of the buyer and so diminished the differences that stood in the way of the sale.

Around this union of commercial minds the scientific salesman's efforts revolved. Although not all commentators made selling the focus of such intense psychological activity that they defined a sale as "the fusion and agreement of two Minds," as William Atkinson did in a 1910 book entitled *The Psychology of Salesmanship,* most acknowledged that salesmanship required "knowing how to make minds meet." On the one hand, commercial writers encouraged salesmen to plumb the depths of every customer's mind—and manipulate it—while, on the other, observers like William Maxwell, writing for *Collier's* in 1913, frankly admitted that such control "is largely a delusion," for the salesman "evolves a more or less uniform method of presenting his subject" based on how customers have treated him. Maxwell denied that salesmen could "read character" and thus advanced a somewhat different notion of salesmanship and human nature than did those who hoped to divine their economic future by scanning the faces of their customers.[70]

Conscious psychologizing was indeed a part of scientific salesmanship, but if it smacked of Freudian theory, modern salesmen seldom acknowledged their debt to contemporaneous influences. In fact, notwithstanding occasional references to William James or Thorstein Veblen, scientific salesmanship often seemed curiously grounded in earlier, nineteenth-century conceptions of the self.[71] Surprisingly, not a few early twentieth-century salesmen clung to the once-hallowed, but now discredited, principles of phrenology. Although few went as far as John Dearing did in his 1913 memoir, *A Drummer's Experience,* where he declared that "the science of phrenology should be taught in every school" because "it is one of the deepest studies known to man," vestiges of the popular antebellum science appeared throughout modern salesmanship literature.[72]

To modern salesmen intent on understanding their customers' habits and proclivities, phrenology offered a universal system for reading character. For instance, although J. Fred Larson, a salesmen for John Wanamaker, apologized at the outset for discussing "the two so-called sciences of phrenology and physiognomy," he based his entire 1905 *Salesmanship* article, "How to Read a Customer," on the "generally admitted notion" that "the shape of heads and their bumps mean something and that the contour of the face is invariably indicative of character according to what may be regarded as fixed rules." Even more indebted to phrenology is Charles Lindgren's 1909 book, *The New Salesmanship.* Not new at all, it is prefaced with a cross section of the human skull labeled to show the particular area of the brain where "amativeness" and other attributes reside—an illustration that would have been familiar to antebellum Americans. Lindgren's manual exhibits the deep cultural roots of this presumably modern, scientific profession. Reading a customer's head and spotting his "rather large Cautiousness," he demonstrates the commercial applicability of phrenology but neglects to reveal his sources. Not once does the word *phrenology* appear in *The New Salesmanship.*[73]

Nor does the word appear much in other salesmanship manuals that correlate physical features with mental characteristics. The authors of the *Salesman's Handbook* of the International Correspondence Schools distinguished among three types of men—phlegmatic, nervous, and sanguine—whose outward bearing corresponded to their general behavior. Although they conceded that beyond these broad distinctions "human nature is too complex to be closely classified," they included an analysis of the "mental characteristics appealed to in selling." Without providing a specific map for "reading character" or acknowledging the place of phrenology in salesmanship, the ICS referred to "acquisitiveness" and "approbativeness" familiarly, as if they as-

In charts like this one, modern salesmen betrayed their reliance on nineteenth-century notions of human nature. From Charles Lindgren, *The New Salesmanship* (1909). (Courtesy of Harvard College Library.)

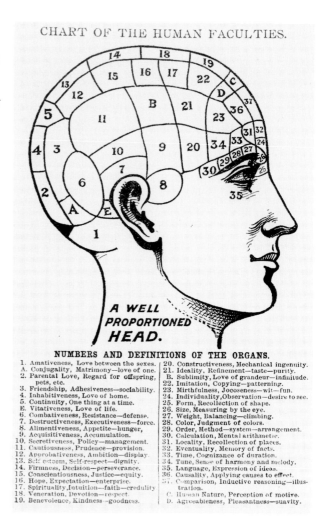

CHART OF THE HUMAN FACULTIES.

A WELL PROPORTIONED HEAD.

NUMBERS AND DEFINITIONS OF THE ORGANS.

1. Amativeness, Love between the sexes.
A. Conjugality, Matrimony—love of one.
2. Parental Love, Regard for offspring, pets, etc.
3. Friendship, Adhesiveness—sociability.
4. Inhabitiveness, Love of home.
5. Continuity, One thing at a time.
E. Vitativeness, Love of life.
6. Combativeness, Resistance—defense.
7. Destructiveness, Executiveness—force.
8. Alimentiveness, Appetite—hunger.
9. Acquisitiveness, Accumulation.
10. Secretiveness, Policy—management.
11. Cautiousness, Prudence—provision.
12. Approbativeness, Ambition—display.
13. Self esteem, Self-respect—dignity.
14. Firmness, Decision—perseverance.
15. Conscientiousness, Justice—equity.
16. Hope, Expectation—enterprise.
17. Spirituality, Intuition—faith—credulity.
18. Veneration, Devotion—respect.
19. Benevolence, Kindness—goodness.

20. Constructiveness, Mechanical ingenuity.
21. Ideality, Refinement—taste—purity.
22. Imitation, Copying—patterning.
B. Sublimity, Love of grandeur—infinitude.
23. Mirthfulness, Jocoseness—wit—fun.
24. Individuality, Observation—desire to see.
25. Form, Recollection of shape.
26. Size, Measuring by the eye.
27. Weight, Balancing—climbing.
28. Color, Judgment of colors.
29. Order, Method—system—arrangement.
30. Calculation, Mental arithmetic.
31. Locality, Recollection of places.
32. Eventuality, Memory of facts.
33. Time, Cognizance of duration.
34. Tune, Sense of harmony and melody.
35. Language, Expression of ideas.
36. Causality, Applying causes to effect.
37. Comparison, Inductive reasoning—illustration.
C. Human Nature, Perception of motive.
D. Agreeableness, Pleasantness—suavity.

sumed their readers knew how to spot these qualities.[74] Even as late as 1923, in *Salesmanship: A Fine Art,* Ross Breniser encouraged real estate men, door-to-door salesmen, and commercial travelers to read character "at a glance" by scanning the noses, eyes, and heads of their customers.[75]

The persistence of phrenology in twentieth-century salesmanship qualifies the descriptive, frequently evaluative term *modern,* revealing the residual influence of lapsed epistemological systems and the endurance of older commercial practices. Barely deviating from the phrenological principles espoused in such nineteenth-century advice books as the 1889 manual *The Art of Selling: With How to Read Character,* whose author called the ability to read character one of "the most valuable faculties for a business man," modern sales experts affirmed, consciously or not, the continued vitality of the selling tradition.[76] Even those who denounced the phrenological method as "folly" or called it "pseudo-psychological" acknowledged the influence of the older way.[77]

In a commercial culture where competition, efficiency, and personality had become bywords, pseudopsychological methods promised a clear path to success. As yet another systematic approach to business, phrenology rationalized selling relationships and, by objectifying the customer's traits, offered salesmen control of them. The aggressive, hurrying salesman had only to glance penetratingly, read carefully, and make his sale. So at least the mechanical sales formula suggested. Most scientific sales manuals, however, offered a more sophisticated view. Assimilated into a wider spectrum of sales strategies and self-improvement plans, the phrenological apparatus appeared transformed and, from the modern salesman's perspective, improved. The salesman, now considered malleable, became capable of cultivating traits, which in the phrenological system remained unchangeable. Being adaptable and flexible, furthermore, the modern salesman carried this spirit of creation into the marketplace, where, by force of personality, he controlled the conditions of selling.

So according to strategies popularized in salesmanship manuals and depending on the mood and temperament of the customer, the salesman suggested and smiled, entreated and commanded—all the time waiting for "the psychological moment" to close the sale. Like an artist, he "sees the completed picture in his mind's eye, his imagination, before he paints." Like an actor, "he speaks the thoughts of other men; he persuades by his manner of speaking, his manner of acting, and by some indescribable force of his own personality which he is able to embody forth as real." Never simply a traveling man, insurance salesman, store clerk, never the mere representative of business enterprise, the modern salesman proved the consummate performer, determined to absorb—and project—everything that his commercial audience knew and loved.[78]

But the acting metaphors that abounded in the literature of modern salesmanship indicated more than the salesman's ability to improvise at will. They spoke finally of a performance in which both salesman and customer had parts. To be sure, persuasion advanced by stages, or acts, as the canny salesman made his samples and his selling pitch the props and script of a convincing performance. On the other side, however, the retail merchant or jobber responded in terms of his own needs, fully conscious that under different circumstances he or his representative would have to get on the consumer's side of the fence and play the role of salesman. Although the traveling man strove to sell to each customer as a sales clerk might persuade a consumer, salesmen and retailers worked together, conspiring by dint of their common selling experience to pass the products on the buying public. Whereas the retailer's relatively sophisticated understanding of selling made him a tougher customer, it also made him a potentially willing partner. For the salesman, as William Maxwell affirmed in the piece he wrote for *Collier's*, the result was a selling script written in part by the collective customer—a drama dictated by the emerging mass market. Linked to a commercial system that stretched beyond the immediate transaction, the salesman's imagination vibrated with the power of modern business enterprise.

The articles that William Maxwell wrote for *Collier's* in 1913 and 1914 dramatize the traveling salesman's role in this increasingly knitted-together enterprise. Once a commercial traveler and a sales manager, Maxwell understood the historical movements that had changed the customs of the road. Describing on the one hand the way the "minds of buyer and salesman . . . appear to synchronize" when they examine a catalog and, on the other, the map-and-tack campaigns aimed at conquering even the smallest out-of-the-way towns, Maxwell traced in the traveling salesman's new role the dynamics of an evolving consumer culture.[79] Embedded in human behavior but shaped by the industrial economy, modern salesmanship, or what Maxwell called rule-of-thumb science, made that evolution appear natural and complete.

Conclusion: The Death
of the Salesman

It is no small irony that at the moment the traveling man became a modern salesman he also entered the American imagination as a nostalgic figure. And yet the logic, or illogic, of this contradiction had always been part of the history of commercial traveling. Beginning with the emergence of the antebellum city drummer, salesmen worked to expand the market through face-to-face encounters, a process that uneasily paired the personal with the impersonal. Given the pressure to efface the personal, to subordinate himself to the objectives of his employer and the needs of his customer, the salesman felt the disciplining limits of the market even as he pursued success through its liberating opportunities. The improvisational, independent personality demanded of traveling men was thus a paradox—in darker terms, a mythic construction threatening to collapse under the weight of occupational necessity. What Arthur Miller termed the death of a salesman was an occupational hazard that concerned the Pearl Street drummer as much as it did the modern commercial traveler. Add to the demands of business the existential perils of the road—loneliness, sickness, and so forth—and the death of the salesman seems a fated, as well as poignant, prospect.

After the turn of the century, however, this prospect was freighted with broad, historical meaning. Not only did the development of scientific sales techniques and modern advertising throw the drummer into relief, but the images and values (of small-town culture and rural landscapes) nostalgically associated with the drummer's obsolescence prepared the way for a furious, if at times ambiguous, attack on mass commercial culture. If for writers like Don Marquis the residual and emergent values that constituted the traveling man's dual image—one old, the other new and modern—initiated meditations on a lost America, for others they begged critical questions of the impact of commercial progress on community, family, and individual identity. These questions differed in tenor from those uttered by previous critical voices. Where nineteenth-century critics had primarily seen the drummer as a threat to established norms and institutions, twentieth-century detractors viewed the salesman as an ally of a powerful corporate economy and a standardized consumer culture—the product and the representative of the status quo that he once challenged. No longer an emerging social type or the embattled agent of a burgeoning market economy, the salesman became the embodiment of modern American culture and a lightning rod for its critics.

Over the course of the twentieth century the nature of this criticism has become familiar. The modern salesman has become a symbol of alienated

With their emphasis on cooperation, fellowship, and boosterism, sales conventions like this one in 1915 at the Lisk Company epitomized the assimilation of salesmanship into mainstream American culture. (Collections of Ontario County Historical Society, Canandaigua, N.Y.)

labor, epitomizing what the sociologist C. Wright Mills called the personality market and what Wendell Berry has more recently termed the revolution of exploitation. Referring to the destruction of farmland by industrial agriculture, Berry warns in his 1977 book, *The Unsettling of America,* that "we are all familiar enough with the nature of American salesmanship to know that [the destruction] will be done in the name of the starving millions, in the name of liberty, justice, democracy, and brotherhood, and to free the world from communism." Here the shared understanding of sales rhetoric lets Berry tie salesmanship itself to a litany of postmodern woes that turn-of-the-century critics would have had to strain to imagine. By 1930 this imaginative gap no longer existed, enabling the Nashville Agrarians, Berry's conservative forebears in the Jeffersonian tradition, to declare in *I'll Take My Stand* that "the producers, disguised as pure idealists of progress, must coerce and wheedle the public into being loyal and steady consumers, in order to keep the machine running. So the rise of modern advertising—along with its twin, personal salesmanship—is the most significant development of our industrialism."[1]

Although such criticism hardly demands interpretation, its didacticism assumes the absorption of the salesman himself into a market system. Indeed, the years between 1900 and 1930, when the number of commercial travelers continued to grow, ironically marked the progress of the salesman's death. No longer a visible target and ubiquitous figure on the landscape, the salesman who once embodied the role of economic and cultural middleman dropped from sight. The terms of his assimilation—the withering away of his mediating function—derive in part from the orchestrated integration of all sales forces under the auspices of modern business enterprises. But they also stem from the perception that the salesman's position within the mass market had stripped him of independence. Now truly a component in a monolithic market economy, the traveling salesman—as Drouet's disappearance into the urban landscape of *Sister Carrie* suggests—seemed little different from a walking advertisement.

The appearance of Dave Singleman in *Death of a Salesman* as part of Willy Loman's own nostalgic recovery of his occupational genealogy signals Arthur Miller's recognition that the emergence of mass commercial culture augured the death of the salesman. An aging salesman whom the youthful Willy meets in the Parker House hotel, Singleman had "drummed merchandise in thirty-one states." Singleman's magnetic "personality," Willy tells his own boss, had inspired him to become a traveling salesman.

> Old Dave, he'd go up to his room, y'understand, put on his green velvet slippers—I'll never forget—and pick up his phone and call the buyers, and without ever leaving his room, at the age of eighty-four, he made his living. And when I saw that, I realized that selling was the greatest career a man could want. 'Cause what could be more satisfying than to be able to go, at the age of eighty-four, into twenty or thirty different cities, and pick up a phone, and be remembered and loved and helped by so many different people? Do you know? when he died—and by the way he died the death of a salesman, in his green velvet slippers in the smoker of the New York, New Haven and Hartford, going into Boston—when he died, hundreds of salesmen and buyers were at his funeral.[2]

Willy's encounter with the old drummer carries all the force of Marquis's and Anderson's recollections of the traveling salesman. Just as he is considering joining his brother and going to Alaska in search of their father and in hopes of making his fortune, Willy adopts Singleman as his mentor. The displacement here of the father by the salesman makes clear how strongly Willy identifies with his chosen profession. Selling means friendship, fraternalism, success—all of which Willy struggles, and generally fails, to attain. But Willy's reasons for this emotional transference are ill founded. By setting the scene in the early twentieth century and by collapsing the portrait of the veteran drummer into a vision of the modern ubiquitous salesman—magically, if electronically, linked to the marketplace—Miller represents the transition from one era of business to another. Singleman's eventual death in the smoker (in his slippers!) confirms this shift while at the same time reenacting the ambivalent reconstitution of home on the road common to generations of salesmen. Willy's longing for this kind of death shapes his life; his choice to live like Dave Singleman is perversely bound to images of his own demise—he, too, wants to be eulogized at his funeral. But with this self-conscious recourse to commercial history, Miller shows Willy to be unconscious of both Singleman's and his own placement in that history. Although by his celebration of personality and comradeship (or cooperation) Willy reveals that he is a product of modern sales theory, he does not understand the drive toward rationalization and efficiency implicit in Singleman's phone conversations. Years of face-to-face improvisations made Singleman's commercial connections possible, but Willy mistakes the phone work for personal work. Furthermore, Miller suggests that Singleman himself is oblivious to the transformations that bring him to do business in a hotel room—wearing his slippers—without ever having to enter or create a commercial landscape. Less a "single man" than a cultural type, Miller's updated, old-fashioned drummer represents the salesman's necessarily inveterate lack of self-consciousness. So when Charley says to Willy, "You're a salesman, and you don't know that," he unwittingly puts his finger on what Miller takes to be one of the central characteristics of the profession—its naturalized commercial identity.[3]

The growth of this sense that the salesman is a cog in modern consumer culture is evident in Sherwood Anderson's writings. Although he wrote nostalgically in his 1942 memoirs of growing up in Ohio and of "standing about listening" with "gaping crowds" as a traveling man "talked in the stores, or talked sitting, on a summer evening, with his chair tilted back against the front wall of our Empire House, speaking so freely of faraway places and of strange mechanical wonders to come," still, his fiction offered a different view.[4] *Windy McPherson's Son* (1916), *Winesburg, Ohio* (1919), and *Poor White* (1920) present a more abstract, critical image of the commercial traveler.

In Anderson's first novel, *Windy McPherson's Son,* he drew his young protagonist into the dreams of success evoked in his 1904 article in *Agricultural Advertising*. The hero, selling newspapers at the local hotel, develops a talent for getting people to talk about themselves and begins to "cultivate" traveling men. "From them, he got into his nostrils a whiff of the city and, listening to them, he saw the great ways filled with hurrying people, the tall buildings touching the sky, the men running about intent upon money-making, and the clerks going on year after year on small salaries getting nowhere, a part of, and yet not understanding, the impulses and motives of the enterprises that supported them. In this picture Sam thought he saw a place for himself."[5] From the drummer's place on this Iowa Main Street, Sam discovers his own place in modern society; the leap in consciousness, moreover, happens quickly with the salesman playing only a limited sensory role. By smelling the salesman's connection to mass urban culture, he anticipates the moment of fulfillment left undescribed in the *Agricultural Advertising* piece. In *Windy McPher-*

son's Son, when that moment arrives after Sam's urban migration, the traveling salesman looks like a successful cultural broker. But Sam McPherson fails to find happiness and, despite experiencing tremendous financial success in Chicago, spends years wandering the country until he returns—still wealthy—to his wife and her small New England hometown, where (bringing the novel full circle) he tries to find peace away from the corruption of the urban commercial world.

Dramatizing the crisis of conscience that often figures in Anderson's writings, where the forces of industrialization are pitted against a free-spirited, artistic consciousness (even the business titan Sam McPherson feels the "power of the artist" stir within him), Anderson, in *Windy McPherson's Son,* implicitly links the traveling salesman to the causes of modern alienation. In *Poor White* the link is stronger still. Anderson gives Hugh McVey, a gangling industrial-inventor, the insight to escape from the oppressive factory town that he helped create by endowing him with incipient artistic awareness, and he condemns Tom Butterworth for his economic rapacity.[6] Anderson implies that without men like Butterworth to promote and sell the mechanical inventions of men like Hugh McVey, the town of Bidwell, Ohio, will remain quiet, fairly insular, and agricultural. Hugh's marriage to Clara Butterworth epitomizes this alliance, while Bidwell's loss of old small-town standards convinces Butterworth that his home "is going to be a city now and a mighty big city."[7] Thus, the boost toward urban modernity becomes part of Bidwell's internal dynamics, a feature of small-town consciousness that facilitates the emergence of mass culture and the erosion of local values.

Traveling men appear throughout *Poor White*—at the sleepy railroad junction where Hugh McVey first works, in Bidwell itself before it changes, and even in the home of the Columbus family where Clara boards while attending college—signaling the inexorable movement of the town toward the twentieth century. In Columbus, Clara receives a suitor who "talked of his experiences as a traveler selling the wares manufactured or merchandized by his father," so that she "grew to feel that she was being merchandized and that they had come to look at the goods."[8] The target of Anderson's outrage over such warpings of self is not simply industrialization but also the mechanics of consumption and the principles of modern salesmanship. More than any other plot turn in *Poor White,* the story of Joe Wainsworth, Bidwell's harness maker, makes this clear. For years Wainsworth happily sold only hand-crafted harnesses in his Main Street shop and even balked at repairing machine-made products, but his life changes when Jim Gibson, a newly hired assistant, determines to bring the merchandise up to date. "The machine-made can be sold cheaper," he tells Wainsworth. "It looks all right and the factories are able to put on a lot of do-dads. That catches the young fellows. It's good business. Quick sales and profits, that's the story." Intimidated and finally paralyzed by Gibson's aggressive, insistent sales talk, Wainsworth resembles the merchant in Anderson's *Winesburg* story named Queer, whose hands "tremble" whenever a traveling man appears. Wainsworth can hardly bear the "flattering wheedling tone" of vendors and resists the change. The assistant nevertheless has his way and, controlling both the store and Wainsworth, boasts to the townspeople that he ordered eighteen sets of harnesses from a traveling man after Joe told the salesman to leave. Jim "called him back" and "made Joe sign the order."[9]

Upon hearing of Wainsworth's defeat, Tom Butterworth feels in "some intangible way" that Jim Gibson had "justified all such men as himself."[10] Displayed for all to see and buy, the harness sets epitomize the union of standardized manufacturing and standardized selling; they signify the emergence of a new era and the passing of the preindustrial age. But the victory does not occur without losses or ironies. Although Gibson brags to onlookers face to face, his listeners no longer evince the ease of manner that once distinguished small-town natives. Rather, they are disgruntled—fully modern —workers, angered by the conditions at Bidwell's new factories. The unease comes to a violent, if not symbolic, conclusion when Wainsworth murders Joe Gibson for stripping him of his livelihood. Yet not even Wainsworth escapes the taint of the marketplace. Awed by McVey's mechanical genius, he invests his savings in an industrial project that fails; he is betrayed by his faith in the very forces that threaten his livelihood.

Anderson's complicitous tale of modernity, encompassing nearly half a century of change, offers few alternatives to the industrial culture that it critiques. Indeed, the conclusion seems just as fated as the transition from old-fashioned drummer to modern salesmen. Given his resolve to depict industrial culture in "subjective" terms, rather than the "objective" terms formerly upheld by James and Howells—a resolve described in "An Apology for Crudity," a 1917 article that he published in the *Dial*—Anderson sought to describe the impact of modernity on consciousness; more specifically, he worked to dramatize the negative effects of the commercial economy on psychological well-being.[11] Anderson's modernist cultural criticism met contradictions, however, when he posited a perspective outside market influence. Like Hugh McVey and, to a lesser degree, Sam McPherson, Anderson fashioned the imperatives of art after a career in business; his alternative aesthetic perspective remained, in this sense, closely allied to the commercial vantage point that he started with. Anderson's evolving representation of the commercial traveler brings this contradictory perspective into focus. Beginning with articles for *Agricultural Advertising*, Anderson's formative identification with the traveling man's mobile perspective and the salesman's historical progression toward modernity led him to incorporate the subjective benefits of modern business in his fiction. Later, as Anderson distanced himself from his celebrations of business efficiency, his representations of salesmen became more negative; still, he never wholly abandoned the perspective of the roving salesman, for only by having a modern commercial consciousness—by extending and embroidering it—could he present a subjectively realistic account of its effects. Anderson shared the perspective that he so poignantly ascribed to George Willard's mother in *Winesburg, Ohio*—who draws from visiting salesmen the hope that there is a bigger, wider, more sympathetic world outside the boundaries of the small town but whose unconscious reaction to the possibilities of the market system renders her grotesque.[12]

If as a whole Anderson's fictional landscapes describe the movement from island communities to mass culture, then Sinclair Lewis assumes at the outset the commodification of the small town. In Lewis's fiction the urban influence theory has little relevance, for the small town rather than the city is the source of commercial power. Places like Gopher Prairie have long since been made by traveling men promoting the values of the marketplace. In *Main Street* (1920) the small town is not "merely provincial, no longer downy and restful in its leaf-shadowed ignorance," but "a force seeking to dominate the earth, to drain the hills and sea of its colors." Stripped of local color and natural vitality, Main Street culture epitomizes the drive to standardize the United States and the rest of the world. "Sure of itself," believing principally in profits and representing cheap commercialism, it "bullies other civilizations, as a traveling salesman in a brown derby conquers the wisdom of China and tacks advertisements of cigarettes over arches for centuries dedicated to the sayings of Confucius." This image of commercial aggression—topped by a "hard derby," the "symbol" among small-town men of "virility and prosperity"—reverberates throughout Lewis's fiction. Carol Kennicott confronts the traveling salesman's "coarseness" and crude humor throughout her tenure in Gopher Prairie, while George F. Babbitt (who sells real estate) makes an appearance in *Arrowsmith* (1925), looking like "an earnest traveling-man who liked to get back to his suburban bungalow every Saturday evening." And in *Free Air,* a novel published in 1919, a callow automobile mechanic tries to attain masculine worldliness by imitating film stars and traveling men.[13]

Lewis's traveling men become ubiquitous through their association with the unremitting drive of the market toward standardization of goods and thought; their place, as the metaphorical alliance of small town, salesman, and advertisement suggests, is everywhere the American economy has an interest. Nor does Lewis hold much hope for alternative ways of life. The traveling man's essence derives from the placeless power of the market, its capacity to mitigate cultural opposition by infecting even critical political viewpoints. Hence, in *Babbitt* (1922), when the socialist lawyer Seneca Doane tells the more radical Dr. Yavitch that he favors standardized industrial products (watches, automobiles, and so forth) but that he opposes "standardization of thought," he hardly realizes just how much his own thoughts and desires may be influenced by corporate advertising and salesmanship. As a consumer, Doane shares George Babbitt's taste for nice new things. "You are a middle-road liberal," Dr. Yavitch tells him, castigating his wishy-washy notion of individualism, "and you haven't the slightest idea what you want."[14]

Nor is the domestic sphere a refuge from imperialistic sales culture. Constructed around a fluid, market-driven image of prosperity, home is any number of standardized places, "nine-tenths" of which, Lewis declares in *Main Street,* "are so alike that it is the completest boredom to wander from one

By easing travel and giving salesmen more independence, automobiles reshaped the landscape of commercial traveling. Advertisement, *World Salesmanship* (June 1917). (Courtesy of Library of Congress.)

The Maxwell Kills the Bogey of Motor-Car Cost for Salesmen

No employer today can afford not to furnish a *Maxwell* for his salesman's use.

The sturdy *Maxwell* roadster — the ideal car for a salesman to get about in— costs only $650, f. o. b. Detroit.

A *Maxwell* can be run on a much smaller expense account than any car made

—thousands of *Maxwell* owners get hard daily service out of their cars on an outlay of $6 to $8 a month.

A salesman's carfare eats up more than that—the *Maxwell* actually saves money for him.

And he can make, with a motor car, at least twice as many business calls as the fellow who goes around with antiquated horse and buggy.

One salesman and a *Maxwell* can do the work of at least two salesmen with old fashioned conveyances.

—and do it with more snap and ginger, too.

Take another, extreme case—that of the salesman himself buying the car.

Certainly, in those circumstances, any employer who was awake at all, would cheerfully pay upkeep cost of an automobile as economical as the *Maxwell*

—and the salesman, moreover, would have a smart car for his own enjoyment after business hours.

Motor cars for salesmen are the modern way of doing business.

Which do you pursue in your business —this modern, efficient, money-saving, money-making method, or the cumbersome, slow, expensive, old fashioned horse and buggy method?

Roadster $650; Touring Car $665; Cabriolet $865; Town Car $915; Sedan $985 completely equipped, including electric starter and lights. All prices f. o. b. Detroit.

Maxwell

Detroit,   *Motor Company, Inc.*   Michigan

to another." Home is where men like Babbitt—in essence, a domesticated version of the drummer and thus ideally suited to selling houses for a living— perpetuate "universal similarity," guaranteeing that both the "physical expression of the philosophy of dull safety" and the philosophy itself remain at the heart of public and domestic happiness.[15] In this way, Lewis brought scientific economy out of commercial establishments and fraternal organizations and into the home.

The truly damning point to this critique, the view that denied the Gopher Prairies any nostalgic or sentimental stature and made Lewis part of what the literary critic Carl Van Doren called the revolt from the village, was that scientific economy had always resided on Main Street. Echoing the condemnation of Puritanical materialism expressed by H. L. Mencken and Van Wyck

Standing by their car in Independence, Kansas, in 1924, these Durham Tobacco salesmen leave no doubt of their confidence or their modernity. (Kansas Collection, University of Kansas Libraries.)

Brooks, Lewis rooted the mechanics of consumption in long-lived communal structures. Rejecting the idea that the hinterland suffered as the colonized victim of a centralized commercial system, he found in Babbitt—and in his commitment to salesmanship and his strong personality—an assuredly modern, but nonetheless prototypical, American man. Unlike Thomas Wolfe, who catalogued the insidious effects of salesmanship but marveled over "the fantastic elasticity of American business," Lewis found in the emergence of modern boosterism little to wonder over. Despite his fascination with the surfaces of American life, he bitterly, if not satirically, viewed standardization in business enterprise as putting old wine in new bottles.[16]

In *Elmer Gantry*, the scurrilous 1927 story of an evangelical preacher, Lewis sensationalized the traveling man's place in the incorporated culture of Main Street. As a seminary student and later as a minister, Gantry remains one of the "boys," but never does his sensual, backslapping nature seem more appropriate than when he is selling agricultural equipment for the Pequot Company. Dressed in "a checked suit, a brown derby, striped socks," wearing "the huge ring of gold serpents and an opal which he had bought long ago, flower-decked ties, and what he called 'fancy vests,'" Gantry "was not unsuccessful." He "was a good talker, a magnificent hand-shaker, his word could often be depended on, and he remembered most of the price-lists and all of the new smutty stories." Closing this fictional personnel report with the efficient, authoritative prose of business English, Lewis ironically adds: "A promising and commendable fellow; conceivably sales-manager some day."[17] No old-fashioned drummer—in fact, Lewis avoids the term—Gantry begins his sales career in 1906, at the age of twenty-six, a fittingly youthful, broad-shouldered example of the modern salesman. Beyond noting the emergence of modern sales practices and poking fun at them, however, Lewis plots Gantry's rise around a more familiar cultural ritual. Gantry's career is reborn when he becomes a traveling salesman within a week of his expulsion from divinity school, on the Friday after Easter Sunday.

Gantry's advance, two years later, back into the ranks of the holy, as an assistant to Sharon Falconer, an evangelical prophet, leads to the crux of Lewis's satire: the commercialization of religion. Targeting some of the same themes that distinguish Harold Frederic's 1896 novel, *The Damnation of Theron Ware,* Lewis burlesques the hypocritical union of soul saving and profit making and, by making religion a business proposition (suggesting, in turn, that American business is a religion), underscores the evangelical nature of salesmanship. In *Elmer Gantry* the spectacle of religious ceremony differs only in content from the spectacle of the marketplace. Conversion becomes another kind of selling when Gantry discovers "the rapture of salvation—yes, and of being the center of interest in the crowd." Later, as Sharon Falconer's assistant, "the new salesman of salvation," he learns how to control that interest and profit by it. As a preacher, Gantry motivates congregations and wins souls, but never for purely spiritual reasons. Integral to Falconer's troupe and to revivalism itself is a sensual love of circuslike effects that springs from the viewer's—and the preacher's—unredeemed natures. At bottom, Elmer and even Sharon—whose Oriental boudoir and sentimental, passionate sermons, presented at "a pulpit shaped like a shell and painted like a rainbow," deny the virtues of Puritan plain style—depend on mundane desires and fears to move their audiences. And their good works, Lewis makes clear, are strictly commercial. When not wearing her "Grecian robe," the "high-priestess" is essentially a "business-woman." Elmer, as his future boss realizes, is only a traveling man. When the salesman begs for a chance to showcase his preaching skills, she suggests as a topic "Getting the Goods with a Gideon Bible." Gantry's sermon on business temptations, in the end called "Increasing Sales with God and the Gideons," addresses the persuasive, even coercive wiles that bind customers to salesmen, preachers to congregations, and Americans to heaven.[18] Ultimately, Elmer's sermons are sales talks.

In highlighting this evangelical sales idiom, Lewis darkened Bruce Barton's view of muscular Christianity, showing a culture duped rather than enriched by the conjunction of business and faith. Gantry's carnivalized faith healing follows the logic of modern salesmanship; by addressing issues of the soul in psychological terms, he drums up converts in the same way a salesman persuades customers and closes a sale. At one point, when he is struggling for work, Elmer teaches Prosperity Classes on the "Wonder Power of Suggestion" and the "Aggressive Personality." Later, as a parish minister, he advertises his Sunday services and initiates "that salesmanship of salvation which was to make him known and respected in every advertising club and forward-looking church in the country." The thrust here and throughout the novel is to collapse salesmanship into the dominant structures of society, to make them indistinguishable and, given the institutional power of modern business enterprises, irresistible.[19]

Although the salesman's personal appeal had always been constituted within a larger cultural system, by the 1920s it seemed to have been wholly assimilated into the dominant consumer society. As drawn by Lewis, Gantry was not only a drummer; he was salesman, preacher, hedonist, con man, and advertiser all at once. But if his critique highlighted the stultifying effects of the mass market, it also contained ironic possibilities for an alternative view. The traveling man's apparent death as an individual underscored his alienation from community and family life; seen as victim and exile, he presented a powerful, if mute, commentary on the demands of the market.

This sense of the traveling man as cut off from humanity pervades two works written during the 1930s, Thornton Wilder's novel *Heaven's My Destination* (1935) and Eudora Welty's short story "Death of a Traveling Salesman" (1936). While each makes different use of the salesman, both stress their protagonists' essential loneliness. Wilder's George Brush is a naive textbook salesman on a quixotic mission of conversion in a secular culture that has little interest in faith. He has little interest in material wealth, and it is this irony—consider his difference from Elmer Gantry—that partly accounts for the element of comedy. Brush is like a Brother Gideon who has given up his commercial ambitions but occasionally reverts to the drummer stereotype, as, for instance, when he sleeps with a farmer's daughter and has a child by her. Wilder's humorous, gentle treatment of the salesman sends the novel back from the tough market culture shaped by Brush's predecessors to find a human faith that has been lost along the way.

Wilder and Welty forgo commercialized representations of salesmen, although the market is rarely far away. Welty has stressed that her story of a lonely salesman's death on the road describes a "journey of errand or search (for some form of the secret of life)" that "was of course nothing new."[20] Like *Heaven's My Destination*, "Death of a Traveling Salesman" unfolds in mythic terms, as Bowman, the salesman, moves steadily toward a final resting place and transcendent understanding of his life. The demands of economic life, however, necessitate this spiritual journey and shape its direction. That his death takes place among strangers who open their home to him and treat him with a warmth that his business life and commercial ways of thinking have prohibited highlights the human costs of making a home on the road and hence the cultural conflicts that shape the history of the profession.

Wilder's and Welty's presentation of the salesman as a transcendent figure, capable of evoking universal themes, may in part be attributed to their effort to recover from the Great Depression some usable past or perspective from the broken market economy. But their fiction was also a rejoinder to a profession that exacted mind, body, and soul from its practitioners. Hence, the death of the salesman in works like Welty's performs a dual function; it highlights the life-sapping demands of the profession and, by returning the salesman to humanity, effaces his singularly commercial identity.

The imaginary work required of this stripping down to essences could be nasty, however. Eugene O'Neill's casting away of "pipe dreams" in *The Iceman Cometh* (1946) is a good example. O'Neill finds in modern salesmanship the discourse sustaining the false idealism that keeps his cast of down-and-outers from confronting the reality of their lives. By telling jokes, treating for drinks, and playing the role of the genial drummer, the salesman Hickey reinforces their illusions; he makes his audience as only a salesman can. But he also strives to unmake them—and himself—first by revealing their deceptions to themselves and then by exposing his own duplicitous rhetoric and empty self. Hickey's confessions are tantamount to suicide, for he is unraveling the fabric of his identity as a salesman. And when he tells his friends that he has killed his wife because he could no longer abide her continual forgiveness of the sins that he has committed on the road, it is clear that for all the metaphysical issues at stake in his violent honesty, Hickey has died the death of a salesman. O'Neill implies, but does not finally explain, whether Hickey (or, for that matter, his friends at Harry Hope's saloon) has a self apart from the sales improvisations that has constituted it. Indeed, although Hickey's willed destruction of his sales personality points to a truer self orchestrating the breakdown, the verbal suicide itself is a display of commercial pyrotechnics. Having in some sense sold his self to his audience, Hickey departs at the end of the play with the police, destined to be executed.

Set in 1912, at the same momentous juncture in commercial history that frames *Death of Salesman,* O'Neill's play suggests that the reasons for the salesman's failure and impending death hang on the incompatibility of commercial culture with the domestic culture that ultimately makes it possible. In fact, Hickey's inability to live with this complicitous relationship precipitates his breakdown. Unlike Lewis's Babbitt, he cannot simultaneously hold in opposition both the male self, whose transgressions commercial culture winks at and even conventionalizes, and the domestic self that his wife works so hard to prop up. A similar contradiction shapes Miller's play: Willy sacrifices his home life for success on the road (and, in one instance, sexual prowess). The more complete portrayal of domestic life in *Death of a Salesman* deepens the sense of complicity between home and work. Not only does Linda let Willy go forth, but she nurtures his illusions of success, while Willy, in turn, strives to inculcate the ebullient sales personality in his sons, urging them to be "well liked" even at the cost of honesty.

Arthur Miller thus returns the story of the traveling salesman to where perhaps it had always been—the home. If, as Miller has urged, the crucial question that all great dramas ask is "How may a man make of the outside

Like the drummer of old, the modern salesman continued to command the admiration of onlookers. (Minnesota Historical Society.)

world a home?" then *Death of a Salesman* answers this question in the ironically tragic terms inherent to its hero's occupation: by showing Willy's misguided, perhaps unconscious, but finally inevitable confusion of home and market.[21] As critic after critic has argued, Miller makes Willy's dreams speak for all upwardly mobile Americans. Yet it is Willy's assimilation as a salesman into this doctrine of success that gives the drama its conflicted, dream-infused atmosphere of self-creation. On the one hand, Willy's Yiddish grammatical constructions give away his immigrant background, pointing to Miller's own ethnic heritage, and, on the other, his role as a salesman reinforces his effort to invent the self and forget the past. *Death of a Salesman* is a modern assimilation drama. Drawing from American commercial and ethnic culture, Miller parallels and overlaps the making of an American with the making of a salesman, striving, as he once put it, to illuminate Willy's search for his "immortal soul."[22] Viewed this way, Willy's failures only emphasize the breadth of his ambition, while his death as a salesman confirms his humanity within a world poised to take it away. By returning us constantly to the past and urging us to identify with Willy's dreams and believe that they might have turned out differently, Miller tempts us to see the salesman's life and death as our own.

Notes

Preface

1 A sustained scholarly treatment of English or European commercial traveling does not exist. Consult the brief but often illuminating discussions in Mantoux, *Industrial Revolution in the Eighteenth Century,* 122; D. Alexander, *Retailing in England During the Industrial Revolution,* 133; Fraser, *Coming of the Mass Market,* 144–46; McKendrick et al., *Birth of a Consumer Society,* 86–89; Mui et al., *Shops and Shopkeeping in Eighteenth-Century England,* 15–17. Two helpful articles published in business periodicals are A. Stimson, "Commercial Travellers"; and Miltoun, "Getting the Business of France." Firsthand accounts of British commercial traveling include *Hints on Commercial Travelling by a Veteran Highwayman;* Crick, *Sketches from the Diary of a Commercial Traveller;* A. Allen, *Ambassadors of Commerce* (1885); Gandon, *Sixty Years "On the Road."*

2 Barthes, *Mythologies,* esp. 109–59. In thinking about the institutional formation of types, I have benefited from Berger and Luckmann, *Social Construction of Reality.*

3 A. Miller, *Timebends,* 127.

4 Chandler, *Visible Hand,* 219. Among Atherton's several studies of merchants, see *Frontier Merchant in Mid-America* and *Southern Country Store;* and see T. Clark, *Pills, Petticoats, and Plows.*

5 Strasser, *Satisfaction Guaranteed;* Zunz, *Making America Corporate.* An exception to the traveling man's exclusion from scholarship is Susan Strasser's essay "'The Smile That Pays.'"

6 A. Miller, *Death of a Salesman,* 138.

7 Boorstin, *Americans,* 135.

8 Marchand, *Advertising the American Dream;* Lears, "Some Versions of Fantasy," 397; Schudson, *Advertising,* 209, 210. On the rise of modern advertising, also see Ewen, *Captains of Consciousness;* Fox, *Mirror Makers.* Also relevant is Lears's influential essay "From Salvation to Self-Realization," 3–38.

9 Lears, "Truth, Power, Consequences," 223.

10 Rourke, *American Humor,* 11; Agnew, *Worlds Apart,* 6. Lears discusses the peddler in "Stabilization of Sorcery" and in "Beyond Veblen: Rethinking Consumer Culture in America," in Bronner, ed., *Consuming Visions.* On Hermes see N. Brown, *Hermes the Thief.* For discussions of the peddler's cultural and literary importance also see R. Wright, *Hawkers and Walkers;* and Hoffman, *Form and Fable,* 49–55. More recent examinations of commercial itinerants are David Jaffee, "One of the Primitive Sort," in Hahn and Prude, eds., *Countryside in the Age of Capitalist Transformation,* 103–38; Benes, ed., *Itinerancy in New England and New York.* For an illuminating discussion of the importance of commercial itinerancy in the book industry—and the need for further scholarship in that area—consult James Gilreath, "American Book Distribution," in Hall and Hench, eds., *Needs and Opportunities,* 103–85. Perhaps the best-known fictional depictions of the antebellum peddler are Thomas Chandler Haliburton's tales of *The Clockmaker; or, the Sayings and Doings of Samuel Slick.*

11 I refer here not only to the trend in literary studies that has come to be called New Historicism—and the many theories and statements of purposes (both for and against) that have attended its emergence—but also to the "textualizing of history" and the perceived loss of objectivity in historical inquiry. Although the disciplines (generally) remain separate and their debates highlight different concerns, the common focus on the meaning of history, as well as the use of theory and the treatment of text and context, suggests a good deal of overlap. For a discussion related primarily, though not exclusively, to literary studies, see the essays in Veeser, *New Historicism;* Thomas, *New Historicism.* On the historian's perspective see Novick, *That Noble Dream;* and the round-table debate over "the old History and the new" in the *American Historical Review* 94 (Summer 1989). Christopher P. Wilson surveys these recent developments from an American studies point of view in "Containing Multitudes."

12 Such a history charts "those eruptions into consciousness and passion that define and give shape to societal change. . . . Perception has the virtue of referring to a whole range of environmental responses, of thinking, feeling, and seeing." W. Taylor, *Cavalier and Yankee,* 9.

13 Susman, *Culture as History,* 271–85. Even as scholars have cited Susman's important work, they have been busy pushing back to the origins of this modern self. See, e.g., Halttunen, *Confidence Men,* and Kasson, *Rudeness and Civility,* both of which suggest the presence of personality in antebellum urban culture.

14 C. Mills, *White Collar,* 182–88. See Bledstein, *Culture of Professionalism.* Although Mary Ryan in *The Cradle of the Middle Class* and Stuart Blumin in *The Emergence of the Middle Class* depart from Bledstein in their methods and emphases, both associate self-control and intellectual abstraction with middle-class values—Ryan by looking at child-rearing practices and Blumin by distinguishing nonmanual from manual labor.

15 Halttunen, *Confidence Men and Painted Women.* The central theme of Agnew's *Worlds Apart* is that by the end of the eighteenth century, the marketplace had become an abstract, placeless process, an argument that Susan Strasser takes up in *Satisfaction Guaranteed,* 124–25.

16 On this score the sociological and anthropological literature is abundant. I have found useful N. Elias, *History of Manners;* Goffmann, *Presentation of Self;* Geertz, *Interpretation of Cultures,* esp. the chapter "Deep Play Notes on the Balinese Cockfight"; M. Douglas, *Purity and Danger.* Among the various applications of such theory by cultural historians, I have profited from Robert Darnton's books, *The Literary Underground of the Old Regime* and *The Great Cat Massacre,* and John Kasson's *Rudeness and Civility.* In highlighting the importance of the built environment for commercial traveling, I take my cue from the historians John Brinckerhoff Jackson and John R. Stilgoe.

17 One of the most illuminating discussions of the increased importance of visual spectacle in consumer culture is Leach, "Transformations in a Culture of Consumption."

18 Porter and Livesay, *Merchants and Manufacturers,* 145–47, 161–65, 197–98, 214–15.

19 Simmel, *On Individuality and Social Forms,* 143.

20 Hahn, *Roots of Southern Populism.* See, e.g., Halttunen, *Confidence Men and Painted Women;* Kasson, *Rudeness and Civility;* Levine, *Highbrow/Lowbrow;* Fabian, *Card Sharps.*

21 James, *American Scene*, 424–29.
22 Gilmore, *American Romanticism and the Marketplace*, 153.
23 A. Kaplan, *Social Construction*, 9. In addition to Kaplan's study of American realism and Gilmore's examination of American romanticism see J. Howard, *Form and History in American Literary Realism*; Michaels, *Gold Standard and the Logic of Naturalism*.
24 In particular, see the introduction to Michaels, *Gold Standard and the Logic of Naturalism*. Michaels scolds Lears, Trachtenberg, Ann Douglas, and other critics of consumer culture for their nostalgic attachment to producer-oriented values—an attack that, to my mind, is blunted by his own unwillingness to examine the historical transition from a culture of production to a culture of consumption. Although less pointed in its emphasis, Howard Horwitz's *By the Law of Nature* likewise flattens the distinctions between apparently oppositional texts. Although Horwitz seeks to avoid portraying culture as a "monolithic entity" (17), his readings tend to highlight the ground shared by acts of representation. On these issues see Christopher Wilson, "Containing Multitudes"; and Jameson, *Postmodernism*, 181–217.
25 Trachtenberg, *Incorporation of America*.

Introduction: A Rare Bird of Passage

1 Dreiser, *Sister Carrie*, 5.
2 Scott, "Psychology of Advertising," 33.
3 Marchand, *Advertising the American Dream*, 37, 73–74, 300, 304. Marchand points out that radio advertising epitomized the effort to recover the intimacy of face-to-face sales encounters; see chap. 4. For a discussion of modern advertising methods in the years leading up to the starting point of Marchand's history, see Lears, "Some Versions of Fantasy." On the personal appeal to "you" in advertising see Spitzer, "American Advertising Explained as Popular Art," 349–56. Spitzer mentions that face-to-face selling methods also make this appeal to "you" but does not examine the historical connections between salesmanship and advertising.
4 Fox, *Mirror Makers*, 50. According to industry legend, John E. Kennedy was the first to intone this magical phrase during a meeting with Albert Lasker at the Chicago offices of the Lord and Thomas agency in 1904, although, as Stephen Fox points out, Charles A. Bates called advertising "printed salesmen" in 1896. Kennedy, *Intensive Advertising*, 5–6.
5 Charles Clark Munn, letter, in "Our Sample Case" (1903).
6 The phrase comes from the title of Veblen's 1904 book, *The Theory of Business Enterprise*.
7 *Confidence* (1922) features an unsuccessful salesman who mistakenly picks up a suitcase filled with money, and *Sunset Legion* (1928) is about a gun salesman who doubles as a masked man. Munden, ed., *American Film Institute Catalog*, vol. F2, pp. 144, 771. There were, no doubt, many other films with traveling men in minor roles. But my understanding of these films depends chiefly on the American Film Institute catalogs, which offer subject indexes and provide plot summaries. As far as I can tell from rental guides and archival sources—in particular, the Library of Congress film catalog—nearly all of these early films are unavailable.
8 Lardner's story appears in his 1926 collection *The Love Nest and Other Stories*, 31–54. Not included in this partial list but pertinent to the traveling salesman's tarnished reputation are Flannery O'Connor's 1955 tale "Good Country People," featuring a

door-to-door Bible agent as a seducer, and Mary McCarthy's "Man in the Brooks Brothers Shirt" (1941), which plays off the image of the traveling man as promiscuous adventurer. For O'Connor's story see her *Complete Stories*, 271–91. Erskine Caldwell, in his short story "Back on the Road," describes how a sedentary office manager is tempted to return to road life during an amorous encounter with a traveling saleswoman in a hotel room. *Complete Stories of Erskine Caldwell*, 224–34. Not all literary depictions of the commercial traveler were negative. For a favorable portrait see Edna Ferber's novels *Roast Beef, Medium; Personality Plus;* and *Emma McChesney and Co.* Ferber's unusual commercial traveler, Emma McChesney, is a divorced woman and a doting mother. Ferber's treatment of Ed Meyers, a rather unscrupulous salesman competing in the same line—women's undergarments—is more typical. A more mundane, even grim depiction of commercial traveling—in an automobile—is John Herrmann's Depression-era novel, *The Salesman*.

9 Consider, for example, Wolfe's *Look Homeward, Angel* (1929) and *You Can't Go Home Again* (1940) and Lewis's *Main Street* (1920), *Babbitt* (1922), and especially *Elmer Gantry* (1927).

10 Mencken, *American Language*, 14; Mencken, *Prejudices: Second Series*, 38; "A Drummer's Prayer."

11 Tarkington, *Penrod*, 46, 71.

12 Tebbel, *George Horace Lorimer*, 6–9.

13 Lorimer, *Letters from a Self-Made Merchant*, 104–5.

14 Cohn, *Creating America*, esp. 3–19. The comparison to Harriet Beecher Stowe's *Uncle Tom's Cabin* is in Tebbel, *George Horace Lorimer*, 32.

15 Williams, "Base and Superstructure."

16 Barton, *Man Nobody Knows*, 139, 104.

17 Crissey, "Modern Commercial Traveler," 22.

18 Belasco, *Americans on the Road*, 47; Chapman, "Automobile in Business"; Hiscox, "Telephone: A Traveling Salesman's Accessory."

19 Crissey, "Modern Commercial Traveler," 22–23, 27. For another view of the commercial traveler's busy pace see Goodrich, "Day's Work of a Traveling Man."

20 Crissey reminded readers that the salesman "is part of a great system, one wheel of a big machine, and must conform to the routine of that system or become a disturbing element in the organization." "Modern Commercial Traveler," 24. On technology and perception see, e.g., Tichi, *Shifting Gears*.

21 Jameson, *Marxism and Form*, 61. On aura see Benjamin, *Illuminations*, 221.

22 Anderson, "Business Types—the Traveling Man," 39–40. In other *Agricultural Advertising* articles, Anderson describes more efficient, modern alternatives to the old-time traveling man: "Rot and Reason: The New Job," 14, 16; "Sales Master and the Selling Organization." On Anderson's career as an adman and business writer see I. Howe, *Sherwood Anderson*, 32–38; Townsend, *Sherwood Anderson*, 43–53; Sutton, "Sherwood Anderson."

23 Anderson, "Business Types—the Traveling Man," 39.

24 Anderson, "Business Types—the Traveling Man," 39.

25 Marquis, "My Memories," 20, 153–54.

26 Marquis, "My Memories," 20.

27 Wiebe, *Search for Order*, 4.

28 Marquis, "My Memories," 20, 152–53.

29 *American Heritage Dictionary*, 2nd college ed., s.v. "nostalgia"; *Webster's New International Dictionary*, 2nd ed., s.v. "nostalgia." On the concept of nostalgia and its history

see Starobinski, "Idea of Nostalgia," esp. 84–86, 100–103; Lowenthal, "Past Time, Present Place," 1–5; F. Davis, "Nostalgia, Identity and the Current Nostalgia Wave," 414–15; Kern, *Culture of Time and Space,* 129; Jacoby, *Longing for Paradise,* 4–9. Also pertinent to the discussion of memory and space is Bachelard, *Poetics of Space,* esp. 56–59. As Starobinski and Jacoby make clear, nostalgia continues to play a role in psychiatry. See, e.g., McCann, "Nostalgia: A Review of the Literature."

30 Marquis, "My Memories," 20.

31 Lears, *No Place of Grace,* esp. 32–58. In "From Salvation to Self-Realization," Lears emphasizes the therapeutic benefits that the past had for Bruce Barton and other modern Americans, but his understanding of nostalgia is not cast in geographical terms.

32 Hull, "Fourth Profession," 412.

33 Geyer, "Oldest Traveling Salesman," 53; "Our Sample Case" (December 1915), 389–93; Munn, "Oracles of Christmas Cove," 527.

34 L.S.S., "1872 to 1903," 85.

35 Modern sales experts continually warned against telling bawdy or long stories to busy customers. See "Do You Want to Be a Knight of the Grip," 31; Fife, "Phoenix of the Drummer," 215–18.

36 See Skidelsky, *Tales;* Peak, *Ranger;* F. Smith, *Beyond the Swivel Chair.* Other early twentieth-century memoirs include E. Briggs, *Fifty Years;* Jacobs, *Thirty Years;* Page, *Recollections;* Bartelle, *Forty Years;* Nisbet, *Footprints.* In substance and especially in tone, these works differ from such accounts as Horn, *Drumming,* and Plummer, *Leaves,* which predate the economic transformations that made commercial traveling part of modern business enterprise.

37 F. Smith, *Beyond the Swivel Chair,* 5, 42; Carleton, "It Is Not Like the Old Days," 916. Other veteran salesmen who acknowledged the benefits of modern sales methods include Nisbet, *Footprints,* 244–46, 283–86; Skidelsky, *Tales,* 30–31.

38 Nisbet, *Footprints,* 20, 21.

39 Page, *Recollections,* 59–60; Skidelsky, *Tales of a Traveler,* 29–30; Peak, *Ranger,* 75–6.

40 Page, *Recollections,* 46–47; E. Briggs, *Fifty Years,* 86–89; Bartelle, *Forty Years,* 143–45; F. Smith, *Beyond the Swivel Chair,* 39–44.

41 Palmer, *Forty Years,* 7. A similar account, though somewhat chastened in tone and lacking a comparable historical perspective, is Weldon, *Twenty Years.*

42 Jacobs, *Thirty Years,* 82; Nisbet, *Footprints,* 299.

43 Nisbet, *Footprints,* 146.

44 Nisbet, *Footprints,* 147; Page, *Recollections,* 51; Skidelsky, *Tales,* 58.

45 In this respect, veteran salesmen resembled immigrants whose memory of Old World traditions played a vital role in the construction of their American ethnic identities. As the sociologists Vladimir C. Nahirny and Joshua A. Fishman have observed: "To dismiss this as a lachrymose nostalgia for a bygone past and as nothing but another instance of *Schwaermerei* is simply to disregard the significance of concrete experiences for the continuity of personal identity." Nahirny and Fishman, "American Immigrant Groups," 316.

46 Bartelle, *Forty Years,* 160–61.

47 Similarly, Joel Page's *Recollections of Sixty Years in the Shoe Trade* appeared in the *Shoeman,* while J. P. Bartelle's *Forty Years on the Road* was first published in the trade journal *Wood Construction.*

48 Cather, *My Ántonia,* 372.

1 The Perils of Pearl Street

1 On the derivation of *drummer* see the Peter Tamony Collection, Accession 4710, MHM.

2 Holmes, *Account of the United States of America*, 355.

3 Irving, *Bracebridge Hall*, 1:114. In 1839 the English system of commercial traveling was "in its wane," according to A. Stimson, in "Commercial Travellers," 29.

4 McKendrick et al., *Birth of a Consumer Society*, 41, 143.

5 Blumin, *Emergence of the Middle Class*, 26.

6 Chandler, *Visible Hand*, 36–40; Horlick, *Country Boys and Merchant Princes*, esp. chaps. 3 and 4.

7 Wiebe, *Opening of American Society* 259, 258.

8 Jaffee, "Peddlers of Progress"; Lears, "Beyond Veblen: Rethinking Consumer Culture in America," in Bronner, *Consuming Visions*.

9 Chandler, *Visible Hand*, 56, 217; Jaffee, "Peddlers of Progress," 533–35. Jaffee argues that peddlers created rural marketing networks that "provided a model for the post–Civil War manufacturers who developed internal sales forces that employed traveling salesmen" (534). On the other hand, I emphasize the importance of wholesale jobbers in the creation of both antebellum and postbellum marketing structures.

10 Sellers, *Market Revolution*.

11 Atherton, *Frontier Merchant*, 81–83. Although Boston wholesalers soon began to offer country merchants domestically milled textiles, by the 1840s New England manufacturers were also sending their domestic goods to New York for sale. For this information and the general summary of the importance of New York City as a commercial and transportation center I have depended on Albion's *Rise of New York Port*, esp. 12–13, 42–43, 60–64, 76–77, 90–91.

12 Atherton, *Frontier Merchant*, 81. The estimate comes from a partisan source, the *New York Globe*, cited in "Miscellaneous."

13 Chandler, *Visible Hand*, 27–28.

14 Atherton, *Pioneer Merchant in Mid-America*, 54–55, 63–64, 69–70. New York's dominance of the western and southern markets in the 1830s and 1840s by no means precluded wholesale merchants in Philadelphia, Baltimore, and even St. Louis from supplying retail traders with goods. For a comprehensive discussion of this network and its history see Atherton, *Frontier Merchant*, 59–114.

15 Wiebe, *Opening of American Society*, 300, 298–303.

16 Antebellum wholesalers generally granted merchants six months of free credit, but in extending bills another six months they charged 6–10 percent interest. See Atherton, *Frontier Merchant*, 149. For anecdotes about the "the art of dunning"— battles in which dunning clerks struggled to bring recalcitrant debtors to honor their financial obligations—see Kirkland, *Cyclopedia of Commercial and Business Anecdotes*, 2:418.

17 An example in fiction is C. Briggs, *Adventures of Harry Franco*.

18 Atherton, *Southern Country Store*, 127–28; White, "Before the Traveler," 541; Atherton, "Predecessors of the Commercial Drummer in the Old South," 24. Even in 1858, when traveling men had already begun to carry product samples, their primary responsibility was to collect money that interior merchants owed their firms. See *Commercial Bulletin* [Boston], Feb. 7, 1874. On the early appearance of traveling salesmen see also Marburg, "Manufacturer's Drummer, 1832."

19 Norris, *R. G. Dun and Co*, esp. 7–14, 18–19, 22–27; Wyatt-Brown, "God and Dun and Bradstreet," 436–44; and Wyatt-Brown, *Lewis Tappan*, 234–37.

20 This point is driven home by reading any one of the thousands of handwritten evaluations of business character that fill the Dun and Bradstreet credit ledgers, now housed at the Baker Library, Harvard Business School.

21 Wiebe, *Opening of American Society*, 300–301; Sellers, *Market Revolution*, 267–68.

22 A. Stimson, "Commercial Travellers," 30.

23 Foster, *New York Naked*, 119. Tappan's Mercantile Agency was acquired by R. G. Dun in the 1870s and later merged with the Bradstreet Agency to become Dun and Bradstreet.

24 "Philadelphia Dun." To be called a dandy was no great compliment. As one critic explained in 1830, the dandy is a "locomotive automaton," a "weathercock turning in the variable atmosphere of fashion—soulless, heartless, and effeminate—a direct libel on the human species." See "Dandy."

25 See, e.g., "Passages in the Life of a Merchant," 506–7.

26 On traditional clerical duties see Blumin, *Emergence of the Middle Class*, 68; Chandler, *Visible Hand*, 36–40. The best contemporaneous description of the city drummer is in Greene, *Perils of Pearl Street*. For a discussion of the drummer's place in the antebellum commercial system and references to period descriptions of his function see Nystrom, *Economics of Retailing*, 94; F. Jones, *Middlemen*, 16–17; Albion, *Rise of New York Port*, 280; Atherton, *Frontier Merchant in Mid-America*, 30–31; Atherton, "Predecessors of the Commercial Drummer in the Old South," 18; Atherton, *Southern Country Store*, 134–36; Friedman, "Drummer in Early American Merchandise Distribution," 40–43; Carson, *Old Country Store*, 135–58; Ries, "American Salesman," 23.

27 Greene, "Mercantile Drumming" (May 5). The *Constellation* piece later became part of Asa Greene's *Perils of Pearl Street* (1834), which, according to the 1933 edition of the *Oxford English Dictionary*, is where the word *drummer* first appeared in American print. Greene was also editor of the *Constellation*.

28 See Susman, *Culture as History*, 271–85.

29 On adaptability in nineteenth-century cities see Konvitz, *Urban Millennium*, 96–130.

30 Blumin, *Emergence of the Middle Class*, 68; Chandler, *Visible Hand*, 36–40.

31 Horlick, *Country Boys and Merchant Princes*, 107. Carroll Smith-Rosenberg extends Horlick's findings from New York to antebellum cities in general and locates the changing social structure of the mercantile city within the larger economic and demographic revolution that reshaped American society between 1790 and 1850. See her *Disorderly Conduct*, 80–81.

32 *New York Transcript*, June 22, 1836.

33 Horlick, *Country Boys and Merchant Princes*, esp. chap. 10.

34 "Wages of Clerks." In this regard, critics were concerned with the impact of low wages on the morality of all mercantile clerks. See also "Clerk's Salaries" and "Inadequate Salaries of Clerks."

35 For vague allusions to drummers' moral shortcomings and a more specific complaint that drumming opened the door to "bad customers," that is, merchants who could not pay, see "Loss and Gain of Drumming for Custom."

36 Horlick, on the other hand, in *Country Boys and Merchant Princes*, stresses the New York merchant's accommodation to economic and social change.

37 Blumin, *Emergence of the Middle Class*, 76–78. Blumin also points out that aspiring

clerks willingly settled for relatively low salaries because they knew that they would have the opportunity to rise in position and improve their incomes (112–13).

38 Blumin refers in passing to drummers as upwardly mobile, nonmanual workers and hence part of a emerging middle class. Blumin, *Emergence of the Middle Class,* 112, 149–50, 271.

39 Blumin, *Emergence of the Middle Class,* 83–107.

40 Mathews, *Big Abel and the Little Manhattan,* 66.

41 Frothingham, "Stewart, and the Dry Goods Trade of New York," 529; "New York Daguerreotyped," 125.

42 Enton, "Old Street of New York," 75; Dodge, "A Great Merchant's Recollections," 155–56.

43 Dodge, "A Great Merchant's Recollections," 156.

44 Albion, *Rise of New York Port,* 421. Like the Bowery or Five Points, Pearl Street was one of several "symbolic zones" in the city that, according to Stuart Blumin, demanded interpretation. See Blumin, "Explaining the New Metropolis," 23, 24. Blumin's discussion of the New York City landscape does not include Pearl Street.

45 Even as late as the 1850s, when merchants were moving to areas west and north of the original wholesale district, Pearl Street continued to confound observers. "It is a haunting nightmare to a stranger in town, this long narrow alley, meeting him at every turn and leading him into inextricable confusion," noted a contributor to *Putnam's Monthly* in 1853. "New York Daguerreotyped," 124.

46 Mathews, *Big Abel and the Little Manhattan,* 66–67.

47 The relation between Mathews's novel and Cooper's fiction is explored in P. Miller, *Raven and the Whale,* 141–45.

48 Greene, *Perils of Pearl Street,* 49.

49 Stephens, *High Life in New York,* 14.

50 In contrast to fictional portrayals of the visual disorder of Pearl Street, Albion stresses the sense of order and routine in the mercantile establishment. *Rise of New York Port,* 260–62.

51 C. Briggs, *Adventures of Harry Franco,* 1:20; Kimball, *Was He Successful?* 138; Beecher, *Lectures to Young Men,* 225–26.

52 J. Alexander, "Merchant's Clerk Cheered and Counselled," 21–22. Also see the report on the Reverend Brownlee's sermon in "Young Men of New York" for a similar warning against drummers.

53 *Notes on the Road.* Atherton describes the efforts of merchants to avoid drummers in Baltimore, Philadelphia, and New York in *Frontier Merchant,* 31–32.

54 "Borers and Drummers"; also cited in Thornton, *American Glossary,* 272. For another discussion of Philadelphia "bores" see Mudge, "Open Letter," 73.

55 Freedley, *United States Mercantile Guide,* 204. During the 1850s Boston drummers likewise made the rounds of the principal hotels in the city, promising dinners and theater tickets and "hunting up customers." Page, *Recollections,* 22.

56 Wyse, *America,* 1:376.

57 Halttunen, *Confidence Men and Painted Women,* 1–32.

58 Harris, *Humbug,* chap. 3.

59 On hothouse dynamics see Demos, "Oedipus and America," 27–29; G. Brown, *Domestic Individualism.*

60 A. Miller, *Death of a Salesman,* 138; "Loss and Gain of Drumming for Custom," 389; Freedley, *United States Mercantile Guide,* 204; Wyse, *American,* 2:376.

61 On Greene see A. Reed, *Asa Greene;* on Briggs see P. Miller, *Raven and the Whale,* esp. 47–58; Bender, *New York Intellect,* 161–66.

62 Greene, *Perils of Pearl Street,* 71, 105.

63 C. Briggs, *Adventures of Harry Franco,* 1:22, 35. This episode looks forward to those stock scenes in jokes and fiction in which traveling salesmen approach unaccompanied women.

64 C. Briggs, *Adventures of Harry Franco,* 2:205.

65 Greene, *Perils of Pearl Street,* 231.

66 A Yankee from western Massachusetts, Greene edited the *Constellation* from November 29, 1829 until September 8, 1832. He went on to edit other New York penny newspapers, including the *Citizen* and the *Transcript.* Although articles rarely included bylines, Greene may very well have been responsible for many of the mercantile sketches in these newspapers. Reed argues that Greene's experience on the *Transcript* acquainted him with the topic of *The Perils of Pearl Street;* however, he says nothing of the series of articles on drumming in the *Constellation.* A. Reed, *Asa Greene,* 81–93.

67 Greene, "Mercantile Drumming," May 5, June 2, and June 30, 1832. The installments preceded the publication of *The Perils of Pearl Street* by two years.

68 Greene, *Perils of Pearl Street,* 122, 124.

69 For other period descriptions of Peter Funk see Foster, *New York in Slices,* 33, 34; "Auction Sketch"; C. Briggs, "Peter Funk's Revenge."

70 Greene, *Perils of Pearl Street,* 50–51.

71 Greene, *Perils of Pearl Street,* 57–61. "The easiest persons to be drummed are those who have nothing to lose." See "Loss and Gain of Drumming," 390.

72 Greene, *Perils of Pearl Street,* 60–61.

73 Here I follow William Cronon's powerful analysis of economic culture in *Nature's Metropolis,* xvii, 62, 72, 267–68. Although Cronon focuses on the emergence of Chicago as the entrepôt of the American West, his view of how boosters of the city understood and imagined commercial processes has relevance, I suspect, for much of nineteenth-century America and, in particular, antebellum New York. Cronon also notes that the economic centrality of New York during the early nineteenth century made the rise of Chicago possible. See 60–63. For a corroborating discussion of how nature functioned as a source of absolute value in nineteenth-century discourse, but from the perspective of literary analysis, see Horwitz, *By the Law of Nature.* Thomas Bender argues that until the nineteenth century New Yorkers "were inclined to interpret culture as proceeding directly from commerce." *New York Intellect,* 55–56. On New Yorkers' faith in commerce see also Sellers, *Market Revolution,* 19–20.

74 "Review of the Market"; "New York as It Is."

75 "Western Merchants Coming to Town"; "Broadway."

76 "Western Merchants Coming to Town." From a westerner's perspective, the spring season posed particular problems. Melting snow and rain made roads "miry," a condition that, as a guide to migrants put it, compelled travelers to wade through mud and water "ancle [*sic*] deep, knee deep, and peradventure deeper than that." A dry spring, on the other hand, meant low water levels and dangerous steamboat travel. See "Hints to Emigrants," 49–50.

77 Friedman, "Drummer," 40; Atherton, "Predecessors," 18.

78 J. Jones, *Western Merchant,* 116, 164. Commenting on Jones's book, Atherton points

out that Missouri and Kentucky retail merchants regularly favored the Philadelphia and Baltimore markets. *Frontier Merchant,* 83.

79 "New York and Philadelphia."

80 Belden, *New York,* 76. On New York guidebooks during the antebellum years see Marx, *This Is the City.*

81 Halttunen, *Confidence Men and Painted Women,* chaps. 1 and 2.

82 For instance, in *New York in Slices,* George G. Foster warned that trusting merchants who bought goods by sample might discover later, after opening the bales, that they had purchased "a pig in a poke" (34).

83 J. Jones, *Western Merchant,* 165–66. Watch scams are also described in Foster, *New York in Slices,* 35.

84 "Country Merchants." Atherton argues that by 1840 New York had almost monopolized the western market. *Frontier Merchant,* 81. The *New York Globe* and the *United States Gazette* are cited in "Miscellaneous."

85 Blumin, "George G. Foster," 9; Stansell, *City of Women,* chap. 9, esp. 172–75, 183–84. Stansell suggests that country merchants were among the streetwalkers' principal customers.

86 Baker, *Glance at New York,* 4.

87 Briggs's protagonist is conned into "commercial speculation" when he purchases a "valuable" casket at a New York auction, while Redburn parts with his father's fowling piece for a pittance when an unscrupulous New York pawnbroker presses him into the deal. C. Briggs, *Adventures of Harry Franco,* 1:46, 51; Melville, *Redburn.*

88 On middle-class anxiety see Halttunen, *Confidence Men and Painted Women,* 1–32. During the 1830s and 1840s New York theater audiences were still a heterogeneous mixture of classes because theater had not yet become the respectable, middle-class institution that it would be in the 1850s. R. Allen, *Horrible Prettiness,* 51–73.

89 On the popularity of Mose see Dorson, "Mose the Far-Famed and World Renowned." Stuart Blumin also emphasizes the rural perspective in Baker's play. Blumin, "George G. Foster," 55–57.

90 Here I mean to draw a line between those actively engaged in face-to-face sales transactions and those whose jobs, though financial in nature, were insulated from such transactions.

91 On Shillaber see J. Reed, *Benjamin Penhallow Shillaber.*

92 Shillaber, *Drummer,* 73, 70, 73, 26.

93 Shillaber, *Drummer,* 19.

94 Shillaber, *Drummer,* 32–34.

95 Shillaber, *Drummer,* 18.

96 Shillaber, *Drummer,* 5.

97 Shillaber, *Drummer,* 24.

98 J. Jones, *Western Merchant,* 167–69.

99 J. Jones, *Western Merchant,* 167–70.

100 Shillaber, *Drummer,* 20, 18, 19, 10, 9.

101 Sellers, *Market Revolution,* 245–46, 258–59, 261–63.

102 Shillaber, *Drummer,* 69.

103 For a discussion of "turning the world inside out" and the conservative effects of the transgressive in mercantile culture see Stallybrass and White, *Politics and Poetics of Transgression,* 37.

2 But One Country

Epigraphs: John Kirk, letter to his wife, Mar. 3, 1853, in John Kirk Letter Books, 1:202, CHS; William Hutton, letter to Lineus L. Hutton, Oct. 11, 1884, Hutton Family Papers, MHS. Hutton scrawled "Come out and see the world" on an enclosed business card.

1 Kirk, letter to his mother, Mar. 13, 1853, in John Kirk Letter Books, 1:247, CHS; Kirk, letter to Lippincott Co., Mar. 17, 1853, in John Kirk Letter Books, 1:267, CHS. On the development of this view from a train throughout the late nineteenth and early twentieth centuries see Stilgoe, *Metropolitan Corridor,* esp. chap. 9.

2 Kirk, letter to his mother, Sept. 27, 1858, in John Kirk Letter Books, 5:109, CHS.

3 Hutton, letter to Lineus L. Hutton, Mar. 3, 1887, Hutton Family Papers, MHS.

4 Hutton, letters to Lineus L. Hutton, Jan. 18, 1890; Apr. 8, 1891; Mar. 3, 1887, Hutton Family Papers, MHS.

5 Cited in Faragher, *Sugar Creek,* 242 n. 3.

6 Hutton, letter to Lineus L. Hutton, Mar. 3, 1887, Hutton Family Papers, MHS.

7 Gilbert, *Perfect Cities,* 8–9.

8 See the comparative statistics for 1870 to 1900 in U.S. Bureau of the Census, *Occupations at the Twelfth Census* (Washington, D.C., 1904), xxxvi–xxxvii.

9 Society of Commercial Travellers, *System,* 18, 17. Brockett cites the same figures in *Commercial Traveller's Guide Book,* 27, 67.

10 "Samples" (October 1883), 189.

11 U.S. Industrial Commission, *Reports on Trusts and Industrial Combinations* (1900), 1:25.

12 Bledstein, *Culture of Professionalism,* 87; Ryan, *Cradle of the Middle Class,* chap. 4, esp. p. 161.

13 Zunz discusses professional advancement within corporations in *Making America Corporate,* 189–91.

14 K. Brown, "Memories," 241. In 1902 the average weekly wage for traveling salesmen working out of Boston was about $30.00 (the high was $100.00 and the low, $10.00), roughly $1,200 per year—a salary topped only by managers—with some salesmen earning as much as $5,000 per year. Kocka, *White Collar Workers in America,* 77.

15 K. Brown, "Memories," 241, 229–30; Twyman, *History of Marshall Field and Co.,* 73–74.

16 Hollander, "Anti-Salesman Ordinances," 347.

17 G. Wright, *Moralism and the Modern Home,* 83. These statistics pertain specifically to Chicago.

18 Baym, *Woman's Fiction,* 27. "Home," the historian Elizabeth Fox-Genovese has observed, "is a modern and ideologically charged term." *Within the Plantation Household,* 31.

19 N. Saunders, *Forty Years,* 93.

20 Chandler, *Visible Hand,* 216 (quotation), 88–89, 215–19; Pred, *Urban Growth and City Systems in the United States,* 62–65; Nystrom, *Economics of Retailing,* 90–95; "Samples," 189; F. Jones, *Middlemen.*

21 On the relative infrequence of manufacturers' salesmen see Page, *Recollections,* 38; Goddard, *Art of Selling,* 50–51. Goddard points out that competition increasingly compelled manufacturers to employ their own sales staff.

22 Porter and Livesay, *Merchants and Manufacturers*, 28.

23 Chandler, *Visible Hand*, 287–88, 312, 314.

24 Strasser, *Satisfaction Guaranteed*, 228. For her discussion of designing markets see chap. 5.

25 Porter and Livesay, *Merchants and Manufacturers*, 227. The statistics were cited in Blackford, *History of Small Business*, 53. Strasser notes that as late as 1923 "over two-thirds of American retail business was still done through general stores and small, single-unit stores selling one line of goods, such as hardware, drugs, groceries, clothing, or furniture." *Satisfaction Guaranteed*, 230.

26 Strasser, *Satisfaction Guaranteed*, 125.

27 Cronon, *Nature's Metropolis*, 264, 318. Cronon discusses the wholesaler's role in the urban-rural synthesis in chaps. 6 and 7. His painstaking examination suggests a rethinking of the emphasis that scholars have recently placed on corporate dominance. The phrase "island communities" is Robert Wiebe's in *Search for Order*, 3–4.

28 Harris, *Cultural Excursions*, 26.

29 Society of Commercial Travellers, *System*, 18–19. For discussions on the predominance of eastern commercial travelers in the 1860s and early 1870s see E. Briggs, *Fifty Years*, 33, 53; K. Brown, "Memories," 238.

30 E. Briggs, *Fifty Years*, 32–33; K. Brown, "Memories," 238. For a more detailed discussion of the wholesaler's role between 1860 and 1900 see Moeckel, *Development of the Wholesaler*.

31 "Dry Goods Exchange." Also in the *Commercial Bulletin* see "Drumming"; "Recollections of an Old Merchant"; and an untitled article of Feb. 7, 1874.

32 T. Clark, *Pills, Petticoats, and Plows*, 11–15.

33 Moeckel notes the role that small cities played as wholesale centers, in *Development of the Wholesaler*, 94–106. Cronon argues that the case he has made for the commercial power of Chicago over the hinterland is "representative" of other cities' influence. *Nature's Metropolis*, 383–84. T. Clark's *Pills, Petticoats, and Plows*, in particular chap. 1, suggests that this urban-rural hierarchy likewise existed in the post–Civil War South.

34 Dreiser, *Sister Carrie*, 15–16; Cronon, *Nature's Metropolis*, 281–82; Moeckel, *Development of the Wholesaler*, 65–75.

35 Twyman, *History of Marshall Field and Co.*, 51–56, 92–95. Twyman shows that between 1873 and 1906 Marshall Field and Company increased expenditures on traveling men from $2,276 to $597,693.

36 Higinbotham, *Making of a Merchant*, 42–43.

37 V. Wright, *Ten Years*, 12–13; Plummer, *Leaves*, 18–19.

38 N. Saunders, *Forty Years*, 57.

39 E. Briggs, *Fifty Years*, 59. See also the argument of A. Schilling and Company in 1884 that by selling Schilling tea a merchant gained profit and prestige. *Advice to Traveling Salesmen*, 4.

40 Cudahy Pharmaceutical Company, *Travelers' Manual*, 16. Becker stresses these lines of communication in "Wholesalers of Hardware and Drugs," 122 n. 14.

41 Kirk, letter to Edward Morris, Dec. 14, 1852, in John Kirk Letter Books, 1:10, CHS.

42 P. J. Willis and Brother, letter to E. I. Dupont and Co., Apr. 6, 1878, E. I. DuPont De Nemoors and Company Papers, HML.

43 Twyman, *History of Marshall Field and Co.*, 94.

44 For an overview of new products and late nineteenth-century consumption patterns see Schlereth, *Victorian America*, 141–67; Boorstin, *Americans*, esp. 89–164,

307–58. A view of rural consumption is in Schlereth, "Country Stores, County Fairs, and Mail-Order Catalogues: Consumption in Rural America" in Bronner, ed., *Consuming Visions*, 349–56. Concerning the rise of brand-name products and their marketing, Strasser's *Satisfaction Guaranteed* offers a valuable, wide-ranging synthesis.

45 Chandler, *Visible Hand*, 291.

46 V. Wright, *Ten Years*, 152. It is not clear whether Martin sold the furniture for his primary employer, P. J. Willis, or for another concern. By 1882 he was working for more than one firm and worrying about meeting his obligations to all of them. See Martin, letters to Julia G. Martin, Jan. 19, 1880; Feb. 13, 1882; Feb. 20, 1884, E. Barton Martin Papers, PL.

47 E. Barton Martin, letter to his wife, Apr. 6, 1877, E. Barton Martin Papers, PL. For another account of antebellum commercial traveling—in New England—see Page, *Recollections*, 26–27, 59–60.

48 Becker, *Wholesalers of Hardware and Drugs*, 127–31. Moeckel notes that the difficulties surrounding price-cutting were especially acute in the 1860s but that wholesales gradually moved to a one-price system.*Development of the Wholesaler*, 38–39.

49 "On the Road," 18.

50 Becker, *Wholesalers of Hardware and Drugs*, 132–34.

51 Society of Commercial Travellers, *System*, 4, 5. On the missionary spirit among modern advertisers see Marchand, *Advertising the American Dream*, chap. 2.

52 Horn, *Drumming*, 10.

53 Belcher, *What I Know*, 11.

54 "Commercial Travelers and Commercial Traveling," 1.

55 Commercial Travelers' Home Association of America, *Official Souvenir*, 93.

56 Brockett, *Commercial Traveller's Guide Book*, 44.

57 R. Miller, *American Apocalypse*, 30; Cronon, *Nature's Metropolis*, 31–46. Such rhetoric was not unique. An organic language of uplift characterized such well-known efforts as Walt Whitman's, in *Democratic Vistas* (1871), to reconcile the economic realities of the new era with the Republic's promise of a democratic millennium.

58 Horwitz, "Standard Oil Trust as Emersonian Hero," 105. These issues are taken up at greater length in Horwitz's book *By the Law of Nature*.

59 On the advertiser's modernity see Lears, "Some Versions of Fantasy," 354–63; Marchand, *Advertising the American Dream*, esp. the introduction and chap. 1, tellingly entitled "Apostles of Modernity."

60 Commercial Travelers National Association, *Descriptive Handbook*, 7–21.

61 R. G. Dun and Co., *Mercantile Agency Reference Book*, n.p.

62 Norris, *R. G. Dun and Co., 1841–1900*, 54–55, 87–88, 111–13; Blackford, *History of Small Business*, 55.

63 E. Briggs, *Fifty Years*, 126–29.

64 Battle, *Tributes*, 195.

65 Maher, *Man of Samples*, 130.

66 "Lamentations of the Traveling Man," in Streeter, *Gems*, 33.

67 William A. White, letter to John White, May 23, 1875, White Family Papers, NYPL.

68 V. Wright, *Ten Years*, 342.

69 Horn, *Drumming*, 52.

70 Samuel Nesbit, letter to parents, Aug. 25, 1907, Hotels, Box 18, Warshaw Collection.

71 E. Howe, *Man Story,* 40–41. Also see Howe's description of Joe Bush in *Anthology of Another Town,* 84.

72 U.S. Bureau of the Census, *Statistics of the Population of the United States* (Washington, D.C., 1872), 676–77.

73 Nearly all of Babcock's letters written during his career as a traveling man reflect his loneliness at being separated from his family. In particular, see Joseph Weeks Babcock, letter to his wife, Mary F. Babcock, May 7, 1876, Joseph Weeks Babcock Papers, SHSW.

74 Martin, letters to Julia G. Martin, Apr. 6, 1877, E. Barton Martin Papers, PL.

75 Sources for these lists include state codes, court opinions, salesmen's guidebooks and autobiographies, and Stanley C. Hollander's article (which I did not discover, alas, until after I spent many hours poring over statute law) entitled "Nineteenth Century Anti-Drummer Legislation in the United States."

76 Ga. Code, sec. 1631 (Stanton, Cobb, and Irwin 1873); 1879 Mont. Laws, sec. 3, p. 5; Ky. Gen. Stat., chap. 83, sec. 3, p. 276 (Stanton 1867).

77 Speer v. The Commonwealth, 23 Grat. 935 (Va. Ct. of Appeals 1873); E. Briggs, *Fifty Years,* 48–49.

78 Cited in Elias Ward v. The State of Maryland, 31 Md. 279 (Md. Ct. of Appeals 1869); Society of Commercial Travellers, *System,* 6–7.

79 Hollander, "Anti-Salesman Ordinances," 348.

80 Keller, *Affairs of State,* 409–10, and more generally 409–38. States had the right, as Justice Taney put it, to exercise "power over their internal police and improvement, which is so necessary to their well being and prosperity." Cited in Warren, *Supreme Court in United States History* 2:34–35.

81 Baldwin, *Travelling Salesmen,* 8, 5, 23, 19.

82 Ga. Code, sec. 1634 (Stanton, Cobb, and Irwin 1873); Me. Rev. Stat., chap. 44, sec. 2, p. 389 (1871).

83 Thomas v. City of Hot Springs, 34 Ark. 553 (Ark. Sup. Ct. 1879).

84 Hollander, "Nineteenth-Century Anti-Drummer Legislation," 483. Of the states that revised older, peddler laws and inserted the proper terms Michigan was typical. It simply supplemented its 1871 statute by enlarging the definition of a hawker or peddler to include anyone who exposes for sale "any goods, wares or merchandise, by sample lists or catalogues." Mich. Comp. Laws. (Dewey 1871), secs. 1148–57.

85 Commonwealth v. Jones, 7 Bush 502 (Ky. Ct. of Appeals 1870); City of Kansas v. John T. Collins, 34 Kan. 434 (Kan. Sup. Ct. 1885).

86 Society of Commercial Travellers, *System,* 15; Becker, *Wholesalers of Hardware and Drugs,* 264; Hollander, "Nineteenth-Century Anti-Drummer Legislation," 488.

87 Ga. Code, sec. 1631 (Stanton, Cobb, and Irwin 1873); Ind. Rev. Stat., sec. 5629 (1888); Ky. Gen. Stat., chap. 83, sec. I, p. 276; Me. Rev. Stat., chap. 44, sec. 21, p. 396; 1867 Md. Laws, chap. 413, sec. 37; 1870–71 Va. Laws, chap. 72, sched. A, sec. 101, p. 98; W.Va. Rev. Stat., sec. 13, p. 1135 (1879). A Missouri peddler law favoring home manufactures was struck down in 1877 Mo. Laws, p. 292.

88 1859 Ga. Laws, tit. 16, sec. 74, p. 58.

89 James W. Owens, letter to H. Tillard Smith, Jan. 4, 1868, H. Tillard Smith Papers, PL.

90 Robert W. Dryden and Son, letter to H. Tillard Smith, Feb. 18, 1868, H. Tillard Smith Papers, PL.

91 Weldon, *Twenty Years,* 222–23.

92 Plummer, *Leaves*, 62–65; Hayes, *Twenty Years*, n.p. Hayes was arrested by "spotters" in a Richmond store when his "Northern cut" suit gave him away. For a law that rewarded informers see 1870–71 Va. Acts, chap. 72, sched. A, sec. 101, p. 98.

93 "Samples" (September 1883), 79; and "Samples" (December 1883), 375. According to Charles Plummer, licensing laws gave drummers the chance to play practical jokes, as, for instance, when unlicensed drummers tiptoed down streets to avoid detection. "If a friend stepped up behind and tapped one on the shoulder," he recalled, "the face became pale at once, and the knees trembled in fear of the dreaded officer with his demand to see the license." *Leaves*, 64–65.

94 Forbush, "Familiar Legal Talks," 50–51.

95 E. Briggs, *Fifty Years*, 49; Society of Commercial Travellers, *System*, 19, 22.

96 Society of Commercial Travellers, *System*, 5–8, 19–22; "Samples" (September 1883), 79; *Bradstreet's Pocket Atlas of the United States*, 5–9; Travelers' Protective Association, Kentucky Division, *Commercial History of the State of Kentucky*, n.p. See also Brockett, *Commercial Traveller's Guide Book*, 28–42.

97 See *License Laws;* Gash, *Rights of Agents;* Aluminum Cooking Utensil Company, *Briefs;* Bryan et al., *Salesman's Rights;* Real Silk Hosiery Mills, *Condensed Legal Facts*.

98 Aluminum Cooking Utensil Company, *Briefs*, 1.

99 Forbush, "Familiar Legal Talks, No. II," 167.

100 Ex Parte Taylor, 58 Miss. 478 (Miss. Sup. Ct. 1880).

101 Ex Parte Taylor.

102 Robbins v. Shelby County Taxing District, 120 U.S. 489 (U.S. Sup. Ct. 1886). Nineteenth-century Supreme Court drummer cases that followed and depended on Robbins include Corson v. Maryland, 120 U.S. 502; Asher v. Texas, 128 U.S. 129; Stoutenburgh v. Hennick, 129 U.S. 141; Brennan v. Titusville, 153 U.S. 289. For twentieth-century affirmations of the *Robbins* decision see Real Silk Hosiery Mills v. City of Portland et al., 268 U.S. 325, and Nippert v. City of Richmond, 327 U.S. 416.

103 Ward v. Maryland.

104 Robbins v. Shelby County.

105 Trachtenberg, *Incorporation of America;* Moeckel, *Development of the Wholesaler*, 40–41, 157–58.

106 Real Silk Mills v. Portland, 268 US 325 (U.S. Sup. Ct. 1924).

107 Hemphill, "House to House," 642.

108 Hutton, letters to Lineus L. Hutton, July 1, 1892, and Aug. 14, 1892, Hutton Family Papers, MHS.

3 A Grip on the Land

1 Denham, *For Traveling Salesmen Only*, 13, 14.

2 White, letter to John White, May 23, 1875, White Family Papers, NYPL.

3 Maher, *On the Road to Riches*, 30–32.

4 Eaton, *How To Succeed as a Drummer*, 21.

5 Horn, *Drumming*, 112–14.

6 Castelow, *Only a Drummer*, 32, 33.

7 Castelow, *Only a Drummer*, 34.

8 Jewett and Butler's letter to James Eaton, June 22, 1864, Jewett and Butler Letters, CHS.

9 *Oxford English Dictionary*, 2nd ed., s.v. "canvas" and "make."

10 K. Brown, "Memories," 231; E. Barton Martin, letter to his wife, Julia G. Martin, Feb. 10, 1880, E. Barton Martin Papers, PL; Caldwell, *How to Become a Commercial Traveler,* n.p.; Street, *Abroad at Home,* 119.

11 Bourdieu, *Outline,* esp. 78–83.

12 The phrase "inland imagination" is Herman Melville's, in *Redburn,* 2. Claremont Manufacturing Company, *Commercial Traveler's Pocket Companion,* 1; Brockett, *Commercial Traveller's Guide Book,* 155; Breyfogle, *Commercial Traveler,* n.p.

13 Skidelsky, *Tales,* 6.

14 Plummer, *Leaves,* 14.

15 Daniel W. Groh, letter to John Groh, Nov. 9, 1887, Daniel Webster Groh Papers, PL. Similarly, in traveling across Missouri, Illinois, and Indiana in the autumn of 1881, Edward P. Clark moved from one road to another, changing direction only when he reached important rail junctions. Clark, letter to Charles W. Clark, Nov. 15, 1881, Charles W. Clark Papers, MHM.

16 Lindsay, *Handy Guide for Beggars,* 20–21.

17 Clark, letter to Charles W. Clark, May 13, 1879, Charles W. Clark Papers, MHM.

18 Peak, *Ranger,* 46.

19 E. Briggs, *Fifty Years,* 56.

20 Peak, *Ranger,* 13; Hamilton, *Footprints,* 113–14.

21 T. H. Young, Journal, Alfred Decker Papers, CHS.

22 Augustus D. Ayling Diary, vol. 1: Jan. 7, Feb. 5 and 13, 1867, NHHS.

23 Joseph Weeks Babcock, letter to Mary F. Babcock, Aug. 24, 1876, Joseph Weeks Babcock Papers, SHSW.

24 William A. White, letter to John White, May 23, 1875, White Family Papers, NYPL. For his description of another occasion that required livery rental see his letter to his sister Julia, May 4, 1876, White Family Papers, NYPL.

25 Castelow, *Only a Drummer,* 13.

26 Burough, "Drummer of Today," 202.

27 Jewett and Butler's letter to James Eaton, May 6, 1864, Jewett and Butler Letters, CHS.

28 Maxwell, "Traveling Salesman," 23.

29 *Oxford English Dictionary,* 2nd ed., s.v. "territory"; Caldwell, *How to Become a Commercial Traveler,* 19.

30 Caldwell, *How to Become a Commercial Traveler,* 50.

31 T. H. Young, Journal, 1892, Alfred Decker Papers, CHS.

32 N. Saunders, *Forty Years,* 93; National Salesmen's Training Association, *How to Become "A Knight of the Grip,"* 81.

33 Streeter, *Gems,* 11–12; Peak, "Ode to an Old Grip Sack," 209.

34 Peak, *Ranger,* 24; Belcher, *What I Know,* 130; K. Brown, "Memories," 262, 264, 265. Other descriptions of hotel life include F. Mills, "Early Commercial Travelling in Iowa," 333; V. Wright, *Ten Years,* 285. For a description of this life and a poignant story of one salesman's death on the road see Onion, "Drummers Accommodated."

35 "American Commercial Traveler," 373; Albro, "'C. T.': His Story," 27.

36 N. Saunders, *Forty Years,* 37, 49.

37 Caldwell, *How to Become a Commercial Traveler,* 34; Plummer, *Leaves,* 13.

38 Martin, letters to Julia G. Martin, Jan. 4, 1880, and June 20, 1880, E. Barton Martin Papers, PL; N. Saunders, *Forty Years,* 37; Caldwell, *How to Become a Commercial Traveler,* 14–15; Crewdson, *Tales of the Road,* 110.

39 F.H.F., "What Are You Going to Do About It? " 151; Crandall, "Baggage," 81.

40 Crandall, "Liability of Railroads for Lost Baggage," 555.

41 Crandall, "Baggage," 82.

42 K. Brown, "Memories," 229–31; Young, Journal, Alfred Decker Papers, CHS. The physical description comes from Isaac A. Alling and others v. Boston and Albany Railroad Company, 126 Mass. 121 (Mass. Sup. Ct. 1879).

43 Plummer, *Leaves*, 47.

44 N. Saunders, *Forty Years*, 51, 92; Nisbet, *Footprints*, 255.

45 To guard against theft, shoe salesmen carried only odd shoes and even pasted decals on them. Here I am indebted to Malcolm Levison for discussing his experiences as a traveling shoe salesman during the automobile age. Personal interview, Sept. 2, 1987.

46 Inscription on the stationery in Babcock, letter to Mary F. Weeks, Aug. 24, 1876, Joseph Weeks Babcock Papers, SHSW.

47 See, e.g., the stationery for the Giradin House for Martin, letter to Julia G. Martin, Mar. 16, 1877, E. Barton Martin Papers, PL; the advertisement for Reese's Commercial Rooms, in White, letter to Julia White, May 4, 1876, White Family Papers, NYPL.

48 Plummer, *Leaves*, 171–72.

49 Tarkington, *Gentleman from Indiana*, 53, 9.

50 Jacobs, *Thirty Years*, 38.

51 Maxwell, "Traveling Salesman," 25; V. Wright, *Ten Years*, 297. The Cudahy Pharmaceutical Company even urged its salesmen to skip "country towns" and confine their movements to bigger cities during the winter months, when orders were, it was believed, more difficult to attain. *Travelers' Manual*, 19.

52 The story comes from E. Briggs, *Fifty Years*, 39–40. For other examples of parlors–turned–sample rooms see Jacobs, *Thirty Years*, 43, 50.

53 "Dry Goods Exchange."

54 Weldon, *Twenty Years*, 213. Proprietors who served inedible food, kept dirty hotels, and charged exorbitant rates treated traveling men as "legitimate public plunder," according to K. Brown, "Memories," 283.

55 Schaefer, "Commercial Traveler, the Prey of the Hotel," 101; "Fifty Cents for Sample Rooms," 139.

56 "Should Extra Charge Be Made for Sample Rooms?" 21; "Wisconsin's Seventh Annual," 24; "Airing of Ideas," 20–21.

57 See Wagner, "Statler Idea: Typical Floor Plan," 165; Wagner, "Statler Idea: Sample Room Floors," 15–16; Wagner, "Hotel Statler in Detroit," 339.

58 Wagner, "Statler Idea: Sample Room Floors," 18.

59 "Travelers' Methods," 27.

60 F. Smith, *Beyond the Swivel Chair*, 10.

61 Weldon, *Twenty Years*, 264.

62 Palmer, *Forty Years*, 302–5. Hamlin Garland recalls witnessing this trick as a boy. *Son of the Middle Border*, 176.

63 A. Schilling and Company, *Advice*, 3–7. For further instructions see A. Schilling's *Contract* and *Reply to Your Letter*.

64 N. Saunders, *Forty Years*, 57.

65 E. Briggs, *Fifty Years*, 59. See also the argument of A. Schilling and Company that by selling its tea a merchant gained profit and prestige. *Advice*, 4.

66 Throughout the late nineteenth and early twentieth centuries commercial travelers

indignantly emphasized that they were not peddlers. See, e.g., Marquis, "My Memories," 152.

67 Johnston, *Twenty Years*, 547–48.

68 Caldwell, *How to Become a Commercial Traveler*, 28. The development of business etiquette in a culture of transition, movement, and anonymity dovetails with the establishment of middle-class social conventions. As Karen Halttunen has argued, by the second half of the nineteenth century "middle-class Americans were coming to accept the idea of a social system filled with liminal men in pursuit of the main chance." For a discussion of the need to express sincerity through formal conventions see Halttunen, *Confidence Men and Painted Women*, 198. Such etiquette was not indigenous to the United States. According to an 1837 book published in Scotland, "natural" and "quiet" manners improved a commercial traveler's chances of success. See *Hints*, 20.

69 Martin, account book, undated, E. Barton Martin Papers, PL; R. G. Dun and Company Collection, BL, Texas, 15:98, 100, and Kentucky, 38:55.

70 Belcher, *What I Know*, 62–64; G. Douglas, *Experiences*, 18–19.

71 Plummer, *Leaves*, 39–40.

72 Horn, *Drumming*, 68; W. F. Main Company, *Instructions*, 19.

73 Lorimer, *Letters*, 177–78.

74 Susan Strasser also notes the traveling man's geniality in her aptly named essay "The Smile That Pays," 156.

75 Hochschild, *Managed Heart*, 20.

76 A bibliographical survey of humor books is Weiss, "Brief History of American Jest Books," 273–89.

77 See esp. Rourke, *American Humor*, chap. 1.

78 According to a writer for *Texas Siftings*, an illustrated weekly of the 1880s, the salesman's profanity gave "the air a sulphurous odor for miles around." Sweet and Knox, *Sketches from Texas Siftings*, 10.

79 Parker, *Kansas Man Abroad*, iv. A similar view of the drummer's propensity for telling stories may be found in *A Drummer's Diary*. "When drummers are engaged in swapping stories," its pseudonymous author writes, "veracity became of less importance than picturesqueness of detail." "Milton," *Drummer's Diary*, 6.

80 Hayes, *Twenty Years*, n.p.

81 E. Briggs, *Fifty Years*, 46.

82 On joke telling and cultural contexts see Douglas, *Implicit Meanings*, 90–114.

83 *Oxford English Dictionary*, 2nd ed., s.v. "craftsmanship"; "landscape"; "salesmanship"; "shape"; and "-ship." Although the *OED* shows *salesmanship* entering the vocabulary in 1880, it was, like other commercial terms, probably in use earlier.

84 Ducker, *Selling Journeys*, 115.

4 Only a Drummer

1 Marshall, *O'er Rail and Cross-Ties*, 13. A staff writer for *American Heritage* gives this more ironic reading of the painting; see "Happy Ending." The recent title is also cited in Gordon, "*Spirit of '76*." Given the dearth of information about Willard and most of his paintings (with the prominent exception of *The Spirit of '76*), the creation of *The Drummer's Latest Yarn* remains a mystery. In 1895, according to an article by Willard's promoter, James F. Ryder, the painting still retained its original title. See Ryder, "Painter of 'Yankee Doodle,'" 485–86.

2 Jackson Lears has argued with reference to modern advertising that "under capitalism, visual and verbal signs become detached from all traditional associations and meaning in general is eroded." Lears, "From Salvation to Self-Realization," 21.

3 Berthoff, *Ferment of Realism*, 12. As part of the nostalgic literature of local color, however, drummers much more gently evoked the contemporaneous impulse to tell the story of "the way we live now" (23–30).

4 The phrase is a chapter title in Van Doren, *Contemporary American Novelists*, 147–71.

5 On the other hand, in puzzling over this fragmented identity, I have been struck by how the salesman's visual presence generated some of the same attributes (which I evoke here) that Frederic Jameson associates with postmodernism. For my purposes, naming the paradigm is not so nearly important as the fact that the late nineteenth-century economy gave way, however incidentally, to its own brand of marketplace aesthetics. See Jameson, "Post-Modernism," esp. 55–64.

6 Orvell, *Real Thing*, 35. Orvell also discusses the tremendous popularity of chromolithographs (36–38). On Willard's relationship with Ryder see Pauly, "In Search."

7 Jay, *Trade Card*, 39–40. Prang is cited in Marzio, *Democratic Art*, 99.

8 Borus, *Writing Realism*, 67, 95.

9 Adams, "Der Drummer," in Adams, *Leedle Yawcob Strauss and Other Poems*, 64, 67. For a similar contemporaneous treatment in Dutch dialect see "Mr. Kroutsmeyer on 'Drummers,'" 37–38.

10 Burdette, *Hawk-Eyes*, 99; G. Peck, *Peck's Fun*, 152. The origins of such humor in small-town newspapers are suggested by reports in the *Lafayette* [Indiana] *Daily Courier* (July 3 and 15, 1876) on a "festive bummer" or "Mr. bummer" who was jailed by local authorities for his drunken escapades.

11 Burdette, *Chimes from a Jester's Bells*, 226–27.

12 Dewey, "Americanism and Localism," 687.

13 "Burdette on Commercial Travelers," in Brower, *Complete Traveling Salesman's Joke Book*, 10–12.

14 Ade, "The Fable of the Slim Girl Who Tried to Keep a Date That Was Never Made," in Ade, *Fables in Slang*, 12; Ade, "The Fable of What Happened the Night the Men Came to the Women's Club," in Ade, *More Fables in Slang*, 81–82.

15 Ade, *Fables in Slang*, 123–26, 132–33.

16 Ade, *True Bills*, 113–15.

17 Sweet and Knox, *Sketches from Texas Siftings*, 10.

18 Gunnison, *Rambles Overland*, 231–32. The Englishman Samuel Hole likewise classified the genus drummer by including a two-column list comparing American words to British nomenclature in his description of a trip through the United States in 1890s. See Hole, *A Little Tour in America*, 170.

19 "Studies in the South," 752, 751; "The Trip of *The Mark Twain*," 401; Morgan, "Problems of Rural New England," 582.

20 Meriwether, *Tramp at Home*, 60; R. Davis, *West from a Car-Window*, 225–26, 6.

21 Kipling, *American Notes*, 197–200.

22 Twain, *Life on the Mississippi*, 465–67. Miles Orvell notes Twain's attention to imitative products. *Real Thing*, 53.

23 Powell, "The Man from High Hat," 558; Bishop, *House of a Merchant Prince*, 2. For a similar treatment see Ellsworth, "The Man from Maine," 25–28.

24 Howells, *Their Wedding Journey*, 65. More mundanely, Howells described his own encounter with a traveling man on a train near Albany, New York. By this time, Howells had written *Their Wedding Journey* and took pleasure in observing the

Mohawk Valley and knowing that he "had got it all right." Howells, *Selected Letters* 1:372.

25 In *David Harum*, Edward Noyes Wescott depicted the traveling man as a conduit of commercial information, whose word to his New York City wholesale house determined the credit—and the fate—of local merchants. In Lydia Perkins's 1903 story "The Hat Pharmacy," drummers are responsible for the economic growth of a small town. Wescott, *David Harum*, 192–94; Perkins, "Hat Pharmacy," 24–26.

26 Stuart, "Unlived Life of Little Mary Ellen," 697; Dreiser, *Sister Carrie*, 5; Cather, "Death in the Desert," 199.

27 Garland, "Up the Coule," in Garland, *Main-Travelled Roads*, 51.

28 Walworth, "Three Miss Merritts," 4. For a similar case of mistaken identity see Sarah Orne Jewett, "King of Folly Island," 103.

29 Deland, "Fourth-Class Appointment," 266.

30 Late in *John March, Southerner*, as John March and Barbara Garnet, Cable's Reconstruction-era lovers, begin their affair on a North-bound train, two commercial travelers provide mistaken analyses throughout the journey. The drummers pride themselves on their sharp eyes and worldly knowledge but, lacking both, provide humor every time they appear and earnestly doff their hats to the two southerners. The comedy continues until one drummer's father meets March on a train and, without knowing his identity, tells him that his son loves a Southern woman—in fact, Barbara Garnet—and that people often mistake his son for the famous John March. Cable brings the novel full circle when the father discloses how he found the young John March stuck in a hollow log when returning home after the Civil War.

31 Cable, *Bonaventure*, 153.

32 Cable, *Bonaventure*, 161–62. For another literary evocation of a fraternal gathering among salesman see K. Clark, "At the Sign of the Wildcat," 40–48.

33 LaFrance, *Reading of Stephen Crane*, 211–13; Wolford, *Stephen Crane*, 28–30.

34 Crane, "Bride," 366–70. Crane's story first appeared in *McClure's Magazine* 10 (February 1898).

35 Gibson, *Fiction of Stephen Crane*, 126.

36 Crane, "Bride," 370–71.

37 Crane, "Bride," 370.

38 Garland, "A Stop-Over at Tyre" and "A Fair Exile," in Garland, *Other Main-Travelled Roads*, 144, 254. In the southern village in Ruth McEnery Stuart's local-color fiction, similar scenes take place. When the village belles walk or drive past the storefronts, drummers "sit forward in supposed parlor attitudes, and easily doff their hats with a grace that the Simpkinsville boys fiercely denounce while they vainly try to imitate it." Such imitations fail, Stuart laments, for "a country boy's hat will not take on that repose which marks the cast of the metropolitan hatter." "Unlived Life," 697.

39 Garland, *Rose of Dutcher's Coolly*, 42.

40 Suggestive here is Garland's attitude toward literary agents, whom he reviled—in Daniel H. Borus's words—as "another species of middleman." Borus, *Writing Realism*, 55.

41 Wister, *Virginian*, 13, 14, 45, 26, 22.

42 Wister, *Virginian*, 22, 4, 45, and passim.

43 Wister, *Owen Wister Out West*, 90, 97.

44 Wister, *Virginian*, 2, 3.

45 Hale, *G.T.T.; or, The Wonderful Adventures of a Pullman*, 10. G.T.T. stands for "gone to Texas."

46 Stimson, "Alabama Courtship," 551.

47 Bartlett, *Commercial Trip*, 90–91, 128. For another illustration of the difficulty that authors had integrating drummers into stories see Demetrak, *Unfortunate Merchant*.

48 These two novels were written, respectively, by George C. Jenks and Joseph Badger. Other titles include Badger's *The Grip-Sack Sharp* (1889), *Silver-Tongued Sid* (1889), *The Gripsack Sharp's Even-Up* (1890), and *The Get-There Sharp* (1890). Edward Willett's *Drummer Sport* (1890) differs from the preceding novels in its depiction of the drummer as a humorous, joke-playing figure, rather than a crime solver. On western heroes in dime novels see H. Smith, *Virgin Land*, 90–111.

49 Badger, *Get-There Sharp*, 2–3.

50 Badger, *Gripsack Sharp's Even-Up*, 2.

51 The play's obscure history is briefly told in Hubert Heffner's introduction to Jessop, *Sam'l of Posen*, xx–xxi.

52 "'Drummer's' Haven," 229.

53 Jessop, *Sam'l of Posen*, 162.

54 *St. Paul Dispatch*, Aug. 19, 1894. The following newspaper reviews also call attention to Curtis's depiction of a general type. Some of them are missing precise dates: *Chicago News*, 1894, and *Boston Transcript*, October 1894?. See the *Sam'l of Posen* Clippings File, HTC.

55 Jessop, *Sam'l of Posen*, 157.

56 Curtis revised the play and copyrighted it with a new title—*Drummer on the Road; A Comedy in Four Acts*—but Heffner notes that the surviving version is probably the revised one, still leaving it without any scenes from the road. See Jessop, *Sam'l of Posen*, xx–xxi.

57 Playbill for *Sam'l of Posen; or, The Commercial Drummer*, in the *Sam'l of Posen* Clippings File, HTC. Although the play is set in Philadelphia in 1854, the program describes a modernized landscape, more in keeping with the 1890s.

5 For the Good of the Order

Epigraph: Wilcox, "Commercial Traveler," in Wilcox, *Poems of Power*.

1 Benson, *Counter Cultures*, 178–80. These percentages are based on U.S. census figures collected between 1870 and 1910. See the following sources from the Bureau of the Census: *The Statistics of the Population of the United States* (Washington, D.C., 1872), 706; *Statistics of the Population of the United States at the Tenth Census* (Washington, D.C., 1883), 746–47; *Compendium of the Eleventh Census: 1890* (Washington, D.C., 1897), 396; *Occupations at the Twelfth Census* (Washington, D.C., 1904), cxiv: *Thirteenth Census of the United States. Population, 1910* (Washington, D.C., 1914), 4:93. For a discussion of the cultural imperatives that made domestic work the occupation of choice for women who could afford not to work outside the home, see Kessler-Harris, *Out to Work*, 128–41.

2 Kerber, "Separate Spheres," 39.

3 Lears, "Beyond Veblen: Rethinking Consumer Culture in America," in Bronner, ed., *Consuming Visions*, 79–82; Lears, "Stabilization of Sorcery."

4 Ryan, *Cradle of the Middle Class*.

5 Edward P. Clark, letter to Charles W. Clark, Mar. 6, 1883, Charles W. Clark Papers,

MHM. Clark represented the H. J. Johnson Company and sold works by Shake-speare, as well as a variety of histories. Because Clark covered cities and towns in several states, as was frequently the custom among book agents, his experiences on the road resembled a commercial traveler's—enough so that he identified with the commercial travelers whom he met on the road.

6 E. Barton Martin, letter to John Glascock, Mar. 31, 1874, E. Barton Martin Papers, PL. These records consists primarily of Martin's letters to his wife and a fly-bespattered list of dry-goods and general-store owners. Although the list of accounts is undated, the customer names and a corresponding examination of Dun's credit ratings for the area suggest that it was written sometime in 1874.

7 Martin, letter to Julia G. Martin, June 19, 1876, E. Barton Martin Papers, PL.

8 Martin, letter to John Glascock, Mar. 31, 1874, E. Barton Martin Papers, PL.

9 Martin, letters to Julia G. Martin, Jan. 4, 1880; June 20, 1880; Aug. 28, 1875, E. Barton Martin Papers, PL.

10 Martin, letter to Julia G. Martin, Apr. 9, 1880, E. Barton Martin Papers, PL.

11 Martin, letters to Julia G. Martin, Apr. 17 and 21, 1880; May 18, 1882; Jan. 4, 1880; June 19, 1876, E. Barton Martin Papers, PL.

12 Martin, letter to Julia G. Martin, Aug. 19, 1882, E. Barton Martin Papers, PL.

13 Martin, letter to Julia G. Martin, Apr. 9, 1880, E. Barton Martin Papers, PL.

14 John Dewitt, "Drummer's Constancy," in Streeter, comp., *Gems.*

15 George H. Hood, letter to Henrietta J. Hood, Apr. 13, 1862, George Henry Hood Papers, PL; William A. White, letter to his sister, Julia, May 4, 1876, White Family Papers, NYPL; Peak, *Ranger,* 20.

16 Clark, letter to Charles W. Clark, Nov. 15, 1881, Charles W. Clark Papers, MHM.

17 J. Ford, "'Drummer' vs. the 'Bagman,'" 31–32; Gandon, *Sixty Years "On the Road,"* 33–35. Also see the description of the commercial room in Anthony Trollope's 1862 novel *Orley Farm,* 48–62, 84–94.

18 E. Anthony Rotundo, "Boy Culture" in Carnes, ed., *Meanings for Masculinity.* See "Boys," 29; Munn, "Boys," 225–28.

19 Crewdson, *Tales of the Road,* 96–98.

20 Caldwell, *How to Become,* 83; V. Wright, *Ten Years,* 397. For other declarations of the drummer's charitable, fraternal disposition see Horn, *Drumming,* 36–37, 105–7; Plummer, *Leaves,* 7–8, 18–19; Peak, *Ranger,* 115–16, 153–54.

21 James Whitcomb Riley, "The Traveling Man," in Riley, *Complete Works,* 3:445. The poem first appeared in the *Saturday Review* on Feb. 12, 1881, according to Russo, *Bibliography of James Whitcomb Riley,* 85.

22 "'Drummer's' Haven," 229. The illustration appears on p. 233.

23 "What Fraternities Have Accomplished," 362.

24 Brockett also pointed out that English commercial travelers had successfully created their own insurance societies. Brockett, *Commercial Traveller's Guide Book,* 65–66.

25 Ultimately, most fraternal insurance societies had to adopt these more sophisticated methods to survive. Schmidt, *Fraternal Organizations,* 5–6, 10–13, 16–17; Basye, *History and Operation of Fraternal Insurance,* 9–46; Kip, *Fraternal Life Insurance,* 4–6, 31–36. Fraternal insurance associations for traveling men likewise evolved according to emerging standards. See, e.g., the discussion of the Order of United Commercial Travelers' insurance policy making in "Report of Supreme Attorney," 106–13.

26 Both Schmidt and Kip argue that the ritual content of fraternal benefit societies

diminished considerably in the twentieth century. In 1919, however, according to Basye, ritualistic work was still an important aspect of these societies. Schmidt, *Fraternal Organizations*, 4; Kip, *Fraternal Life Insurance*, 6; Basye, *History and Operation of Fraternal Insurance*, 45–46.

27 Commercial Travelers' National Association, *Descriptive Handbook*, 3, 4; Commercial Travelers' Protective Association, *Commercial Travelers' Protective Association*, 2, 12–13. One writer, F. B. Goddard, credits the Commercial Travelers National Association with being the first organization for traveling men but claims that it dissolved a couple years after its 1870 founding. *Art of Selling*, 87–88. I have found no mention of the Commercial Travelers Protective Association after 1877.

28 Commercial Travelers Club of New York, *Trade and Travel*, 11. In addition to the Commercial Travelers Club of New York, which was established in 1891, other wholly fraternal clubs and their foundation dates are as follows: Michigan Knights of the Grip (1889), Commercial Travelers' Club of Springfield, Massachusetts (1895), Gideons (1899), Egyptian Hustlers (1903), and National Travelers' Association of America (1908). See "Insurance and Fraternal Association Notes," 83–93; Commercial Travelers' Club of Springfield, *Third Annual Hand-Book*.

29 Rochester Commercial Travelers' Mutual Benefit Association, *Rochester*, 5 (emphasis deleted).

30 "Samples" (September 1883), 78–79; (October 1883), 185–86; (December 1883), 376. Also see "For the Good of the Order," 135–36.

31 In 1883 most fraternal associations were "mutual insurance societies." "Commercial Travelers," *National Agent* 3 (August 1883): n.p., in Salesmanship, Oversize Folder, Warshaw Collection. For a more complete list of fraternal associations see "Insurance and Fraternal," 83–93; "For the Good of the Order," 31–42; "Short Review of the Work of the Association," 12–13.

32 "What Fraternities Have Accomplished," 362. Some fraternal insurance societies survived well into the twentieth century; see International Federation, *Proceedings*.

33 Travelers Insurance Company, *Accident Department*, Accident Policy Pamphlet (Hartford, Conn.: Travelers Insurance Company, 1886), in Insurance, Box 29, Warshaw Collection.

34 Commercial Travelers Mutual Accident Association of America, *Fifth Annual Report*, 5. The continued success of the association is emphasized in its annual reports. The *Fortieth Annual Report* was issued in 1923.

35 By 1922 the association insured over 170,000 traveling men. Commercial Travelers Mutual Accident Association of America, *Fortieth Annual Report*, 10.

36 Commercial Travelers Mutual Accident Association of America, *Eighth Annual Report*, 9–16, and *Fifth Annual Report*, 31.

37 See, e.g., Travelers' Protective Association, Kentucky Division, *Commercial History of the State of Kentucky*, n.p.; "Traveling Men That Get Hurt," advertisement for the Iowa State Traveling Men's Association, *Sample Case* 21 (November 1902): n.p.; "The Order of United Commercial Travelers," advertisement, *Sample Case* 21 (August 1902): 189; Travelers' Protective Association, Indiana Division, *Travelers' Protective Association of America*, 21. Of these fraternal insurance associations, the United Order of Commercial Travelers paid the most money for a death claim— $6,300.

38 "Traveling Men," advertisement for the Iowa State Traveling Men's Association, *Sample Case* 21 (October 1902): n.p.; "Order of United Commercial Travelers," advertisement.

39 Dickerson, "When Chapin Changed His Mind," 278–82; Fitzgerald, "Mary Jane's Traveling Man," in National Association of Traveling Men, *First Annual Announcement,* 66.

40 The following discussion is based on an examination of trade journals published between 1883 and 1920. Devoted to the interests of traveling men and fraternal associations, they exemplify the impact of domestic morality—and fraternalism— on commercial traveling.

41 "Commercial Travelers," 20.

42 This motto derives from the name of a regularly featured section of the Minnesota-based periodical *Traveling Man* in which the editors discussed news from the various fraternal associations.

43 This combination proved even more elaborate as the order made clear by its explanation of "Our Tenets And Colors." It stressed that "UNITY, its color BLUE, denotes STABILITY. CHARITY, its color GOLD, denotes FIDELITY. TEMPERANCE, its color WHITE, denotes PURITY." Masthead of *Sample Case* 21 (August 1902): n.p. Also see "Two Southern Banquets," 207–8.

44 Briscoe, *Angels of Commerce,* 95, 216.

45 Dewitt, "I'll Meet You in the Morning," 335–37.

46 "Sam," 338–43; "Hypocrite," 481–82; "Orphans Story," 5–7.

47 According to the charter, the two-dollar membership fee would help finance these plans. See "C. T. Home Special Charter," 3; Commercial Travelers' Home Association of America, *Official Souvenir* (1896), 73. See also the *Official Souvenir* for 1898. In the end, the Home movement failed because, according to one critic, the organization poured too much money into its magazine. "Commercial Travelers' Home Association."

48 Thurber, *Quaint Crippen,* 11, 116, 89, 90, 19, 48, 253.

49 For histories and descriptions of this organization see "National Society of Christian Traveling Men," 626–27; "For the Good of the Order," 31–34; "Insurance and Fraternal," 90–91; Gideons, *Twenty-Two Years' History of the Gideons;* Crosby, "Gideons," 417–25. Also consult the *Gideon Quarterly* (or the *Gideon,* which it later became), the official organ, which began publication in September 1900.

50 "Rules and Regulations of the Gideons," 7.

51 L. Smith, "Convention Sermon" (1901), 32; Betts, "Some Forms of Temptation," 18–19. See also "Chaplain's Department," 29; Lundy, "Loyalty," 12–13; "Obscene Story Telling," 37; Teetzel, "Are All Gideons Christians?" 28–29; "Card Playing in Hotels," 8.

52 L. Smith, "Convention Sermon" (1901), 32. This point is also emphasized in Betts, "Some Forms of Temptation," 18–19; and in "Obscene Story Telling," 37.

53 L. Smith, "Sermon," 44–45.

54 L. Smith, "Convention Sermon" (1900), 32, 36, 35. On the traveling man's need for salvation also see "Report of the Second Annual Convention," 15.

55 L. Smith, "Convention Sermon" (1900), 36. These phrases are repeated in Phelps, "Chicago Rally," 23.

56 Darner, "From Our Iowa State Superintendent," 10; Phelps, "Chicago Rally," 25. The organization also made it a policy to refuse advertising from hotels that served liquor. See the note on advertising in the *Gideon Quarterly* 1 (December 1900): 22.

57 "Each One Win One," 10; "Work of the Gideons," 20; N. Ford, "Traveling Men of the Bible," 22.

58 Gideons "harangued fellow drummers on every occasion," according to Crosby, "Gideons," 420. Warren Susman explores the influence of Barton and the importance of salesmanship as part of a "secular religion" that during the 1920s eased American culture "from an older, more producer-centered system with its traditional value structure to the newer, more consumer-oriented system with its changed value structure." I find that this secular, evangelical salesman evolved even earlier. Susman, "Culture Heroes: Ford, Barton, Ruth," in Susman, *Culture as History,* 123; see also 122–31. On Barton's therapeutic role in twentieth-century advertising see Lears, "From Salvation to Self-Realization," 29–38.

59 "Executive Committee Meeting," 18; Bowen, "Outlook," 15.

60 "Council Records," 46–47. On membership policies see Order of United Commercial Travelers of America, Grand Council of Ohio, *Proceedings of the Seventh Annual Session,* 14.

61 Daniel, "Ask the Man," 348. The commitment to domestic virtue was strong from the start of the organization. For early declarations of fraternal piety see "Our Traveling Salesmen," 148; Patterson, "Annual Sermon," 425–29. Other statements of the idealistic purposes of the association include Waller, "Fraternity," 121–22; "Two Southern Banquets," 207–8; "Travelers of To-Day," 221–22. From the *Crescent and Grip,* the journal published by Minnesota UCT members, see "The Necessity and Methods of Bringing the Members Up to a Just Appreciation of the Principles of U.C.T.ism," 133–34, and "The Great U.C.T. Meeting: Thirteenth Annual Session at Albert Lea," 335–36.

62 In nineteenth-century America conceptions of masculinity were generally shaped by this conflict between aggressiveness and Christian piety or chivalry. See Filene, *Him/Her/Self,* 77-104; Charles E. Rosenberg, "Sexuality, Class, and Role in Nineteenth Century America," in E. and J. Peck, eds., *American Man,* 229–31, 235, 241–42.

63 The specific remark comes from an untitled article in the *Crescent and Grip* 3 (October 1905): 57. For similar complaints see "The 'How' and the 'Why,'" 86–87; "Causes of Suspension," 213.

64 "Travelers of To-Day," 221; Order of United Commercial Travelers, Grand Council of Ohio, *Proceedings of the Twenty-First Annual Session,* 56.

65 "Let Them Wallow," 50. The same historical perspective shapes an anonymous poem, "The Traveling Man," published in a 1918 issue of the *Commercial Travelers Magazine,* 146–49.

66 "Our Sample Case," 490.

67 W. A. Johnson, "Proscription nor Prejudice or Barriers of Birth or Creed in the Brotherhood of Traveling Men," in Order of United Commercial Travelers of America, Grand Council of Illinois, *Souvenir Program,* 14; "Fraternity," 21; "Application for Membership in the Travelers Protective Association of America," 47. The National Association of Traveling Men invited "any white man actively engaged as a traveling man" to be a member. "Constitution," in National Association of Traveling Men, *First Annual Announcement,* 19. In researching this project, I encountered no written record of African American commercial travelers.

68 See, e.g., Tansill's Punch trade card, Jews, Box 2, Warshaw Collection; Jay, *Trade Card in Nineteenth Century America,* 67–76. Lears discusses anti-Semitic sentiment directed against Jewish peddlers, in "Stabilization of Sorcery."

69 Cahan, *Rise of David Levinsky,* 327–29.

70 C. Howard, "Fellowship," 105, 106; Lou G. Adams, "Cooperation and Reciprocity Among Traveling Salesmen," in National Association of Traveling Men, *First Annual Announcement*, 93–95.

71 Wiebe, *Search for Order;* Neil Harris, "The Lamp of Learning: Popular Lights and Shadows," in Oleson and Voss, eds., *Organization of Knowledge in Modern America*, 430–39.

72 Barker, "'Youngster,'" 124–25. For another, more dramatic fictional conversion that leads to business success see Barker, "Reformation of Bonner," 8–13.

6 *Sister Carrie* and the Logic of Salesmanship

1 Dreiser, *Sister Carrie*, 58; Moers, "Finesse of Dreiser," 109–14; Michaels, *Gold Standard and the Logic of Naturalism*, 29–58.

2 Dreiser, *Sister Carrie*, 60.

3 Dreiser, *Sister Carrie*, 59–60, 127–28.

4 Shapiro, *Theodore Dreiser*, 13; Matthiessen, *Theodore Dreiser*, 66; Moers, *Two Dreisers*, 132.

5 Michaels, *Gold Standard and the Logic of Naturalism*, 43; Dreiser, *Sister Carrie*, 449; Fisher, *Hard Facts*, 163, 129.

6 A. Kaplan, *Social Construction*, 140, chap. 6 in general.

7 H. Smith, "Search for a Capitalist Hero," 89.

8 Howells, *Rise of Silas Lapham*, 290. On moral economy see, e.g., Wai-Chee Dimock, "The Economy of Pain: Capitalism, Humanitarianism, and the Realistic Novel" in Pease, ed., *New Essays*.

9 Howells, *Day of Their Wedding*, 128, 136. The crucial chapters for this discussion are 9–12. I am indebted to Michael Anesko for bringing this novel to my attention.

10 This view is forcefully expressed in Michaels, "*Sister Carrie*'s Popular Economy," in Michaels, *Gold Standard and the Logic of Naturalism*.

11 For another realist novel whose author opposes domestic virtue to commercial traveling see E. W. Howe's 1888 novel, *A Man Story*. Howe's principal character, Tom Saulsbury, spends long periods away from his family and midwestern village, ostensibly traveling for a nearby urban merchant. But Saulsbury is not a commercial traveler, nor are his domestic arrangements what they appear. Tom turns out to be a managing partner in his mercantile firm and the reluctant husband of an estranged wife who refuses to recognize their divorce. The drama of *A Man Story* turns on exposing this duplicitous life while at the same time relying on the presumed threat of commercial traveling to a stable home life. "I regret that love is not like the true religion," Tom tells his wife during one of his visits home, "but it isn't; every man who has deserted his wife has probably felt love as keenly as I do, and expressed it in almost exactly the same words" (83). Although Tom's heresy has nothing to do with commercial traveling itself, his worldly realism speaks to the temptations of a drummer's life. The resolution to this conflict is hardly surprising. After a brief separation, Saulsbury rejoins his second wife and becomes the owner of a general store—an independent, settled businessman. Now that appearance follows substance, confidence in the novelist's implied true religion—domestic harmony—can be restored.

12 Dreiser, *Sister Carrie*, 93, 107; Alan Trachtenberg, "Who Narrates? Dreiser's Presence in *Sister Carrie*," in Pizer, ed., *New Essays*, 116 n. 2.

13 Dreiser, *Sister Carrie*, 3.

14 A. Kaplan, *Social Construction*, 145. Trachtenberg also emphasizes Drouet's role as tempter. "Who Narrates?" in Pizer, ed., *New Essays*, 94.

15 *Newark Sunday Times*, Sept. 1, 1901; Louisville *Courier-Journal*, Feb. 13, 1901; *Interior*, Feb. 21, 1901; Syracuse *Post-Standard*, ca. February 1901. All are quoted in Salzman, *Theodore Dreiser*, 16, 14, 13, 13.

16 Dreiser, *Dawn*, 352, 361; Dreiser, *Book of Myself*, 362.

17 Dreiser, *Jennie Gerhardt*, 462; Dreiser, *Hoosier Holiday*, 191. For a discussion of Paul Dresser's influence on young Dreiser see R. Elias, *Theodore Dreiser*, 11–12.

18 Dreiser, *Dawn*, 71.

19 Dreiser, *Sister Carrie*, 4.

20 R. Elias, *Theodore Dreiser*, 5.

21 Dreiser, *Sister Carrie*, 22, 5, 90, 6.

22 Dreiser, *Sister Carrie*, 3–7.

23 Dreiser, *Sister Carrie*, 5–6.

24 Dreiser, *Sister Carrie*, 3.

25 The title of chapter 6 is "The Machine and the Maiden: A Knight of Today."

26 Dreiser, *Sister Carrie*, 5.

27 Dreiser, *Sister Carrie*, 5.

28 Dreiser actually cut out Ade's fable and pasted it on his manuscript. See Moers, *Two Dreisers*, 130–31; Salzman, "Dreiser and Ade."

29 Dreiser, *Sister Carrie*, 5. When asked what he thought of Dreiser's theft, Ade told the *Chicago Herald-Tribune* in 1926 that "while some of us have been building chicken coops, or possibly, bungalows, Mr. Dreiser has been creating skyscrapers." Ade, *Best of George Ade*, 241.

30 Dreiser, *Sister Carrie*, 56, 166. The term *ginger* designates the vigor that salesmen brought to their selling techniques. On the importance of acting and the anticipated self see Fisher, *Hard Facts*, 157–69. For a discussion of Carrie's position as pupil see Bader, "Dreiser's Sister Carrie." Bader says little about Drouet's role as teacher in the novel.

31 Dreiser, *Sister Carrie*, 60, 42, 54, 430, 449.

32 Dreiser, *Sister Carrie*, 94.

33 Dreiser, *Sister Carrie*, Pennsylvania ed., 105–6. The initial version was published by the University of Pennsylvania Press in 1981.

34 Dreiser, *Sister Carrie*, Pennsylvania ed., 100; Dreiser, *Sister Carrie*, 94, 114, 94.

35 Dreiser, *Sister Carrie*, 60, 71, 134. In the Pennsylvania edition, Dreiser emphasizes the visual aspect of Drouet's influence, calling him an "enlivening spectacle" (64).

36 Dreiser, *Sister Carrie*, Pennsylvania ed., 146.

37 For a discussion of erotic merchandising see Fisher, *Hard Facts*, 166.

38 Dreiser, *Sister Carrie*, 144, 167. On Drouet's collaborative role in helping Carrie assume this acting role see Barbara Hochman, "A Portrait of the Artist as a Young Actress: The Rewards of Representation in *Sister Carrie*," in Pizer, ed., *New Essays*, 48–52.

39 Dreiser, *Sister Carrie*, 160. Both Fisher and Michaels note Carrie's anticipation of the future—and future selves. Fisher, *Hard Facts*; and Michaels, *Gold Standard and the Logic of Naturalism*.

40 Dreiser, *Sister Carrie*, 88.

41 Dreiser, *Sister Carrie*, 254; Thomas P. Riggio, "Carrie's Blues," in Pizer, ed., *New Essays*.

42 Dreiser, *Sister Carrie*, 74, 56.

43 Dreiser, *Twelve Men*, 1018.
44 For a discussion of its publishing history see John C. Berkey et al., "*Sister Carrie:* Manuscript to Print," in Dreiser, *Sister Carrie*, Pennsylvania ed., 503–41.
45 Dreiser, *Sister Carrie*, 5, 449.
46 Dreiser, *Sister Carrie*, 181–82.

7 The Mechanics of Consumption

1 Veblen, *Theory of Business Enterprise*, 11, 316–17.
2 Veblen, *Theory of Business Enterprise*, 53.
3 On the corporate maturity and the infrastructural transformations that accompanied it see Chandler, *Visible Hand*, 285–76.
4 The ensuing discussion of modern salesmanship is based on a comprehensive reading of trade literature, how-to-sell manuals, and business ephemera published between 1900 and 1920.
5 Strong, *Psychology of Selling and Advertising*, 8.
6 Droke, *Making a Success of Salesmanship*, 7–8. On the same point, similarly expressed, see Whitehead, *Principles of Salesmanship*, 41.
7 Chalmers, "Science of Selling Goods," 34–35. Also see Lewis, *Creative Salesmanship*, 5; Whitehead, *Principles of Salesmanship*, 7; Alexander Hamilton Institute, *Salesmanship*, 3.
8 Collins, "Limiting Opportunity," 4; Moody, *Men Who Sell Things*, 14.
9 Olerich, *Cityless and Countryless World*, 398; B. Peck, *World a Department Store*, 84–85. For a description of a world with "no lightning rod peddlers and no book agents" and no "street fakirs" see Chambless, *Roadtown*, 166, 167.
10 My discussion of the mail-order business draws on Chandler, *Visible Hand*, 230–33; and Emmet and Jeuck's history of Sears, Roebuck and Company, *Catalogues and Counters*, esp. chap. 10, which deals with the commercial traveler's point of view.
11 Bellamy, *Looking Backward*, 64; Schaefer, "Commercial Traveler," 166. On traveling salesmen's reactions also see Hiscox, "Meeting Mail Order Competition"; Norvell, "Catalogue House Competition"; Harwood, "Parcels Post Bill."
12 Chandler, *Visible Hand*, 233; Emmet and Jeucks, *Catalogues and Counters*, 157–58.
13 So far as I can tell, all but two of these quotations are addressed to retail merchants—the one from Lincoln, Leonard and the promise of Dixie Bargain House that "our only salesman is our catalogue." All of the following sources are found in the Warshaw Collection: B. and A. Galland catalogue for 1879, Ladies Clothing, Unnumbered Box; Lincoln, Leonard and Company circular, Furniture and Furnishings, Box 5; John Davenport and Company, *Davenport's Booklet on Modern Methods of Selling Merchandise* (New York, 1908?), 3, Mercantile, Box 1; Dixie Bargain House catalogue for fall and winter 1914, Dry Goods, Box 31; Butler Brothers business card, Dry Goods, Box 35; M. P. Ansorge circular for fall and winter 1903–4, Men's Clothing, Box 1; Baker and Company advertising letter, June 22, 1907, Coffee, Box 1.
14 Moody, *Men Who Sell Things*, 14–17.
15 Charles Clark Munn, letter, in "Our Sample Case," 412; Bullard, "When Is a Salesman? " 289. On the differences between the drummer and the modern salesman also see Carleton, "Views of a Sales Manager," 319–20; Elliot, "Satirical Shots at Salesmen," 157–58; A. Douglas, *Traveling Salesmanship*, 4; Stowe, *Winning the Trade*, 54–55.

16 Canfield, "What I Think of Commercial Travelers," 753, 754.

17 Lacher, "Travelers of To-day and Yesterday," 221.

18 On the use of organic language, ideas, and imagery see R. Williams, *Culture and Society*, esp. 37, 138–39, 258–60, 263–64.

19 U.S. Industrial Commission, *Reports,*1:26, 33.

20 U.S. Industrial Commission, *Reports,* 1:26, 28.

21 McCraw, *Prophets of Regulation,* 77–78.

22 U.S. Industrial Commission, *Reports,* 1:28.

23 Lorimer, *Letters,* 128, 131; Tinelli, *"Pointers" to Commercial Travellers,* 17.

24 Alexander Hamilton Institute, *Sales Management,* 246–47. On the preference for younger salesmen also see "A Chat with Mr. George S. Dana," 165.

25 Holman, *Ginger Talks;* "Be a Salesman" advertising circular [1908?] for the National Salesmen's Training Association, Salesbooks, Box 1, Warshaw Collection.

26 Connolly, "Necessity of Correct Dress in Business," 292. One sales expert urged older salesmen not to let youth "disqualify" them and encouraged them to adopt the "Pompeian of energy and get Youth-i-fied." Withers, *Salesmanship: An Artistic Science,* 29–30.

27 May, *Screening Out the Past,* 74–75, 114–15, 124–26, 188–89, 235.

28 Here I follow John Higham, "The Re-Orientation of American Culture in the 1890s," in Higham, *Writing American History;* and, in particular, Jackson Lears's argument in *No Place of Grace.*

29 Moody, *Men Who Sell Things,* 14, 16; Knox, *Salesmanship and Business Efficiency,* 93.

30 Sheldon, *Science of Successful Salesmanship,* 1:32; Knox, *Salesmanship and Business Efficiency,* 44; Marden, *Selling Things,* 8; Johnson, *Hints on Salesmanship,* 17.

31 International Correspondence Schools, *Salesman's Handbook,* 6–7. Other reminders that salesman are made and not born include Sheldon, "How the Salesman Is Made"; Sheldon, *Art of Selling,* 32; W. A. Waterbury, "Training for Selling: How the Principles of Salesmanship Are Applied," in Macbain, *Selling,* 2; Russell, *Ethics and Principles of Salesmanship,* 12; Willis, "Are Salesmen Born or Made?"

32 Knox, *Science of Applied Salesmanship,* 163.

33 Benson's *Counter Cultures* is especially effective in showing the impact of scientific management on sales clerks in department stores.

34 Searles, "Handling of Salesmen," 76–77.

35 Hiscox, "System for Commercial Travelers"; Alexander Hamilton Institute, *Sales Management,* 296–308; W. B. Waterbury, "System and the Salesman," in Macbain, *Selling,* 140–59. The importance of systems is stressed throughout *How to Increase Your Sales,* published by the System Company.

36 "Taking the Office Along."

37 Taylor, *Principles of Scientific Management,* 36.

38 Hoyt, *Scientific Sales Management,* 3–5.

39 These are central themes in Hoyt's book.

40 W. Davis, "Salesman of the Coming Ten Years," 97; B. C. Bean, "Science Versus Empiricism in Selling," in Macbain, *Selling,* 26, 27, 28.

41 Clifford, "Matching Salesmen with Territory"; Macready, "Analysis of Sales Management and Organization." Hanson's short story "Along the Line of Least Resistance" shows a sales manager learning of a traveling man's mediocre sales from office records and joining him on the road to criticize his performance.

42 Selz, "System in Selling"; advertisement for Sales Department Map System in Shaw-Walker Company, *Card Index Systems and Supplies,* 37.

43 Banning, "Military System for the Sales Campaign," 6904.

44 Hanson, "Salesman Who Lacked Courage," 268; Selden, "Crew That Worked Dubuque," 181–82.

45 Hanson, "Selling Moses Irons," 165.

46 "Use Modern Arms and Ammunition," cartoon, *Salesmanship* 6 (April 1906): 166; Aleshire, "Climb Up on the Friendly Shoulders," cartoon, *Salesmanship* 8 (January–February 1907): 6. The boast in advertisements addressed to sales organizations was that cartoons in the magazine "keep ever before the salesman's mind in striking fashion the truths that only by incessant energy, perseverance, hard study, loyal effort, and careful use of time could he get his best results in the field." Back cover of *Salesmanship* 6 (January 1906).

47 The martial ideal, as Jackson Lears has pointed out, became particularly important to educated Americans during the late nineteenth and early twentieth centuries. *No Place of Grace*, 98–139.

48 Holman, *Ginger Talks*, 44, 48, 100, 45, 98.

49 Holman, *Ginger Talks*, v. For other testimonies to the influence influence of the National Cash Register Company see Bean, "Science Versus Empiricism," 28; "Sales Schools," 175.

50 For a detailed discussion of these developments see Crowther, *John H. Patterson*, 103–12, 124–36, 152–60; Marcosson, *Wherever Men Trade*, 34–39, 109–19; Gibbs, "How N.C.R. Gets 100 Percent Efficiency."

51 Gibbs, "How N.C.R. Gets 100 Percent Efficiency," 17–18. Gibbs also points out that the older salesmen typically had the most difficulty memorizing the sales pitch. See the first installment of his series in *Printer's Ink* 75 (June 29, 1911): 4–5.

52 Johnson, *Hints on Salesmanship*, 6.

53 On the transition from "character" to "personality" during the early twentieth century see Warren Susman's essay "'Personality' and the Making of Twentieth-Century Culture," in his *Culture as History*, 271–85. Ironically, Susman's discussion of the personality manuals written in a modern consumer culture—which, he argues, gradually "move away from an interest in business" (281)—includes little of the business literature that would lend overwhelming support to his argument. I argue, however, that personality development was crucial to salesmanship and that commercial traveling encouraged this modern view of the self, even during the nineteenth century.

54 Marden, *Selling Things*, 53. On the instruction of high school students in salesmanship see Moulton, "Course in Salesmanship"; Towsley, "Training in Salesmanship"; Hoover, *Science and Art of Salesmanship*, v–xi.

55 On Marden's tremendous popularity see Parker, *Mind Cure in New England*, 28–32.

56 Marden, *Selling Things*, 8, 53.

57 Marden, *Selling Things*, 5.

58 Woodworth, *Success in Salesmanship*, 30, 81, 14; "How To Study Salesmanship," 83–84.

59 James, "Greatest Ginger Talk Ever Written," 116.

60 Sheldon, "How the Salesman Is Made," 423; Marden, *Selling Things*, 9; Sheldon, "Evolution of Success," in Sheldon, *Science of Successful Salesmanship*, 2:37–38. For other charts and lists see Knox, *Salesmanship and Business Efficiency*, 33–35, 113; Moran, "Self-Development of a Salesman"; National Salesmen's Training Association, *How to Become "A Knight of the Grip,"* 63.

61 Ferris, *Business Adventures of Billy Thomas*, 1, 29. Ferris included several of these

adventures in a series of tales about Pete Crowther, Salesman, which appeared in *Outlook* magazine in 1911–14.

62 Ferris, *Adventures of Billy Thomas*, 7, 4; Ferris, "Contentment, Psychology, and Salesmanship," 282–83.

63 Munsterberg, *Business Psychology*, 5. Perhaps the most familiar—but hardly the first—guide to business psychology is Dale Carnegie's 1936 book *How to Win Friends and Influence People*. Carnegie's famous discussions on how to influence people followed a long line of modern self-help books that began to appear around the turn of the century.

64 Munsterberg, *Psychology and Industrial Efficiency*, 295.

65 Barcus, *Science of Selling*, 68, 69. Holman expressed the later perspective when he pointed out that there are two kinds of people: those ruled by reason and those ruled by impulse. *Ginger Talks*, 131.

66 Stowe, *Winning the Trade*, 10. On the relation between advertising and salesmanship also see "True Relation of Advertising to Salesmaking"; Nicholson, "How Advertising Helps the Profession"; Sheldon, *Art of Selling*, 177–78.

67 Most salesmanship literature that I have seen defines the sales transaction according to these or similar steps. See, e.g., Dukesmith, "Publisher's Announcement"; Russell, *Ethics and Principles of Salesmanship*, 67; Pierce, *Scientific Salesmanship*, 3; Sheldon, "What Is Salesmanship? " 216; F. Hamilton, "Working Principles of Systems," 896; Johnson, *Hints on Salesmanship*, 6; Woodworth, *Success in Salesmanship*, 9; Knox, *Salesmanship and Business Efficiency*, 96; International Correspondence Schools, *Salesman's Handbook*, 56; National Salesmen's Training Association, *How to Become "A Knight of the Grip,"* 61; M. Smith, "Teaching Is Salesmanship," 339.

68 Dukesmith, "Publisher's Announcement," 2. According to one contributor, *Salesmanship* was "the first attempt ever made to create a literature on the science of salesmanship." "In Reading Salesmanship."

69 F. Hamilton, "Working Principles of Systems," 896–97; Holman, *Ginger Talks*, 168. Knox also encouraged salesmen to "Get on Customer's Side of Fence." *Salesmanship and Business Efficiency*, 97.

70 Atkinson, *Psychology of Salesmanship*, 28; Maxwell, "Salesmanship," 18. Atkinson did indeed suggest that salesmen should read character when, like the writers discussed below, he cited the usefulness of phrenology (76–77).

71 See, e.g., Ducker's discussion of James and Veblen in *Selling Journeys*, 47. And Ducker was addressing door-to-door book salesmen, not commercial travelers.

72 Dearing, *Drummer's Experience*, 429.

73 J. Larson, "How to Read a Customer," 14. Lindgren, *New Salesmanship*, 25.

74 International Correspondence Schools, *Salesman's Handbook*, 39, 42. A similar perspective is provided in Hoover, *Science and Art of Salesmanship*, 59–67.

75 Breniser, *Salesmanship: A Fine Art*, 39. Breniser mentioned nothing about phrenology or physiognomy. Other twentieth-century texts that encouraged salesmen to read character include Johnson, *Hints on Salesmanship*, 14–17; Edwin Morrell, "The Science of Judging Men," in Knox, *Salesmanship and Personal Efficiency*, 300–438. Although Morrell's 1917 discussion rests on contemporaneous psychological and "scientific" analyses of racial types, his vocabulary and his conclusion—that salesmen can assess a customer's character by assessing facial features and other physical traits—owes much to phrenology and physiognomy.

76 Goddard, *Art of Selling*, 31.

77 Holcomb, *Salesology of the Butter-Kist Popcorn Machine*, 15; Whitehead, *Principles of Salesmanship*, 138.

78 Knox, *Salesmanship and Business Efficiency*, 100 (artist); Sheldon, "What Is Salesmanship?" 217 (actor). The word *performance* and other acting metaphors abound in the literature of salesmanship. See Holman, *Ginger Talks*, 143; Whitehead, *Principles of Salesmanship*, 233; Collins, *Human Nature in Selling Goods*, 86.

79 Maxwell, "Salesmanship: Rule-of-Thumb Science, Part Two," 21. Also see his "Salesmanship: Rule-of-Thumb Science" and "Traveling Salesman."

Conclusion: The Death of the Salesman

1 Mills, *White Collar*, 182–88; Berry, *Unsettling of America*, 11, 10; Ransom, *I'll Take My Stand*, xlv–xlvi.

2 A. Miller, *Death of a Salesman*, 81.

3 A. Miller, *Death of a Salesman*, 97.

4 Anderson, *Sherwood Anderson's Memoirs*, 90–91.

5 Anderson, *Windy McPherson's Son*, 66–67. For the earlier evocation of such dreams see Anderson, "Business Types—the Traveling Man."

6 For a reading of *Poor White* as a critique of industrial technology see Tichi, *Shifting Gears*, 184–94.

7 Anderson, *Poor White*, 342.

8 Anderson, *Poor White*, 164. Clara's father even tries to market her to an unscrupulous suitor.

9 Anderson, *Poor White*, 209, 339; Anderson, *Winesburg, Ohio*, 190–92.

10 Anderson, *Poor White*, 352.

11 Anderson, "Apology for Crudity," 438.

12 Anderson, *Winesburg, Ohio*, 46.

13 Lewis, *Main Street*, 267, 289, 60, 184; Lewis, *Arrowsmith*, 93; Lewis, *Free Air*, 85–89.

14 Lewis, *Babbitt*, 100–101.

15 Lewis, *Main Street*, 268.

16 Van Doren, *Contemporary American Novelists*, 146–71; Wolfe, *Look Homeward, Angel*, 210. In chapter 8 of his 1940 novel, *You Can't Go Home Again*, Wolfe describes a company very much like National Cash Register and highlights the aggressive, false geniality of the salesmen.

17 Lewis, *Elmer Gantry*, 151.

18 Lewis, *Elmer Gantry*, 48, 191, 156, 160, 166, 170.

19 Lewis, *Elmer Gantry*, 229, 294.

20 Welty, "Looking Back at the First Story," 752. "Death of a Traveling Salesman" first appeared in *Manuscript* 3 (June 1936) and has been republished with minor changes in *The Collected Stories of Eudora Welty*.

21 A. Miller, "Family in Modern Drama," 73.

22 Salesmen, Miller went on to say, "have an intimate understanding of this problem"; they "have to get up in the morning and conceive a plan of attack and use all kinds of ingenuity all day long, just the way a writer does." *"Death of Salesman: A Symposium,"* in Bloom, ed., *Willy Loman*, 45–56. For a discussion of Willy's Jewish identity see Louis Harap's comments in the same volume, pp. 29–30.

Bibliography

Manuscripts and Archival Material

Augustus Davis Ayling Diary. New Hampshire Historical Society Collections, Concord (NHHS).

Joseph Weeks Babcock Papers. State Historical Society of Wisconsin, Madison (SHSW).

Charles W. Clark Papers. Joint Collections, University of Missouri Western Historical Manuscripts Collection–Columbia and State Historical Society of Missouri Manuscripts, Columbia (MHM).

Alfred Decker Papers. Chicago Historical Society, Chicago (CHS).

R. G. Dun and Company Collection. Baker Library, Harvard University Graduate School of Business Administration, Cambridge, Mass. (BL).

E. I. DuPont De Nemoors and Company Papers. Hagley Museum and Library, Wilmington, Del. (HML).

Daniel Webster Groh Papers. Manuscript Department, Perkins Library, Duke University, Durham, N.C. (PL).

George Henry Hood Papers. Manuscript Department, Perkins Library, Duke University, Durham, N.C. (PL).

Hutton Family Papers. McLean County Historical Society Collections, Bloomington, Ill. (MHS).

Jewett and Butler Letters. Chicago Historical Society, Chicago (CHS).

Lilburn A. Kingsbury Collection. Joint Collections, University of Missouri Western Historical Manuscripts Collection–Columbia and State Historical Society of Missouri Manuscripts, Columbia (MHM).

John Kirk Letter Books. Chicago Historical Society, Chicago (CHS).

E. Barton Martin Papers. Manuscript Department, Perkins Library, Duke University, Durham, N.C. (PL).

Sam'l of Posen; or, The Commercial Drummer Clippings File. Harvard Theatre Collection, Pusey Library, Harvard University, Cambridge, Mass. (HTC).

H. Tillard Smith Papers. Manuscript Department, Perkins Library, Duke University, Durham, N.C. (PL).

Peter Tamony Collection. Joint Collections, University of Missouri Western Historical Manuscripts Collection–Columbia and State Historical Society of Missouri Manuscripts, Columbia (MHM).

Warshaw Collection of Business Americana. National Museum of American History, Smithsonian Institution, Washington, D.C. (WC).

White Family Papers. Manuscripts and Archives Division, New York Public Library (NYPL).

Books, Articles, and Dissertations

The *Commercial Travelers Magazine* published in the early 1880s is not the same periodical as the *Commercial Travelers Magazine* that appeared in the early twentieth century. Similarly, two magazines shared the title *Salesmanship.* The first, which ran from roughly 1903 to 1908, should not be confused with the second, which ran from 1915 to 1919.

A. Schilling and Company. *Advice to Traveling Salesmen Introducing Perfection Canned Teas.* San Francisco: A. Schilling, 1884.

———. *Contract Between " " as Traveling Representative with A. Schilling and Co.* San Francisco: A. Schilling, 1880.

———. *A Reply to Your Letter.* San Francisco: A. Schilling, 1896.

Adams, Charles Follen. *Leedle Yawcob Strauss and Other Poems.* Boston: Lee and Shepard, 1877.

Ade, George. *The Best of George Ade.* Ed. A. L. Lazarus. Bloomington: Indiana University Press, 1985.

———. *The County Chairman: A Comedy Drama.* New York: Samuel French, 1924.

———. *Doc' Horne: A Study of the Streets and Town.* Chicago: Herbert S. Stone, 1900.

———. *Fables in Slang.* Chicago: Herbert S. Stone, 1899.

———. *More Fables in Slang.* Chicago: Herbert S. Stone, 1900.

———. *True Bills.* New York: Harper, 1904.

"Advertising." *Public Ledger* [Philadelphia], Apr. 22, 1836.

Agnew, Jean-Christophe. *Worlds Apart: The Market and the Theater in Anglo-American Thought, 1550–1750.* Cambridge, Eng.: Cambridge University Press, 1986.

"An Airing of Ideas." *Hotel Monthly* 12 (September 1904): 20–22.

Albion, Robert Greenlagh. *The Rise of New York Port.* New York: Scribner's, 1939.

Albro, John. "The C. T.: His Story." *Commercial Travelers Magazine* 1 (September 1883): 26–28.

Alexander, David. *Retailing in England During the Industrial Revolution.* London: Athlone, 1970.

Alexander, James W. *Forty Years' Familiar Letters of James W. Alexander.* Ed. John Hall. New York: Scribner, 1860.

———. "The Merchant's Clerk Cheered and Counselled." In *The Man of Business, Considered in His Various Relations,* by Alexander et al. New York: Anson D. F. Randolph, 1857.

Alexander Hamilton Institute. *Sales Management.* Modern Business, 2. New York: Alexander Hamilton Institute, 1918.

———. *Salesmanship.* Modern Business, 1. New York: Alexander Hamilton Institute, 1918.

Allen, A. P. *The Ambassadors of Commerce.* London: T. Fisher Unwin, 1885.

Allen, Robert C. *Horrible Prettiness: Burlesque and American Culture.* Chapel Hill: University of North Carolina Press, 1991.

Aluminum Cooking Utensil Company. *Briefs, Decisions and Opinions Pertaining to the Collection of License Taxes by States and Municipalities from Salesmen and Deliverymen Engaged in Soliciting Orders for Future Delivery.* New Kensington, Pa.: Aluminum Cooking Utensil Co., 1914.

"The American Commercial Traveler." *Commercial Travelers Home Monthly Magazine* 1 (October 1893): 372–73.

"And I Was Sure Going to Like Being a Traveling Man." *Commercial Travelers Magazine* 22 (March 1916): 24–47.

Anderson, Sherwood. "An Apology for Crudity." *Dial* 63 (Nov. 8, 1917): 437–38.

———. "Business Types—the Traveling Man." *Agricultural Advertising* 11 (April 1904): 39–40.

————. *Poor White*. New York: B. W. Huebsch, 1920.

————. "Rot and Reason—the New Job." *Agricultural Advertising* 10 (February 1903): 13–16.

————. "The Sales Master and the Selling Organization." *Agricultural Advertising* 12 (April 1905): 306–8.

————. *Sherwood Anderson's Memoirs*. New York: Harcourt, Brace, 1942.

————. *Windy McPherson's Son*. [1916]. Reprint. Chicago: University of Chicago Press, 1965.

————. *Winesburg, Ohio: A Group of Tales of Small Town Life*. New York: Viking, 1960.

Anesko, Michael. *"Friction with the Market": Henry James and the Profession of Authorship*. New York: Oxford University Press, 1986.

Annan, J. "From the Diary of a Traveling Salesman." *Outlook* 122 (Aug. 20, 1919): 605ff.

"Application for Membership in the Travelers Protective Association of America." *T.P.A. Magazine* 12 (November 1917): 47–48.

Arkins, Frank J. "The Merchant Who Cannot Travel." *Harper's Weekly* 37 (April 5, 1913): 18ff.

Atherton, Lewis E. *The Frontier Merchant in Mid-America*. Columbia: University of Missouri Press, 1971.

————. "Itinerant Merchandising in the Antebellum South." *Bulletin of the Business Historical Society* 19 (April 1945): 35–59.

————. *The Pioneer Merchant in Mid-America*. New York: Da Capo, 1969.

————. "Predecessors of the Commercial Drummer in the Old South." *Bulletin of the Business Historical Society* 21 (February 1947): 17–24.

————. *The Southern Country Store, 1800–1860*. Baton Rouge: Louisiana State University Press, 1949.

Atkinson, William Walker. *The Psychology of Salesmanship*. Chicago: Progress Co., 1910.

"An Auction Sketch." *New-York Saturday Emporium,* Dec. 14, 1844.

Austrian, Joseph E. *"We Need the Business."* New York: Frederick A. Stokes, 1919.

Bachelard, Gaston. *The Poetics of Space*. Trans. Marie Jolas. [1958]. Reprint. Boston: Beacon, 1969.

Bacon, C. W. "Are Women Successful as Commercial Travelers?" *Commercial Travelers Magazine* 18 (December 1912): 513–14.

Bacon, Isabel E. "Women Commercial Travelers." *Commercial Travelers Magazine* 18 (March 1912): 129–31.

Bader, Rudolph. "Dreiser's Sister Carrie, More Pupil than Victim." *International Fiction Review* 12 (Summer 1985): 74–78.

Badger, Joseph Edwards. *The Get-There Sharp; or, Grip-Sack Sid at Rocky Comfort*. New York: Beadle and Adams, 1890.

————. *The Grip-Sack Sharp; or, The Seraphs of Sodom*. New York: Beadle and Adams, 1889.

————. *The Grip-Sack Sharp's Even-Up; or, The Boss Racket at Solid City*. New York: Beadle and Adams, 1890.

————. *Silver-Tongued Sid; or, The Grip-Sack Sharp's Clean Sweep*. New York: Beadle and Adams, 1889.

Baker, Benjamin. *A Glance at New York*. [1848]. Reprint. New York: Samuel French, n.d.

Bakhtin, Mikhail M. *The Dialogic Imagination*. Trans. Michael Hoquist and Caryl Emerson; ed. Michael Holquist. Austin: University of Texas Press, 1981.

Baldwin, William H. *Travelling Salesmen: Their Opportunities and Their Dangers*. Boston: Nathan Sawyer, 1874.

Balzac, Honoré de. *The Illustrious Gaudissart. The Human Comedy*. Vol. 4 of *Studies of Customs: Scenes from Provincial Life*. Philadelphia: George Barrie, 1898.

Banning, Kendall. "A Military System for the Sales Campaign." *World's Work* 11 (November 1905): 6902–4.

Barcus, J. S. *Science of Selling for Canvassers, Drummers and Clerks*. New York: Clarke and Barcus, 1895.

Barker, Charles Edmund. "The Reformation of Bonner." *Sample Case* 20 (January 1902): 8–13.

———. "The 'Youngster'" *Sample Case* 20 (March 1902): 123–25.

Barrett, Fred W. *From a Diary*. Springfield, Ohio: F. W. Barrett, 1934.

Bartelle, J. P. *Forty Years on the Road; or, The Reminiscences of a Lumber Salesman*. Cedar Rapids, Iowa: Torch Press, 1925.

Barthes, Roland. *Mythologies*. Trans. Annette Lavers. New York: Hill and Wang, 1972.

Bartlett, George H. *A Commercial Trip with an Uncommercial Ending*. New York: Putnam's, 1884.

Barton, Bruce. "As Prophets Are Your Salesmen a Loss?" *Commercial Travelers Magazine* 27 (July 1921): 101–8.

———. *The Man Nobody Knows*. Indianapolis: Bobbs-Merrill, 1924.

Basye, Walter. *History and Operation of Fraternal Insurance*. Rochester, N.Y.: Fraternal Monitor, 1919.

Battle, Jesse Mercer. *Tributes to My Father and Mother*. St. Louis: Mangan, 1911.

Baym, Nina. *Woman's Fiction: A Guide to Novels By and About Women in America, 1820–1870*. New York: Cornell University Press, 1978.

Becker, William H. "The Wholesalers of Hardware and Drugs, 1870–1900." Ph.D. diss. Johns Hopkins University, 1969.

Beecher, Henry Ward. *Lectures to Young Men on Various Important Subjects*. Salem, Mass..: J. P. Jewett, 1846.

———. *New Star Papers; or, Views and Experiences of Religious Subjects*. New York: Derby and Jackson, 1859.

Belasco, Warren James. *Americans on the Road: From Autocamp to Motel, 1910–1945*. Cambridge: MIT Press, 1979.

Belcher, Alexander Emerson. *What I Know About Commercial Travelling*. Toronto: Hunter, Rose, 1883.

Belden, E. Porter. *New York: Past, Present, and Future; Containing a History of the City of New York, a Description of Its Present Condition and an Estimate of Its Future Increase*. New York: Putnam, 1849.

Bell, Michael. *The Salesman in the Field*. Geneva: International Labour Office, 1980.

Bellamy, Edward. *Looking Backward, 2000–1887*. Ed. Robert C. Elliott. Boston: Houghton Mifflin, 1966.

Bender, Thomas. *New York Intellect*. New York: Knopf, 1987.

Benes, Peter, and Jane M. Benes, eds. *Itinerancy in New England and New York*. Proceedings of the Dublin Seminar for New England Folklife. June 16–17, 1984. Boston: Boston University, 1986.

Benjamin, Walter. *Illuminations*. Trans. Harry Zohn; ed. Hannah Arendt. New York: Schocken, 1969.

Benson, Susan Porter. *Counter Cultures: Saleswomen, Managers, and Customers in American Department Stores, 1890–1940*. Urbana: University of Illinois Press, 1987.

Berger, Peter L., and Thomas Luckmann. *The Social Construction of Reality: A Treatise in the Sociology of Knowledge.* New York: Doubleday, 1966.

Berry, Wendell. *The Unsettling of America: Culture and Agriculture.* San Francisco: Sierra Club Books, 1977.

Berthoff, Rowland T. *An Unsettled People: Social Order and Disorder in American History.* New York: Harper and Row, 1971.

Berthoff, Warner. *The Ferment of Realism: American Literature, 1884–1919.* New York: Free Press, 1965.

Betts, T. G. "Some Forms of Temptation Peculiar to Traveling Men." *Gideon Quarterly* 2 (June 1902): 18–19.

Bigelow, L. Adda. *Reminiscences, by L. Adda Nicholas Bigelow.* Chula Vista, Calif.: Denrich, 1917.

Biggers, Earl Derr. "But Home Was Never like This." *Collier's* 72 (Aug. 4, 1923): 9–10.

Bishop, William Henry. *The House of a Merchant Prince.* Boston: Houghton Mifflin, 1882.

Blackford, Mansel G. *A History of Small Business in America.* New York: Twayne, 1991.

Bledstein, Burton. *The Culture of Professionalism: The Middle Class and the Development of Higher Education in America.* New York: Norton, 1976.

Bloom, Harold, ed. *Willy Loman.* New York: Chelsea, 1991.

Blumin, Stuart M. *The Emergence of the Middle Class: Social Experience in the American City, 1760–1900.* Cambridge: Cambridge University Press, 1989.

———. "Explaining the Metropolis: Perception, Depiction, and Analysis in Mid-Nineteenth-Century New York City." *Journal of Urban History* 11 (1984): 9–38.

———. "George G. Foster and the Emerging Metropolis." In *New York by Gaslight and Other Urban Sketches,* by George G. Foster; ed. Stuart M. Blumin. Berkeley: University of California Press, 1990.

Boorstin, Daniel J. *The Americans: The Democratic Experience.* New York: Random House, 1973.

"Borers and Drummers." *Public Ledger* [Philadelphia], Aug. 23, 1836.

Borough, Rube. "The Drummer of Today." *Independent* 65 (July 23, 1908): 199–204.

Borus, Daniel H. *Writing Realism: Howells, James and Norris in the Mass Market.* Chapel Hill: University of North Carolina Press, 1987.

Bourdieu, Pierre. *Outline of a Theory of Practice.* Trans. Richard Nice. Cambridge: Cambridge University Press, 1977.

Bowen, W. J. "The Outlook." *Gideon Quarterly* 2 (March 1902): 14–15.

"The Boys." *Commercial Travelers "Home" Monthly Magazine* 1 (August 1893): 29.

Bradstreet Company. *Bradstreet's Pocket Atlas of the United States.* New York: Bradstreet, 1882.

Braudel, Fernand. *The Wheels of Commerce.* Trans. Sian Reynolds. New York: Harper and Row, 1982.

Breniser, Ross D. *Salesmanship: A Fine Art.* Ross D. Breniser, 1923.

Breyfogle, L. C., comp. *The Commercial Traveler, Being a Hotel Guide and Gazetteer of the United States. . . .* Lockport, N.Y.: United States Hotel Register Publishing Co., 1881.

Briggs, Charles Frederick. *The Adventures of Harry Franco: A Tale of the Great Panic.* [1839]. Reprint. New York: Garrett, 1969.

———. "Peter Funk's Revenge." *Knickerbocker* 27 (January 1846): 58–61.

Briggs, Edward P. *Fifty Years on the Road: The Autobiography of a Traveling Man by Edward P. Briggs.* Philadelphia: Lyon and Armor, 1911.

Briscoe, George H. *Angels of Commerce; or, Thirty Days with the Drummers of Arkansas.* New York: Press of the Publishers' Printing Co., 1891.

"Broadway." *New York Saturday Emporium: A Family Gazette of Literature, Art, Science, Agriculture, General Intelligence and Amusement,* Sept. 21, 1844.

Brockett, Linus Pierpont. *The Commercial Traveller's Guide Book. . . .* New York: H. Dayton, 1871.

Bronner, Simon, ed. *Consuming Visions: Accumulation and Display of Goods in America, 1880–1920.* New York: Norton, 1989.

Brower, Bill. *The Complete Traveling Salesman's Joke Book.* New York: Stravon, 1952.

Brown, Gillian. *Domestic Individualism: Imagining Self in Nineteenth-Century America.* Berkeley: University of California Press, 1990.

Brown, Kendrick W. "Memories of a Commercial Traveler." *Palimpsest* 52 (May 1971): 225–86.

Brown, Norman O. *Hermes the Thief: The Evolution of a Myth.* New York: Random House, 1947.

Bryan, McCormick, and Wilber. *The Salesman's Rights Under Federal and State Laws as Applied to Interstate Commerce.* Chicago: Hitchcock-Hill, 1920.

Bullard, Benjamin F. "When Is a Salesman?" *Commercial Travelers Magazine* 19 (June 1913): 288–93.

Bunnell, Sterling H. "The Functions of the Engineer as a Salesman." *Engineering Magazine* 34 (January 1908): 613–16.

Burdette, Robert J. *Chimes from a Jester's Bells.* Indianapolis: Bowen-Merrill, 1897.

———. *Hawk-Eyes.* New York: G. W. Carleton, 1879.

Burke, Peter. *Popular Culture in Early Modern Europe.* New York: Harper and Row, 1978.

"The C.T. Home Special Charter." *Commercial Travelers "Home" Monthly Magazine* 1 (August 1893): 3.

Cable, George W. *Bonaventure: A Prose Pastoral of Arcadian Louisiana.* New York: International Association of Newspapers and Authors, 1887.

———. *John March, Southerner.* New York: Scribner's, 1894.

Cahan, Abraham. *The Rise of David Levinsky.* [1917]. Reprint. New York: Harper and Row, 1966.

Caldwell, E. *How to Become a Commercial Traveler; or, The Art of Selling Goods.* Syracuse, N.Y.: D. Mason, 1893.

Caldwell, Erskine. *The Complete Stories of Erskine Caldwell.* New York: Duell, Sloan and Pearce, 1953.

Canfield, James H. "What I Think of Commercial Travelers." *Sample Case* 7 (September 1895): 753–54.

"Card Playing in Hotels." *Gideon* 5 (February 1905): 8.

Carey, Thomas J. *Drummer's Yarns.* New York: Excelsior, 1886.

———. *"That Reminds Me": A New Crop of Drummer's Yarns.* New York: Excelsior, 1894.

Carleton, August. "It Is Not like the Old Days." *Traveling Man* 2 (January 1909): 915–16.

———. "Views of a Sales Manager." *Traveling Man* 1 (June 1908): 319–22.

Carnegie, Dale. *How to Win Friends and Influence People.* New York: Simon and Schuster, 1936.

Carnes, Mark Christopher. *A Pilgrimage for Light: Fraternal Ritualism in America.* Ann Arbor, Mich.: University Microfilms, 1982.

Carnes, Mark Christopher, and Clyde Griffen, eds. *Meanings for Manhood: Constructions of Masculinity in Victorian America.* Chicago: University of Chicago Press, 1990.

Carson, Gerald. *The Old Country Store.* New York: Oxford University Press, 1954.

Casson, Herbert N. *Tips for Traveling Salesmen.* New York: B. C. Forbes, 1927.

Castelow, Wilbur Elijah. *Only a Drummer: A Short History of the Commercial Travelling Salesman's Life.* Meriden, Conn.: Wilbur Elijah Castelow, 1903.

"The Causes of Suspension." *Crescent and Grip* 3 (March 1906): 212–13.

Cather, Willa. "A Death in the Desert." *Scribner's* 33 (January 1903): 109–21.

———. *My Ántonia.* Boston: Houghton Mifflin, 1918.

———. *O Pioneers!* Boston: Houghton Mifflin, 1913.

Cawelti, John G. *Apostles of the Self-Made Man.* Chicago: University of Chicago Press, 1965.

Chalmers, Hugh. "The Science of Selling Goods." *Collier's* 45 (Apr. 16–23, 1910): 18ff, 32ff.

Chamberlain, John. "The Businessman in Fiction." *Fortune* 38 (November 1948): 134–38.

———. *The Enterprising Americans: A Business History of the United States.* New York: Harper and Row, 1961.

Chambers, Talbot W. *The Noon Prayer Meeting of the North Dutch Church, Fulton Street, New York: Its Origin, Character and Progress, with Some of Its Results.* New York: Reformed Protestant Dutch Church, 1858.

Chambless, Edgar. *Roadtown.* New York: Roadtown Press, 1910.

Chandler, Arthur D. *The Visible Hand: The Managerial Revolution in American Business.* Cambridge: Harvard University Press, 1977.

Chapin, E. H. *Moral Aspects of City Life.* New York: Henry Lyon, 1854.

"Chaplain's Department." *Gideon Quarterly* 1 (December 1900): 29–32.

Chapman, Clowry. "The Automobile in Business." *System* 8 (December 1905): 545–53.

"A Chat with Mr. George S. Dana, of the Utica Travelers' Association." *Salesmanship* 1 (December 1903): 164–66.

Claremont Manufacturing Company. *The Commercial Traveler's Pocket Companion, for a Business Trip Through Vermont and New Hampshire. . . .* Claremont, N.H.: Claremont Manufacturing Co., 1871.

Clark, Katherine P. "At the Sign of the Wildcat." *Black Cat* 4 (August 1899): 40–48.

Clark, Thomas D. *Pills, Petticoats and Plows: The Southern Country Store.* Indianapolis: Bobbs-Merrill, 1944.

Clawson, Mary Ann. *Brotherhood, Class and Patriarchy: Fraternalism in Europe and America.* Ann Arbor, Mich.: University Microfilms, 1980.

"Clerk's Salaries." *New York Transcript,* June 29, 1836.

Clifford, W. G. "Matching Salesmen with Territory." *System* 26 (October 1914): 392–97.

Cohn, Jan. *Creating America: George Horace Lorimer and the Saturday Evening Post.* Pittsburgh: University of Pittsburgh Press, 1989.

Collins, James H. *Human Nature in Selling Goods.* Philadelphia: Henry Artemus, 1909.

———. "Limiting Opportunity: The Salaried Man." *Saturday Evening Post* 179 (Feb. 16, 1907): 3–5.

"Commercial Travelers." *American Pottery and Glassware Reporter* 8 (Dec.14, 1882): 20.

"Commercial Travelers and Commercial Traveling." *Commercial Travelers Magazine* 1 (September 1883): 1–7.

Commercial Travelers Club of New York. *Trade and Travel: An Illustrated Volume Descriptive of the Commercial, Financial, Transportation and Hotel Interests of the United States.* New York: Commercial Travelers Club of New York, 1895.

Commercial Travelers Club of Springfield, Mass. *Third Annual Handbook of the Commer-*

cial Travelers Club of Springfield, Massachusetts. Springfield: Commercial Travelers Club of Springfield, Mass., 1899.

"Commercial Travelers' Home Association." *Salesmanship* 4 (January–February 1905): 23–24, 87–88.

Commercial Travelers' Home Association of America. *The Official Souvenir of the Commercial Travelers' Fair, Held Under the Auspices of the Commercial Travelers' Home Association of America, to Aid in Completing the Home and Hospital for Worthy Indigent Commercial Travelers, Their Dependent Wives or Widows and Children.* Ed. William Mill Butler. New York: Frederick M. Crossett, 1896.

———. *The Official Souvenir of the Commercial Travelers' Fair, Held Under the Auspices of the Commercial Travelers' Home Association of America, to Aid in Completing the Home and Hospital for Worthy Indigent Commercial Travelers, Their Dependent Wives or Widows and Children.* Ed. Allen S. Williams. New York: Frederick M. Crossett, 1898.

Commercial Travelers Mutual Accident Association of America. *Eighth Annual Report.* Utica, N.Y.: Commercial Travelers Mutual Accident Association of America, 1891.

———. *Fifth Annual Report.* Utica, N.Y.: Commercial Travelers Mutual Accident Association of America, 1888.

———. *Fortieth Annual Report and Story of the First Forty Years of Service of the Commercial Travelers Mutual Accident Association of America.* Utica, N.Y.: Commercial Travelers Mutual Accident Association of America, 1923.

———. *Seventh Annual Report.* Utica, N.Y.: Commercial Travelers Mutual Accident Association of America, 1890.

Commercial Travelers National Association. *Descriptive Handbook and Abstract of the Advantages, Privileges and Franchises of the Commercial Travelers National Association.* New York: Commercial Travelers National Association, 1872.

Commercial Travelers Protective Association. *Commercial Travelers Protective Association.* New York: Commercial Travelers Protective Association, 1877.

"The Commercial Travellers' Fair." *Harper's Weekly* 40 (Dec. 26, 1896): 1282.

Connolly, C. M. "The Necessity of Correct Dress in Business." *Success* 6 (May 1903): 292ff.

"The Contributors' Club—Our Town." *Atlantic Monthly* 102 (August 1908): 282–83.

Cooper, James Fenimore. *Home as Found.* [1838]. Reprint. New York, W. A. Townsend, 1860.

"Council Records." *Sample Case* 21 (July 1902): 26–27.

"Country Merchants." *Sun* [New York], Mar. 26, 1835.

Crandall, F. W. "Baggage—Sample—Personal Excess Baggage." *Commercial Travelers Magazine* 20 (April 1914): 81–88.

———. "The Liability of Railroads for Lost Baggage." *Commercial Travelers Magazine* 17 (December 1911): 551–59.

Crane, Stephen. "The Bride Comes to Yellow Sky." In The Red Badge of Courage *and Selected Prose and Poetry.* Ed. William M. Gibson. New York: Holt, Rinehart, and Winston, 1950.

Crewdson, Charles N. *Tales of the Road.* Chicago: Thompson and Thomas, 1905.

Crick, Throne. *Sketches from the Diary of a Commercial Traveller.* London: Joseph Masters, 1847.

Crissey, Forest. "Experiences of a Salesman." *World's Work* 10 (August 1905): 6569–70.

———. "The Modern Commercial Traveler." *Everybody's Magazine* 21 (July 1909): 22–31.

Cronon, William. *Nature's Metropolis: Chicago and the Great West.* New York: Norton, 1991.

Crosby, W. C. "The Gideons." *American Mercury* 14 (August 1928): 417–25.

Crowther, Samuel. *John H. Patterson: Pioneer in Industrial Welfare.* Garden City, N.Y.: Garden City Publishing, 1926.

Cudahy Pharmaceutical Company. *Travelers' Manual.* South Omaha, Nebr.: Cudahy Pharmaceutical Co., 1894.

"The Dandy." *Constellation* [New York], Oct. 30, 1830.

Danforth, Emma. "On the Road." *Woman's Home Companion* 50 (March 1923): 44–45.

Daniel, Charles G. "'Ask the Man.'" *Sample Case* 22 (November 1903): 347–49.

Darner, W. H. "From Our Iowa State Superintendent." *Gideon Quarterly* 1 (December 1900): 10–11.

Darnton, Robert. *The Great Cat Massacre and Other Episodes in French Cultural History.* New York: Vintage, 1984.

———. *The Literary Underground of the Old Regime.* Cambridge: Harvard University Press, 1982.

———. "The Symbolic Element in History." *Journal of Modern History* 58 (March 1986): 218–34.

David, Beverly R. "Selling the Subscription Book." *Hayes Historical Journal* 1 (Spring 1977): 192–200.

Davis, Dorothy. *A History of Shopping.* London: Routledge and Kegan Paul, 1966.

Davis, Fred. "Nostalgia, Identity and the Current Nostalgia Wave." *Journal of Popular Culture* 11 (Fall 1977): 414–24.

Davis, Richard Harding. *The West from a Car-Window.* New York: Harper, 1892.

Davis, W. E. "The Salesman of the Coming Ten Years." *Salesmanship* 2 (March 1904): 94–97.

Day, W. L. "The Traveling Man." *Sample Case* 8 (February 1896): 88–90.

Dearing, John Samuel. *A Drummer's Experience.* Colorado Springs: Pike's Peak Publishing, 1913.

Deland, Margaret. "A Fourth-Class Appointment." *Harper's New Monthly Magazine* 84 (January 1892): 265–92.

Delbanco, Andrew. "The Rise and Fall of American Regionalism." *Bennington Review,* no. 16 (Spring 1984): 75–79.

Demetrak, Charles. *The Unfortunate Merchant and Experiences of Drummers.* Berkeley, Calif.: World Publishing, 1898.

Demos, John. "Oedipus and America: Historical Perspectives on the Reception of Psychoanalysis in the United States." *Annual of Psychoanalysis* 6 (1978): 23–39.

Denham, Earl Lanham. *For Traveling Salesmen Only.* Boston: Meador, 1932.

Dewey, John. "Americanism and Localism." *Dial* 68 (June 1920): 684–88.

Dewitt, John. "I'll Meet You in the Morning." *Commercial Travelers "Home" Monthly Magazine* 1 (October 1893): 335–37.

"The Diamond Salesman." *Harper's Weekly* 56 (Sept. 7, 1912): 24.

Dickens, Charles. *The Pickwick Papers.* Ed. James Kinley. New York: Oxford University Press, 1988.

Dickerson, B. Winona. "When Chapin Changed His Mind. *Commercial Travelers Magazine* 18 (June 1912): 278–82.

"Do You Want to Be a Knight of the Grip." *Commercial Travelers Magazine* 22 (March 1916): 28–33.

Dodge, William Earl. "A Great Merchant's Recollections of Old New York." In *Valentine's Manual of Old New York*, n.s. 5, ed. Henry Collins Brown. New York: Valentine's Manual, 1920.

Dolan, J. R. *The Yankee Peddlers of Early America.* New York: Bramhall, 1964.

Dorson, Richard M. "Mose the Far-Famed and World-Renowned." *American Literature* 15 (November 1943): 288–300.

———. "The Yankee on Stage—a Folk Hero of American Drama." *New England Quarterly* 13 (September 1940): 467–93.

Dougall, Lily. "Commercial Traveller." *Living Age* 210 (Aug. 22, 1896): 478–86.

Douglas, A. W. "Sensing Public Opinion." *Independent* 83 (Sept. 13, 1915): 372–73.

Douglas, Archer Wall. *Traveling Salesmanship.* New York: Macmillan, 1919.

Douglas, George Anson. *The Experiences of a Veteran Salesman of Memorial Monuments.* Cincinnati: C. O. Ebel, 1906.

Douglas, Mary. *Implicit Meanings.* London: Routledge and Kegan Paul, 1975.

———. *Purity and Danger: An Analysis of the Concepts of Pollution and Taboo.* London: Routledge and Kegan Paul, 1966.

Dreiser, Theodore. *A Book of Myself.* New York: Boni and Liveright, 1922.

———. *Dawn.* London: Constable, 1931.

———. *Hoosier Holiday.* New York: John Cane, 1916.

———. *Jennie Gerhardt.* New York: Library of America, 1987.

———. *Sister Carrie.* Philadelphia: University of Pennsylvania Press, 1981.

———. *Sister Carrie.* New York: Library of America, 1987.

———. *Twelve Men.* New York: Library of America, 1987.

Droke, Maxwell. *Making a Success of Salesmanship.* Chicago: Dartnell Corp., 1922.

"A Drummer's Haven." *Frank Leslie's Illustrated Newspaper,* Nov. 28, 1885.

"A Drummer's Prayer." *Captain Billy's Whiz Bang* 3 (Oct. 1, 1921): 21.

"Drumming." *Commercial Bulletin* [Boston], Oct. 6, 1860.

"A Dry Goods Exchange." *Commercial Bulletin* [Boston], Oct. 28, 1876.

Ducker, W. H. *Selling Journeys: A Handbook for Representatives of Journeys Through Bookland.* Chicago: Bellows-Reeve, 1914.

Dukesmith, F. H. "Publisher's Announcement" *Salesmanship* 1 (June 1903): 1–3.

Dwight, Timothy. *Travels in New England and New York.* Ed. Barbara Miller Solomon. [1821–22]. Cambridge: Harvard University Press, 1969.

"Each One Win One." *Gideon* 5 (February 1905): 10.

Eaton, Seymour. *How to Succeed as a Drummer.* Boston: Oxford, 1891.

Elias, Norbert. *The History of Manners.* Trans. Edmund Jephcott. New York: Pantheon, 1978.

Elias, Robert H. *Theodore Dreiser: Apostle of Nature.* New York: Knopf, 1949.

Elliot, Berton. "Satirical Shots at Salesmen." *Commercial Travelers Magazine* 16 (June 1910): 157–60.

Elliott, Sarah Barnwell. "Squire Kayley's Conclusions." *Scribner's Magazine* 22 (November 1897): 758–69.

Ellis, Charles M. *The Argument of Charles M. Ellis, Esq., in Favor of the Metropolitan Police Bill Before the Joint Special Committee of the Legislature, Wednesday, March 18, 1863.* Boston: Wright and Potter, 1863.

Ellsworth, J. D. "The Man from Maine." *Black Cat* 1 (November 1895): 25–28.

Emmet, Boris, and John E. Jeuck. *Catalogue and Counters: A History of Sears, Roebuck and Company.* Chicago: University of Chicago Press, 1950.

Enton, James V. "An Old Street of New York." *American Historical Magazine* 3 (January 1908): 68–77.

Ewen, Stuart. *Captains of Consciousness: Advertising and the Social Roots of Consumer Culture.* New York: McGraw-Hill, 1975.

"Executive Committee Meeting." *Gideon Quarterly* 1 (December 1900): 18–19.

F. H. F. "What Are You Going to Do About It?" *Commercial Travelers Magazine* 1 (October 1883): 150–52.

Fabian, Ann. *Card Sharps, Dream Books, and Bucket Shops.* Ithaca: Cornell University Press, 1990.

Faragher, John Mack. *Sugar Creek: Life on the Illinois Prairie.* New Haven: Yale University Press, 1986.

Feld, Rose C. "Spoon Rivers with the Full Quality of America." *New York Times Book Review,* Sept. 7, 1924.

Ferber, Edna. *Emma McChesney and Co.* New York: Grosset and Dunlap, 1915.

———. *Personality Plus: Some Experiences of Emma McChesney and Her Son Jock.* New York: Frederick A. Stokes, 1914.

———. *Roast Beef, Medium.* New York: Frederick A. Stokes, 1913.

Ferris, Elmer E. *The Business Adventures of Billy Thomas.* New York: Macmillan, 1915.

———. "Contentment, Psychology, and Salesmanship." *Outlook* 97 (Feb. 4, 1911): 279–83.

———. "Pete Crowther, Salesman." *Outlook* 101 (Aug. 24, 1912): 921–28; 105 (Dec. 27, 1913): 889–95; 106 (Jan. 24, 1914): 193–99; 107 (Aug. 1, 1914): 809–15.

Fife, George Buchanan. "Phoenix of the Drummer." *Commercial Travelers Magazine* 19 (June 1913): 213–21.

"Fifty Cents for Sample Rooms." *Sample Case* 22 (March 1903): 139.

Filene, Peter Gabriel. *Him/Her/Self: Sex Roles in Modern America.* New York: Harcourt Brace Jovanovich, 1974.

Findlay, John H. *Dwight L. Moody: American Evangelist, 1837–1899.* Chicago: University of Chicago Press, 1969.

Fisher, Philip. *Hard Facts: Setting and Form in the American Novel.* New York: Oxford University Press, 1985.

Fogg, Lawrence Daniel. "The Drummer as I Know Him." *Commercial Travelers Magazine* 18 (June 1912): 246–55.

———. "The Troublesome Tip." *Commercial Travelers Magazine* 19 (June 1913): 193–202.

"For the Good of the Order." *Traveling Man* 1 (January–February 1908): 31–43, 131ff.

Forbush, George S. "Familiar Legal Talks." *Commercial Travelers Magazine* 1 (September 1883): 49–52.

———. "Familiar Legal Talks, No. II." *Commercial Travelers Magazine* 1 (October 1883): 167–70.

Ford, James L. "The 'Drummer' vs. the 'Bagman.'" *Saturday Evening Post* 175 (June 20, 1903): 31–32.

Ford, Nathan. "Traveling Men of the Bible." *Gideon Quarterly* 2 (March 1902): 21–23.

Foster, George G. *New York in Slices, by an Experienced Carver: Being the Original Slices Published in the* N.Y. Tribune. New York: William H. Graham, 1849.

———. *New York Naked.* New York: Robert M. DeWitt, 1855.

Fox, Stephen. *The Mirror Makers: A History of Modern Advertising and Its Creators.* New York: Vintage, 1984.

Fox-Genovese, Elizabeth. *Within the Plantation Household: Black and White Women of the Old South.* Chapel Hill: University of North Carolina Press, 1988.

Franklin, Benjamin. *Autobiography and Other Writings.* Ed. Russel B. Nye. Boston: Houghton Mifflin, 1958.

Fraser, W. Hamish. *The Coming of the Mass Market, 1850–1914.* Hamden, Conn.: Archon, 1981.

"Fraternity." *T.P.A. Magazine* 12 (January 1918): 21.

Freedley, Edwin T. *United States Mercantile Guide: Leading Pursuits and Leading Men.* Philadelphia: Edward T. Young, 1856.

Friedman, Lee M. "The Drummer in Early American Merchandise Distribution." *Bulletin of the Business Historical Society* 21 (April 1947): 39–44.

Frothingham, W. "Stewart, and the Dry Goods Trade of New York." *Continental Monthly* 2 (November 1862): 528–34.

Fryer, Judith. *Felicitous Space.* Chapel Hill: University of North Carolina Press, 1986.

Fuller, Margaret. *Margaret Fuller, American Romantic: A Selection from Her Writings and Correspondence.* Ed. Perry Miller. New York: Doubleday, 1963.

Gandon, James. *Sixty Years "On the Road."* London: Mitre, [1950s].

Gardiner, Paul. *A Drummer's Parlor Stories.* New York: Modes and Fabrics, 1898.

Gardner, F. K. "How I Watch Expense Accounts." *System* 33 (February 1918): 199.

Garland, Hamlin. *Main-Travelled Roads.* Ed. Thomas A. Bledsoe. New York: Holt, Rinehart and Winston, 1954.

———. "A Man Story." *Boston Evening Transcript,* Nov. 7, 1888.

———. *Other Main-Travelled Roads.* New York: Harper, 1892.

———. *Rose Of Dutcher's Coolly.* New York: Harper, 1895.

———. *A Son of the Middle Border.* New York: Grosset and Dunlap, 1917.

Gash, A. D., comp. *Rights of Agents.* Chicago: Chicago Crayon Co., 1905.

Geertz, Clifford. *The Interpretation of Cultures.* New York: Basic Books, 1973.

Geyer, O. R. "The Oldest Traveling Salesman." *American Magazine* 81 (March 1916): 53.

Gibbs, E. D. "How N.C.R. Gets 100 Percent Efficiency Out of Its Men." *Printer's Ink* 75 (June 29, 1911): 3–6; 76 (July 6, July 13, July 27, and Aug. 24, 1911): 3–6, 17–20, 34–40, 9–11.

Gibson, Donald B. *The Fiction of Stephen Crane.* Carbondale: Southern Illinois University Press, 1968.

The Gideons. *Twenty-Two Years' History of the Gideons, the Christian Commercial Travelers' Association of America.* Chicago: Gideons, 1921.

Gilbert, James. *Perfect Cities: Chicago's Utopias of 1893.* Chicago: University of Chicago Press, 1991.

Gilmore, Michael T. *American Romanticism and the Marketplace.* Chicago: University of Chicago Press, 1985.

Gist, Noel P. *Secret Societies: A Cultural History of Fraternalism in the United States.* Columbia: University of Missouri Studies, 1940.

Goddard, F. B. *The Art of Selling: With How to Read Character; Laws Governing Sales, etc.* New York: Baker and Taylor, 1889.

Goffman, Erving. *The Presentation of Self in Everyday Life.* New York: Doubleday, 1959.

Goodrich, Arthur. "A Day's Work of a Traveling Man." *World's Work* 2 (June 1901): 885–88.

Gordon, Willard F. *"The Spirit of '76" . . . an American Portrait: America's Best Known Painting, Least Known Artist.* Fallbrook, Calif: Quail Hill Associates, 1976.

"The Great U.C.T. Meeting: Thirteenth Annual Session at Albert Lea." *Crescent and Grip* 3 (July 1906): 325–39.

[Greene, Asa]. "Mercantile Drumming." *Constellation* [New York], May 5, June 2, June 30, 1832.

————. *The Perils of Pearl Street, Including a Taste of the Dangers of Wall Street, by a Late Merchant.* New York: Betts and Anstice, 1834.

Greenleaf, A. B. *Ten Years in Texas.* Selma: William G. Boyd, 1881.

Gunnison, Almon. *Rambles Overland.* Boston: Universalist Publishing House, 1883.

Hahn, Steven. *The Roots of Southern Populism: Yeoman Farmers and the Transformation of the Georgia Upcountry, 1850–90.* New York: Oxford University Press, 1983.

Hahn, Steven, and Jonathan Prude, eds. *The Countryside in the Age of Capitalist Transformation: Essays in the Social History of Rural America.* Chapel Hill: University of North Carolina Press, 1985.

Hale, Edward Everett. *G.T.T.; or, The Wonderful Adventures of a Pullman.* Boston: Roberts, 1877.

Haliburton, Thomas Chandler. *The Clockmaker; or, The Sayings and Doings of Samuel Slick, of Slickville.* [1836–40]. Reprint. London: Richard Bentley, 1853.

Hall, David D., and John B. Hench, eds. *Needs and Opportunities in the History of the Book: America, 1639–1876.* Worcester, Mass.: American Antiquarian Society, 1987.

Halsey, Van R. "Fiction and the Businessman: Society Through All Its Literature." *American Quarterly* 11 (Fall 1959): 391–402.

Halttunen, Karen. *Confidence Men and Painted Women: A Study of Middle-Class Culture in America, 1830–1870.* New Haven: Yale University Press, 1982.

Hamilton, F. H. "Working Principles of Systems." *Traveling Man* 2 (January 1909): 895–98.

Hamilton, Henry Raymond. *Footprints.* Chicago: Lakeside Press, 1927.

Handlin, Oscar, and Mary Handlin. *The Dimensions of Liberty.* Cambridge: Harvard University Press, 1961.

Hanson, Daniel Louis. "Along the Line of Least Resistance." *System* 12 (October 1907): 345–48.

————. "The Salesman Who Lacked Courage." *System* 11 (March 1907): 268–70.

————. "Selling Moses Irons." *System* 27 (February 1915): 160–65.

"Happy Ending." *American Heritage* 33 (April–May 1982): 86–87.

Harris, Neil. *Cultural Excursions: Marketing Appetites and Cultural Tastes in Modern America.* Chicago: University of Chicago Press, 1990.

————. *Humbug: The Art of P. T. Barnum.* Boston: Little, Brown, 1973.

Harwood, John S. "The Parcels Post Bill." *Traveling Man* 1 (March 1908): 238–40.

Haskin, Frederic J. "Stopping the Tipping Evil." *Commercial Travelers Magazine* 19 (June 1913): 234–39.

Hawthorne, Nathaniel. *Nathaniel Hawthorne: Selected Tales and Sketches.* Ed. Hyatt H. Waggoner. New York: Holt, Rinehart and Winston, 1950.

Hayes, George M. *Twenty Years on the Road; or, The Trials and Tribulations of a Commercial Traveler by One of Them.* Philadelphia: Baker and Hayes, 1884.

Heise, M. E. "Protest from Commercial Travelers Against Cummins Baggage Law." *Commercial Travelers Magazine* 21 (July 1915): 168–69.

Hemphill, John. "The House to House Canvasser in Interstate Commerce." *American Law Review* 60 (September–October 1926): 641–48.

Henri, Hurst, and McDonald. "—*Like the Message to Garcia.* Chicago: Henri, Hurst, and McDonald, 1925.

Herrick, Robert. "The Background of the American Novel." *Yale Review* 3 (January 1914): 213–33.

———. *The Memoirs of an American Citizen.* [1905]. Reprint. Ed. Daniel Aaron. Cambridge: Harvard University Press, 1963.

Herrmann, John. *The Salesman.* New York: Simon and Schuster, 1939.

Herron, Ima Honaker. *The Small Town in American Literature.* Durham, N.C.: Duke University Press, 1939.

Higham, John. *Writing American History.* Bloomington: Indiana University Press, 1970.

Higinbotham, Harlow N. *The Making of a Merchant.* 2nd ed. Chicago: Forbes, 1906.

Hints on Commercial Traveling by a Veteran Highway Man. Glasgow, Scot.: John Symington, 1837.

"Hints to Emigrants." *Illinois Monthly Magazine* 14 (November 1831): 49–55.

Hiscox, W. W. "Meeting Mail Order Competition." *Crescent and Grip* 4 (October 1906): 37–38.

———. "System for Commercial Travelers." *Crescent and Grip* 3 (February 1906): 167–69.

———. "The Telephone: A Traveling Salesman's Accessory." *Salesmanship* 3 (July 1904): 13–14.

Hochschild, Arlie Russell. *The Managed Heart: The Commercialization of Human Feeling.* Berkeley: University of California Press, 1983.

Hoffman, Daniel G. *Form and Fable in American Fiction.* New York: Oxford University Press, 1961.

Holcomb, J. I. *Salesology of the Butter-Kist Popcorn Machine.* Indianapolis: Holcomb and Hoke Manufacturing Co., 1917.

———. "System for Commercial Travelers." *Crescent and Grip* 3 (February 1906): 167–69.

Hole, Samuel Reynolds. *A Little Tour in America.* London: Edward Arnold, 1895.

Hollander, Stanley C. "Anti-Salesman Ordinances of the Mid-Nineteenth Century." In *Toward Scientific Marketing,* ed. Stephen Greyser. Chicago: American Marketing Association, 1964.

———. "Nineteenth Century Anti-Drummer Legislation in the United States." *Business History Review* 38 (Winter 1964): 479–500.

Holman, Worthington C. *Ginger Talks: The Talks of a Sales Manager to His Men.* Chicago: Salesmanship Co., 1905.

Holmes, Isaac. *An Account of the United States of America, Derived from Actual Observation, During a Residence of Four Years in That Republic: Including Original Communications.* London: Caxton, 1823.

Hoover, Simon Robert. *The Science and Art of Salesmanship.* New York: Macmillan, 1917.

Horlick, Allan Stanley. *Country Boys and Merchant Princes: The Social Control of Young Men in New York.* Lewisburg, Pa.: Bucknell University Press, 1975.

Horn, Henry A. *Drumming as a Fine Art.* New York: G. W. Carleton, 1882.

Horwitz, Howard. *By the Law of Nature: Form and Value in Nineteenth-Century America.* New York: Oxford University Press, 1991.

———. "The Standard Oil Trust as Emersonian Hero." *Raritan* 6 (Spring 1987): 97–119.

"The 'How' and 'Why.'" *Sample Case* 20 (February 1902): 86–87.

How to Increase Your Sales. New York: System, 1908.

How to Introduce the Personal Memoirs of U. S. Grant. R. S. Peale, 1885.

"How to Study Salesmanship." *Salesmanship* 1 (October 1903): 81–84.

Howard, Clarence H. "Fellowship of True Relation Between Employer and Employee." *Commercial Travelers Magazine* 26 (June 1920): 105–8.

Howard, June. *Form and History in American Literary Naturalism*. Chapel Hill: University of North Carolina Press, 1985.

Howe, E. W. *The Anthology of Another Town*. New York: Knopf, 1920.

———. *A Man Story*. Boston: Ticknor, 1889.

Howe, Irving. *Sherwood Anderson*. New York: William Sloan, 1951.

Howells, William Dean. *The Day of Their Wedding*. New York: Harper, 1896.

———. *The Rise of Silas Lapham*. [1971]. Reprint. New York: Viking Penguin, 1983.

———. *Selected Letters*. Ed. George Arms et al. Boston: Twayne, 1979.

———. *Their Wedding Journey*. Boston: Riverside, 1871.

Hoyt, Charles W. *Scientific Sales Management: A Practical Application of the Principles of Scientific Management to Selling*. New York: George B. Woolson, 1912.

Hull, R. N. "The Fourth Profession." *Sample Case* 23 (December 1903): 411–12.

Humphrey, Heman. *Revival Sketches and Manual*. New York: American Tract Society, 1859.

Hyde, Lewis. *The Gift: Imagination and the Erotic Life of Property*. New York: Random House, 1979.

"The Hypocrite." *Commercial Travelers "Home" Monthly Magazine* 1 (November 1893): 481–82.

"In Reading Salesmanship." *Salesmanship* 1 (July–August 1903): 36.

"Inadequate Salaries of Clerks." *New York Transcript,* July 20, 1836.

The Instruction Book of the Southwestern Publishing House. 1883.

"Insurance and Fraternal Association Notes." *Commercial Travelers Magazine* 17 (March 1911): 83–93.

International Correspondence Schools. *The Salesman's Handbook*. Scranton, Pa.: International Textbook Co., 1912.

International Federation of Commercial Travelers' Organizations. *Proceedings of the Twenty-Fourth Annual Convention*. Mackinac Island, Mich.: International Federation of Commercial Travelers' Organizations, 1923.

Irving, Washington. *Bracebridge Hall; or, The Humorists*. London: John Murray, 1822.

Jackson, Thomas W. *On a Slow Train Through Arkansaw*. Chicago: Thomas W. Jackson, 1903.

Jacobs, Victor. *Thirty Years of Ups and Downs of a Commercial Traveler*. Chicago: Victor Jacobs, 1911.

Jacoby, Mario. *The Longing for Paradise: Psychological Perspectives on an Archetype*. Trans. Myron B. Gubitz. Boston: Sigo, 1985.

Jaffee, David. "Peddlers of Progress and the Transformation of the Rural North, 1760–1860." *Journal of American History* 78 (September 1991): 511–35.

James, Henry. *The American Scene*. [1907]. Reprint. Bloomington: Indiana University Press, 1968.

James, R. L. *Letters from an Old Time Salesman to His Son*. Chicago: Dartnell, 1922.

James, William. "The Greatest Ginger Talk Ever Written." *Salesmanship* 5 (September 1905): 115–20.

Jameson, Frederic. *Marxism and Form: Twentieth-Century Dialectical Theories of Literature*. Princeton: Princeton University Press, 1971.

———. "Postmodernism, or the Cultural Logic of Late Capitalism." *New Left Review,* no. 146 (July–August 1984): 53–92.

————. *Postmodernism, or the Cultural Logic of Late Capitalism.* Chapel Hill, N.C.: Duke University Press, 1991.

Jarman, Rufus. *A Bed for the Night.* New York: Harper, 1952.

Jay, Robert. *The Trade Card in Nineteenth Century America.* Columbia: University of Missouri Press, 1987.

Jefferson, Thomas. *The Portable Thomas Jefferson.* Ed. Merrill D. Peterson. New York: Viking, 1975.

Jenks, George Charles. *The Drummer Detective; or, The Dead Straight Trail.* New York: Beadle and Adams, 1888.

Jessop, George H. *Sam'l of Posen; or, The Commercial Drummer, Davy Crockett and Other Plays.* Ed. Isaac Goldberg and Hubert Heffner. Princeton: Princeton University Press, 1940.

Jewett, Sarah Orne. "The King of Folly Island." *Harper's New Monthly Magazine* 74 (December 1886): 102–16.

Johnson, Adolph. *Hints on Salesmanship.* Stockton, Calif.: Adolph Johnson, 1911.

Johnson, Paul E. *A Shopkeeper's Millennium: Society and Revivals in Rochester, New York, 1815–1837.* New York: Hill and Wang, 1978.

Johnston, J. P. *Twenty Years of Hus'ling.* Chicago: Hallet, 1888.

Jones, Fred Mitchell. *Middlemen in the Domestic Trade of the United States, 1800–1860.* Illinois Studies in the Social Sciences, vol. 21, no.3. Urbana: University of Illinois Press, 1937.

Jones, John Beauchamp. *The Western Merchant.* Philadelphia: Grigg, Elliot and Co., 1849.

Kaplan, Amy. *The Social Construction of American Realism.* Chicago: University of Chicago Press, 1988.

Kaplan, Louis, ed. *Bibliography of American Autobiographies.* Madison: University of Wisconsin Press, 1961.

Kasson, John F. *Rudeness and Civility: Manners in Nineteenth-Century Urban America.* New York: Hill and Wang, 1990.

Kazin, Alfred. *On Native Grounds: An Interpretation of Modern Prose Literature.* New York: Harcourt, Brace, 1942.

Keayne, Robert. *The Apologia of Robert Keayne.* Ed. Bernard Bailyn. Gloucester, Mass.: Peter Smith, 1970.

Keller, Morton. *Affairs of State: Public Life in Late Nineteenth Century America.* Cambridge: Harvard University Press, 1977.

Kelly, John F. *Drummers Samples: A Series of Short Stories Told on the Rails.* New York: J. S. Ogilvie, 1903.

Kelly, John F. "Will Soliciting Orders Constitute a Person a Hawker and Peddler Under the Various State Statutes?" *Central Law Journal* 15 (Nov. 10, 1882): 362–64.

Kennedy, John E. *Intensive Advertising.* [1940]. Reprint. New York: Associated Business Publications, 1956.

Kerber, Linda K. "Separate Spheres, Female Worlds, Woman's Place: The Rhetoric of Woman's History." *Journal of American History* 75 (June 1988): 9–39.

Kern, Stephen. *The Culture of Time and Space, 1880–1918.* Cambridge: Harvard University Press, 1983.

Kessler-Harris, Alice. *Out to Work: A History of Wage-Earning Women in the United States.* New York: Oxford University Press, 1982.

Kimball, Richard B. *Was He Successful?* New York: Carleton, 1864.

Kip, Richard de Raismes. *Fraternal Life Insurance in America.* Philadelphia: Richard de Raismes Kip, 1953.

Kipling, Rudyard. *American Notes.* London: Classic, 1889.

Kirkland, Frazar [Richard Miller Devens]. *Cyclopedia of Commercial and Business Anecdotes.* New York: D. Appleton, 1864.

Knox, James Samuel. *Salesmanship and Business Efficiency.* Des Moines: James Samuel Knox, 1912.

————. *Salesmanship and Personal Efficiency.* Cleveland: Knox School of Salesmanship and Business Efficiency, 1917.

————. *The Science of Applied Salesmanship.* Des Moines: James Samuel Knox, 1911.

Kocka, Jürgen. *White Collar Workers in America, 1890–1940: A Social-Political History.* Trans. Maura Kealey. London: Sage, 1980.

Konvitz, Josef W. *The Urban Millennium: The City-Building Process from the Early Middle Ages to the Present.* Carbondale: Southern Illinois University Press, 1985.

L.S.S. "1872 to 1903." *Sample Case* 22 (February): 85.

Lacher, J. H. A. "Travelers of To-Day and Yesterday." *Sample Case* 23 (September 1903): 221–22.

LaFrance, Marston. *A Reading of Stephen Crane.* Oxford: Oxford University Press, Clarendon Press, 1971.

Landis, J. M. "The Commerce Clause as a Restriction on State Taxation." *Michigan Law Review* 20 (1921–22): 50–85.

Lardner, Ring. *The Love Nest and Other Stories.* New York: Scribner, 1926.

Larson, J. Fred. "How to Read a Customer." *Salesmanship* 5 (July 1905): 13–17.

Leach, William. "Transformations in a Culture of Consumption: Women and Department Stores, 1890–1925." *Journal of American History* 71 (September 1984): 320–42.

Lears, T. J. Jackson. "From Salvation to Self-Realization: Advertising and the Therapeutic Roots of the Consumer Culture, 1880–1930." In *The Culture of Consumption: Critical Essays in American History, 1880–1980,* ed. Lears and Richard Wightman Fox. New York: Pantheon, 1983.

————. *No Place of Grace: Antimodernism and the Transformation of American Culture, 1880–1920.* New York: Pantheon, 1981.

————. "Some Versions of Fantasy: Toward a Cultural History of American Advertising, 1880–1930." *Prospects* 9 (1984): 349–405.

————. "The Stabilization of Sorcery: Antebellum Origins of Consumer Culture." Paper Presented to the Organization of American Historians Annual Meeting, Philadelphia, Apr. 3, 1987.

————. "Truth, Power, and Consequences." *Nation* 243 (Sept. 13, 1986): 220–24.

"Let Them Wallow." *Traveling Man* 1 (January 1908): 50–51.

Levine, Lawrence. *Highbrow/Lowbrow: The Emergence of Cultural Hierarchy in America.* Cambridge: Harvard University Press, 1988.

Lewis, E. St. Elmo. *Creative Salesmanship.* Pittsfield, Mass.: Caxton Society, 1911.

Lewis, Sinclair. *Arrowsmith.* New York: Harcourt, 1925.

————. *Babbitt.* New York: Harcourt, 1922.

————. *Elmer Gantry.* New York: Harcourt, 1927.

————. *Free Air.* New York: Grosset and Dunlap, 1919.

————. *Main Street.* New York: Harcourt, 1920.

License Laws. Chicago: J. A. Shepard, 1894.

Lindberg, Gary. *The Confidence Man in American Literature.* New York: Oxford University Press, 1982.

Lindgren, Charles. *The New Salesmanship and How to Do Business by Mail.* Chicago: Laird and Lee, 1909.

Lindsay, Vachel. *A Handy Guide for Beggars, Especially Those of the Poetic Fraternity.* New York: Macmillan, 1916.

Lloyd, Nelson. *The Chronic Loafer.* New York: J. F. Taylor, 1900.

Lockhart, William B. "The Sales Tax in Interstate Commerce." *Harvard Law Review* 52 (1939): 617–44.

London, Jack. *Novels and Social Writings.* Ed. Donald Pizer. New York: Library of America, 1982.

Lorimer, George Horace. *Letters from a Self-Made Merchant to His Son.* Boston: Small, Maynard, 1902.

———. *Old Gorgon Graham: More Letters From a Self-Made Merchant to His Son.* New York: Doubleday, 1904.

"The Loss and Gain of Drumming for Custom." *Journal of Mining and Manufactures* 32 (March 1855): 389–90.

Lowenthal, David. "Past Time, Present Place: Landscape and Memory." *Geographical Review* 65 (January 1975): 1–36.

Lundy, N. W. "Loyalty." *Gideon Quarterly* 2 (March 1902): 12–13.

McArthur, Benjamin. *Actors and American Culture, 1880–1920.* Philadelphia: Temple University Press, 1984.

Macbain, A. L., ed. *Selling.* Chicago: System, 1905.

McCann, Willis H. "Nostalgia: A Review of the Literature." *Psychological Bulletin* 38 (March 1941): 165–82.

McCarthy, Mary. "The Man in the Brooks Brothers Shirt." *Partisan Review* 8 (July–August 1941): 279–88, 324–43.

McCraw, Thomas K. *Prophets of Regulation.* Cambridge: Harvard University Press, 1984.

McKendrick, Neil, et al. *The Birth of a Consumer Society: The Commercialization of Eighteenth-Century England.* London: Europa, 1982.

Macready, W. L. "Analysis of Sales Management and Organization." *Salesmanship* 7 (July 1906): 37–39.

Maher, William H. *Drum Taps.* Toledo, Ohio: Toledo Book Co., 1890.

———. *A Man of Samples. Something About the Men He Met on the Road.* Chicago: L. E. Crandall, 1888.

———. *On the Road to Riches.* Toledo, Ohio: T. J. Brown, 1876.

Mantoux, Paul. *Industrial Revolution in the Eighteenth Century.* Trans. Marjorie Vernon. New York: Macmillan, 1927.

Marburg, Theodore F. "Manufacturer's Drummer, 1832." *Bulletin of the Business Historical Society* 22 (April 1948): 40–56.

Marchand, Roland. *Advertising the American Dream: Making Way for Modernity, 1920–1940.* Berkeley: University of California Press, 1985.

Marcosson, Isaac F. *Wherever Men Trade: The Romance of the Cash Register.* New York: Dodd, Mead, 1945.

Marden, Orison Swett. *Selling Things.* New York: Thomas Y. Crowell, 1916.

Marquis, Don. "My Memories of the Old-Fashioned Drummer." *American Magazine* 107 (February 1927): 20ff.

Marshall, George L. *O'er Rail and Cross-Ties with Gripsack.* New York: G. W. Dillingham, 1891.

Marx, Leo. *The Machine in the Garden: Technology and the Pastoral Ideal in America.* New York: Oxford University Press, 1964.

Marx, Paul. *This Is the City: An Examination of Changing Attitudes Toward New York as Reflected in Its Guidebook Literature, 1807–1860.* Ann Arbor, Mich.: University Microfilms, 1983.

Marzio, Peter C. *The Democratic Art.* Boston: Godine, 1979.

Mason, Walt. "Drummers." *System* 27 (January 1915): 63.

Mathews, Cornelius. *Big Abel and the Little Manhattan.* [1845]. Reprint. New York: Garrett, 1970.

Matthiessen, F. O. *Theodore Dreiser.* New York: William Sloane, 1951.

Maule, Harry E., and Melville H. Cane, eds. *The Man from Main Street.* New York: Random House, 1953.

Maxwell, William. "Salesmanship: Rule-of-Thumb Science." *Collier's* 51 (July 12, 1913): 18ff.

———. "Salesmanship: Rule-of-Thumb Science, Part Two." *Collier's* 51 (July 19, 1913): 21–22.

———. *The Training of a Salesman.* Philadelphia: Lippincott, 1919.

———. "The Traveling Salesman." *Collier's* 53 (Sept. 5, 1914): 22–24.

May, Lary. *Screening Out the Past: The Birth of Mass Culture and the Motion Picture Industry.* New York: Oxford University Press, 1980.

Melville, Herman. *Redburn: His First Voyage.* New York: Russell and Russell, 1963.

Mencken, H. L. *The American Language: A Preliminary Inquiry into the Development of English in the United States.* New York: Knopf, 1919.

———. *Prejudices: Second Series.* New York: Knopf, 1920.

Meriwether, Lee. *The Tramp at Home.* New York: Harper, 1889.

Merrill, Kenneth Griggs. "The Hobby of a Traveling Man." *Atlantic Monthly* 139 (April 1927): 519–23.

Meystre, Frederick J. *The Salesman in the American Novel of the Twentieth Century.* Ann Arbor, Mich.: University Microfilms, 1959.

Michaels, Walter Benn. *The Gold Standard and the Logic of Naturalism: American Literature at the Turn of the Century.* Berkeley: University of California Press, 1987.

Miller, Arthur. *Death of a Salesman: Certain Private Conversations in Two Acts and a Requiem.* New York: Viking, 1949.

———. *The Theater Essays of Arthur Miller.* Ed. Robert A. Martin. New York: Viking, 1978.

———. *Timebends: A Life.* New York: Grove, 1987.

Miller, Floyd. *Statler—America's Extraordinary Hotelman.* New York: Statler Foundation, 1968.

Miller, Perry. *The Life of the Mind in America.* New York: Harcourt Brace Jovanovich, 1965.

———. *The Raven and the Whale.* New York: Harcourt, Brace, 1955.

Miller, Ross. *American Apocalypse: The Great Fire and the Myth of Chicago.* Chicago: University of Chicago Press, 1990.

Mills, Borden H. "Easy Money." *Black Cat* 11 (September 1906): 22–25.

Mills, C. Wright. *White Collar: The American Middle Classes.* New York: Oxford University Press, 1951.

Mills, Frank M. "Early Commercial Travelling in Iowa." *Annals of Iowa*, 3rd ser., 11 (April 1914): 328–35.

"Milton." *A Drummer's Diary Containing Twenty-Five Stories as Told by a Traveling Man.* New York: J. S. Ogilvie, 1906.

Miltoun, Francis. "Getting the Business of France." *Salesmanship* 4 (November 1916): 366–70.

"Miscellaneous." *Niles Weekly Register,* Dec. 8, 1832.

Moeckel, Bill Reid. *The Development of the Wholesaler in the United States, 1860–1900.* New York: Garland, 1986.

Moers, Ellen. "The Finesse of Dreiser." *American Scholar* 33 (Winter 1963–64): 109–14.

———. *Two Dreisers.* New York: Viking, 1969.

Moody, Walter D. *Men Who Sell Things.* Chicago: A. C. McClurg, 1907.

Moore, Truman E. *The Traveling Man: The Story of the American Traveling Salesman.* Garden City, N.Y.: Doubleday, 1972.

Moran, Richard. "Self-Development of a Salesman." *Salesman* 1 (September 1909): 41–42.

Morgan, Philip. "The Problems of Rural New England." *Atlantic Monthly* 79 (May 1897): 577–87.

Morrill, Henry H. "Drummers Old and New." *Commercial Travelers Magazine* 16 (September 1910): 321–31.

Mott, Frank Luther. *A History of American Magazines, 1885–1905.* Cambridge: Harvard University Press, 1957.

Moulton, Leonard B. "A Course in Salesmanship." *School Review* 20 (January 1912): 56–59.

"Mr. Kroutsmeyer on 'Drummers.'" *Furniture Trade Journal* 6 (April 1879): 37–38.

Mudge, G. W. "An Open Letter." *Commercial Travelers Magazine* 1 (December 1883): 372–73.

Mui, Hoh-Cheung, and Lorna H. Mui. *Shops and Shopkeeping in Eighteenth-Century England.* Kingston, Ont.: McGill–Queen's University Press, 1989.

Munden, Kenneth W., ed. *The American Film Institute Catalog.* New York: Bowker, 1971.

Munn, Charles Clark. "The Boys." *Commercial Travelers Magazine* 23 (September 1917): 225–28.

———. "The Oracles of Christmas Cove." *Commercial Travelers Magazine* 17 (December 1911): 527–39.

Munsterberg, Hugo. *Business Psychology.* Chicago: LaSalle Extension University, 1915.

———. *Psychology and Industrial Efficiency.* Boston: Houghton Mifflin, 1913.

Nahirny, Vladimir C., and Joshua A. Fishman. "American Immigrant Groups: Ethnic Identification and the Problem of Generations." *Sociological Review,* n.s., 13 (1965): 311–26.

National Association of Traveling Men. *First Annual Announcement.* Chicago: National Association of Traveling Men, 1912.

National Salesmen's Training Association. *The Art and Science of Selling.* Chicago: National Salesmen's Training Association, 1918.

———. *How to Become "A Knight of the Grip."* New York: National Salesmen's Training Association, 1917.

"A National Society of Christian Traveling Men." *Outlook* 72 (Nov.15, 1902): 626–27.

"The Necessity and Methods of Bringing the Members Up to a Just Appreciation of the Principles of U.C.T.ism." *Crescent and Grip* 3 (January 1906): 133–34.

"New Profession for Young Men." *Scientific American* 79 (Oct. 22, 1898): 258.

"New York and Philadelphia." [New York], Nov. 6, 1833.

"New York as It Is." *New York Transcript,* May 20, 1835.

"New York Daguerreotyped." *Putnam's Monthly* 1 (April 1853): 121–36.

Nicholson, R. M. "How Advertising Helps the Profession." *Traveling Man* 2 (November 1908): 714–16.

Nisbet, Harry T. *Footprints on the Road.* New York: Martin B. Brown, 1919.

Norris, James D. *R. G. Dun and Co., 1841–1900: The Development of Credit-Reporting in the Nineteenth Century.* Westport, Conn: Greenwood, 1978.

Norvel, S. "Catalogue House Competition." *Salesmanship* 7 (August 1906): 97–98.

Notes on the Road; by a Canadian "Guerilla" Alias Commercial Traveler. Toronto: Telegraph Printing, 1868.

Novick, Peter. *That Noble Dream: The "Objectivity Question" and the American Historical Profession.* Cambridge: Cambridge University Press, 1988.

Nystrom, Paul H. *Economics of Retailing.* Rev. ed. New York: Ronald Press, 1930.

"Obscene Story Telling." *Gideon Quarterly* 2 (June 1902): 37.

O'Connor, Flannery. *The Complete Stories.* New York: Farrar, Straus and Giroux, 1971.

Olerich, Henry. *A Cityless and Countryless World: An Outline of Practical Co-Operative Individualism by Henry Olerich.* [1893]. Reprint. New York: Arno, 1971.

Oleson, Alexandra, and John Voss, eds. *The Organization of Knowledge in Modern America, 1860–1920.* Baltimore: Johns Hopkins University Press, 1979.

"On the Road." *Pottery and Glassware Reporter* 17 (Aug. 25, 1887): 18.

O'Neill, Eugene. *The Iceman Cometh.* New York: Vintage, 1957.

Onion, Margaret Kent. "Drummers Accommodated: A Nineteenth Century Salesman in Minnesota." *Minnesota History* 46 (Summer 1978): 59–65.

Order of United Commercial Travelers of America, Grand Council of Illinois. *Souvenir Program, Grand Council Meeting of Illinois.* Indianapolis: Order of United Commercial Travelers of America, Grand Council of Illinois, 1915.

Order of United Commercial Travelers of America, Grand Council of Ohio. *Proceedings of the Seventh Annual Session.* Cedar Point, Ohio: Order of United Commercial Travelers, Grand Council of Ohio, 1906.

———. *Proceedings of the Twenty-first Annual Session.* Cincinnati: Order of United Commercial Travelers, Grand Council of Ohio, 1910.

"The Orphans Story." *Commercial Travelers "Home" Monthly Magazine* 1 (August 1893): 5–7.

Orvell, Miles. *The Real Thing: Imitation and Authenticity in American Culture, 1880–1940.* Chapel Hill: University of North Carolina Press, 1889.

"Our Sample Case." *Commercial Travelers Magazine* 18 (December 1912): 485–507.

———. *Commercial Travelers Magazine* 21 (December 1915): 389–415.

———. *Commercial Travelers Magazine* 22 (December 1916): 389–414.

"Our Traveling Salesmen." *Sample Case* 5 (October 1894): 148.

Page, Joel C., and A. W. Gage. *Recollections of Sixty Years in the Shoe Trade.* Ed. Arthur L. Evans. Boston: Arthur L. Evans, 1916.

Palmer, Edward E. *Forty Years of Hustling.* Wooster, Ohio: Edward E. Palmer, 1942.

Parker, Gail Thain. *Mind Cure in New England from the Civil War to World War I.* Hanover, N.H.: University Press of New England, 1973.

Parker, Jo A. *The Kansas Man Abroad.* Lagrange, Ky.: Jo A. Parker, 1889.

"Passages in the Life of a Merchant." *Hunt's Merchant's Magazine and Commercial Review* 18 (May 1848): 506–10.

Patterson, Rev. "Annual Sermon." *Sample Case* 6 (April 1895): 425–29.

Pauly, Thomas H. "In Search of 'The Spirit of '76.'" *American Quarterly* 28 (Fall 1976): 444–64.

Peak, Howard Wallace. "Ode to an Old Grip Sack." *Commercial Travelers Magazine* 23 (September 1917): 209.

———. *A Ranger of Commerce; or, Fifty-Two Years on the Road.* San Antonio, Tex.: Naylor, 1929.

Pease, Donald E., ed. *New Essays on the Rise of Silas Lapham.* Cambridge: Cambridge University Press, 1991.

Peck, Bradford. *The World a Department Store: A Story of Life Under a Cooperative System.* Lewiston, Me.: Bradford Peck, 1900.

Peck, Elizabeth H., and Joseph H., eds. *The American Man.* Englewood Cliffs, N.J.: Prentice-Hall, 1980.

Peck, George W. *Peck's Fun.* Comp. V. W. Richardson. Chicago. Belford, Clarke, 1880.

Perkins, Lydia Felicia. "The Hat Pharmacy." *Black Cat* 8 (April 1903): 24–27.

Phelps, A. "Chicago Rally." *Gideon Quarterly* 1 (December 1900): 23–27.

"The Philadelphia Dun." *Constellation* [New York], Dec. 11, 1830.

Pierce, Carl Horton. *Scientific Salesmanship.* New York: Horton and Motley, 1906.

Pizer, Donald, ed. *New Essays on Sister Carrie.* Cambridge: Cambridge University Press, 1991.

Plummer, Charles S. *Leaves from a Drummer's Diary; or, Twenty-Five Years on the Road.* Chicago: Belford, Clarke, 1889.

Poe, Edgar Allan. "The Business Man." *Broadway Journal* 2 (Aug. 2, 1845): 49–52.

Pogue, John Fleming. "The Philosophical Drummer." *Commercial Travelers Magazine* 18 (September 1912): 460–65.

Porter, Glenn, and Harold C. Livesay. *Merchants and Manufacturers: Studies in the Changing Structure of Nineteenth-Century Marketing.* Baltimore: Johns Hopkins University Press, 1971.

Porter, Kenneth W. "The Business Man in American Folklore." *Bulletin of the Business Historical Society* 18 (November 1944): 113–30.

Powell, Richard Stillman. "The Man from High Hat." *Munsey's Magazine* 16 (February 1897): 558–59.

Pred, Allan. *Urban Growth and City Systems in the United States, 1840–1860.* Cambridge: Harvard University Press, 1980.

Prime, Samuel Irenaeus. *The Power of Prayer, Illustrated in the Wonderful Displays of Divine Grace at the Fulton Street and Other Meetings in New York and Elsewhere, in 1857 and 1858.* New York: Scribner, 1859.

Quincy, Thomas S. *The Traveling Man; or, What Are the Little Ones Doing at Home?* Minneapolis–St. Paul: Dyer and Howard, 1884.

R. G. Dun and Company. *The Mercantile Agency Reference Book.* New York: R. G. Dun, 1876.

Ransom, John Crowe, et al. *I'll Take My Stand: The South and the Agrarian Tradition.* Baton Rouge: Louisiana State University Press, 1958.

Real Silk Hosiery Mills. *Condensed Legal Facts on Local License Ordinances.* Indianapolis: Real Silk Hosiery Mills, 1922.

"Recollections of an Old Merchant; or, Experiences, Facts and Anecdotes of the Last Fifty Years." *Commercial Bulletin* [Boston], Nov. 10, 1866.

Reed, Arthur Lachlan. *Asa Greene, New England Publisher, New York Editor and Humorist.* Ann Arbor, Mich.: University Microfilms, 1954.

Reed, John Q. *Benjamin Penhallow Shillaber.* New York: Twayne, 1972.

Relph, E. *Place and Placelessness.* London: Pion, 1976.

"Report of Supreme Attorney." *Sample Case* 23 (July 1903): 106–13.

"Report of the Second Annual National Convention, Held in Madison, Wis., Last July." *Gideon Quarterly* 2 (December 1901): 8–16.

"Review of the Market." *New York Journal of Commerce,* Mar. 11, 1833.

Reynolds, David S. *Beneath the American Renaissance: The Subversive Imagination in the Age of Emerson and Melville.* New York: Knopf, 1988.

Rhodes, Harrison. "The Hotel Guest." *Harper's Monthly Magazine* 138 (May 1919): 753–64.

Ries, Raymond Edward. "The American Salesman: A Study of a Direct Sales Organization." Ph.D. diss. University of Illinois, 1958.

Riley, James Whitcomb. *The Complete Works of James Whitcomb Riley.* Ed. Edmund Henry Eitel. Indianapolis: Bobbs-Merrill, 1913.

Rochester Commercial Travelers' Mutual Benefit Association. *Rochester Commercial Travelers' Mutual Benefit Association, Rochester, N.Y.* Rochester: Rochester Commercial Travelers' Mutual Benefit Association, 1899.

Rolker, A. W. "Imagination in Making Sales." *Saturday Evening Post* 184 (Aug. 5, 1911): 12–14.

Rourke, Constance. *American Humor: A Study of National Character.* New York: Harcourt, Brace, 1931.

"Rules and Regulations of the Gideons." *Gideon Quarterly* 1 (September 1900): 7–10.

Russell, Edgar Alexander. *Ethics and Principles of Salesmanship.* Philadelphia: Benjamin F. Emery, 1905.

Russo, Anthony J., and Dorothy Russo. *A Bibliography of James Whitcomb Riley.* Indianapolis: Indianapolis Historical Society, 1944.

Ryan, Mary P. *Cradle of the Middle Class: The Family in Oneida County, New York, 1790–1865.* Cambridge: Cambridge University Press, 1981.

Ryder, James F. "The Painter of 'Yankee Doodle.'" *New England Magazine,* n.s., 13 (December 1895): 482–94.

"Sales Schools." *Salesmanship* 1 (April 1915): 175–76.

Salzman, Jack. "Dreiser and Ade: A Note on the Text of *Sister Carrie.*" *American Literature* 40 (January 1969): 544–48.

———, ed. *Theodore Dreiser: The Critical Reception.* New York: David Lewis, 1972.

"Sam." *Commercial Travelers "Home" Monthly Magazine* 1 (October 1893): 338–43.

"Samples." *Commercial Travelers Magazine* 1 (September–December 1883): 74–85, 184–92, 272–82, 374–81.

Saunders, E. C. "The Pioneers of Commerce." *Commercial Travelers Magazine* 27 (July 1921): 97–100.

Saunders, Norvell. *Forty Years of Hardware.* New York: Hardware Age, 1924.

Schaefer, Anton. "The Commercial Traveler: The Prey of the Hotel." *Crescent and Grip* 3 (December 1905): 101–2.

———. "Commercial Traveler and Country Merchant or Catalogue House. Which?" *Crescent and Grip* 3 (February 1906): 165–66.

Schinto, Jeanne. "Drummer Days and Nights." *American West* 15 (March–April 1978): 10–17.

Schlereth, Thomas J. *Victorian America: Transformations in Everyday Life, 1876–1915.* New York: HarperCollins, 1991.

Schlesinger, Arthur M. *The Rise of the City, 1878–1898.* New York: Macmillan, 1933.

Schmidt, Alvin J. *Fraternal Organizations.* Westport, Conn.: Greenwood, 1980.

Schudson, Michael. *Advertising, the Uneasy Persuasion.* New York: Basic Books, 1984.

Scott, Walter Dill. "The Psychology of Advertising." *Atlantic Monthly* 93 (January 1904): 29–36.

Scull, Penrose, and Prescott C. Fuller. *From Peddlers to Merchant Princes: A History of Selling in America.* Chicago: Follett, 1967.

Searles, P. W. "The Handling of Salesmen." *System* 4 (June 1904): 76–77.

Selden, F. J. "The Crew That Worked Dubuque." *System* 9 (February 1906): 181–83.

Sellers, Charles. *The Market Revolution: Jacksonian America, 1815–1860.* New York: Oxford University Press, 1991.

Selz, J. Harry. "System in Selling." *System* 4 (May 1903).

Shapiro, Charles. *Theodore Dreiser: Our Bitter Patriot.* Carbondale: Southern Illinois University Press, 1962.

Shaw-Walker Company. *Card Index Systems and Supplies.* Muskegon, Mich.: Shaw-Walker Co., 1909.

Sheldon, Arthur Frederick. "Are All Salesmen Born?" *Traveling Man* 1 (June 1908): 317–18.

———. *The Art of Selling.* Chicago: Sheldon School, 1911.

———. "How the Salesman Is Made." *Traveling Man* 1 (July 1908): 421–24.

———. *The Science of Successful Salesmanship.* Chicago: Arthur Frederick Sheldon, 1904.

———. "What Is Salesmanship?" *Traveling Man* 1 (March 1908): 215–17.

Shillaber, Benjamin Penhallow. *The Drummer; or, New York Clerks and Country Merchants.* Milwaukee: Job Press of Cary and Rounds, 1851.

———. *Partingtonian Patchwork.* Boston: Lee and Shepard, 1873.

"Short Review of the Work of the Association." *Official Bulletin: Pacific Coast Commercial Travelers' Association* 6 (January 1906): 12–15.

"Should Extra Charge Be Made for Sample Rooms?" *Hotel Monthly* 9 (June 1901): 21.

Simmel, Georg. *On Individuality and Social Forms.* Ed. Donald N. Levine. Chicago: University of Chicago Press, 1971.

Simms, William Gilmore. *Guy Rivers: A Tale of Georgia.* New York: Harper, 1834.

Skidelsky, Simon S. *The Tales of a Traveller: Reminiscences and Reflections from Twenty-Eight Years on the Road.* New York: A. T. De La Mare, 1916.

Smith, F. Hopkinson. "Five Meals for a Dollar." *Harper's Monthly Magazine* 91 (October 1895): 803–6.

Smith, Frank Will. *Beyond the Swivel Chair: Sixty Years of Selling in the Field.* New York: Pacific, 1940.

Smith, Harriet Lummis. "Competitors." *Commercial Travelers Magazine* 18 (June 1912): 259–66.

Smith, Henry Nash. "The Search for a Capitalist Hero: Businessmen in American Fiction." In *The Business Establishment,* ed. Earl F. Cheit. New York: Wiley, 1964.

———. *Virgin Land: The American West as Symbol and Myth.* Cambridge: Harvard University Press, 1950.

Smith, L. C. "Convention Sermon." *Gideon Quarterly* 1 (September 1900): 29–37.

———. "Convention Sermon." *Gideon Quarterly* 2 (September 1901): 27–35.

———. "Sermon by the Rev. L. C. Smith, at Indianapolis, July 4th, 1903." *Gideon* 4 (September 1903): 44–48.

Smith, M. Ellwood. "Teaching Is Salesmanship." *Outlook* 118 (Feb.27, 1918): 339–41.

Smith, Stephe, ed. *Romance and Humor of the Rail.* New York: G. W. Carleton, 1873.

Smith-Rosenberg. *Disorderly Conduct: Visions of Gender in Victorian America.* New York: Knopf, 1985.

Society of Commercial Travellers. *The System of Commercial Travelling in Europe and the*

United States: Its History, Customs, and Laws. Prep. Melancthon M. Hurd, Henry Levy, and Lyman H. Hay. Boston: Riverside, 1869.

Spitzer, Leo. "American Advertising Explained as Popular Art." In *Leo Spitzer: Representative Essays,* ed. Alban K. Forcione et al. Stanford: Stanford University Press, 1988.

Spears, Timothy B. "'All Things to All Men': The Commercial Traveler and the Rise of Modern Salesmanship." *American Quarterly* 45 (December 1993): 524–57.

———. "A Grip on the Land." *Chicago* 17 (Fall–Winter 1988–89): 4–25.

Stallybrass, Peter, and Allon White. *The Politics and Poetics of Transgression.* Ithaca: Cornell University Press, 1986.

Stansell, Christine. *City of Women: Sex and Class in New York, 1790–1860.* New York: Knopf, 1986.

Starobinski, Jean. "The Idea of Nostalgia." *Diogenes* 54 (1966): 81–103.

Stephens, Anne S. [Jonathan Slick, pseud.]. *High Life in New York.* New York: Bunce, 1854.

Stilgoe, John R. *Metropolitan Corridor: Railroads and the American Scene.* New Haven, Conn.: Yale University Press, 1983.

Stimson, A. L. "Commercial Travellers." *Merchant's Magazine and Commercial Review* 1 (1839): 29–33.

Stimson, F. J. "An Alabama Courtship." *Scribner's Magazine* 9 (May–June 1891): 551–62, 713–24.

Stokes, I. N. Phelps. *The Iconography of Manhattan Island.* New York: Robert H. Dodd, 1915.

Stowe, A. Peter. *Winning the Trade.* Business Man's Publishing Co., 1913.

Strasser, Susan. *Satisfaction Guaranteed: The Making of the Mass Market.* New York: Pantheon, 1989.

———. "'The Smile That Pays': The Culture of Traveling Salesmen, 1880–1920." In *The Mythmaking Frame of Mind: Social Imagination and American Culture,* ed. James Gilbert, Amy Gilman, Donald M. Scott, and Joan W. Scott. Belmont, Calif: Wadsworth, 1993.

Street, Julian. *Abroad at Home.* New York: Century, 1914.

Streeter, N. R., comp. *Gems from an Old Drummer's Grip.* Groton, N.Y.: N. R. Streeter, 1889.

Stribling, T. S. *Birthright.* New York: Century, 1922.

———. *The Store.* [1932]. Reprint. University: University of Alabama Press, 1985.

Strong, Edward K. *The Psychology of Selling and Advertising.* New York: McGraw-Hill, 1925.

Stuart, Ruth McEnery. "The Unlived Life of Little Mary Ellen." *Harper's New Monthly Magazine* 93 (October 1896): 697–709.

"Studies in the South." *Atlantic Monthly* 49 (June 1882): 740–52.

Susman, Warren I. *Culture as History: The Transformation of American Society in the Twentieth Century.* New York: Pantheon, 1973.

Sutton, William A. "Sherwood Anderson: The Advertising Years, 1900–1906." *Northwest Ohio Quarterly* 22 (Summer 1950): 120–57.

Sweet, Alexander E., and Jarmoy Knox. *Sketches from Texas Siftings.* New York: Texas Siftings Pub., 1882.

"Taking the Office Along." *System* 31 (February 1917): 155.

Tallant, Robert. *Southern Territory.* Garden City, N.Y.: Doubleday, 1951.

Tarkington, Booth. *The Gentleman from Indiana.* New York: Doubleday, 1899.

————. *Penrod*. New York: Doubleday, 1914.

Taylor, Frederick Winslow. *Principles of Scientific Management*. New York: Harper, 1911.

Taylor, John. "Versatility and the Realm of Career." *New England Quarterly* 60 (December 1987): 584–95.

Taylor, William R. *Cavalier and Yankee: The Old South and the American National Character*. Cambridge: Harvard University Press, 1979.

Tebbel, John. *George Horace Lorimer and the Saturday Evening Post*. Garden City, N.Y.: Doubleday, 1948.

Teetzel, W. H. "Are All Gideons Christians?" *Gideon Quarterly* 3 (September 1902): 28–29.

Thomas, Brook. *The New Historicism and Other Old-Fashioned Topics*. Princeton: Princeton University Press, 1991.

Thornton, Richard H. *An American Glossary*. [1911–13]. Reprint. New York: Frederick Ungar, 1962.

Thurber, Alwyn M. *Quaint Crippen, Commercial Traveler*. Chicago: A. C. McClurg, 1896.

Tichi, Cecelia. *Shifting Gears: Technology, Literature, Culture in Modernist America*. Chapel Hill: University of North Carolina Press, 1987.

Tinelli, Frank B. *"Pointers" to Commercial Travellers; or, How to Become a Successful Salesman Interspersed with a Few Reminiscences, Experiences and Witticisms*. South Norwalk, Conn: Schumann Art Print, 1906.

Townsend, Kim. *Sherwood Anderson*. Boston: Houghton Mifflin, 1987.

Towsley, W. B. "Training in Salesmanship." *Journal of Proceedings and Addresses of the Fiftieth Annual Meeting* [of the National Education Association of the United States] *Held at Chicago, Illinois, July 6–12, 1912* (1912): 1043–46.

Trachtenberg, Alan. *The Incorporation of America: Culture and Society in the Gilded Age*. New York: Hill and Wang, 1982.

"Travelers' Methods—the Secret of Selling Goods." *Pottery and Glassware Reporter* 18 (Oct. 27, 1887): 12.

Travelers' Protective Association of America. *Commercial History of the State of Kentucky*. Ed. T. Edgar Harvey. Louisville: Courier Journal Job Printing Co., 1899.

Travelers' Protective Association of America. Indiana Division. *Thirteenth Annual State Convention of the Indiana Division*. Indianapolis: Indiana Division of the Travelers' Protective Association of America, 1920.

Travelers' Protective Association of America. Kentucky Division. *Commercial History of the State of Kentucky*. Ed. T. Edgar Harvey. Louisville: Kentucky Division of the Travelers' Protective Association of America, 1899.

"The Traveling Man." *Commercial Travelers Magazine* 24 (June 1918): 145–46.

"The Trip of *The Mark Twain*." *Century* 25 (January 1883): 399–403.

Trollope, Anthony. *Orley Farm*. Ed. David Skilton. New York: Oxford University Press, 1985.

"The True Relation of Advertising to Salesmaking." *Salesmanship* 2 (January 1904): 6–9.

Twain, Mark [Samuel Clemens]. *Life on the Mississippi*. New York: Library of America, 1982.

"Two Southern Banquets." *Sample Case* 21 (September 1902): 207–8.

Twyman, Robert W. *History of Marshall Field and Co., 1852–1906*. Philadelphia: University of Pennsylvania Press, 1954.

Underwood, Earl. *Representing John Marshall and Co.; Being Confessions of Edward R. Ward, Drummer*. New York: G. W. Dillingham, 1905.

U.S. Industrial Commission. *Reports on Trusts and Industrial Combinations.* Washington, D.C.: Government Printing Office, 1900.

Van Doren, Carl. *Contemporary American Novelists, 1900–1920.* New York: Macmillan, 1922.

———. *The Viking Portable Library: Carl Van Doren.* New York: Viking, 1945.

Van Meter, Charles E. "Tales from the Road Told by Traveling Men Themselves." *Commercial Travelers Magazine* 19 (December 1913): 377–85.

Veblen, Thorstein. *Absentee Ownership and Business Enterprise in Recent Times.* New York: B. W. Huebsch, 1923.

———. *The Portable Veblen.* Ed. Max Lerner. New York: Viking, 1948.

———. *The Theory of Business Enterprise.* [1904]. Reprint. New Brunswick, N.J.: Transaction Books, 1978.

———. *The Theory of the Leisure Class.* New York: New American Library, 1953.

Veeser, H. Aram, ed. *The New Historicism.* New York: Routledge, 1989.

W. F. Main Company. *Instructions and Hints to Salesmen.* Iowa City: W. F. Main Co., 1895.

W.S.H. "The Itinerant Merchant." *Indiana Law Journal* 16 (1940–41): 247–51.

"Wages of Clerks." *New York Transcript,* Feb. 24, 1836.

Wagner, W. Sydney. "The Hotel Statler in Detroit: George B. Post and Sons, Architects." *Architectural Record* 37 (April 1915): 320–39.

———. "The Statler Idea in Hotel Planning and Equipment: Sample Room Floors and Restaurant Service." *Architectural Forum* 28 (January 1918): 15–18.

———. "The Statler Idea in Hotel Planning and Equipment: The Development of the Typical Floor Plan." *Architectural Forum* 27 (December 1917): 165–70.

Waller, Hiram. "Fraternity." *Sample Case* 20 (March 1902): 121–22.

Walworth, Jeanette H. "The Three Miss Merritts." *Ladies' Home Journal* 12 (March 1895): 3–4.

Warren, Charles. *The Supreme Court in United States History.* Rev. ed. Boston: Little, Brown, 1926.

Watts, Emily Stipes. *The Businessman in American Literature.* Athens: University of Georgia Press, 1982.

Weiss, Harry B. "A Brief History of American Jest Books." *Bulletin of the New York Public Library* 47 (April 1943): 273–89.

Weldon, S. James. *Twenty Years a Fakir.* Omaha, Nebr.: Gate City Book and Novelty, 1899.

Welty, Eudora. *The Collected Stories of Eudora Welty.* New York: Harcourt Brace Jovanovich, 1983.

———. "Looking Back at the First Story." *Georgia Review* 33 (Winter 1979): 751–55.

Wescott, Edward Noyes. *David Harum, a Story of American Life.* New York: D. Appleton, 1898.

"Western Merchants Coming to Town." *Sun* [New York], Apr. 13, 1835.

"What Fraternities Have Accomplished." *Sample Case* 23 (November 1903): 362.

White, Edgar. "Before the Traveler Came." *Traveling Man* 1 (August–September 1908): 540–42.

Whitehead, Harold. *Principles of Salesmanship.* New York: Ronald Press, 1917.

Whitman, Walt. *The Portable Walt Whitman.* Ed. Mark Van Doren. New York: Viking, 1945.

Wiebe, Robert H. *The Opening of American Society: From the Adoption of the Constitution to the Eve of Disunion.* New York: Knopf, 1984.

———. *The Search for Order, 1877–1920.* New York: Hill and Wang, 1967.

Wilcox, Ella Wheeler. *Poems of Power*. Chicago: W. B. Conkey, 1901.

Wilder, Thornton. *Heaven's My Destination*. New York: Harper, 1935.

Willett, Edward. *The Drummer Sport; or, Captain Dasher's Droll Dilemma*. New York: Beadle and Adams, 1890.

Williams, Raymond. "Base and Superstructure in Marxist Cultural Theory." *New Left Review* 82 (November–December 1973): 3–16.

———. *Culture and Society, 1780–1850*. [1958]. Reprint. New York: Columbia University Press, 1983.

Williamson, Harold. "Sarah Harrison Has Taken 4,000 Traveling Men to Church." *American Magazine* 103 (February 1927): 66–67.

Williamson, Jefferson. *American Hotel*. [1930]. Reprint. New York: Arno, 1975.

Willis, Harry. "Are Salesmen Born or Made?" *Salesman* 1 (September 1909): 29–30.

Wills, Sheldon. "Why Folks Drive Sixty Miles to Trade with Us." *System* 37 (April 1920): 729ff.

Wilson, Charles. *The History of Unilever*. New York: Praeger, 1954.

Wilson, Christopher P. "Containing Multitudes: Realism, Historicism, American Studies." *American Quarterly* 41 (September 1889): 466–95.

Wisby, Johannes Hrolf. "The Commercial Traveler's Work of Civilization." *Arena* 23 (March 1900): 308–14.

"Wisconsin's Seventh Annual." *Hotel Monthly* 10 (September 1902): 22–25.

Wister, Owen. *Owen Wister Out West*. Ed. Fanny Kemble Wister. Chicago: University of Chicago Press, 1958.

———. *The Virginian*. New York: Macmillan, 1902.

Withers, Elliot [James Withers Elliot]. *Salesmanship: An Artistic Science*. New York: Sales Talk Co., 1913.

Wolfe, Thomas. *Look Homeward, Angel*. New York: Scribners, 1929.

———. *You Can't Go Home Again*. New York: Harper and Row, 1940.

Wolford, Chester L. *Stephen Crane: A Study of the Short Fiction*. Boston: Twayne, 1989.

Woodworth, Stanley. *Success in Salesmanship*. Chicago: American School of Commerce, 1912.

"The Work of the Gideons." *Gideon Quarterly* 1 (September 1900): 17–21.

Wright, Gwendolyn. *Moralism and the Model Home: Domestic Architecture and Cultural Conflict in Chicago, 1873–1913*. Chicago: University of Chicago Press, 1980.

Wright, Lyle H. *American Fiction, 1876–1900: A Contribution Toward a Bibliography*. San Marino, Calif: Huntington Library, 1966.

Wright, Richardson. *Hawkers and Walkers in Early America: Strolling Peddlers, Preachers, Lawyers, Doctors, Players, and Others from the Beginning to the Civil War*. Philadelphia: Lippincott, 1927.

Wright, Virgil M. *Ten Years on the Road*. Ed. Aurelius Smith. Indianapolis: F. H. Smith, 1893.

Wyatt-Brown, Bertram. "God and Dun & Bradstreet, 1841–1851." *Business History Review* 40 (Winter 1966): 432–50.

———. *Lewis Tappan and the Evangelical War Against Slavery*. Cleveland, Ohio: Case Western Reserve University Press, 1969.

Wyse, Francis. *America, Its Realities and Resources*. London: T. C. Newby, 1846.

"The Young Men of New York." *New York Transcript,* June 14, 1836.

Ziff, Larzer. *The American 1890s: Life and Times of a Lost Generation*. Lincoln: University of Nebraska Press, 1966.

Zunz, Olivier. *Making America Corporate, 1870–1920*. Chicago: University of Chicago Press, 1990.

Index

Castelow, Wilbur, 115; *Only a Drummer*, 81–82, 85

Cather, Willa, 5, 15; *My Ántonia*, 20–21

Chalmers, Hugh, 196

Chandler, Alfred D., Jr., viii, 26, 56

Claremont Manufacturing Co.: *Pocket Companion*, 84

Clark, Charles Munn, 198

Clark, Edward, 147–148

Clark, Thomas D., viii

Collins, James H., 196

"The Commercial Drummer's Thanksgiving," 155–156, *156*

commercial rhetoric, 39–41, 45–46, 121, 123, 126, 135–136

commercial travelers: adaptability to change, 198–202; and commercial spectacle, xiii, 101; as cultural type, vii–viii, xi–xiv, 3–5, 55, 113–120, 137–141, 175, 178, 182–183, 189; relationships with customers, 19, 60–62, 119; demographics of, 53, 170; and drinking, 109, 151–152, 163, 166; in England and Europe, vii, 23–24, *24*, 152–153; and ethnic stereotypes, 134, 136–137, *138–140*, 139, 165, 170; and fraternal relations, 152–55 (*see also* Fraternal organizations); and gambling, 151–152; independence diminished, 205–208, 223; understanding of landscape, 82–88, 97–98; and modernity, 2, 7–12, *10–11*, 57–59, 65–67, *193;* old-fashioned drummer vs. modern salesman, 2, 6–13, 169, 197–199; painting of, 113–117; and physical labor, 88; resistance to and criticism of, xiv–xvi, 53–56, 115–120, 125–126, 131–134, 197, 221–233; salaries of, 55; veteran, 16–20, 199–200; women, 145. *See also* Commercial travelers, representations of; Commercial traveling; Dunning clerks

commercial travelers, representations of: in drama, 136–138, 223–224, 232–233; in fiction, vii, xiv–xvii, 3–7, 20–21, 126–136, 164–165, 173–191, 224–232; in film, 3, 5; in literary sketches, 7–13, 120–123; in music, 149; in painting and other visual texts, 113–117 and passim; in poetry, 68–69, 136–138, 143, 154; in travel literature, 124–125

Commercial Travelers' Association of the State of New York, 157

Commercial Travelers Club of New York, 157

Commercial Travelers' Home Association of Syracuse, 164–165

Commercial Travelers' "Home" Monthly Magazine, 164–165

Commercial Travelers' Mutual Accident Association of America, 158–159

Commercial Travelers National Association, 157

Commercial Travelers' Protective Association of America, 159

Commercial Travelers' Protective Organization, 157

commercial traveling: boosterism, 64–66; competition, 62–63, 196–200; effect on home life, 69–70, 147–149 (*see also* Domestic ideology); hardships and conflicts of road life, 51–52, 62–64, 68–69; making towns, 82–87, *83;* as military campaign, 208–210; and modernity, 65–67; modes of travel, 8, *83*, 84–87, *86, 90, 228–229;* naturalistic designations of, 198–200, 203–204; and professional identity, 54–56, 145; progressive development of, 194, 198–199; reform of, 145–146, 200–203; and scientific methods, 206–207; as system, 65–67, 77, 194, 205–208; work culture, 145–147, 151–154, 170–171; and youth, 201–203, *204*. *See also* Commercial rhetoric; Commercial travelers; Culture; *and specific organizations by name*

confidence man, x–xi, 36

Connolly, C. M.: "The Necessity of Correct Dress in Business," 202

corporation, xviii, 57, 66–67, 200

Crane, Stephen: "The Bride Comes to Yellow Sky," 129–131, *130*

credit agencies, 28, 67–68

Crewdson, Charles N.: *Tales of the Road*, 154, *155*

Crissey, Forrest, 8–9

Cronon, William, 57, 65

Cudahy Pharmaceutical Co., 61

culture: commercial (defined), xii; mass, ix–x, 1–3, 57–59, 79–80, 223–224

Daniel, Charles G., 168

Dearing, John S.: *A Drummer's Experience*, 217

"death" of the salesman, viii–ix, 1–3, 9–

improvisation, 47–49, 79–80, 101–106, 109–110; defined, 82. *See also* Personality

International Correspondence Schools: *The Salesman's Handbook*, 204–205, 217–218

Iowa State Traveling Men's Association, 160

Irving, Washington: *Bracebridge Hall*, 23–24

Jacobs, Victor, 17, 94–97

Jaffee, David, 25

James, Henry, xv–xvi

James, R. L.: *Letters from an Old Time Salesman to His Son*, 201

James, William: "Greatest Ginger Talk Ever Written," 213

Jameson, Frederic, 9

Jessop, George: *Sam'l of Posen*, 136–138, *138–140*

John Wanamaker, 60

Johnson, Adolph: *Hints on Salesmanship*, 204

Johnston, J. P.: *Twenty Years of Hus'ling*, 103

jokes and jest books, 6, 79, 88, 106–107, *107–108*, 109–110, 114–115, 166, 169, 201, 243*n*63, 249*n*93

Jones, John Beauchamp, 43

The Kansas Man Abroad, 107–109

Kaplan, Amy, xv, 175, 178

Keayne, Robert: "Apologia," 36–37

Kerber, Linda, 146

Kimball, Richard: *Was He Successful?* 35

Kipling, Rudyard, 125

Kirk, John, 51–52, 61, 148

Knox, James, 203, 205

Lacher, J. H. A., 198, 200–201

"Lamentations of the Traveling Man," 68–69

Lardner, Ring, 3

Larson, J. Fred: "How to Read a Customer," 217

Lears, T. J. Jackson, x, xvi–xvii, 25

Lewis, Sinclair, 3, 20–21, 49, 168, 170; *Arrowsmith*, 227; *Babbitt*, 227–228; *Elmer Gantry*, 229–231; *Free Air*, 227; *Main Street*, 227–228

Leyendecker, J. C., 202, *204*

licensing laws, 53, 70–77; judicial review of, 75–77

"*—Like the Message to Garcia*," 201

Lindgren, Charles: *The New Salesmanship*, 217

Livesay, Harold C., xiv, 57

Lorimer, George H., 7; *Letters from a Self-Made Merchant to His Son*, 5–6, 104–105, 201–202; *Old Gorgon Graham: More Letters from a Self-Made Merchant to His Son*, 201

Maher, William H., 106; *A Man of Samples*, 68; *On the Road to Riches*, 80–81, 212

mail-order houses, 197

Mann-Elkins Act, 89

maps and guidebooks, 67–68, 84–85. *See also names of specific guidebooks and their authors*

Marchand, Roland, x, 1–2

Marden, Orison Swett: *Selling Things*, 212–213

market: as abstract, xiii–xiv, 57; fluidity of urban, 31–34, 40–41; and hegemony, x–xiii, xvi–xvii; literary representation of, xvi–xvii; as marketplace, xiii–xiv, 14; development of national, ix–x, 1–2, 53, 56–57; opposition to, xiv–xvii; utopian conceptions of, 196–197

Marquis, Don, 57, 221; "My Memories of the Old-Fashioned Drummer," 12–14, 20

Marshall Field and Co., 60–61

Martin, E. Barton, 62, 70, 82, 103, 148–149

Martin, Julia, 148–149

Marx, Karl, 196

"Mary Jane's Traveling Man," 161

masculinity, 48–49, 147, 153–154

Mathews, Cornelius: *Big Abel and the Little Manhattan*, 32–33

Matthiessen, F. O., 174, 179

Maxwell, William, 216–217, 219–220

McKendrick, Neil, 24

Melville, Herman: *The Confidence Man*, x–xi; *Redburn*, 44

Mencken, H. L., 3–4, 228

merchants: all-purpose, 25; country, 23, 26–27, 41–45, 47; retail (postbellum), *2*, 19, 60–64, *100*, 101–103, *104*, *181*, 219–220. *See also* Wholesalers

Michaels, Walter Benn, xvii, 173–174

middle class, xiii, xv, 31, 36, 54–55

Milburn, William F., 206

Miller, Arthur, viii–ix, xii, 21, 117, 221;